Johann Jakob Moser

and the Holy Roman Empire

of the German Nation

MACK WALKER

and the Holy Roman Empire

of the German Nation

The University of North Carolina Press Chapel Hill

© 1981 The University of North Carolina Press

All rights reserved

Manufactured in the United States of America

ISBN 0-8078-1441-5

Library of Congress Catalog Card Number 79-27720

Library of Congress Cataloging in Publication Data

Walker, Mack.
  Johann Jakob Moser and the Holy Roman Empire of the German nation.

  Bibliography: p.
  Includes index.
  1. Moser, Johann Jakob, 1701–1785. 2. Political scientists—Germany.
3. Holy Roman Empire—Constitutional history. 4. Holy Roman Empire—
History—1648–1804. I. Title.
JX2333.W34   340'.092'4 [B]   79-27720
ISBN 0-8078-1441-5

Contents

Illustrations

Argument and Acknowledgments

"Germany is a state no longer," wrote the young Hegel in a political essay on the constitution of the German Empire. "What cannot be grasped does not exist." The German constitution Hegel meant was the one expounded by a Stuttgart neighbor of his boyhood, the then aged but still famous constitutional jurist Johann Jakob Moser. Hegel's verb *begriffen* carries both the rational sense of "systematically comprehended" and the political sense of "seized" or "laid hold of"; and the political and rational meanings were for him inseparable. The natural lawyer Samuel Pufendorf, writing a century and a half before, had taken much the same view of the German constitution. For Moser, though, the essence and even the merit of the German constitutional or public law was that it could not be wholly "grasped." For him too rational comprehension seemed bound together with political power and manipulation; but for him that was cause to distrust and to fear the political uses of juridical reason. Hegel's proof of the empire's nonexistence was its incapacity to summon up and to order military force. Moser thought military force, and especially the political means and motives for mobilizing it, were the supreme threats to the German constitutional order.

Most of us are far more nearly the intellectual heirs to Hegel than to Moser. A thought underlying this book at its inception was that it is not practicable, by means presently available, to bring together that complex of public and personal relations, the constitution of the Holy Roman Empire of the eighteenth century, into a coherent and manageable compass—not while retaining any sense of how it was lived. So I have tried to strike a path through it. Whoever tries to understand German public life between Luther and Napoleon finds himself, whenever he takes his eyes from a handful of courts, ministries, and soldiers, contemplating a maze. It is not a trackless maze, for it is crisscrossed with a thousand tracks going everywhere and sometimes nowhere; not an impenetrable maze, for most of the paths and corners are easy enough to penetrate, so to lose sight of the rest; not a hopeless maze surely, for, after all, people moved about in it at least with no more bewilderment or despair than people commonly feel. In Moser I have chosen a guide for this exploration: somebody who traveled through more of it, more parts and at more levels, than almost anybody else—at least, than anybody else who left such voluminous reports of his travels and experiences.

Johann Jakob Moser was of the profession which grew up to conduct the public business of Germany in the maze, that mix of administrator, politician, and scholarly jurist who arranged, negotiated, and formalized its disposition of rights and authority. What I have seen on this journey and describe here has been seen, on the whole, through his eyes. An important advantage in this, besides the breadth of his experience, is Moser's determination and conviction, as jurist, that he must see and describe things exactly as they were. A cardinal principle of his profession was to restate, in law, the realities of political transactions and relations. But this is a deceptive advantage too. I did not expect, at first, to give much attention to his private life, experience, or beliefs. Still, to understand his place as a jurist it seemed necessary to know something of his professional relations with other academic jurists and of his everyday administrative and political circumstances. To understand these it has seemed important to know something of his personal character and of his religious faith. This is so despite his lifelong efforts to keep these several spheres of his life separate—indeed, much of the most revealing biographical and even constitutional detail I have found has come from the intellectual and moral strains these efforts imposed upon him. The severely chronological scheme I adopted for this book has proved essential for discovering and interpreting these tensions and crossovers at compartmental boundaries; and they in turn have carried the story along.

In this mode I find that I have touched on themes of wider import than I had supposed as I worked; but I have treated them mainly in the workaday terms and protean forms in which Moser discerned them. At the end I find I have arrived at a sense of analogy or integrity between Moser's own dispersed and errant career, and the law and empire to which he was committed. The mass of detail, and the extraordinary difficulty of ordering it by mind or might, was itself an essential characteristic of the German imperial constitution, inseparable from its true nature and achievement; it ought not be ignored or dismissed. Much the same was true of Moser, whose own style and thought embodied that quality of the empire. I have tried neither to romanticize nor to rationalize the Holy Roman Empire. It was a political and legal structure with many merits, but neither romance nor rationality was notable among them. And as biography, this is one without a hero in a literary sense, for I conceive that the trivialities and frailties apparent in Moser's work and person were interwoven with his courage and honor, not departures from them, so that right representation of each depends on the other. Readers should not expect a protagonist who always knew what he was about, nor a political institution with clear deduction of power and right.

I have discovered a great deal about that world, though, following

Moser about in it. There are very many nooks and openings along the way that I have been unable adequately to explore. To others who may wish to learn about it too, I offer here a stroll through the public life of the Germany of the Old Law, made in the company of someone the reader may come to know.

The debts I have incurred and the free gifts I have had along the way are many, as always, and some of the most important ones as always are surely now forgotten. The book could not have been written if Helmut Haecker and Frau Haecker of Urach had not made available to me the manuscript autobiography of Moser preserved in the family. Recent books on Moser by Reinhold Rürup and Erwin Schömbs I have used confidently and gratefully, though I think they will see this is a different book. Serious research began with the aid of a grant from the National Endowment for the Humanities in 1972–73. The American Philosophical Society in 1977 helped support another visit to German libraries and archives to clear up detail. Part I of the book was drafted at Cornell University in 1974, parts II and III at the Johns Hopkins University in 1976–77, and part IV at the Institute for Advanced Study in Princeton in 1977; the contributions of all these institutions to the work are palpable and valued. Walter M. Pintner read the manuscript at an early stage with the critical generosity I have come to expect of him. Publisher's referees—anonymous in an eighteenth-century sense—may be sure of my appreciation, whatever my behavior. I have profited from comment by members of the History Seminar at the Johns Hopkins University, by members of my family, by Terry Butler, Marion Matrician, and many others. Officers of the libraries and archives I have consulted did their duties generously and well on my behalf. Daryl Jensen, Julie Gillern, Lawrence Klein, James McNaughton, Doris McCloskey, and Bozena Lamparski worked patiently and intelligently with manuscripts of an impatient and sometimes unintelligible author. In the reading of proofs, Cameron Munter and Barbara Walker made so many rescues of syntax, sense, and substance that they wholly deserve editorial credit. Irma Walker made the collection of illustrations a happy and fruitful excursion. Katarina Rice, Gwen Duffey, and Lewis Bateman have been altogether cooperative and helpful, and I am grateful too to other associates of The University of North Carolina Press whose names are not known to me but whose work is apparent in the book.

This is a book not easy to dedicate in the usual way, and I shall not do so. But I hope it honors my teachers, my colleagues, and my profession, for what they have brought to my understanding and concern for the life here recounted.

Mack Walker

Johann Jakob Moser
and the Holy Roman Empire
of the German Nation

Preamble. Hohentwiel
Fortress, September 1763

STATE Councillor Moser had been shut four years in his room high in the Hohentwiel, prisoner of his duke, nearly always alone, forbidden books to read or pen and paper with which to write. That was time enough to think back to how he had come there—the lifetime taken up with compulsive writing, study, and administrative work, the career he presumed to be finished. It was time enough for the floating fragments of memory that seemed to say something about him to come to the surface and to drift to the places that gave them meaning. He was old and felt old; he did not know whether he would leave this place alive. He had been very ill the winter before. When he got better and found a way to write despite the prohibition, he set about putting his memories down. This was to edify his children and descendants, but also because he was still compelled to write everything down. At this he got sick again, but by some intervention of will he recovered and went to work.

His life had three parts, Moser decided in the manner of a lawyer and a Christian—not sequential sections laid end to end in historical time but three separate compartments in which he, or the three parts of him, simultaneously had lived. These analytical parts were his natural life, his spiritual life, and his civic life. Now after setting down the headings and getting the preliminaries out of the way, he wrote: §Birth. Now he needed an opening sentence.

The conventions of autobiography called for something portentous here, something adorned maybe with prophetic planetary conjunctions, earthquakes, or remarkable circumstances of weather. But the old man was too studiously prosaic, and too shrewdly pious, for supernatural symbolism. Besides, birth was in the compartment of natural life, and there he must let facts speak for themselves as he always had, as Lutheran and jurist. God alone knew how the facts went together and what they signified, and God's place was in the compartment on spiritual life. Here Moser must tell what naturally happened: "§Birth. I was born in the year 1701, on the eighteenth of January, between eleven and twelve in the forenoon at Stuttgart, capital city of Württemberg. So I have gone with the age of the present century, and am exactly as old as the Kingdom

3

of Prussia; for the first King in Prussia was crowned on the day of my birth."[1]

Another circumstance of his birth was in his mind, but in this private memoir for posterity he kept it apart for the spiritual compartment. When years later he came to take parts of this manuscript "Account" for a published Life History to justify himself to contemporaries, there was a leakage between compartments, and the combined passage read: "I was born in Stuttgart in the year 1701, 18th of January, on the day of the first Prussian royal coronation, and learned only many years later rightly to value the baptism I immediately received."[2] Still the facts were there for themselves, though here the new Kingdom of Prussia and Moser's belated appreciation of sacramental grace came somehow together into the one sentence on natal auspices. Moser did not say why. To learn the meaning of events in Moser's life, and also the meaning of facts in the law that was his work, a reader often must depend on odd associations, on eccentric ordering of things, on discontinuous and seemingly irrelevant anecdotes or precedents that came into his mind and out on paper as he wrote and wrote and wrote. It is never certain how much conscious cunning there was in this, or how aware he was of the tricks memory and composition played on his principle of stating only positive facts however they arose and leaving their further meaning, if any, to a higher Intelligence. To doubt the apparent disorder and naivety of his Life History—a superb eighteenth-century autobiography—is to begin a reconstruction of his life.[3] Much the same is true of his jurisprudence, where despite his characteristically dispersed and disjointed exposition Moser became one of the last and greatest authorities on Germany's Old Law.

The sentence from the published Life History that I have just quoted is the nearest Moser even came to naming a key link among the compartments of himself: that sure salvation and forgiveness of sin had coincided,

1. "Nachricht von meinem natürlichen, bürgerlichen und geistl: Leben, Für meine Kinder und Nachkommen" (dated Hohentwiel, 12 September 1763; manuscript in the possession of Helmut Haecker at the Hirsch-Apotheke in Urach/Württemberg), p. 2.

2. *Lebensgeschichte Johann Jacob Mosers . . . von ihm selbst beschrieben.* 3d ed., 4 parts (Frankfurt/Main, 1777–83), I, p. 4.

3. Moser's patronizing great-grandson Robert von Mohl wrote in 1846: "Wir mögen lächeln über das Eingehen in manche kleinliche Einzelheit, über die öffentliche Mittheilung von Zuständen und Gewohnheiten welche sonst kaum unter Hausgenossen gesprochen werden; die Naivetät des ehrwürdigen Greises geht zuweilen weit." *Monatsblätter zur Ergänzung der Allgemeinen Zeitung* (1846), p. 363. Moser in fact used naivety and indiscrimination in order to say things he otherwise might not say.

in time, with serious bodily illness, and with his greatest professional disaster—humiliation and dismissal by the Prussian crown at the end of the 1730s. The first quarter of this book is about the first career, the learned official's career, from birth at Stuttgart to failure and salvation at Frankfurt on Oder.

PART I
The Learned Official

§1. Childhood

THE Swabian Moser, who shared his birthday with the Prussian kingdom at the far corner of Germany, was baptized Johann Jakob after his father. It had been a traditional family name for many generations, though the 1701 Moser, curiously, was to break the chain, passing the name to none of his sons. His father had been a middling fiscal official of the Württemberg duchy and then, at the time of the son's birth, auditor of the Swabian Circle of the Holy Roman Empire, a post at which he achieved modest but solid distinction.[4] A particular distinction seems to have been that he did not enrich himself from the public purse during the Spanish succession war, something he apparently thought he might have done if he had tried; anyway, this was a topic at the Moser household, and it was all that the son grown old found to mention about his father's career.

Little Johann—if he was ever called Hans or Hannesle we shall not know it—was the first child of his father's second marriage. The elder Moser's first wife had died childless in 1699. The forty-year-old widower was promptly remarried, to Helena Katherina Misler, twenty-eight, orphaned daughter of a line of theologically trained scholars, pastors, and ecclesiastical officials from Frankfurt on Main. Helena Katherina had been living as a poor relation with a Stuttgart family connected with her mother; her father had died in the service of the Swedish crown, as superintendent of the bishopric of Verden and cathedral preacher at Stade. Moser's marriage into that family was mildly unusual in that the six generations of Mosers before him in the direct paternal line, all Württemberg civil servants, had all married the daughters of Württemberg civil servants. The reasons for this matrimonial adventurousness do not appear. Her family was probably a shade better than his, but she was a spinster nearing thirty, and poor. The mother seems to have made little impression on young Johann Jakob, though she lived until 1742; she appears in his recollections of childhood mainly as an audience for his own exploits and adventures. He did in retrospect attribute his mental vigor and "choleric nature" to his mother, but that probably says more about his father than about her. And portraits show that he looked very much like her. This second Frau Councillor Moser produced nine more children after Johann Jakob, of whom seven survived childhood, but these hardly figure at all in his childhood memories or in his career.[5]

4. Peter-Christoph Storm, *Der Schwäbische Kreis als Feldherr* (Berlin, 1974), pp. 180–81 and passim.

5. "Nachricht," pp. 1–3; *Lebensgeschichte*, I, pp. 1–4; Friedrich Bauser, *Geschichte der Moser von Filseck* (Stuttgart, 1911), pp. 6–50; Erwin Schömbs, *Das Staatsrecht Johann*

Councillor Moser found he had a clever late and firstborn son. He was proud of him and tried to provide him with a good education. The little boy had a French governess for a while, unusual for a family in the Mosers' circumstances; then from age eleven at least he attended good schools in Stuttgart and sporadically had tutors at home as well—the indigent theology students who filled such posts at a pittance. But although the boy showed mental virtuosity and energy, no distinguishing talent or interest appeared during childhood and adolescence to guide him toward a career. Intentionally or not, his father seems not to have framed his education with any specific calling in mind, nor to have tried to shape the boy's personality or ambition. Here to be sure we have only the son's own testimony, given late in life when he wanted to explain a career then seeming uncertain in direction, and an intellect then appearing without sure form. Disorder as biographical, intellectual, or political principle is not easy to compose, nor altogether palatable; and in the 1760s and 1770s Moser was inclined to blame it on his own childhood experience and training.

After the French governess (whom Moser mentions only as evidence of his father's vaguely good intentions), there was no real effort to provide him with the graces of social conduct either—a failing in *conduite* that Moser grown old liked to blame for some of his failures in the great world. Religious exercises and training seem to have been regular but perfunctory, though here too there is room for skepticism of Moser's later testimony, which dramatized his adult reception of grace with the contrasting irreligiosity of his youth.[6] That too was a part of making sense of his life and times.

In 1712 Johann entered the Gymnasium Illustre at Stuttgart, which probably offered the best academic education that a boy his age could have in that town; three years later he was enrolled at the Obergymnasium.[7] As a schoolboy he was moderately precocious and very obnoxious —a smart aleck who delighted and dared to talk back to his teachers and outwit them before the class. Alongside this, though, he wanted to please and was sensitive to slights. Two recollections of those days found place in both his autobiographies: One tells how, when praised by a favorite

Jakob Mosers (1701–1785) (Berlin, 1968), pp. 23–24; Reinhard Rürup, *Johann Jacob Moser: Pietismus und Reform* (Wiesbaden, 1965), pp. 17–18.

6. "Nachricht," pp. 10, 26–27; *Lebensgeschichte*, IV, p. 3.

7. It seems likely that Johann had had earlier formal schooling at a German school and was shifted to the Gymnasium Illustre, a Latin school, when his talents and energy became apparent: "Nachricht," p. 83; Rürup, *Moser*, p. 24. Schömbs, *Staatsrecht Mosers*, pp. 25–33, provides the best description of these schools at the time Moser attended them.

teacher for voluntarily composing a hundred Latin verses for a recitation, he went out and composed a thousand for the next week's class; the teacher called him a fool and threw the copybook at him across the room, demanding to know whether Johann supposed that he, the teacher, was paid to do nothing better than read these reams of hasty doggerel. Another story has to do with Johann's effort to learn Greek, with the childish thought of becoming a pastor; and besides the instructor in Greek was another favorite of his. But one day Johann spelled $\alpha\nu\theta\rho\omega\pi\sigma\varsigma$ with a delta instead of a theta—the two sounds probably came out about the same in that Stuttgart classroom—and the teacher ridiculed him and told him to forget about Greek. There ended his Greek studies and his pastoral ambitions. It may be that the favorite teacher did not think Johann was cut out to be a Swabian parson.[8]

He was a boy eager to learn but difficult to teach; he hungered for praise but resisted direction. Though he was fluent at Latin reading and composition (once he won a wager for his father at a wedding banquet by composing a Latin nuptial hymn ex tempore; the father was proud and fifty years later the son remembered), he seemed untouched by the humanistic graces presumed to flow from the study of that tongue. The story of how he abandoned Greek was probably kept alive in his mind and memoirs by awareness of his ignorance of classical philosophy. He enjoyed music and drawing in a casual way but had, as he later said, "no real disposition for that."[9] Once he persuaded his father to buy a whole library, twelve hundred volumes at a kreuzer apiece, mostly law and theology, and he read them all one after another. His appetite was indiscriminate and undisciplined, old Moser recalled, without conscious limits or tastes. In 1717 the father, on his deathbed, reproached Johann bitterly for his frivolity and his inattention to the serious matter for preparing for a career. He now adjured his eldest son to follow in his footsteps as civil servant and jurist. This conventional deathbed scene came in a context of sexual anxieties and shame from which the boy was suffering at the time (described in a different part of the memoirs, though), and as soon as the father was dead, Johann determined that he must put an end to his childhood.[10]

He announced that he would immediately leave home and the Gymnasium to enter the university at Tübingen. This rather traditional and rustic university, about a day's journey south from Stuttgart, provided

8. "Nachricht," pp. 83–84; *Lebensgeschichte*, I, p. 5; IV, pp. 3–4.
9. "Nachricht," p. 84.
10. "Nachricht," pp. 26–27, 83–85; *Lebensgeschichte*, I, pp. 6–7; Otto Häcker, "Neues über Johann Jakob Moser," *Schwäbischer Schillerverein, Rechenschaftsbericht*, XXXIV (1930), p. 112.

that part of Germany with most of its public offficials, clergymen, and physicians, and then educated their sons in those pursuits. It was a natural place for Johann to go, and his father had in fact submitted the boy's name there in 1714. But in 1717 there was some doubt, at school and at home, whether Johann was prepared for university studies, and whether he was mature enough to choose among the faculties of instruction there, a choice that would determine his lifetime career. He was barely sixteen, had not completed his course of studies at the Gymnasium, and had shown no signs of stability of purpose. But Johann insisted, and threatened to go into the military service of Venice (then at war with the Ottoman Turks) unless he had his way. The family appealed to an influential relative named Johann Andreas Frommann, a jurist who had been rector at Tübingen and was now a Württemberg privy councillor at Stuttgart, to temper Johann's haste and to help set him on the track to an appropriate and useful profession. Frommann shared the feeling that the boy was not ready. He told Johann that the choice of careers was for him to make, but first he must prove to Frommann that he had thought thoroughly and objectively about his abilities, interests, and his professional options; and he must satisfy Frommann that he was in fact prepared for university study.[11]

Johann produced a formal argumentation, with orderly pros and cons, about the suitability of the three careers open to him—law, medicine, or theology, for no other was considered—and this is the earliest document from his hand to survive. The law had been his father's wish, Moser wrote, and God had provided now a preceptor (Privy Councillor Frommann) well qualified to guide his entry into that pursuit. But it was a profession full of deceit, where success must be paid for with a bad conscience. "To be an advocate means a mouth full of lies most of the time, conscious or unconscious, because the parties give you lying information." Medicine offered a better conscience and better income, and theology brought one closest to God and to the weal of others. But he would have to start learning physics and Greek for medicine, and Greek and Hebrew for theology, and at sixteen it was too late; besides, either of these professions would require him to buy a great many new and expensive books. Also his lack of physical stamina (Moser was anxious about this all his life, into his eighties), and the propensity to gout to which his family was heir, might handicap the work of a pastor or physician, whereas a lawyer could write briefs and opinions at home. His list of the advantages offered by the lawyer's profession concluded, "The

11. "Nachricht," p. 85; *Lebensgeschichte*, I, p. 10; Schömbs, *Staatsrecht Mosers*, pp. 10–11.

authorities are instituted of God, and there are even some pious jurists among them"; and the list of drawbacks ended with, "I cannot be as political as jurists have to be."[12]

But in the end it was the law, if there had ever really been a question. Young Moser's brief sounds oddly more like the reflections of the old man about a career coming to an end than a boy's about one not yet begun. But that probably owes more to conversations with Frommann and to family talk about the deceased father's more successful colleagues than to young Johann's prophetic powers or even self-knowledge. The choice made, Frommann now put a test to see whether Johann was ready to begin: he must write a Latin oration examining whether a Christian ruler (implicitly France) might properly form an alliance with an unbeliever (the Ottoman Turks). Moser worked hard on the oration, but when Frommann had read it he said, very well, now go write another with a different argument and better style. This temporizing from the privy councillor spurred Johann's impudence. He went home and composed a new oration out of the obscurest and most flowery phrases he could cull from the ancient authors, loaded it with documentation from modern scholarly authorities, and embellished it with a Latin verse dedication. It was a fearful composition, but everything in it could be checked, endlessly, back to sources. Frommann threw up his hands; the boy was beyond him; Johann could go to Tübingen.[13]

§2. University

MOSER always disparaged the importance of his student career at Tübingen, and the published Life History tends to heavy jocularity about his formal studies there. But it seems clear, from anecdotal associations and from other circumstances noted in his "Natural Life," that the freshly orphaned teenager who arrived in 1717 at the Swabian university town was a very anxious and self-conscious young man. His last recollections of boyhood in Stuttgart tell how a neighbor boy jealous of his academic prowess—so Moser

12. Häcker, "Neues über Johann Jakob Moser," pp. 112–14.
13. "Nachricht," p. 86; *Lebensgeschichte*, I, pp. 10–11; Schömbs, *Staatsrecht Mosers*, pp. 33–38.

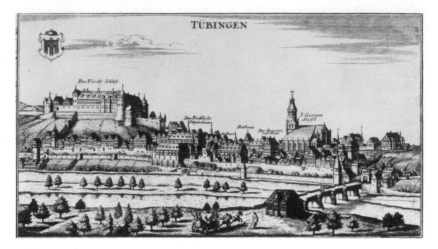

TÜBINGEN
"The water grew ever deeper . . . I looked toward the town of Tübingen, and realized I was not at the ford . . . I got dizzy, and my senses left me. When I came to myself again I was on the other side, all wet." Moser, Lebensgeschichte, I, p. 19.
Württembergische Landesbibliothek, Stuttgart

surmised—tried to shoot him dead from ambush, and how another attacked him with a dagger. Then during his first weeks at the university he fell into a fever so violent that a physician told him to prepare for death. But the terror of death and eternity brought on a heavy sweat that drowned his fever in blessed relief; fear of death, opined the physician, had freed Moser of death. Another anecdote, with religious and prophetic echoes, opens the Life History's description of the Tübingen years. It tells how Moser tried to wade across the Neckar to reach the town, leading a companion; but he missed the ford and found himself in deep water and a strong current. He sank beneath the water and lost consciousness, then came to himself safe somehow on the far shore. The cries of his companion had aroused his spirit, blind and unconscious though he was, to bring him through the water to life on the other bank.[14]

Johann was allowed free lodgings in a hostel maintained by endowment for students of his background and circumstances. That was fortunate, for there was very little money; the widowed mother had her large family to maintain back in Stuttgart. Poverty, he believed, helped preserve him from the customary student dissipation and drunkenness of the time; this conventional moralism may be true without excluding effects from

14. "Nachricht," pp. 6, 15; *Lebensgeschichte*, I, pp. 8–12.

his own personality. He had few friends and was temperamentally incapable of idleness or quiet contemplation. That left work. He worked from long before dawn till late at night, reading omnivorously in whatever books he could find to borrow or afford to buy, writing down summaries and comments about what he read. He went from lecture to lecture, seminar to seminar, and he seems never to have engaged in the kind of intellectual play, the undergraduate bull session, that might have stimulated his speculative capacity in sorting out what he had learned and thought and putting it into a view of the world and himself.[15]

The Tübingen faculty of that time as Moser later described it represents an academic menagerie in full decadence—a caricature of German university life, along with the roistering fellow students and lascivious chambermaids that accompany them in Moser's account (especially the morally edifying manuscript version). Here was Professor Neu, who lectured on history "and who took ten or twelve years to get as far as the ninth century A.D., but died before he got to the Interregnum [of the thirteenth century]." Here was Helferich on German history, who spent a semester on the period before Charlemagne and a year for all the rest. On the other hand Scheffer, on the history of the Reich, covered the reigns of the three most recent emperors, from Leopold I to the presently reigning Charles VI, in one summary lecture.

Historical studies were an important source and discipline for training in the public law, partly by default. Jurisprudence itself was in a confused state at Tübingen then, probably because the system of Roman law, which for some centuries had brought organizing principles to the corpus of German law, had lost its primacy and its organizing capacity; yet the natural-law schools developing at Halle and elsewhere to take its place had not penetrated to the Tübingen law faculty, although there were signs of it among the theologians. Thus neither the systematic codes and commentaries of Justinian nor the rationalist deductive schemes of Leibniz and Christian Wolff were there to give coherence to the law curriculum. The main professional exercises for the fledgling lawyers were disputations, *collegia disputatorum*, presided over by senior professors. Moser described one such session in the Life History: the paltry abstract themes that nobody could take seriously (deliberately chosen to avoid real controversy so as to focus on the argumentation); the pompous Latin formulas of debate; the final dissolution of the whole exercise into helpless laughter, in which the presiding professor joined, at the absurdity of it all. "So I may surely say," concluded Moser, "that whatever I know, even the basic principles of it, I know not from soaking it up from my

15. Schömbs, *Staatsrecht Mosers*, p. 39; "Nachricht," pp. 27, 86–87; *Lebensgeschichte*, I, pp. 12–14.

teachers, but I got it from my own thinking, experience, and reading in the works of others."[16]

But Moser was never the man to admit willingly his intellectual debts to others, nor even, perhaps for that reason, to perceive them. Nor was the Tübingen faculty of his student years, according to the carefullest recent judgment made of it, as trivial and arid as Moser made it out to be. In any case, as the Tübingen months and years went by, a pattern emerged which characterized Moser's intellectual life and even his political life ever afterward, and which conformed to the doctrines, talents, and interests of the professors who dominated academic life at Tübingen when he was there.[17] This circumstantial evidence of their forming effect on him is really confirmed by his own deprecations, his omissions, and his excessive boasts to the contrary. Throughout his life Moser claimed that his entire concern was for practical things, facts of law and politics, taken from actual experience and circumstances rather than from doctrines or speculation. But like many men who talk of experience as the best teacher, Moser was exceedingly resistant to learning in that way, at least until his old age, when experience itself seemed to fail him and he turned to rational modes to understand and to explain why. His guiding interest at Tübingen, to be sure, was to equip himself to be a working jurist—that is, a public official and a legal scholar, professions so intertwined in that day that hardly anyone not of noble birth could pursue one without the other. But what he thought practical and useful to that end depended on what he was taught and the models he saw: his cousin Frommann, Chancellor Pfaff at Tübingen, and later the vice-chancellor of the empire, Friedrich Karl von Schönborn. If he had attended other universities—the vigorous new Prussian one at Halle, for example—then other models and other professors might have led him to suppose that quite other things were practical and useful for an ambitious jurist.

Moser's most striking denial of scholarly influence is his treatment of Gabriel Schweder, professor of the German public law; for if influence is to be discerned in continuity of styles and intent, Schweder's influence on Moser must be considered greater than any other. Modern historians of jurisprudence place Schweder in a main line in the development of German public law that runs from Conring through Schweder to Moser's own mature works. A short digression into the history of German law may help to appreciate this. Hermann Conring's historical research, published as *De origine iuris Germanici* in 1643, had refuted the prevailing

16. "Nachricht," pp. 86–87; *Lebensgeschichte*, I, pp. 14–17.
17. The excellent examination of Tübingen in the 1710s and Moser's student career there in Schömbs, *Staatsrecht Mosers*, pp. 39–122, denies the autodidactic claims in Moser's autobiographical and other writings.

theory that Roman imperial law had been introduced in a body as German imperial law by Emperor Lothar in the twelfth century. Rather, Conring showed, certain specific doctrines from Roman law had been introduced piecemeal into German practice where they were convenient, mainly since the fifteenth century. Conring's scholarly feat had removed the theoretical primacy of the Justinian corpus over native German positive law, and thenceforth—though dissent and variations remained— Roman law got validity not from any general mandate or systematic effect, but only insofar as pieces of it were severally applied or cited in authoritative practice, along with German law, customs, statutes, treaties, and the like.

This had helped launch a vast research and publication of German laws and precedents, a geological enterprise largely subsidized by political leaders and dynasties who wanted to be sure that the right metals were boiled out of the heterogeneous constitutional ores that lay buried in the hundreds and thousands of public and private archives of Germany. Gabriel Schweder's first and most important work, *Introductio in ius publicum* (1681), had undertaken to set forth a general public law—that is, definitions of political rights and relations—out of these German sources alone. At a time when almost all legal scholarship was designed to support the interests of the particular families, courts, or towns that subsidized it, Schweder worked hard and quite successfully to free his legal data of partisan taint. This probably speaks well for the small, quiet university that retained him, but tells even more about the greater ones that did not seek him out. Finally and more important here: to emphasize and preserve the integrity of his sources, Schweder's *Introductio* had deliberately rejected not only the dogmatic and systematic mode of exposition traditional in treatises on Roman law, but also had similarly rejected or ignored the newer German schools that argued deductively to cases from principles of natural law. System inevitably distorted facts. So Schweder chose a loose compendium of legal artifacts, categorically arranged by subject matter, without much regard to their derivation or their logical relation. A law was a law not because it fit with others in a code, and not because it sustained a principle, but because it was demonstrably and authoritatively cited and applied. The great multivolume works of Moser's maturity, the *Teutsches Staats-Recht* (1737–53) and the *Neues Teutsches Staats-Recht* (1766–75), were a culmination of this positivist direction in the public law launched by Conring a century before. They follow closely Schweder's principles and methods, carrying them indeed beyond the threshold where their defects and limitations seemed obvious to nearly everybody. Letting the juridical facts speak for themselves, free of the political bias of advocacy and the intellectual bias of system, was something Moser boasted of all his days, on the whole justifiably—albeit tiresomely.[18]

These circumstances point to the Tübingen professor Schweder as a primary influence on Moser the scholar. But not Moser's testimony. The published Life History mentions Schweder only as one of the staler dishes at the Tübingen academic cafeteria. It dismisses his seminars as useless. It concedes that his forty-year-old *Introductio*, whose existence Moser could hardly ignore or deny in public print (but there is no mention of it in the manuscript version), helped attract his attention to the public law field, "because I was looking for nothing but useful things and real cases and circumstances, and thought I could find them in this discipline." But Moser took pains to describe how he found this book by himself, how he noticed it in a fellow student's room and read it on his own. Johann Jakob Moser would be beholden to nobody.[19]

Whatever Schweder's eventual scholarly influence and Moser's attitude toward it, clearly enough the most important personal influence over Moser's university career and professional beginning was that of Christoph Matthäus Pfaff. Pfaff arrived at Tübingen as a professor in the spring of 1717, just after Johann Jakob's father's death and just before his own entry at the university. For part of the story of Moser's relations with Pfaff we have Moser's own testimony; but much more of it, and by far the more interesting part, emerges from the researches of Erwin Schömbs in the archives of the university and in other esoterica of the cultural and political life of the time.[20]

Pfaff in 1717 was thirty-one years old, but this was his first academic appointment. Scion of a prominent Württemberg theological family, he had had a brilliant school and university career, and then had embarked on a full decade of travel and study in many parts of Europe, supported by subsidies from Duke Eberhard Ludwig (who reigned 1698–1733). He had studied at Hamburg and Halle, Oxford and Cambridge; he had spent several years as travel companion and pastor to the heir apparent, young Friedrich Ludwig, at the courts of Turin and Paris. In 1714 Duke Eberhard Ludwig appointed him professor of theology at Tübingen, and

18. Roderich Stintzing and Ernst Landsberg, *Geschichte der deutschen Rechtswissenschaft*, II (Munich, 1884), pp. 165–88; Hanns Gross, *Empire and Sovereignty: A History of the Public Law Literature of the Holy Roman Empire* (Chicago, 1973), pp. 255, 292, 392–426; Schömbs, *Staatsrecht Mosers*, pp. 92–101.

19. "Nachricht," p. 86; *Lebensgeschichte*, I, p. 15. The manuscript, written for private edification of posterity, dismissed Schweder as a useless teacher and does not mention the *Introductio* at all; but apparently Moser realized that this would raise eyebrows among scholarly contemporaries, and added the minimal acknowledgment of the *Introductio* for the published version.

20. Schömbs, *Staatsrecht Mosers*, passim, but especially pp. 70–92, 122–31.

three years later, at the end of the stay in Paris, Pfaff arrived to take up his post. In 1720 he was made chancellor.

Pfaff was a man of great energy, presence, and vanity, with an ambition that often outran discretion and even scholarly scruples. For example, in 1715 he had published some fragments, ostensibly found in the Turin library, that he attributed to the second-century church father Irenaeus; these were promptly denounced by church historians as inauthentic and seem in fact to have been forged by Pfaff.[21] He had strong and vocal convictions against rigidly orthodox Lutheranism and also against the logical rationalism of the Leibniz-Wolff school, regarding both, orthodoxy and reason, as relapses into medieval scholasticism; he openly warned students to stay away from professors of those persuasions, and as chancellor he blocked their appointments and promotions. But he admired Christian Thomasius, whom he had heard at Halle in 1706–7, for his empirical and historical conception of natural law and for his spirit of toleration. Pfaff's own scholarly specialty—though he was ready to lecture and write about anything—was religious history.

Young Moser, newly orphaned, insecure and ambitious, fell readily into the orbit of the magnetic Pfaff. He became a special protégé and took his mentor's advice about which lecturers to attend and which to shun. The established faculty, though, was not at all pleased by this academic whirlwind of a Pfaff who had descended upon them, and there can be little doubt that Moser was caught in a web of professional jealousies that he took some time to recognize. Indeed the politics of the matter were not limited to Tübingen. Pfaff owed his appointment not only to the duke himself but to the Grävenitz party centered around the duke's mistress, which then dominated the court. Moser wrote hardly a line that I have seen about the Grävenitz scandal, but it dominated Württemberg politics throughout his early career there.[22]

Christiane Wilhelmine von Grävenitz had been brought from Mecklenburg in 1706 by her brother, an enterprising young courtier at Stuttgart who saw opportunity in the wandering eye of Duke Eberhard Ludwig. There was a secret marriage in 1707—despite the existence of an emphatically live and legitimate duchess—and the affair soon became notorious. The privy council of the duchy joined with the estates, and with the outraged duchess, in an effort to oblige Eberhard Ludwig to invalidate

21. That was the view, extreme but apparently authoritative, of the Protestant theologian and church historian Adolf v. Harnack: *Die Pfaff'schen Irenäus Fragmente als Fälschungen Pfaffs nachgewiesen* (Leipzig, 1900).

22. For the Grävenitz affair generally, Walter Grube, *Der Stuttgarter Landtag 1457–1957* (Stuttgart, 1957), pp. 380–97; Eugen Schneider, *Württembergische Geschichte* (Stuttgart, 1896), pp. 333–37.

the marriage and so to dislodge "the Grävenitz." They were supported on a larger stage by the duchess's Baden relatives and by the emperor at Vienna. The emperor's motives were probably not moralistic—at Eberhard Ludwig's request and for a fee of twenty thousand gulden he himself had recently raised both Grävenitzes to the rank of count—but it was his office to try to solve local disorders of this kind. Under these constraints the duke renounced the marriage but demanded that the diet, the estates of Württemberg, compensate Christiane Wilhelmine (by now countess of Urach) with a settlement of a hundred thousand gulden; this the diet refused, despite imperial pressure to settle it that way. In 1710 a new complaint from the duchess to the emperor brought formal reconciliation within the house of Württemberg and exile to the Grävenitz; but then Eberhard Ludwig got her back by marrying her to a debt-ridden Count von Würben, as whose legitimate spouse she returned to Stuttgart, though unaccompanied by Würben, who as part of the arrangement stayed out of the way and enjoyed his emolument elsewhere.

During the next decade, Grävenitz and her growing entourage progressively seized control of Württemberg politics, purging the duke's retinue of earlier favorites and associates and infiltrating state offices with her nominees. Finally she set up a court "ministry" of her own to rival the privy council, a body of outlanders pitted against the traditional Württemberg worthies in the council; she herself assumed the chair in this new ministry. She challenged the claims of native Württemberger to the posts, powers, and patronage of the duchy. She demanded to be included in the official prayers (which inspired one ecclesiastical wag to comment that she already was, in the part "Deliver us from evil"). The brother became a leading councillor of the duke and later, in 1729, himself prime minister of the duchy.

There will be more to say of the bearing of all this on Moser's early professional career later on. Here note that from his first days at Tübingen, the politics of the duchy was dominated by a split between a court party led by the siblings Grävenitz, and an opposition centered in the pietistically inclined diet or estates of Württemberg, and in the old privy council, and among the university traditionalists. There were widespread fears in the duchy that the duke would convert to Catholicism so as to legitimize his relations with the Grävenitz—the Lutheran official court preacher now refused communion to Eberhard Ludwig—and thus throw the ecclesiastical settlement into turmoil, including control over church properties and endowments, appointments, and doctrine. In such circumstances the habitual fiscal reluctance of the estates and of the Protestant religious establishment, two main sources of public revenue in Württemberg, was aggravated to the point of impasse. The court party took to the sale of office and other irregular financial dealings to meet its expenses; and under the Grävenitz regime these were considerable.

There is no reason to suppose that Pfaff's appointment at Tübingen was financially corrupt, but neither is there any doubt that he was perceived by the other Tübingen professors to be the court party's nominee, an ambitious and arrogant and even unscholarly one at that; and his particular favorites among the students were suspect accordingly.[23] For Pfaff openly courted student allegiances in this atmosphere of partisan intrigue. Moser was one who came under his sway, out of what proportions of ambition and of naivety it is not possible to say; another was Christoph Friedrich Harpprecht, scion of the distinguished clan of Tübingen jurists, and Moser's best and maybe his only friend among the students. These two young men were put to work exploring the history of the Tübingen professoriate—part of the reconnaissance in which Chancellor-to-be Pfaff was engaged—and Moser's first published work, which appeared in 1718 when he was seventeen years old and which bore Pfaff's endorsement, was a collection of biographies of Tübingen theologians. Harpprecht got to do the jurists.[24] By 1720, Pfaff's sponsorship had encouraged Moser to decide for an academic career, and to get started he set himself to obtain a Tübingen professorship of law.

---

§3. Professor at Tübingen

MOSER'S decision to seek a professorship at age nineteen met with derision from fellow students and professors, and he later admitted that he possessed neither the training nor the maturity for the post. He went after the appointment with a perilous blend of guile and innocence that seems almost suicidal, so that one would put it down to youthful inexperience, except that he brought the same combination to like situations throughout his long life. And in his autobiographies he wrote down the many odd and otherwise unrelated stories that enable us to see the pattern—seeing through the man with our own superior and worldlier perception.

One reason for haste was his shortage of funds. His stipend at the

23. Schömbs, *Staatsrecht Mosers*, pp. 70–92.
24. "Nachricht," p. 87; *Lebensgeschichte*, I, p. 18; Schömbs, *Staatsrecht Mosers*, pp. 39–43.

hostel would run out after three years, and his mother was still burdened with the many younger children. A paying position in the regular civil service, an alternative for which he was better qualified, ordinarily required a fee paid to the ducal treasury, which he could not afford. But what brought the matter to a head was Christoph Matthäus Pfaff's offer of his sister's hand to young Moser. Julianne Pfaff was two years older than Moser, and she was her brother's responsibility, the father having died during the preceding winter. Such a marriage would have been an altogether sensible and normal way of fulfilling Pfaff's duty to his sister while providing young Moser with the connections he needed to launch his carreer.

Moser was reluctant. For a time his reluctance appeared tactical and ritualistic. First, he said, he would have to pass the examination for the Licentiat, his certification as a lawyer. This was accomplished by the end of March 1720, in an oral examination for which Moser found himself quite ill prepared but which, he gleefully related forty years later, he passed by setting his examiners to quarreling over an obscure point of legal doctrine—specifically, a debate pitting the views of Christian Thomasius, admired by Pfaff, against a position generally held by the Tübingen law faculty.[25] However Moser may or may not have outwitted his examiners, he got his Licentiat; and as soon as he got it he was promptly approached again by Pfaff about the marriage. Oh, replied Moser, but still I have no position, no income with which to support her. Perhaps, Pfaff replied, I can see to that as well. And thereabouts, apparently, Moser decided to try for the Tübingen professorship.

But that is where he broke the ritual, too. He resolved to go to Stuttgart himself and seek the appointment directly from the ducal court. There is a hint that he did this because of the widespread ridicule of his ambitions, and especially because of a rash claim he made that he could achieve them without bribery. And clearly it was important to Moser's pride that he owe his career to his own initiatives and not to a bartered bride, with the future dependency she implied. His direct approach to the court got him his professorship, to be sure, but involved him in political jealousies and maneuvers that made it worthless by ruining his position at the university, with Pfaff's enemies and with Pfaff as well.

We cannot work through the details of this confidently, and maybe Moser himself never fully understood them; but in the spring of 1720 he presented himself before a ducal cabinet minister, Baron von Schunck, a colleague of the brother Grävenitz with whom, however, Schunck was currently squabbling. As evidence of his scholarly qualifications Moser presented a modest treatise on the Württemberg coat of arms. The profes-

25. "Nachricht," p. 88.

CHRISTOPH MATTHÄUS PFAFF
"He said: I had referred to Dr. Schweder as Magnificum in my disputation; that was improper; there was only one Magnificus in Tübingen: namely, the Rector of the University." Moser, "Nachricht," p. 91.
Universitätsbibliothek, Tübingen

sorial appointment followed with astounding speed, costing him only, Moser boasted, the one-kreuzer tip he had given Schunck's servant to let him in to see Schunck. He can hardly have got the post, though, despite these gestures of independence, without a presumption of Pfaff's support. Pfaff's relations with the court were close and of long standing, whatever the quarrels within the Grävenitz party; he became chancellor at Tübingen at just that time, and he was trying to consolidate his hold on his faculty and particularly the faculty of law; and he still planned to cement Moser's allegiance through the marriage with Julianne. The faculty had just been treated to their new chancellor's inaugural lecture, "On Reforming Academic Universities and Purging Them of Bookish Pedantry";[26] now they were informed by ducal decree that a nineteen-year-old student, one who had never visibly admired or flattered them and who was a known ally of this alarming new chancellor, was to be made professor extraordinary of law. He had no doctorate, even.

But he had the appointment. The next step, before he could actually assume the professorship, was the inaugural disputation to be held before the whole faculty, scheduled for mid-September; that would be faculty innings, as Moser knew. On the eve of this *disputatio pro loco*, Pfaff for the third time proposed the marriage with his sister Julianne. Moser now refused altogether, saying (or so he remembered it) "that I had no wish for a wife who could hold it over me that it was she who had made a man of me."[27]

Moser had planned to present for the public disputation a treatment of the prerogatives of the counts of Montbéliard—one of the more controversial titles of the Württemberg house—but that was forbidden by the censors of the privy council as being politically too perilous a subject. It stirred some nasty frictions with the Kingdom of Prussia. So belatedly he chose instead a topic in imperial public law, concerning certain rights of the emperor.[28] What he put together was not, he knew, much of a legal treatise; but then the disputation was ordinarily intended more for the display of verbal and logical virtuosity than for the serious examination

26. *De universitatibus scholasticis emendandis et pedantismo literario ex iisdem eliminando* (Tübingen, 1720); Karl Klüpfel, *Geschichte und Beschreibung der Universität Tübingen* (Tübingen, 1849), especially pp. 146–47, 186–87.

27. For Moser's activities from the decision to seek a professorship until the eve of the inaugural disputations, Schömbs, *Staatsrecht Mosers*, pp. 122–28; *Lebensgeschichte*, I, pp. 21–23; "Nachricht," pp. 88–90.

28. *Dissertatio de potestate Imperatoris circa concessionem Privilegiorum* (Tübingen, 1720). The Montbéliard thesis was never published. On its political background, August Schmid, *Das Leben Johann Jakob Mosers* (Stuttgart, 1868), pp. 22–23; and on the ecclesiastical, Hermann Tüchle, *Die Kirchenpolitik des Herzogs Karl Alexander von Württemberg (1733–1737)* (Würzburg, 1937), pp. 116–18.

of an issue or of a candidate's learning. Moser delivered his thesis. The first to respond was Pfaff.

The chancellor attacked Moser harshly and personally. Moser replied in kind. Pfaff reminded Moser that he was addressing a rector and chancellor. Moser reminded Pfaff that he was addressing not a student but a professor. Pfaff then turned to the law faculty, which he knew to be hostile to him, and accused Moser of having used the title "Magnificus" in speaking of Professor Schweder in the dissertation: let it be understood that there was only one Magnificus at Tübingen, and that was the Magnificus Chancellor Pfaff. Moser said that if he had known that Pfaff was master of ceremonies at Tübingen, he would have checked the point of protocol with him before; perhaps, Moser conceded, he should have used the predicate "Illustre" for Professor Schweder, an honorific he surely deserved for his many decades of distinguished service to the university. In Moser's account, which is all there is to go on—or rather, in his two accounts, which differ in some small details—he gave Pfaff blow for blow and came out ahead in each exchange. Pfaff concluded by derisively congratulating the university and especially the law faculty on the brilliance and splendor it had found in the person of its newest member.

Now it happens that one lecture with which Chancellor Pfaff had recently favored his faculty was about the vanity of titles and petty jealousy over formal preeminence. That would make Pfaff doubly a fool if in fact titles and honorifics were all the debate was about. Moser never says there was more to it, or what the more may have been. He describes the events of the disputation without apparent nuance—in the usual undetermined proportions of innocence and guile. But the sequence of events leaves hardly a doubt that Pfaff's wrath began with Moser's avoidance of Pfaff's patronage for the professorship, his renunciation of allegiance, and the frustration of Pfaff's plan to establish his sister domestically while inserting a dutiful brother-in-law on the Tübingen faculty of law. Pfaff directed his attack against Moser's ostentatious respect for an elderly and quite decent professor who by Moser's own estimation was a poor teacher and whose important scholarship lay decades in the past; and Moser now defiantly took his stand there, against his former patron.

When Pfaff was finished, Michael Grass, the dean of the law faculty, rose to take his turn. Grass was a remote connection of the Mosers, married to Johann Andreas Frommann's sister, but he had not theretofore shown Moser special favor. When he began to speak he used German, not Latin, apparently to show that this was now something other than a formal academic disputation. He professed to be astonished at the chancellor's intemperate behavior, and predicted that this young man, inexperienced indeed but with a good beginning, might seriously fulfill the distinction and honor that Pfaff had prophesied in sarcasm. Then he delivered a brief disquisition on the proper usages of the term Magnificus, and concluded with some mild criticism of Moser's thesis.

Next came the turn of Schweder himself, who by Moser's account was not very quick at debate. Schweder tried to bring the disputation back to properly scholarly terms, objecting to a phrase Moser had used, *electores, principes et status Imperii inclusa nobilitate immediata imperii*—"electors, princes, and estates of the empire including immediate nobility." This, now, Schweder said, seemed to mean that Moser included imperial knights among the imperial estates, but they weren't, as Schweder then proceeded to argue. Moser replied that he did not in fact consider imperial knights to be imperial estates, but the phrase in question was a direct translation from the German of the Imperial Electoral Capitulation, a main source of imperial law. Therefore whatever conclusions were to be drawn from Moser's words were drawn from the Electoral Capitulation, and whatever could not be asserted on the basis of the capitulation could not be drawn from Moser's words. This tour de force seems to have left Schweder speechless; he passed.[29] Finally there came a Professor Majer, another elderly gentleman who, in Moser's words, was cousin to rabbits, "einen Hasen zum Vetter hatte." Majer set forth some criticisms of Moser's thesis, breaking intermittently into nervous laughter; when Moser began to reply, Majer interrupted to say, don't bother, because my objections are irrefutable, and laughed all the harder. The audience began to laugh and Moser to shout; then it was two in the afternoon; Moser was too hoarse to talk anymore, and the exercise ended. Moser's special relation with Chancellor Pfaff was ended. But that did not make the other professors love this cuckoo's egg of a Moser any better. It only set them free to express their dislike and resentment without worrying about Pfaff.[30]

With the *disputatio pro loco* out of the way, it was time to begin the business of lecturing and teaching. Moser's inaugural lecture was on a subject that a fledgling professor of jurisprudence ought surely to be thinking about but was rather a big one for him to be pontificating

29. Imperial knights were imperial estates in the sense of being estates immediate to the empire, but not in the sense of having seat and voice in the imperial diet. The *Wahlkapitulation* was the agreement sworn by each emperor at the time of his election—generally standardized by the eighteenth century—to respect and uphold a variety of rights appertaining to imperial estates. See below, §15.

30. For the disputation scene, *Lebensgeschichte*, I, pp. 23–27; "Nachricht," pp. 90–92; Schömbs, *Staatsrecht Mosers*, pp. 79–84, 115–18.

about: "On the Relation of Critical Method with the Science of Public Law"—*De nexu studii critici cum prudentia iuris publici.*[31] The lecture was immediately published, and here is the first evidence (apart from Moser's own autobiographical hindsight) of the patterns his jurisprudence was taking. He argued that the way to understand the meaning of legal sources was not verbal exegesis and analysis but rather historical and philological criticism—not on account of any primacy of the past, though, but on the contrary to get to the real meaning of the texts and rid them of musty mysteries. Only by accepting the historicity of language could legal sources be correctly understood and ordered; only thus could their places in modern jurisprudence be established. By this consciously anti-antiquarian use of history, Moser claimed, it might finally be possible to make a complete critical collection of the sources of the public law of the German Empire—"the labor of a Hercules," to be sure, "to clean the Augean stables." These opinions and ambitions seem unexceptionable, but the dedication of the published lecture surely was not: Moser inscribed it in fulsome terms to Count Grävenitz at the court.

It is hard to say whether this dedication was an acknowledgment of court patronage, or expressed hope of future patronage; or how much of it was bravado aimed at the Tübingen faculty; or what Moser may have expected Pfaff to make of it. Moser's manuscript autobiography mentions it only to deny that it meant he owed his appointment to Grävenitz, though the language of the dedication comes close to asserting that he did.[32] At the very least, Moser herewith publicly associated himself with the Grävenitz party. Perhaps he hoped that this public association with the court might attract the interest and attachment of the future civil servants and academics who composed the law student body at Tübingen, and whose fees and whose attention must be his resource, especially in the presence of hostile colleagues and an angry chancellor.

But when it came to students Moser was no Abelard. His efforts to establish himself at Tübingen as a teacher were a sorry failure. In the Life History he claimed that the senior professors steered students away from his lectures and seminars, and moreover that his elders had all the popular courses staked out for themselves and left him with only the dullest and most perfunctory of subjects. Indeed it would have been surprising if they had behaved otherwise toward this bumptious figure, three years out of the Stuttgart Gymnasium, foisted on them by a corrupt outside

31. Published at Tübingen, 1720; analyzed in Schömbs, *Staatsrecht Mosers,* pp. 147–55.

32. "Nachricht," p. 92; Schömbs, *Staatsrecht Mosers,* pp. 122–28, quotes the dedication and believes it proves that Moser's professorship came from Grävenitz. But Schömbs apparently did not use the "Nachricht," which contains Moser's only subsequent mention of the matter that I have noted.

authority, and having no sensible claim on the corporate amenities of the community of scholars. Moser's published list of offerings shows him ready to hold lectures or seminars on almost any subject students might pay to hear or to talk about—the Golden Bull, current legislation, specialized topics in public law, a seminar on Schweder's *Introductio* (respecting which he apparently did not consult Schweder himself), Roman constitutional history, or interesting recent books. At first a few students came; then, for whatever reasons, there were none. Probably there were substantial reasons for this, apart from the jealousy of the Tübingen community. Moser's professional knowledge of this random collection of fields was necessarily superficial and undigested. It might perhaps have sufficed for that kind of intellectual personality who from bits of information and impressions can forge a coherent effective statement of his own, or pretend to; but Moser by nature was not such a one, nor did he believe that to be what the study of law was about. The telling characteristic of the curricula he proposed was their casual eclecticism, the supposition that all that was needed for the study of almost any subject was the time and work of collecting the materials; there is no trace of any pedagogical notion that subjects taught and studied should be integral in the intellectual processes and personality of the scholar and teacher.[33]

But even if young Moser had been endowed with greater intellectual force and talent for teaching, and even if he had possessed more political prudence and better grace for flattery and ingratiation than he did, still to break down the barriers that excluded him from the academic community at Tübingen would have taken time and patience—and Moser had no time or patience, either. Before the first year was out he was sure there was no future for him as a Tübingen professor and was casting about for something else. Perhaps that same denial of loyalties and lack of intellectual focus that blighted his precocious academic career meant that he always had to be casting about for something else. And around the end of 1720 or early in 1721, when he had not quite given up his effort to establish himself as a professor at Tübingen but when the future was growing critically uncertain, Johann Jakob decided he must marry.

His motives, Moser confided to posterity, were "purely carnal, though there was this much good to it: that I did not wish to go whoring, and I rejected any marriage made for the sake of temporal fortune, and guided my search neither by status, nor riches, nor beauty, but only virtue, insofar as I understood it."[34] By this description the pious older Moser

33. *Lebensgeschichte*, I, pp. 27–28; "Nachricht," pp. 92–93; the lecture plans are analyzed in Schömbs, *Staatsrecht Mosers*, pp. 161–77.
34. "Nachricht," p. 28; *Lebensgeschichte*, II, p. 176.

meant to distinguish the worldly marriage of his youth, however righteous, from true marriage based on religious intimacy in grace. In 1720 he was looking for a stable and decent relationship, one that he could be sure of and that did not threaten his dignity—and that would forfend the possible resurgence of Julianne Pfaff. In his "Natural Life" he described how he went about it.

The celebration of a sister's marriage brought "almost the whole assemblage of Stuttgart young ladies together," and Moser asked his sister to recommend one to him. She pointed out a Fräulein Vischer, who, she observed, was a patient girl with a peaceable temper. Moser scrutinized the girl all day, and when at midnight he saw another Stuttgart swain making ready to escort her home in a coach he accosted her, saying, "Mademoiselle Vischerin, I have a little something to tell you." He led her back into the crowd and said into her ear, "Tomorrow morning I shall come to you and ask whether you will take me as your Schatz," and then he restored her to her escort and turned away. He did go in the morning, and after a few days she said yes. The marriage was delayed for another year and a half, ostensibly because of the girl's delicate health, but also probably because of her brothers' and sisters' skepticism about Moser's prospects, and perhaps their personal hostility toward him as well. Moser himself spent most of this time in Vienna, but she stayed faithful to her promise, despite what Moser conceded to be a certain lack of *galanterie* in his bearing and behavior.[35]

Friderica Rosina Vischer came from another endless line of Württemberg civil servants, going back for at least five generations in both her mother's and her father's families.[36] Her father had died when she was two years old, leaving her the youngest of six children; then her mother had died, and Friderica had been sent to distant relatives, where she lived in cramped quarters under the roof, not quite ill treated but quite ready at age seventeen to accept the brash young Moser. For Moser's part it was a suitable marriage, appropriate to his social and professional position, but yet one in which she must be dependent and obliged to him rather than the other way around. She was a loyal wife and mother all her life, managed his household and raised his children; she followed him from place to place on his peripatetic path, and that was not the custom among Württemberg civil servants' wives. Marriage to her shielded Moser from sexual and familial contingencies that might have been harder for him to manage with another partner. But apart from appreciating these domestic virtues and services he seems to have taken little

35. "Nachricht," p. 20.
36. Johann Jakob Moser, *Vischerische Ahnen-Tafeln* (Tübingen, 1728).

interest in her, until a religious component entered their relationship with the severer crises of his later career.[37]

---

§4. Reconnaissance at Vienna, 1721–1722

B Y early 1721 Moser's position at Tübingen was one that neither his purse nor his pride could easily bear. He had a "head full of projects," though. One was to establish a Swabian historical academy, with himself as head; but although he drafted and printed a prospectus and a statute for it, and although he enlisted dignitaries in Berlin and Leipzig to become "outside members," nothing came of it. He started to publish a journal called "Weekly News of the Swabian Learned World," but—laconically—"soon I ran out of material, and the circulation did not cover publication costs."[38] If his countrymen would have none of him, then he must do them one better; he decided to try his fortune at Vienna itself, at the court of the Holy Roman Emperor of the German Nation. He knew nobody at Vienna, to be sure, and nobody knew him. So he exhumed a lapsed family title and began calling himself Moser von Filseck; he prepared a historical treatise showing how the Grand Duchy of Tuscany had not really been freed of imperial sovereignty in the thirteenth century (Tuscany's relation with the empire through the Habsburg house was then being hotly debated); and he betook himself to the Württemberg court to procure the title of state councillor (Regierungsrat) to carry with him to Vienna.

It is just possible that in asking for this distinction Moser was hoping for a real position in the Württemberg government, guarding himself against failure and more humiliation by the claim that he was only after the formal title—which in any case is all he got. He found the Württemberg court at the sour springs at Deinach, and there accosted the Baron von Schüz, promenading in the square. Schüz, whose official position was ducal emissary to the imperial diet, the Reichstag at Regensburg, had become the leading figure in the cabinet after the fall of that Schunck from whom Moser had got his professorship. The minister demurred at

37. "Nachricht," pp. 21–22.
38. *Statuta et Oeconomia Suevicae Historiarum Academiciae* (Tübingen, 1721, anon.); *Wochentliche Relationes von Schwäbischen gelehrten Neuigkeiten* (Tübingen, 1721, anon.); "Nachricht," p. 93.

Moser's proposal; but then Moser unrolled a theory he had developed
out of his historical studies, that Württemberg was too heavily assessed
in its regular fiscal contribution to the empire, the Reichs-Matricular. It
was assessed at the high rate that electors paid, though Württemberg did
not hold electoral rank. This derived from a peculiar set of political
circumstances in the early sixteenth century; these conditions no longer
prevailed, and so the high assessment was not valid. The idea caught
Schüz's fancy, and he took another look at young Moser. This might not
be a bad fellow to have at Vienna. Here, anyway, was a proposal that
might bring honor to the duchy's representative at the Reichstag. Musing
aloud that he should have liked to have had that bit of lore at hand
during the last negotiations on the imperial contribution, Schüz asked
Moser to write it up and let him have the draft. Could the ingenious
Moser perhaps not also make a case that the ducal house of Württemberg
was descended from the great old Zähringen dukes, rather than the un-
seemly Lords Beutelsbach? Now Moser demurred, saying that nowadays
people would demand documentation and footnotes for such a claim.
Well, said Schüz, let me have a written application for the appointment
you want. Moser hastily prepared three alternative ones, along a rising
scale of dignity. Schüz went in to see the duke, and two hours later Moser
had the appointment as state councillor, with simultaneous permission to
go to Vienna. Schüz summoned Moser to receive the documents from his
own hands. Moser thanked him profusely. There was an expectant and
stubborn silence. Then Schüz stamped out of the room to his inner office
and slammed the door. "I perceived," wrote Moser to his descendants,
"that he had expected somthing additional from me. But I couldn't and
wouldn't, and after waiting for a while I went away."[39] Schüz had an
experience to share with Chancellor Pfaff of Tübingen.

Now the young Swabian jurist, with his Württemberg office and his
defense of the empire's Tuscan claims in his scanty baggage, was ready
for the imperial court. He came to Vienna, he says, "with almost no
money, a very poor *Equipage*, without having asked or got anybody's
advice on how to manage such a journey or how to behave at the imperial
court, without recommendation or introduction, without knowing a soul
in Vienna"—without any commission from Württemberg and without
any knowledge of the structure of the imperial court or access to it. If this
is true, and there is no apparent reason to doubt it, the fact is remarkable
that young Moser was promptly noticed and even cultivated by the vice-

39. "Nachricht," pp. 93–94; *Lebensgeschichte*, I, pp. 28–30. The published version
leaves out the final scene with Schüz, concluding with the bare remark that Moser got the
post without paying for it; but see the later supplementary remarks in *Lebensgeschichte*, IV
(1783), p. 4.

chancellor of the empire, Friedrich Karl von Schönborn. Moser offers no real explanation of how this came about. He only says that he had read in a newspaper that this Count Schönborn was imperial vice-chancellor, whatever that meant, and so presented himself at one of Schönborn's semiweekly public audiences. There he flourished his vindication of the imperial Tuscan claims and engaged Schönborn in a discussion of them, to which the count attended "with a patience that even now [1763] seems amazing." And so Schönborn "honored me with his grace."[40]

It is not credible that Moser, however parochial his experience and however faulty his education, should not have known what the office of imperial vice-chancellor meant in Vienna affairs or who Schönborn was —especially not a Moser on his way to make his fortune at Vienna. The vice-chancellor was chief administrative officer of the empire, after the emperor himself and the formal absentee chancellorship of the arch-bishop of Mainz, who was Schönborn's uncle. Moreover, this Friedrich Karl von Schönborn was a particularly energetic and controversial in-cumbent of that office. Indeed, his administration makes him one of the notable just-might-have-beens of eighteenth-century German imperial history, on account of his efforts to establish imperial institutions and imperial policies free of the compromises imposed by the dynastic and confessional entanglements that were a main source of debility in the empire's political constitution. Schönborn, unlike the politicians and dip-lomats who mainly preceded him, was a skilled jurist, and conceived the empire as a juridical structure, hoping thereby to surmount the failings of its dynasts and diplomats. For him, the public law was the Reich's equivalent for sovereign majesty; this was a conception readily impressed on the young jurist from Stuttgart and Tübingen.[41]

Schönborn's task was twofold. First, he must revitalize the institutions of the empire itself, those instrumentalities in which the princes and prelates and other dignitaries designated as imperial estates participated —most notably the Reichstag, chief deliberative and legislative body of the empire, and of the Reichskammergericht, its highest judicial tribunal. Second, he had to establish and sustain the preeminence of the "imperial" party at Vienna, led by himself, in competition with the "Austrian" party, institutionally based on the government of the Habsburg house for its family holdings and led by the court chancellery (Hofkanzlei), for the ear and favor of the emperor, who reigned over both systems. Schön-born's ambitions had begun to fail around 1719, when a confessional quarrel over a forced conversion of Palatine Protestants (the Ryswick

40. "Nachricht," pp. 94–95; *Lebensgeschichte*, I, p. 30.
41. Hugo Hantsch, *Reichsvizekanzler Friedrich Karl von Schönborn (1674–1746)* (Augs-burg, 1929), pp. 355 and passim.

Clause controversy) brought about a boycott and immobilization, led by the Protestant estates, of the imperial institutions that Schönborn hoped to revitalize;[42] and his failure seemed certain after about 1725, when an Austrian-Spanish rapprochement in international affairs, followed by a North German-French-British alliance, brought a victory for the Austrian party in its perpetual competition with the imperial party at Vienna.[43] Whichever date or issue seems decisive in hindsight, by all accounts Schönborn was at a critical point in his struggle when the young Moser arrived in the early 1720s.

Whether Moser had any direct commission from the Württemberg government or not, he arrived at Vienna with a fresh appointment as Württemberg state councillor, from the hands of the leading minister there, and he had associations with the Grävenitz party; and he arrived at a time when Schönborn had urgent reasons to conciliate and to attract the Protestant estates, of which Württemberg was a smallish but significant member—and one very conscious of confessional issues, for reasons that will appear shortly. Schönborn was much interested in Württemberg affairs and knew a great deal about them.

These factors can hardly have been absent from Schönborn's mind when he contemplated the young newcomer from Stuttgart and Tübingen, although Moser's account, which is all we have, makes no allusion to them and indeed makes no inquiry at all into the sources of Schönborn's interest.[44] Neither does Moser give any clear account of the stages of development of his connection with Schönborn. Instead, after describing the first encounter with the vice-chancellor at the public audience, he goes on to tell about the warm receptions he had from Catholic scholars, monks, and bishops-to-be, at least some of whom enjoyed Schönborn's particular favor. They tried to persuade him of the greater merits of the Roman Catholic faith. The Benedictine Abbot Gottfried von Göttweig, who was reputed to have effected the conversion of the duke of Braunschweig-Wolfenbüttel to Catholicism, a major stroke in confessional politics, tried to convert Moser, intimating that this would raise Moser in Schönborn's favor and encourage the emperor himself

42. On the Ryswick Clause controversy, below, §7.

43. Lothar Gross, *Geschichte der deutschen Reichshofkanzlei von 1559 bis 1806* (Vienna, 1933), pp. 62–71, 348–50; Hanns Gross, *Empire and Sovereignty*, pp. 306–7; Hans E. Feine, "Zur Verfassungsentwicklung des Heil. Röm. Reichs seit dem Westfälischen Frieden," *Zeitschrift der Savigny-Stiftung für Rechtsgeschichte, Germanische Abteilung*, LII (1932), pp. 82–83.

44. Rürup, *Moser*, p. 121, attributes Schönborn's interest in Moser to a shared sense of imperial patriotism; Karl S. Bader, "Johann Jakob Moser," *Lebensbilder aus Schwaben und Franken*, VII (Stuttgart, 1960), pp. 99–100, remarks on Moser's willing energy at Vienna in writing briefs for all and sundry.

to appoint Moser to high position. By Moser's account he confounded this "political abbot" in debate, replying that these proposed bribes in worldly things suggested an insufficiency of the abbot's spiritual wares. In later writings Moser made much of this and similar incidents, not to illustrate strong religious faith (which at least retrospectively he denied having at this time), but as gestures of his independence and firmness of character. Still, the account he gives of his principled resistance to these blandishments ends, in the published Life History, with the dry sentence, "Meanwhile for all that the imperial vice-chancellor remained my gracious lord."[45]

Schönborn's personal favor did not, however, provide him with a steady post or income. Moser spent the winter of 1721–22 roaming the libraries and archives of Vienna making notes and extracts of legal documents, charters, privileges, and such manuscripts, the knowledge of which was the stock in trade of public lawyers. He prepared legal memoranda on matters affecting the house of Habsburg, and handed them over to Emperor Charles VI at a public audience. His most fruitful work, though, was to write a series of reviews of scholarly books, begun that winter in the hope of making money with them, and continued through 1725; these ultimately were published anonymously in six installments under the title *Unpartheyische Urtheile*, "Unpartisan Opinions of Juridical and Historical Books."[46]

The *Unpartheyische Urtheile* were very vigorous and opinionated reviews, in number eventually some two hundred, ranging from a paragraph to several pages in length. They express the attitudes toward jurisprudence which Moser had begun to develop at Tübingen and which were hardly to change in sixty more years. His praise is for useful legal information, stuff so put together that it is easy to find when needed for a lawyer's argument. He cares only to learn of the presently valid positive state of a legal question, ridiculing the opposite poles of antiquarian detail and the formal abstraction of principles. Thus an early review praised his Tübingen mentor Schweder (later disparaged in the Life History) for his impartiality—Unpartheylichkeit—and for his concern for the legal fact, "and not getting stuck in mere history or empty reasoning."[47] Moser had no patience with interdisciplinary irrelevancies and

45. "Nachricht," pp. 28–29, 95; *Lebensgeschichte*, I, pp. 31–34. Moser's Catholic contacts seem mostly to have been with an anti-Jesuit party at Vienna, which probably bears some murky relation with the political constellations around Schönborn; but here the political thickets are too thick for me.

46. Frankfurt/Main and Leipzig, 1722–25.

47. Review of a 1721 Tübingen edition of Schweder's *Introductio ad Ius Publicum* in *Unpartheyische Urtheile*, I (1722), pp. 20–21.

criticized Johann Peter Ludewig's authoritative treatise on the Golden Bull of 1356, a basic imperial constitutional document, for Ludewig's "frequent digressions into etymology, theology, and many other *Scientien* that do not belong *ad scopum*," and for seeking out hidden mysteries where there were none. Ludewig was mentor of the historical school of jurisprudence at the Prussian university at Halle.[48]

With special enthusiasm Moser attacked the great Christian Thomasius, philosopher-jurist at Halle, whom Chancellor Pfaff admired. Once Moser blamed Thomasius for making functional distinctions of essence among towns, villages, and hamlets while offering "no bases for these definitions, nor do I believe that towns, villages, and markets are distinguishable that way outside the Republic of Plato."[49] Then he tore into Thomasius's "Precautions against Jurisprudential Prejudgments," remarking that "there is more pretended to, in these 'precautions,' than a man could do his life long." Without experience (wrote Moser) there can be no lore, "for often there are principles, especially in the practical disciplines, that seem good but experience shows they are not, while on the other hand others seem paradoxical, but experience validates them"—a kind of *credo quia absurdum* that enabled Moser later to describe the most astonishing legal and political situations without apparent embarrassment or ridicule, only enough touch of innocent irony to remind the reader he is there. The young Moser said Thomasius was "rather lax in his theology; and when something sits badly with him, he blames it either on the pope or on Aristotle, though I doubt the tenth part of it ever entered their minds." Moser criticized Thomasius's plea as jurist for reasonable religion, and asked why he had not issued some of his "precautions" about "how the Bible can be conjoined with the *corpus juris*, or how to get any real use out of it at all, except for snapping up something to use in arguments with churchmen, or to harass them."[50] By contrast, Johann Christian Lünig's *Reichsarchiv*, a twenty-four-volume folio collection of imperial documents just complete in 1722, was the "most wonderful book of all that have appeared in this century anywhere in the world, or that ever has appeared in Germany."[51] Of a documentary

48. Review of Ludewig's *Vollständige Erläuterung der Güldenen Bulle* (Frankfurt/Main, 1716–19), in *Unpartheyische Urtheile*, III (1723), pp. 264–70. Moser sniped at Ludewig's casual historical documentation in *Anmerckungen über Herrn Johann Peters von Ludewig Einleitung zu den Teutschen Müntz-Wesen mittlerer Zeiten* (Stuttgart, 1722).

49. Review of Thomasius's *De Jure Statuum Imperii dandae Civitatis* (Halle, 1715), in *Unpartheyische Urtheile*, II (1722), pp. 153–57.

50. Review of Thomasius's *Cautelae circa praecognita Jurisprudentiae* (Halle, 1710), in *Unpartheyische Urtheile*, III (1723), pp. 270–79.

51. The *Reichsarchiv*, truly a major feat of editorial scholarship, was published at Leipzig, 1710–22; Moser's review is in *Unpartheyische Urtheile*, I (1722), pp. 69–76.

collection that pleased him less, though, he announced that the best title one could have given this work is "*Chaos*, or *foetus abortivus Juris publici*."[52]

In general, the reviews in *Unpartheyische Urtheile* tended to favor the imperial side where it came to a close distinction of rights between emperor and estates, or emperor and Europe, though the tendency is not so marked as to belie the "Unpartisan" title, nor so direct as the examples I have given might suggest in historical retrospect. Still, Moser in the 1720s could find no publisher for them in Vienna. The explanation he gives is that the publisher he approached could not believe that so young a man had really produced such learned work; for this we may read, Vienna publishers doubted that their public would pay money for Moser's opinions. And it seemed to him, in late winter 1722, that he was making little progress toward either public office or scholarly publication. No quick advance in his fortunes seemed likely unless, perhaps, he were to commit and submit himself to converting to Catholicism, something he was no more willing to do than he had been to marry Julianne Pfaff. Vienna was an unhealthy place for him. Attacks of diarrhea and fever were growing more severe. Something had to happen. Moser went to Count Schönborn and said he was going home to Württemberg. Schönborn urged him to attend another audience with the emperor first, a private audience. Moser: For what purpose? Schönborn: To let him know you plan to leave. Moser: Why should His Majesty care what I do? Schönborn: I insist.[53]

The audience was scheduled for six in the evening; but on his way to the palace a wave of Moser's fever overcame him and he went home and got into bed, sending a messenger to bear his apologies to the chamberlain, but it was too late: his name was called and he was not there. Such an event was known to anger the emperor, but Moser put his name in again and it was inscribed for a subsequent evening when, as Moser knew from the remarkable periodicity of his fever (a four-day variety, and there were such malarias in Vienna then) that he would be ill again. But there was no escape this time. He came, and sure enough, "In the antechamber I got the frost and when the audience began I got the heat." As he went into the ceremonial movements that were to culminate in kneeling before the emperor, Charles VI made his customary gesture that Moser should not kneel. Convention required him to kneel anyway, but Moser (fearing, he related, that weakness from fever would have prevented him from getting up again) stayed on his feet. He addressed the

52. Review of the 1708 (Regensburg) edition of *Rapsodia Juris publici*, in *Unpartheyische Urtheile*, II (1722), pp. 128–31.

53. "Nachricht," p. 96.

CAROLUS VI.D.G.ROM. IMPER. S.A. GERM. HISP. UNGAR. ET BOH. REX. A.A.

EMPEROR CHARLES VI
"When he heard me address him in Latin he turned sharply and stared at me. But I kept my composure to the end." Moser, *"Nachricht," p. 97.*
Württembergische Landesbibliothek, Stuttgart

emperor in Latin, the state language of His Majesty's Hungarian crown, whereupon Charles, who customarily averted his face when conversing with subjects so as not to fluster them, turned and stared at Moser full face and then replied in Latin, but a Latin which, Moser said, "after the manner adopted for reasons of state, was so indistinct that I could only understand a few words, like *laudibile* etc." The exchange ended; after a baffled silence Moser did kneel and kiss hands, and wavered out.

Next day Schönborn sent a messenger to say that the emperor would be pleased to do Moser a beneficence, a "Gnade": what should it be? Moser asked for a medal to commemorate the audience; and soon it arrived, with a golden chain worth three hundred gulden. There was some talk around Vienna about this medal and chain. Why these favors for young Moser? The Lichtenstein emissary Harpprecht, of the Tübingen Harpprechts, said he had heard that the chain and medal weren't meant for Moser at all; he had only been given them for delivery to Minister Schüz, back in Stuttgart. Moser's defenders said no, they belonged to him. Meanwhile Moser learned that there was talk of him at home too—that he had become Catholic, that he had been heard to slander the Grävenitz and her entourage. His letters to Friderica Rosina were being opened, or he thought they were. Moser pawned the medal and chain "so as to leave Vienna with honor," and set out for Stuttgart in March 1722, half-crippled with his diarrhea and fever.

On the way there occurred one of those incidents that came to mind forty years later. He stopped to visit the famous monastery at Melk, being particularly anxious to meet two learned brothers at the cloister library with whom he had corresponded. When he had left Vienna, friends had given him two bottles of special Hungarian wine, in consideration of his ill health, and he had stored one in each coattail pocket. But in his haste at Melk he knocked one coattail against a stone pillar so that the bottle broke and the wine ran onto the floor; and when Moser tried to save what he could of that one, he smashed the other.[54]

---

54. "Nachricht," pp. 96–97; *Lebensgeschichte*, I, pp. 34–37; IV, pp. 11–13.

§5. Stuttgart, Wetzlar, Vienna, Stuttgart, 1722–1726

MOSER left Austria by way of Linz and Passau, traveling partly by land and partly in open Danube cargo boats to save money. At Regensburg he looked up Baron von Schüz, Württemberg ambassador to the imperial diet, and Schüz lent him enough money to keep him moving. Moser sent most of the Schüz money back to Vienna to get his medal and chain out of pawn, so as to have them as professional credentials when he got home; and then he got as far as Nürnberg when the remaining cash ran out. There he took a room at an inn, skipped his dinners, and worked over his *Unpartheyische Urtheile* manuscripts and patched together a bibliography of miscellaneous documents he had seen at Vienna. He managed to sell both batches to a printer for enough money to get him to Nördlingen, where he had an aunt. Meanwhile the medal and chain had caught up with him from Vienna. The Nördlingen aunt gave him enough money to get to Stuttgart without pawning them again.[55]

Moser made no effort to return to Tübingen. He hoped that his experience and connections at Vienna would bring him a good post in Württemberg service, but they had the opposite effect, if any. He even had trouble getting his medal and chain back when he sent them in for the duke's inspection. Everybody wanted to know what he had been up to in Vienna, and especially, what unrevealed service he must have done for the emperor to get that golden chain and medal. One rumor, put to him directly by a member of the Schüz political clan (the diet ambassador had a brother and a son both eminent in Württemberg affairs), was that Moser had used his special local information to suggest how the house of Austria could get the directorship of the Swabian Circle away from Württemberg. And what had he been telling the imperial court about Grävenitz and her party? Moser denied all. But in two years of trying at Stuttgart he got no posts and no commissions from the ducal government or from any other public agency there.[56]

Promptly upon his arrival from Vienna, he had married Friderica Rosina; and the next year she was pregnant. Moser's first son, born in

---

55. "Nachricht," pp. 97–98; *Lebensgeschichte*, I, pp. 37–38. The *Unpartheyische Urtheile* were placed from Frankfurt/Main and Leipzig, and were anonymous; the bibliography of manuscripts is *Bibliotheca manuscriptorum, maxime anecdotorum, eorumque historicorum* (Nürnberg, 1722).
56. "Nachricht," pp. 98–99; *Lebensgeschichte*, I, pp. 39–40.

December of 1723, was named Friedrich Karl after the imperial vice-chancellor. How Moser supported them and himself is impossible to tell; the autobiographies do not say, leaving this the most obscure period of his life. He tried fitfully to earn money with his pen. The *Unpartheyische Urtheile* appeared by installment, with enough distribution so that they are not difficult to find today. In 1723 he started publishing a "Living Literary Württemberg," *Wurtembergia literata viva*,[57] but the sales were so poor that he gave it up and it went the way of the "Swabian Learned World" of two years before. The same happened to "Mixed Observations on Württemberg Public Law" in 1724.[58] He wrote two political biographies of Württemberg dukes, which remained unpublished.

As for imperial questions: Moser got one commission from Count Hohenlohe-Pfedelbach, through the agency of a brother of Friderica Rosina's who was in that count's service, which touched imperial affairs in ways unlikely to commend him to the Vienna authorities. The *corpus evangelicorum*, organized Protestant party at the imperial diet, had guaranteed an internal Hohenlohe-Pfedelbach agreement regulating relations between the government and the religious confessions, made on the occasion of the title passing from a Protestant to a Catholic count; in 1723 the emperor declared the *corpus evangelicorum* guarantee to be invalid and without effect, and Moser was enlisted to prepare an argument defending it. His brief was incorporated into the official Protestant reply to the emperor in 1725. Two other legal works of those years may have better suited imperial authorities, or at least the Schönborn party: one was a denial of Spanish pretensions to the Order of the Golden Fleece, the other a defense of Emperor Charles's project of an imperial East India Company operating out of Ostend.[59]

None of these were works of serious sustained scholarship; Moser thought of himself as a career civil servant and public lawyer. He kept on trying for a Württemberg post and meanwhile maintained correspondence with Schönborn and with Abbot Göttweig in Vienna. When summoned before a Württemberg official to explain this correspondence, he replied (or so later recalled) that as long as he had no post in Württemberg he must keep up his contacts with these Vienna patrons; and besides, since his letters were regularly opened, the government must know their

57. Tübingen, 1723 (anon.).
58. *Vermischte, die Württembergische Staats-Rechte . . . betreffend Observationes . . .* (Stuttgart, 1724).
59. "Nachricht," p. 99; *Lebensgeschichte*, I, p. 40; Caeserinus Charitinius (pseud.), *Die Nichtigkeit der Spanischen Prätension auf den Ritter-Orden des güldenen Vliesses* (Esslingen, 1723). Neither the Hohenlohe brief nor the Ostend brief seems to have been published.

innocent nature.[60] Then in the summer of 1724 he thought he saw a chance to get his career moving again, this time on an issue affecting the Imperial Cameral Court, the Reichskammergericht, which sat at Wetzlar.

The Reichskammergericht was one of two supreme courts of the empire. Its twenty-five judges (though their ranks were almost never filled) were nominated by the circles and electors of the empire according to a complicated formula, and twelve were to be Protestant; the emperor named only one member of the court, plus a presiding judge and two deputies. In most cases, therefore, the German princes and other estates, especially the Protestant ones, preferred taking their cases to this Wetzlar court, if to any imperial court at all, rather than its jurisdictional rival, the Imperial Court Council or Reichshofrat, which sat at Vienna, whose members were all chosen by the emperor, and were usually all Catholic. What the princes and estates did not like was paying the expenses of running the court, the so-called Kammerzieler; and their reluctance to do so not only inhibited the work of the court, for lack of funds, but undermined whatever independence the court might have whenever new Kammerzieler had to be granted or even whenever a case affecting a contributor (or briber) came before it. The question of how to finance the court became especially active when a reform measure of 1720 more than tripled the budget of the court and the assessment on the estates.[61]

Moser thought up a plan for funding the court while safeguarding its independence—at least he hoped he had, though the autobiographies concede that it was not a very good plan and he never informed posterity just what it had been. But he was straining for any reentry into the world of affairs. In the autumn of 1724 he journeyed to Wetzlar to present himself and his plan to the chief judges of the court. They (the emperor's appointees) told him that they could do nothing with it; he must take his plan to Vienna, and if it was well received there, then it must go before a plenary diet of the empire. The president of the court provided Moser with a letter to the imperial vice-chancellor, Schönborn. So in the autumn of 1724 Moser traveled to Vienna again. But in Vienna the reception was even chillier. Schönborn avoided seeing Moser and would have nothing to do with his Wetzlar Reichskammergericht financing scheme. Count Windischgrätz, blunt president of the competing Vienna Reichshofrat,

---

60. "Nachricht," p. 99.

61. Johann Stephan Pütter, *Historische Entwicklung der heutigen Staatsverfassung des Teutschen Reichs* II (Göttingen, 1798), pp. 409–19; Moser, *Von der Teutschen Justiz-Verfassung* (= Neues Teutsches Staats-Recht VIII), II (Frankfurt/Main, 1774), pp. 353–71. The constitutional number of *Assessoren* had been reduced from the fifty specified in the Peace of Westphalia to twenty-five in 1719–20, but even that roster was never full. Moser (ibid., p. 390), gives seventeen as the actual number of sitting judges traditional by 1774.

told Moser that if he had nothing better to do in Vienna than peddle this scheme he might as well go home; whatever its merits might be, the emperor in fact had no interest in seeing the Wetzlar court financially independent.[62]

But there was nothing to do at home either, so Moser stayed in Vienna, hanging about anterooms and receptions trying to pick up commissions; he made conversation with the cranky Count Wurmbrand, vice-president of the Reichshofrat, when the latter was laid up with gout and his court was in recess. Eventually Schönborn gave Moser some documents to study and some legal reports to make: one on the ecclesiastical jurisdictions of Catholic princes over their Protestant subjects, another on the *Simultaneum*, meaning the right of a Catholic prince in a constitutionally Protestant state to introduce Catholic religious exercises alongside the Protestant. Most probably these study assignments from Schönborn were more than a slap on the wrist for the Hohenlohe brief. They bore on related but larger political prospects of which Schönborn was quite conscious, and on Moser's home duchy in particular. For next in line of succession to the Protestant duchy of Württemberg, after the single son of the Grävenitz-smitten Eberhard Ludwig, was a cousin who had converted to Catholicism, as befit his career in the military service of the emperor, some twenty years before. The confessional difference between that Catholic line and the Protestant duchy was to bring Württemberg its severest constitutional crisis and Moser his greatest fame thirty years later.[63]

But none of this brought in money in the winter of 1724–25, and Schönborn's anteroom remained a chilly place. Fluctuations in the vice-chancellor's favor resulted, probably, from concurrent changes in the course of imperial confessional and territorial politics, complicated by Schönborn's losing struggle with the Spanish court party at Vienna.[64] Of these matters Moser no doubt had more than an inkling, but no certain knowledge. He was down to his last thaler, faced by an urgent plea for funds from Friderica Rosina back in Stuttgart, when Count Wurmbrand, his Reichshofrat acquaintance, told him that Schönborn wanted to see him. On the vice-chancellor's next scheduled audience day, Moser went.

---

62. "Nachricht," p. 100; *Lebensgeschichte*, I, pp. 40–42.

63. "Nachricht," p. 100; *Lebensgeschichte*, I, p. 43; Sincerus (pseud.), *Die auf das allerbeste gegründete Jurisdictio ecclesiastica Catholischer Landes-Herren über ihre Protestirende Unterthanen* (Nürnberg, 1726). The results of the *Simultaneum* researches were published, according to "Nachricht," p. 101, in part III of Moser's (anonymous) *Reichs-Fama* (23 parts, Frankfurt/Main 1727–38).

64. For the dynastic and international outworks of this, involving the Ostend Company and the Pragmatic Sanction, Max Braubach, *Prinz Eugen von Savoyen*, IV (Munich, 1965), pp. 219–311.

He found the anteroom crowded as usual with people trying to see Schönborn, among them the ubiquitous Schüz, who confided that he had heard that high imperial officers had decided to make something out of Moser; and when the audience opened Moser was summoned first, despite protocol, ahead of his superiors in rank (such as Schüz). When he entered the inner audience room there was no sign of the vice-chancellor, but then Moser heard him in an inner office—counting! Then Schönborn emerged "with his hat full of French money" and said: "Herr von Moser! His Majesty the Emperor has learned that you are in need of money, and has furnished me this for you. When it is gone, more will be provided." Moser was stupefied, but he recovered and stuffed the two hundred gulden (a decent half-year's pay for someone of his standing) into his coat pockets. But now, Schönborn went on, he had a return favor to ask. He had a young brother-in-law, a Count von Nostiz, who had been appointed judge on the Reichshofrat, and who really ought to learn some law: would Moser tutor him? Moser disparaged his own knowledge of that court's procedures, and protested modestly at the thought of teaching law to one of the supreme judges of the Reich; but Schönborn assured him that he needn't feel out of his depth, and let him go. Back in the anteroom Moser let Schüz peep into his pockets and consented to have lunch with him. Schüz spiced the luncheon with sardonic probes into the sources of Moser's good fortune, inquired whether there really was such a place as Filseck for the Mosers to be *von*, and such levities—to Moser's own great satisfaction, for it appeared that he need no longer think much about Schüz.[65]

Moser went to Count Nostiz that very day, and was amiably but languidly received. As you see, said the count, I have a great many books; but *das seye der Teufel*, it won't go into my head. They agreed that Moser would work with him two hours a day, for fifty gulden a week (the full pay of a Württemberg active state councillor). The most convenient time the count found, though, was after midnight when he came home from society: his wife the countess, being dissatisfied with the rank accorded her in Vienna, lived on the family estates in Bohemia, and the count at Vienna was away from his apartments a good many evenings. The sober Swabian Moser found it impossible to stay awake beyond midnight, so the time was changed to midday; but then Nostiz slept all through Moser's instruction. If Moser stopped talking Nostiz would wake up and tell him to go on, he understood every word. On days when there was no session of the Reichshofrat, Nostiz stayed in bed with the curtains drawn, so that Moser expounded the Peace of

65. "Nachricht," pp. 101–2; *Lebensgeschichte*, I, pp. 45–46.

Westphalia to an invisible pupil. Clearly Count Nostiz, who held his post by birth and station, had no notion of making a civil servant of himself to justify it. And Moser's principal duty now became to prepare the reports and opinions assigned Nostiz by the Reichshofrat. This tutelary relation occasionally stimulated the count to assert legal opinions that contradicted those of the omniscient Moser. When Moser complained of it to Schönborn the vice-chancellor told him not to worry, that was only Nostiz's *böhmischer Kopf*, his Bohemian head; just show him who's master. After one or two tries at being master, Moser simply kept quiet whenever Nostiz displayed his Bohemian head.

Moser's greatest annoyance with his count was the latter's underdeveloped sense of the uses of paper and forms. There was a particularly painful scene one day at the Reichshofrat when President Windischgrätz asked Nostiz to supply the verbatim content of a document bearing on an appeal case for which Nostiz was rapporteur; and the count, who customarily made his presentations out of his memory of the general state of things, shuffled through his papers in vain until somebody else came and found the document in question while the president snarled and snapped. Windischgrätz directed Moser to see that the count's homework was done better in the future. Moser in the autobiographies claimed to have learned "many curious and secret things" about the Reichshofrat from his days with Count Nostiz, and perhaps he did; but mainly he seems to have meant by this, apart from the normal ration of gossip and inside politics, the judicial blunders of various members of the court and the waspish observations of President Windischgrätz about his bench's level of judicial learning. Still, Moser got the foundations of a useful series of important Reichshofrat decisions that he published from 1726 to 1732—after he was safely out of Vienna and back in Württemberg service—and a successful textbook on Reichshofrat procedures published in the early thirties.[66]

Meanwhile Moser continued to do odd jobs for Schönborn. Moser got a free run of the vice-chancellor's library in return for straightening it out for him. Schönborn had been in his office for twenty years, and the library was full of the kinds of legal and political materials that every public lawyer hungered for, for they were the main ammunition with which they did the battles that were the public life of the empire. These were the endless juridical disputes fought among political groups and personages too weak and too poor to fight with soldiers, among govern-

66. *Merckwürdige Reichs-Hof-Raths-Conclusa* (8 parts, Frankfurt/Main, 1726–32, anon.); *Einleitung zum Reichs-Hof-Raths-Process* (4 parts, Frankfurt/Main, 1731–37; 2d ed. in 3 parts, Frankfurt/Main, 1734–42). "Nachricht," pp. 103–5; *Lebensgeschichte*, I, p. 46; IV, pp. 8–10.

ments whose substitute for trials of force, which might have put an end to them, was legal negotiation or litigation before the empire's courts and arbiters—juridical processes carried on by officials trained for it, and inflated by them in ways they hoped would commend the importance of what they did to their masters, and give business for hosts of civil servants like themselves, like Johann Jakob Moser. Most of the materials were not strictly secret, but many were rare, unpublished, and hard to come by, so that those who possessed or knew about them were likely to keep them for themselves, for the sake of the competitive advantage this would give them over professional rivals to themselves, or over political rivals to the governments they served. There was no sense giving away intelligence to potential adversaries, and surely no sense arousing the populace at large about matters properly managed within and among people like themselves who understood such matters. Thus even Lünig, in his great compendium of imperial laws, had to excuse his failure to identify his sources on the grounds that to reveal publicly the archives where he had found these valid laws and precedents would endanger the archivists who had permitted him to copy them.[67]

Everywhere Moser went he took his greed for legal information. His avid quest for entry into the libraries and archives of every place he visited, the overabundance of time he had to spend in them, and his unusually retentive verbal memory, supplemented by obsessive note taking, filled his arsenal as German jurist and civil servant. But the professional firepower he was assembling in that way had recoil in the suspicions and doubts he aroused in others—suspicions that he might know too much, about the wrong things. It was not just that Moser might use the information he stored to promote his own professional advantage; more particularly, Moser seemed ready to publish anything. This propensity involved him with the problem of censorship, in its eighteenth-century form as political and juridical counterintelligence, when he tried to publish the results of his researches into Reichshofrat procedures and decisions. Members of the Reichshofrat tried to prevent him from doing so, invoking the imperial censors at Frankfurt on Main. Schönborn supported Moser before the censors on the grounds that "the genius of modern times" made it likely that these materials would get out anyway; severe imperial censorship, said Schönborn, only drove the valuable law-publishing industry away from its center at Frankfurt and into the hands of Prussian and Saxon publishers who paid little attention to imperial censorship anyway. Schönborn's intervention with the censors enabled

67. Moser commented on this in his review of Lünig's *Reichsarchiv* in *Unpartheyische Urtheile*, I (1722), pp. 73–74.

Moser eventually to publish at least some of his Reichshofrat materials after he had left Vienna for good, but even then he published the sensitive items anonymously.[68]

During the winter of 1724–25 Moser lived on Schönborn's patronage; and the vice-chancellor's favor toward him became well enough known so that petitioners began to seek out Moser's influence and access to high places. Persons of rank came to ask him to arrange special favors from Schönborn. In June of 1725 Moser traveled to Württemberg (where his wife and son still awaited his return from the journey that had begun with Wetzlar) and formally requested the post of active state councillor, *Würcklicher Regierungs-Rath*—the appointment immediately, then full pay to start whenever a vacancy occurred. The official reply was an order permitting Moser to remain in Vienna on condition that he remember his duty and not let himself be used in any way detrimental to the duke's interest, and that he return to the duke's service whenever summoned. Moser found this decree, which he attributed to the illwill and tale carrying of the Schüz clan, to be insulting and degrading; without making reply he sold his household goods and set to moving his family to Vienna. The description of their Danube passage tells of storms, the sinking of ships, and the drowning of passengers where the river flows through the cliffs and shoals near Passau: travel by night and an eclipse of the moon. He officially resigned his ceremonial Württemberg councillorship and his lapsed Tübingen professorship as soon as he got to Vienna.[69] It was the third time he had come and he expected to remain, but again he stayed less than a year.

Moser's relation with Schönborn and his work with the feckless Reichshofrat Count Nostiz had already drawn the attention of Reichshofrat President Windischgrätz. Shortly after Moser's return to Vienna, Windischgrätz intimated that he might appoint Moser *Agent* or advocate at the Reichshofrat, one of two dozen or so lawyers licensed to manage the cases of parties appearing before it, and potentially a profitable post especially for Protestants, inasmuch as most advocates appointed were Catholic.[70] The approaches from Windischgrätz put Moser in a situation like the one that had come of his efforts to keep one foot in Stuttgart and one in Vienna, for Schönborn and Windischgrätz were not only political rivals by virtue of the two institutions they headed, but were apparently personal rivals as well. Schönborn himself, however, urged Moser to pur-

68. See note 66, above; also "Nachricht," pp. 106–7; *Lebensgeschichte*, I, pp. 46–50; IV, pp. 5–6.

69. "Nachricht," pp. 108–9; *Lebensgeschichte*, I, pp. 17–18, 52–54.

70. Moser, *Justiz-Verfassung* (= NTSR VIII), II, pp. 63–67.

sue the chance, quoting obscurely from the apostle Paul about timeliness, and knowing good from evil times.[71]

Recall, though, that it was Schönborn who had placed Moser with Nostiz and thus in contact with Reichshofrat affairs in the first place, perhaps for the sake of having a protégé of his in the rival camp. And now Schönborn even promised to support Moser from his own purse until, as advocate, Moser got clients enough to stand on his own. Thus Schönborn's patronage would continue if Moser took the Reichshofrat appointment. Moser demurred, on the grounds, he claimed, that an advocate could serve his clients only if he had full access to legal and political information, but that information could only be gotten from persons whose sworn duty it was to keep it secret. So where would he get clients? Schönborn said he might help there too.[72]

Recall, too, that the Austrian-Spanish alliance of that year, with its implications and consequences for imperial internal politics, had the imperial vice-chancellor under severe political pressure—a penultimate stage, as it turned out, in his loss of authority.[73] Moser made no hint of this or its possible effects on his fortunes in the autobiographies, except for a long anecdote about the secret and nefarious doings of Spanish and papal emissaries at Vienna in those years, loosely associated with Schönborn's Pauline warnings about timeliness and tacked onto the end of the Life History in a 1783 edition; but he was surely aware of the situation by now. Whether the reason was Schönborn's decline, or Moser's fear of being caught between two powerful rivals, or his usual dread of dependency aggravated by these, he was frightened and worried that winter. The surest sign that he knew he was in trouble was that he experienced that year his first attack of what he called the *malum hypochondriacum*, a state of melancholy and confusion that in this instance he attributed to a "disorderly living style," the irregular hours and diet imposed by his services to Nostiz.[74]

And aggravating it all, ironically, was that Moser's perilous game of bargaining by ambiguous allegiances was beginning to succeed at home. The court at Württemberg, having gotten Moser's resignation of his obligations and loyalties there, now became disturbed by his connections

71. Moser in *Lebensgeschichte*, I, p. 54, quotes Schönborn as saying, "Ermahne, es seye zu rechter Zeit, oder zur Unzeit!" This is a slight misquotation from 2 Timothy 4:2; and I suspect the reason Moser kept this particular verbatim memory, despite its variance from the biblical text he surely knew, is its hint of the political events taking place at Vienna at that time. On the enmity between Windischgrätz and Schönborn, see also *Lebensgeschichte*, IV, pp. 13–14; and Hantsch, *Schönborn*, pp. 175–76.

72. "Nachricht," pp. 107–8; *Lebensgeschichte*, I, pp. 54–55.

73. See above, §4.

74. *Lebensgeschichte*, I, pp. 54–55; IV, pp. 18–21.

FRIEDRICH KARL VON SCHÖNBORN
"He had, usually, the phlegmatic temper so needful in a minister; he listened calmly to the arguments made before him, recapitulated them point by point, then replied to each just as calmly, with an articulation and precision one could only admire." Moser, Lebensgeschichte, I, p. 59.
Württembergische Landesbibliothek, Stuttgart

ERNST FRIEDRICH VON WINDISCHGRÄTZ
"But confident in his own uprightness, he was all too open with anybody. . . .
Also his passions were overly strong, so that with best intentions he sometimes
broke out in the assembled Reichshofrat with violent attacks on certain of its
members." Moser, Lebensgeschichte, I, p. 58.
Germanisches Nationalmuseum, Nürnberg

at Vienna; suddenly the ducal government offered him that post of active state councillor it had been unwilling to grant before, when he had asked for it. This in turn speeded things up in Vienna. Windischgrätz offered to confer the advocacy at the Reichshofrat even though no Protestant slot was properly open. Other Vienna oracles told him that Count Nostiz was scheduled to become ambassador to France, which event would make Moser's fortune. Moser even heard, or thought he did, that he was being considered to be judge on the Reichshofrat itself—if, of course, he stayed in Vienna and became Catholic. His friend Abbot Göttweig said to him: "With all the respect due princes of the empire: their courts are little streams for catching minnows. Vienna is the ocean, for catching whales!"

Johann decided for his Swabian stream, nowhere explaining why— whether *malum hypochondriacum*, Friderica Rosina's second pregnancy, or apprehensions about what his situation at Vienna was leading to and what happens in the game of whales. Nowhere is there evidence that he preferred the society or landscape of his native place, that he had an attachment to home for its own sake. The nearest approach to an answer from Moser is his repeated claim that he might have become a great figure in imperial affairs if he had been willing to become Catholic. The inference that he left imperial politics to remain Protestant has been im-proved by pious biographers into the proposition that Moser renounced worldly glory for the sake of his Protestant faith. Moser may have hoped for some such attestation by posterity, but there is little evidence for it and Moser himself never directly claimed it: that religious conviction or emotive faith was the reason. To be sure, there are autobiographical strategies at work here: a later Moser had to disavow religious concerns at this stage of his life so as to dramatize the stages of salvation as they came later. Still, almost certainly religious sentiment was no important part of his life in 1726, and most of his best friends were Catholic. Moreover, confessional changes for political career purposes were com-mon enough among German jurists and officials of the time to make such a step quite possible without injury to Moser's limited religious sensibilities.

Yet religion was surely involved, and here we must begin to consider what religion meant in a choice of this kind. When Moser went to Schön-born to take his leave, most of the interview seems to have been taken up with the question of Moser's religion: Schönborn asking Moser to keep his spirit open to the ancient faith, Moser arguing that if antiquity con-ferred merit to a religion, we should all be Jews, or better, heathens; and the vice-chancellor would surely think the less of him if he put his reli-gious loyalties on the counter to trade for worldly success.[75] Schönborn

75. The last days in Vienna and the final scene with Schönborn are described somewhat differently, in accordance with the respective autobiographical compartments into which

was in fact a firm and devout Catholic, and he may seriously have hoped for Moser's conversion for its own religious sake, just as he may have helped Moser's career out of respect for his gifts and his energy. But Schönborn was also a politician, and religious identity was a political factor of great importance, particularly for the working of imperial institutions like Schönborn's and for the careers of civil servants like Moser. The two great German confessions, Roman Catholic and *evangelisch* or Protestant, played a political role in the empire that was the nearest equivalent to the role played by political parties in more recent polities; but they were more explicitly and more rigidly built into the empire's constitutional system than modern parties are into modern state institutions. Offices bore religious tags that largely controlled their distribution. Confessional parity, or controlled disparity, or exclusiveness, was elaborately worked out and specified in nearly every political or judicial instrumentality in Germany, and so religious adherence determined the career ladder of posts and patronage that a public official like Moser would climb.

When Moser chose Stuttgart in 1726 he was opting not merely for a Württemberg ladder rather than an imperial one, nor mainly perhaps for Württemberg at all; he was opting for the Protestant party and ladder. Schönborn for his part, when he urged Moser to stay open to Catholicism, was not arguing for an imperial versus Württemberg career. Moser had already chosen Württemberg; Schönborn was arguing for the Catholic party and ladder. To be sure, most posts and preferments in the empire's gift were Catholic, and most Protestant posts and preferments were in the gift of Protestant princes, estates, and towns. That fact, finally, gives an important clue to the fate of Schönborn's effort to create a body of imperial institutions that would be coherent, effective, and capable of withstanding both the particularist interest of its princely members and the dynastic needs of the Habsburgs. The system of constitutional confessional parties was fatal for him. Being Catholic by conviction and training, and even constitutionally Catholic as imperial vice-chancellor, Schönborn could hardly become head of the Protestant party and direct its preferments, as Moser surely recognized; in that he could not rival the strong Protestant princes that led the Protestant party. But on the other hand, as imperial vice-chancellor, obliged to work with estates and territories of both confessions and dependent upon both for the effective working of imperial institutions and the success of his plans, he could not

they are introduced, in "Nachricht," p. 30, and *Lebensgeschichte*, I, pp. 56–57; around 1725 the "Nachricht" manuscript on "Bürgerliches Leben" breaks off altogether. See also the recollections of that period in Vienna by the aged Moser in *Lebensgeschichte*, IV (1783), pp. 11–24.

credibly rival the emperor's own house officials and exclusive appointees, and the German Catholic prelates as well, for leadership of the Catholic party and dispenser of its preferments.

That is why such matters as the Palatine confessional quarrel and the Austrian-Spanish alliance were politically such damaging crises for Schönborn. By confirming and intensifying confessional partisanship they took the instruments of influence and patronage farther from his grasp. Moreover, Schönborn needed all the German connections he could hold for support against the Spanish party at Vienna; and his relations with Württemberg Protestantism were important to him particularly as counterweight to Prussian confessional politics from the Hohenzollern base nearby in Franconia.[76]

So Schönborn may have hoped, in his final audience with Moser, to keep Moser as a client still, in a Protestant territory but with a foot on the Catholic ladder. Moser was taking leave of a protector whose authority was declining, a mighty imperial officer who for all his constitutional authority had provided no post comparable to the advocacy at the Reichshofrat offered by Windischgrätz, nor to that of active state councillor of the Duchy of Württemberg.

---

§6. Württemberg State Councillor, 1726–1729

T H E Duchy of Württemberg, sprawled over southwestern Germany in the eccentric shapes ordained by dynastic accidents and jurisdictional compromises over the centuries, held at that time about 350,000 souls, roughly the population of the Duchy of East Prussia, or of London, or double that of New England in America. It was by far the most important Protestant state south of the Main River. The capital and largest town, Stuttgart, had a population of about 15,000. The annual peacetime state revenues of Württemberg were about a twentieth the amount England spent on its navy, or a hundredth the peacetime income of the French crown.[77] The duchy was in fact territorially

76. Hantsch, *Schönborn*, pp. 88-89, 106–7, 134, 239–64, 412.

77. The figures are offered only for the purpose of rough comparison. *Handwörterbuch der Staatswissenschaften*, II (Jena, 1924), p. 673; *Statistisches Handbuch der Stadt Stutt-*

rather stable and compact, as eighteenth-century German principalities went, and, probably both as cause and as consequence of this, its governing institutions were relatively well established and integral with the land and society. The state council or Regierungsrat, of which Moser now became an "actual" or working member, was one of three main state administrative bodies. The others were the Rentkammer, which administered the ducal domains and most other direct revenues, and the Kirchenrat, which oversaw the very substantial Protestant ecclesiastical and monastic endowments and revenues of the duchy. Alongside and above these three main agencies of the duke's government was the privy council or Geheimrat, which was sworn to the constitution of the duchy rather than the duke's person, and which rested politically somewhere between ducal authority and the diet or Landschaft, which represented the towns and districts.[78]

Of these institutions the Regierungsrat, with some fifteen members, was the one most actively engaged in the day-to-day work of legislation and administration. It was responsible for overseeing local administration in the towns and districts—here scraping jurisdictions with the Rentkammer of the duke's domains—and it functioned too as an appellate court of the duchy in civil suits, and also as an adjudicating court, a source of authoritative legal opinion, in criminal and administrative law. Ordinarily several of its members held posts in other governmental agencies and in the Deputations, special committees appointed occasionally for particular investigations or tasks. The council functioned collegially: each matter that came before it was assigned to one member for his investigation and presentation before the whole body, which then voted on the disposition of the case, the majority determining the position of the council.

Much of the council's work was formal and bureaucratic: the processing and presentation of the interminable legal analyses that still lie fossil in archives of eighteenth-century German states. But still council membership was an important post and was a good place to learn about the duchy, about the way it was governed, and about politics. How valuable it was for a civil servant's career depended largely of course

gart (Stuttgart, 1960), p. 19; Marcel R. Reinhard et al., *Histoire générale de la population mondiale* (3d ed., Paris, 1968), pp. 224, 275; Karl O. Müller, "Die Finanzwirtschaft in Württemberg unter Herzog Karl Alexander, 1733–37," *Württembergische Vierteljahrshefte für Landesgeschichte*, NF XXXVIII (1932), pp. 276–317; John Ehrman, *The Navy in the War of King William*, 1689–1697 (Cambridge, England, 1953), pp. 614 and passim; Philippe Sagnac and A. de Saint-Leger, *Louis XIV* (Paris, 1949), p. 636.

78. Alfred Dehlinger, *Württembergs Staatswesen*, I (Stuttgart, 1951), pp. 92–94, 101–7.

upon his relations with his peers and his superiors, and on the kind of assignment he got from the council president and his political masters.

One way to success was professional skill and energy, and this was the route Moser chose, conformably with his personality perhaps but also, probably, in the hope that by adopting a severely professional and unpartisan posture—*unpartheylich*—he might escape the loopings of political snares and intrigues that bedraped the public life of Württemberg. By his own account, which there is every reason to believe, Moser did his work himself, and he did it thoroughly, neatly, and punctually, with righteous relish of the kinds of advantages that his systematic habits and his industry gave him over colleagues and competitors. He was scrupulous and independent. Many of the people he worked with and worked for, it seems clear, disliked and distrusted J. J. Moser—disliked him for the virtues he chose; distrusted him, not for being a cheat or corrupt, but because on the contrary his incorruptibility and his righteousness made him an undependable ally. Perhaps it was quite impossible for a Württemberg public official of the 1720s to be politically nonpartisan. In any event, Moser's obsession with *Unpartheylichkeit* in this part of his Life History clearly has to do with the poor state of his relations with the ruling Grävenitz *Parthey*.

The assignments Moser got were routine cases in civil, criminal, and marriage law; the marriage specialty associated him with the marriage contract of Eberhard Ludwig's Catholic cousin, Karl Alexander—a connection with a possibly rising sun that may not have helped him with the incumbents in power. But whatever Moser's particular assignments, more sensitive political matters managed by others came before the council too for its collegial deliberation, and among these were the various grants of office and perquisites, appurtenances of the duchy, with which the ruling Grävenitz party maintained itself in power—especially important now that the charms of the countess of Urach were beginning to fade, visibly even to the eyes of Duke Eberhard Ludwig. Moser's account leaves uncertain whether his indignation at this traffic was directed at the system of patronage itself, or followed a prudent sense that his allegiance should go to the duchy rather than his present master's ministers and mistress, or was plain workmanlike annoyance that the council should be dragged in to legitimize activities that it or at least Moser might have preferred to ignore. They all fit together in Moser's chosen posture and course as neutral administrative official. But his sense of office did not allow him to accept quietly the recommendations of the council members who reported on such matters to the body. Not only did he argue vigorously in meetings against council actions that extended Grävenitz patronage, he even insisted, contrary to easy custom and the secretary's practice, that his dissents must be recorded and even that his full dissenting opinions must be appended to the official approval by the majority. It was after a council wrangle over this that Moser found himself assigned to be the government's specialist on rafts.[79]

The Life History asserts no connection here. Moser describes the foregoing—in detail—as a purely procedural quarrel with the secretary about the recording of Moser's minority opinions; but then the next item in his account is about his assignment as raft specialist. One need not make light of rafts: for a rural place like Württemberg, and especially the impoverished but heavily forested Black Forest area, the orderly transportation and marketing of timber was economically important, and the ripuarian and foresting rights and marketing franchises of the interested states and parties were complex and in such disarray as to frustrate the development and maintenance of this important resource. Indeed upon reflection it seems a very proper assignment for an energetic, unpartisan civil servant. But to an ambitious young man recently wooed away from the side of the Reichshofrat's president and from the personal friendship and regard of the vice-chancellor of the empire, one who moreover knew nothing whatever about timber or rivers or rafts, the assignment seemed deliberately contrived to frustrate his career and to keep him away from serious matters of state, if not publicly to insult him. Moser took his complaint to brother Grävenitz himself, now prime minister. Grävenitz calmly suggested that Moser might find a specialist in the bureaucracy to mend his own ignorance about rivers and timber, the varieties of trees, the units of measure, and all the rest that the council's raft expert had to know. He ordered Moser to keep the assignment. And then another councillor, who in fact knew something about the business, was given council responsibility for Reichshofrat affairs.[80]

In 1727, in order to escape the influence of the city of Stuttgart and of the legitimate duchess (who had stubbornly refused to evacuate the residential Schloss there), the Grävenitz ministry moved the duke's person and government to Ludwigsburg, site of a hunting seat and of the raw beginnings of a planned residential town; any official who refused to follow was threatened with dismissal. Of all the state council only Moser refused to go, telling his superiors in writing that he'd rather go to Vienna than to Ludwigsburg. At this the duke proposed to make Moser

79. *Lebensgeschichte*, I, pp. 67–69, 73–74. It is possible that Moser really was acting here, consciously or not, in the interest of an heir-presumptive party supported by Vienna; the possible heir, the imperial general Karl Alexander, was Catholic and a personal friend of Prince Eugene. I know no positive evidence for this, but the circumstantial evidence is enough to explain the suspicions of Moser's contemporaries.

80. *Lebensgeschichte*, I, pp. 74–76.

an archivist, retaining present pay and dignity, if Moser would undertake never to leave his service, a proposal that Moser found attractive "but in several respects questionable [bedencklich]." He countered with the suggestion that he might return to Tübingen. The government found that agreeable; but as the university faculty would have none of him, Moser was appointed professor at the Collegium Illustre at Tübingen.[81]

This post was a total sinecure; there was no Collegium Illustre in 1727 except as a source of funds to provide for impecunious princelings vaguely attending the university, or to supplement the salaries of Württemberg officials whom the government did not wish to employ nor the university to accept as professors.[82] In fact, for two years after his appointment began (February 1727) Moser stayed in Stuttgart, away from both the academic life at Tübingen and the effective political capital at Ludwigsburg. What he was doing during those two years is not at all clear; very likely he had no clear idea himself what he was about—except waiting, perhaps. "Wrote books and held seminars" is what the Life History says he did, along with a few odd legal commissions. He edited some legal miscellanies; he published a continuation of his series of imperial court materials, and a kind of documentary history of Württemberg; he prepared a genealogy of his wife's family—no sense of scholarly or professional direction appears in any of these.[83]

But also he continued his correspondence with Vienna acquaintances, and once contemplated returning there when Schönborn, upon the death of his rival Windischgrätz, temporarily took charge of the Reichshofrat; and the seminars or collegia he held at Stuttgart were attended by civil servants still located there. These activities, together presumably with the proximity of the duchess's party at the Schloss while the Grävenitz faithful were entrenched with the duke at Ludwigsburg, revived the suspicions and annoyance of the ruling party, reasonably enough. This was not what they had meant to buy with the Collegium Illustre professorship. The political position at that time was delicate and uncertain, with Madame Grävenitz's personal hold on the duke weakening, with a Catholic heir in the wings who was an imperial general, and with a

81. Schneider, *Württembergische Geschichte*, pp. 335–36; *Lebensgeschichte*, I, pp. 79–80.

82. Eugen Schneider, "Das Tübinger Collegium Illustre," *Württembergische Vierteljahrshefte für Landesgeschichte*, NF VII (1898), pp. 217–45.

83. *Reichs-Fama, oder das merckwürdigste vom Reichs-Convent, Kayserlichen Hof und Ständen des Reichs, mit historischen Erläuterungen* (23 parts, Frankfurt/Main, 1727–38, anon.); *Merckwürdige Reichs-Hof-Raths-Conclusa*; *Vischerische Ahnen-Tafeln*. But probably he also began work on the more important *Bibliotheca Juris publici S. R. German. Imperii* (2 vols., Stuttgart, 1729–34), the first part of which appeared late in 1729 after his return to Tübingen.

strong interest at Vienna—particularly on the part of Schönborn—in the outcome of all these matters. There is no evidence (save the circumstantial) that Moser himself was directly engaged in the ongoing intrigues and maneuvers, if only because he had no idea how they would come out; but he knew most of the maneuverers, their situations, and, since he was neither deaf nor blind, something about what they were doing. He was summoned before Regierungspräsident Pöllnitz, the official who ruled the court administrative establishment at Ludwigsburg, who upbraided him for secret correspondence with Vienna in violation of his duty and the interests of his master the duke; if he didn't want an example made of him, said Pöllnitz, let him betake himself at once to Tübingen where he belonged. And in March of 1729, to Tübingen Moser went.[84]

An important development of these uncertain years at the end of the twenties was the first real sign of the religious interest that later became central to Moser's sense of identity and his peace of mind. In describing these, as usual, Moser's writings make no connection between inward religious events and the events of his outer world, with one partial exception: that his own religious development brought with it a richer and more intimate relation with Friderica Rosina, who now became a more important part of his emotional life. But even here Moser was careful to explain that she and he each experienced their first real religious interests separately, and only confessed them to one another later after a period of parallel development. Thus his turn toward faith and his increased reliance on his wife are fastidiously dissociated, and both are kept clear of the "natural" and "civil" compartments of his life. This was necessary for the religious history to be pure and free of secular accidents, but we need not shun the connection now.

Another reason to be wary about Moser's hindsight account of his religious history is the intervention of the highly conventional formulas of religious development worked out in the pietistic strain of eighteenth-century German Protestants, in stages from indifference through to the reception of grace. These patterns were carefully abstracted from the recorded experience of persons whose true condition of grace seemed beyond doubt; it was important to match one's own experience with the established stages, for a departure from them hinted at corruption by false will, either mortal or diabolical. The conventional sequences or stages of religious consciousness these analyses discerned are not psychologically random or arbitrary; they have their own logic, as well as discernment, and seem quite plausible for persons such as Moser to have followed—once launched on the problem of religious identity. For the launching in Moser's case let us note secular factors of explanation: the

84. *Lebensgeschichte*, I, pp. 80–82, 85.

emphasis on his Protestantism that came from the Vienna experience, the decision for Württemberg, and the confessional issues surrounding the succession there; then the emotional insufficiency of the innominate half-idle years since his departure from the council to take up the Collegium Illustre sinecure; out of this a sense that identity as a Christian and Protestant ought to mean more than a particular political and social identity, the latter so often perfunctorily avowed and not to be depended upon.

Moser's two accounts of his religious experience of the late twenties differ in a way whose significance I shall suggest briefly in a footnote;[85] the version I give will be what seems to me a biographically credible reconstruction from his two accounts. It all began, he wrote in his "Account" for posterity, on a Sunday when he started forward for communion, and found himself suddenly trembling at the thought that "if the Christian religion is true, and if there is a God and a devil, then you deserve to be dragged away from the altar by the devil and delivered to hell."[86] So he prayed fervently to such-a-God-if-one-there-be not to let this happen. Was there one? Moser attributed his first rational conviction that God exists to his reading of William Derham's *Astro-Theology*, an argument from design: that a divine Creator and Purpose is manifest in the intricate perfection of the physical universe.[87] Astro- or physicotheology founded a "natural religion," a "reasonable belief." It did not require Moser to believe in biblical tales or in the divinity of Christ. He

85. Respecting the following account: The *Lebensgeschichte* version of Moser's religious experiences of the late twenties moves (rather too neatly) from a condition of "religiöse Gleichgültigkeit" to the "vernünftige Gottesglauben" based on Derham's arguments, and proceeds to the "gesetzliche Zustand" of prudential observance of Christian ordinance in case it should turn out to be true. Those stages prepared Moser for subsequent "Erweckung" and "Bekehrung": thus the analysis on pp. 32 and 70 of Alo Münch, *Johann Jakob Moser, der Gefangene vom Hohentwiel* (Giessen, 1937), a pious and openly anti-Nazi essay exhorting its readers to follow the example of the prisoner of the Hohentwiel; and Marianne Fröhlich (or Beyer-Fröhlich), *Johann Jakob Moser in seinem Verhältnis zum Rationalismus und Pietismus* (Vienna, 1925), and her *Pietismus und Rationalismus* (Leipzig, 1933). Neither of these authors used Moser's manuscript "Nachricht." Eighteenth-century German conversion literature is endless.

86. "Nachricht," p. 31.

87. *Astro-Theology, Or, A Demonstration of the Being and Attributes of God, from a Survey of the Heavens*, first published in London, 1714; on the influence of Derham and physicotheology in Germany, Wolfgang Philipp, *Das Werden der Aufklärung in theologiegeschichtlicher Sicht* (Göttingen, 1957). The argument from design is quite unlike Moser's as a legal positivist, though to be sure Derham himself perversely mixes the unfathomable God in with the God proven by design, when that helps. I do not really think Derham's influence on Moser was important; it is too neatly and conventionally staged as "natural" and "rational" religion, and too uncharacteristic of Moser's way of thinking about either God or the law.

then arrived at a "lawful condition" by reflecting, without much originality, that he could hardly judge the truth or divinity of Jesus' teachings without following them, in order to see their effect—here came the analogy of the watchmaker's apprentice who rejects the master's instructions without trying them out—and he'd be a foolhardy fellow not to follow them when for all he knew they might be true.

This seems to be as far as Moser's religious sensibility had progressed by 1729, a date he used in other contexts and compartments as one after which he never delivered a *partheylich* or partisan opinion or decision.[88] This level of belief encompassed nothing of the supernatural save fear of it, and might have been blasphemous—surely heathen—if he had progressed no further. Certainly prudent calculations like these left his private righteousness on precarious foundations, vulnerable especially to reasonable and experienced doubts about himself. He had a way and a time to go, some eight or nine years, before the unreasoned bliss of divine righteousness came to him out of torment and humiliation beyond bearing.

When Moser arrived with his family in Tübingen in March of 1729, he cast all his energies into reconstructing, from his Collegium Illustre base, his academic career. Two weary years of limbo at Stuttgart had convinced him that his career in Württemberg government was stymied for the foreseeable future. The news of Schönborn in Vienna was not encouraging either. Now began the great flood of publications that Moser sustained, with a few unavoidable interruptions, for the rest of his life—eight titles in 1729, eleven each in 1730 and 1731, ranging from documentary collections, through serious judicial treatises, to anonymous polemics on current constitutional controversies. He also worked very hard—this time more successfully—at the job of teaching, relying on his reputation and his experience at Stuttgart and Vienna to attract the student interest that the callow university Extraordinarius of ten years before had not evoked.

For his main topic he adopted German constitutional or political law, *Staatsrecht*, meaning the rules and procedures governing political authority and public transactions; and he claimed to teach that subject from practical knowledge of how things really were and how they were done. He made much of the contrast between his practical kind of instruction and such stuff as cloistered law professors thought belonged to the subject. Such irrelevant academic ornaments as constitutional antiquities, general or natural law, and Roman codes were omitted or subordinated to "the way it is, now." Finding no general textbook to his

88. See, for example, the retrospection of extreme old age in *Lebensgeschichte*, IV, p. 196.

liking he prepared one himself, written in German, which came to be used in many places—there were seven editions by 1754—and which laid the basic plan for his own monster works of the 1740s and 1770s.[89] He also devised what he considered a new academic discipline, "Chancellery Practice," giving instruction in "how a chairman, councillor, secretary, registrar, etc., in conferences and committees, where affairs are nonjudicially transacted, must use his tongue and his pen"; for without knowing this (as was generally the case) a young jurist "might have the finest academic studies, but when he came into a chancellery conference as councillor or secretary, it was strange terrain for him." Moser compared this training he offered in chancellery practice with "the way it is with military recruits: the advantage one has, when he was practiced well in exercises and maneuvers before, or the harm he suffers when he has not."[90] And he undertook a "Pragmatic European Law of Nations," meant to describe how European potentates treated with one another, for the instruction of those left unsatisfied by the abstract exhortations of Grotius and hoary recitations of the doings of ancient Greeks and Romans. The book he published out of this study was the basis for the treatises on international law which he published forty years later and which some consider the most original of all his work.[91]

A key to this professional energy from the Collegium Illustre, however, was that a major chair at the university was just coming vacant in 1729— none other than the Ordinarius in constitutional law held by Gabriel Schweder, Moser's former teacher. Quite possibly it was the quest for that chair that had brought Moser to Tübingen in March. But he was not alone in aspiring to it, nor did his efforts to shine from the Collegium Illustre post commend him to the regular university faculty. The main rival for Schweder's chair was Johann Jakob Helferich, another former teacher of Moser's who himself was still waiting in a Collegium Illustre post he had held since Moser's student days.

In his competition for the university chair, Helferich took advantage of Moser's dubious political reputation by helping to launch—so Moser always believed and the modern scholar Erwin Schömbs agrees—a campaign to impugn Moser's scholarly qualifications. To the ducal court,

89. *Compendium juris publici Germanici, oder Grundriss der heutigen Staats-Verfassung des Teutschen Reichs* (Tübingen, 1731).

90. *Lebensgeschichte*, I, pp. 85–88.

91. *Lebensgeschichte*, I, pp. 88–89; Moser, *Anfangs-Gründe der Wissenschafft von der gegenwärtigen Staats-Verfassung von Europa und dem unter denen Europäischen Potenzien üblichen Völcker- oder allgemeinen Staats-Recht* (Tübingen, 1732); Franz J. Holtzendorff, *Handbuch des Völkerrechts*, I (Berlin, 1885), pp. 456–62.

Helferich denounced Moser's writings: for hidden Catholic sympathies, for citing too indiscriminately broad a spectrum of authorities, and for other more esoteric juridical lapses. This not only kept Moser's name unpleasantly controversial and suspect, it also brought the censors down upon him and blocked publication of textbooks. The climax came in December, just a week after Moser had visited Ludwigsburg to beat the bushes—successfully, he had thought—for Schweder's chair. Helferich himself, accompanied by a privy court official, confronted Moser at Tübingen with a command signed by Eberhard Ludwig ordering seizure of all Moser's papers, on the grounds that they had to be examined so as to separate and extract Württemberg state documents from Moser's private papers. Moser followed his papers—they were his life—to Ludwigsburg and retrieved his private correspondence (which he suspected Helferich and his friends to be mainly interested in, in their hope to prove treasonous correspondence with Vienna). But it was a year and a half before he recovered the rest of his notes and manuscripts and got his major works on public and international law into print. By that time Helferich had the Schweder chair.[92]

The choice for Helferich really needs no explanation or recourse to conspiracy—though conspiracy there doubtless was. True, the Tübingen faculty also disliked Helferich, had kept him at arm's length at the Collegium Illustre for fifteen years, and even now blocked payment of his university salary; and Moser was probably right to believe himself the duke's own candidate. But neither the university faculty, nor the court party, nor even those hostile to the court party had any reason to have preferred Moser. It was just at this time that the struggle of the Grävenitz party to stay in place was reaching a climax; there were even serious efforts to dislodge the duke himself, and certain leaders of the estates were in the pay of the court party. In such a situation the position of the imperial authorities at Vienna was bound to be important and might be decisive: that is why everybody was so concerned about what Moser's correspondence with Vienna might contain.[93]

But complicating all this further was the election of Friedrich Karl von Schönborn, upon the death of his uncle, Lothar Franz, to be bishop of Bamberg and of Würzburg, two influential seats that whetted his ambition for the powerful Electorate of Mainz. From that important electoral archdiocese he might regain momentum, recover some of the power that was slipping through his fingers at Vienna. Or if not, he could live the

92. "Nachricht," pp. 32–33; *Lebensgeschichte*, I, pp. 89–94; Schömbs, *Staatsrecht Mosers*, pp. 105–9, 135; Rürup, *Moser*, p. 65.
93. Grube, *Stuttgarter Landtag*, pp. 386–88; L. Gross, *Reichshofkanzlei*, pp. 348–50.

agreeable life of a German prince-bishop of wealth and family. So Schön-born turned over the administration of the imperial vice-chancellorship to lesser figures and quit Vienna.[94] Where that left political calculation in Stuttgart and Tübingen it is impossible to say; but surely it seemed safest to everybody concerned to steer as clear as possible of the unpredictable and unpartisan Moser, who once again found himself without party.

§7. Uncertainty and Belief, 1729–1733

R EBUFF to his professorial ambitions, harassment by suspicious censors, and a hostile political climate left Moser in Tübingen in 1730 hardly better off than he had been at Stuttgart. His papers lay at Ludwigsburg; he had no real friends in Tübingen and no professional commissions. He and Friderica Rosina were in the state of reminding one another that the Lord would provide when a commission arrived—how and why is not apparent—that kept him occupied for two years, revived the prospect of a career in imperial affairs, and brought about his first connection with the powerful Protestant states of northern Germany. It was a problem that conjoined local, imperial, and religious issues, and showed how the confessional patterns that shaped the ladders of official careers at the same time complicated them.[95]

The occasion was a political eruption in the town and bishopric of Hildesheim. The burgomaster of Hildensheim town (Neustadt) wished to appoint a pastor who, an outsider, was suspect to the town council. When the council refused to ratify the appointment, the burgomaster got together a crowd which, proclaiming itself the citizenry, broke in on a council session and forced the approval of the burgomaster's own candidate for the pastorate. The council then retaliated by calling in the cathedral provost, Baron von Twickel, to judge the case in the name of his master, the bishop of Hildesheim, in that bishop's loose capacity of Stadtherr or protector of the town. But the important thing about the bishop of Hildesheim was that he was also archbishop-elector of

---

94. Schönborn had been elected *Koadjutor* at Bamberg "*cum spe futurae successionis*," but his succession at Würzburg was unexpected: Hans J. Berbig, *Das Kaiserliche Hochstift Bamberg und das Heilige Römische Reich, vom Westfälischen Frieden bis zur Säkularisation*, I (Wiesbaden, 1976), pp. 28–32.

95. "Nachricht," p. 35; *Lebensgeschichte*, I, pp. 108–9.

Cologne, a position of real importance in the constitutional and confessional politics of the empire; and Twickel himself was a Cologne privy councillor as well as provost at Hildesheim. As bishop of Hildesheim, moreover, the Catholic elector of Cologne was a member of the Lower Saxon Circle of the empire, which despite the Catholic elector's membership was constitutionally regarded as being purely Protestant, and whose most eminent members were the king in Prussia (as prince of Halberstadt) and the king of England (as duke of Saxe-Lauenburg). And incidentally the Hildesheim diocese, though its bishop was the Cologne archbishop-elector, was part of the archdiocese of Mainz.[96]

Provost Twickel invoked the episcopal protective capacity to dismiss the Hildesheim burgomaster, while retaining and supporting the town council; and he secured a judgment sustaining that action from the Reichshofrat at Vienna. But inasmuch as these events occurred within a constitutionally Protestant circle of the empire, execution of the judgment fell to the reluctant Protestant states of Prussia and Wolfenbüttel. The internal confessional and social politics of the diocese, town, and estates of Hildesheim, in which this 1729 affair was embedded, are complex to the point of opacity; but the events point to a loose association of Catholic sympathies with bishop and town council, and of Protestant sympathies with burgomaster and "citizens." It was just the sort of situation that made the bread and butter and sour wine for constitutional lawyers; and Moser described Provost Twickel's summons, accompanied by a fifty-thaler retainer, as a provision of the Lord to him and Friderica Rosina in an hour of need. During 1730, with the outcome of the final Grävenitz crisis still in doubt, his papers impounded, and hopes for the Tübingen professorship disappearing, Moser feverishly wrote briefs for the Hildesheim provost's case—ten of them were published anonymously at Hildesheim—while fighting off censorship and reinforced suspicions of crypto-Catholicism at home. Around this time Moser began the practice of opening his Bible at random and trying to see into his future from the passage under his thumb—and sure enough, some of these prophecies turned out to be true when hindsight came to explain the puns of Providence. For example, his Bible foretold the fall of the Grävenitz party and especially of the Schüz clan, if he had only understood, by putting under his random thumb a verse from Isaiah: "For thus hath the Lord said unto me, within a year, according to the years of a hireling, and all the glory of

96. Adolf Cardinal Bertram, *Geschichte des Bistums Hildesheim*, III (Hildesheim, 1925), pp. 136–37; Justus Lücke, *Die landständische Verfassung im Hochstift Hildesheim 1643–1802* (Hildesheim, 1968), pp. 41–47 and passim; Johannes H. Gebauer, *Geschichte der Stadt Hildesheim*, II (Hildesheim, 1924), pp. 134–36, 160–61, and passim; Pütter, *Staatsverfassung*, II, pp. 91–92.

Wilhelmine, Reichsgräfin von Grävenitz

WILHELMINE VON GRÄVENITZ
"I was accused, without foundation, of having spoken ill of the then famous Countess of Würben and the Grävenitz party when I was in Vienna." Moser, Lebensgeschichte, I, pp. 39–40.
Landesbildstelle Württemberg, Stuttgart

Kedar shall fail: And the residue of the number of archers, the mighty men [Schützen] of the children of Kedar shall be diminished: for the Lord God of Israel hath spoken it."[97] He issued, pseudonymously, his first religious publication: a collection of deathbed narratives entitled *Erbauliche Todes-Stunden*—"Edifying Hours of Death."[98] Moser was thinking about religion.

In 1731 Wilhelmine Grävenitz, countess of Urach and Würben, finally fell from power in the Württemberg court and state. Apparently her growing burden of years, not to mention Eberhard Ludwig's own, had reduced her influence on the duke; and this in turn had encouraged the party of political opposition until she no longer seemed worth the trouble to him. She refused to go meekly or empty-handed, though, and it cost Eberhard Ludwig and the duchy the immense sum of 340,000 gulden to get her settled in Berlin (a Jewish financier named Süss Oppenheimer made the arrangements); but she was gone. That fact alone made a twenty-five-year pattern of Württemberg politics obsolete. But far more important, in that same year, 1731, Eberhard Ludwig's one son died, opening a dynastic breach. It seems likely that this had as much to do with Grävenitz's fall as had the decay of her charms and of the duke's desires, though I have seen no account that links the events. The exile of Grävenitz was necessary for any reconciliation between the fifty-five-year-old duke and his legitimate duchess. But there is no suggestion that anybody expected another heir from that marriage. The Catholic cousin, eight years younger than the reigning duke, was now heir presumptive. But there was no immediate prospect of his succession either. So if old patterns were obsolete, no clear new ones were apparent. As for Vienna, Schönborn had abdicated direct control of his office there but he had not resigned it, and so he had no successor.

Moser's scholarly work of those years reflects his confused uncertainty about his future and his wish to open up new professional opportunities. There were the Hildesheim tracts of 1730. In 1731 he published a book on Switzerland, arguing from law and from history that the Swiss confederation had been made fully independent of the empire and its courts by the Peace of Westphalia. He dedicated the tract to "the Worshipful Thirteen Cantons of the sovereign, and happiest of all European States, Confederate Republic," and sent copies off to Swiss canton and town governments.[99] The word "sovereignty" was one that Moser almost never

---

97. "Nachricht," pp. 32–33, 40; *Lebensgeschichte*, I, pp. 110–11; Isaiah 21:16–17.

98. Under the pseudonym Christ. Gottl. Erdmann (Tübingen, 1730).

99. *Die gerettete völlige Souveraineté der löblichen Schweitzerischen Eydgenossenschaft* (Tübingen, 1731); Albert Leschhorn, *Johann Jakob Moser und die Eidgenossenschaft* (Zürich, 1965). Leschhorn, p. 96, suggests that Moser hoped this tract would bring him a professorship at Basel.

used, before or after this time, because it was a concept incompatible with his understanding of the German constitution and its laws, state or imperial. But in the 1731 Swiss tract he even made favorable reference to the natural lawyer Pufendorf, whose famous treatise on the German constitution was built around the problem of sovereignty, a treatise Moser described in his own German jurisprudence of the time as having "some good ideas, but most of it no use ... unprovable principles ... only reasoned, with nothing analyzed *juridice*."[100] Moser's own writings of the early 1730s, though, show unwonted attention to the rights and powers of the German states, relating them to the concept of sovereignty in international law.[101]

It seems reasonable speculation to connect these juridical flirtations with Moser's dire need for employment and the wide net he was casting. The main hope at present, however, remained the Cologne connection via Hildesheim, and this, if Moser remained Protestant, could lead only to imperial posts, not archepiscopal. Moser dedicated the *Corpus juris publici Germanici* of 1731 to Provost Twickel, bishop of Botry, recording his satisfaction in the recent services he had been able to render and in the stipend he had received, and hoping further favors for himself and for those co-Protestants who had not participated in the recent troubles. And in the summer of 1732 the elector of Cologne, as bishop of Hildesheim, nominated Moser to a Protestant seat as judge or Assessor on the Reichskammergericht at Wetzlar.

This nomination opened, or reopened, a dispute over patronage reflecting the political character of the empire, and it suggests why Twickel may have brought Moser into the Hildesheim case two years before. The position, roughly, was this. Members of the Lower Saxon Circle had the right to make Protestant presentations or nominations to the Reichskammergericht—which body was itself judge of the credentials of nominees to its own membership—and the powerful elector of Cologne, as bishop of Hildesheim, was a member of the Lower Saxon Circle. Did

---

100. *Gerettete Souveraineté*, pp. 1–5; *Bibliotheca juris publici*, II (1730), p. 698; *Praecognita juris publici Germanici generalissima* (Frankfurt/Main, 1732), p. 145, the latter two quoted in Schömbs, *Staatsrecht Mosers*, p. 220.

101. For example, Moser defined the European principle of sovereignty as "standing subject only to God and the sword," and he used the same phrase in describing the territorial Landeshoheit of German states. He never went so far as to attribute sovereignty in an abstract total sense to German states, even *Reichsstände*; but in the treatments of 1731–32 he was inclined to emphasize internal legal restraints on rulers, as distinguished from his usual emphasis on restraints by imperial courts. *Staatsverfassung von Europa*, especially pp. 56–60; *Compendium juris publici*, especially pp. 449–55, 491–92. For his views in the 1760s and 1770s, after his Württemberg experience of the 1750s, see below, §§26, 29, and 32.

that permit this Catholic archbishop to fill a Protestant seat on the court? With the influence available to the elector, on the court itself and elsewhere (he was a member of the Wittelsbach house), he might actually be able to place his own nominee in a Protestant seat on the court. Indeed, this elector might have done so in Moser's case, if his Lower Saxon Circle colleagues, the prince of Halberstadt and the duke of Saxe-Lauenburg, had not also been king in Prussia and king of England, respectively. Moser, though Protestant, was suspected of Catholic sympathies and ambitions for reasons going back to his Vienna days; and now additionally and in the context of Württemberg affairs, he was believed to enjoy good relations with the Catholic heir presumptive to the Duchy of Württemberg (who in the event did succeed to the dukedom in 1733). The Protestant leaders of the circle, although apparently satisfied with the settlement Moser and Twickel had managed to reach in the matter of the Hildesheim pastoral appointment, drew the line here around the Reichskammergericht: England and Prussia, as Saxe-Lauenburg and Halberstadt, put forward a Prussian privy councillor as countercandidate. The bishop of Lübeck—Germany's only Protestant bishop, for in other Protestant places the secular authorities had episcopal powers—supported Moser. The matter went to the court itself at Wetzlar, which apparently split down the middle on confessional lines: Protestant judges favored the Anglo-Prussian candidate, Catholic judges favored Moser. At that the bishop of Lübeck, who was under pressure from England and Prussia (and who wanted to become, and eventually did become, king of Sweden) withdrew his support for Moser. Then the only legal recourse for Cologne-Hildesheim and Moser was the imperial diet. But the case never reached there because in 1736 Moser, as a condition for the Prussian post he assumed that year, was obliged by King Frederick William I to renounce the Reichskammergericht nomination from Cologne. So Moser never became Assessor at the Imperial Cameral Court at Wetzlar, which in fact might have been the best public office there was in Germany for somebody of his talents and beliefs.[102]

The fate of this nomination has taken us ahead of Moser's story, though. In 1731 and 1732, then still pursuing it, he visited Wetzlar and the spa at Schwalbach, frequented by officials of the Cameral Court, to cultivate his candidacy. An anecdote that stuck in his memory of those

102. Pütter, *Staatsverfassung*, II, pp. 91–92; Moser's constitutional description in *Justiz-Verfassung* (= NTSR VIII), II, pp. 410–12; his autobiographical narrative in *Lebensgeschichte*, I, pp. 97–101; and he published several documents relating to the case in *Nebenstunden von Teutschen Staats-Sachen* (Frankfurt/Main, 1757), pp. 259–81. In 1737 he had a nasty note from the court for addressing his resignation to the king of Prussia rather than to the court itself: *Nebenstunden* (1757), p. 269.

endeavors suggests some doubt, at least after the prize had eluded him, about whether the court was in fact the place for him. At dinner with Count Ingelheim, chief justice of the court (Kammerrichter), his host proposed a glass of wine together; Moser excused himself and asked for water, explaining that he made it a "political rule" to drink only water when he dined at a place where he was not entirely sure he could speak openly. Ingelheim, jovially: But if you cannot drink you cannot become a member of the court! Moser: I never saw that in the regulations, but if it is there I propose a compromise: if another member will do the drinking for me I'll do the work for him. Then Moser, smugly no doubt, reminded Ingelheim of a trivial remark the Kammerrichter had made at table eight years before, and the Kammerrichter exploded angrily: Ja! That's what the damned water drinkers do! When other people take a little glass of wine *in bona charitate*, they always sit there and lurk and make notes on everything that is said![103] Sour grapes for Moser.

Moser never took to drink in 1732 or any other time; but this was a critical year in the development of his religious sensibilities. He resigned his Württemberg office again, "albeit with too much haste," he later allowed, but relying openly now on the favor of Prince Karl Alexander and of the elector of Cologne—both Catholics.[104] The incumbent duke lived on, however; the hope for the Wetzlar judgeship faded, and a minor Hildesheim post offered in consolation paid too little to live on. Feelers that Moser put out to the Reichshofrat at Vienna and to the Danish court at Copenhagen came to nothing. But 1732 was also the year the Salzburg Protestant exiles passed through Tübingen.

On Reformation Day in the autumn of 1731 the archbishop and territorial prince of Salzburg required all his subjects who would not embrace the Catholic faith to leave the territory, declaring them rebels against proper authority and against the true faith. Salzburg Protestantism was associated with resistance to the archepiscopal state, and some Salzburg Protestants at least cherished the hope that a renewed Reformation would come to Salzburg one day from the north, a notion that the archbishop now determined to make an end to, harrying these heretics northward instead. Columns of Salzburg exiles appeared in Franconia and Swabia in the late winter and spring of 1732, igniting by their presence an emotional and compassionate force within German Protestantism probably greater than any since the Thirty Years War. Whatever the state of Moser's religious development when the Salzburger appeared, and however it might have continued had they never appeared, there can be no

103. "Nachricht," p. 7; *Lebensgeschichte*, I, pp. 102–4.
104. *Lebensgeschichte*, I, pp. 104–5.

doubt of the impact they made upon him. It seems one of the clearest sentiments of his life; other religious experiences, for example, always bore a taint of emotional or moral self-interest, however he tried to keep it out.

This is not to say that what he saw in the Salzburg exiles was unrelated to his own condition and circumstances at that time; on the contrary, it was the state of his own concerns that gave him the eyes to see the Salzburger he saw, with their patience, their constancy, their assurance founded on faith—a faith dissociated from the complications of ecclesiastical politics. For the faith of the Salzburg Protestants had lived independently of the ecclesiastical structure of their territorial state and lord. In none of the autobiographical writings did Moser say much about them, however—only an edifying little story about how, when he had given all his cash to a group of Salzburger out of sympathy for their plight, precisely double that sum arrived in the mail as a gift to him from a Catholic Swiss canton, presumably in appreciation of his "Sovereignty Preserved" tract. This showed in not very mysterious ways how Providence felt about the Salzburg affair.[105]

But in a pamphlet published anonymously in 1732 Moser had treated of other things. He dwelt on the amazing fact that the Protestants of Salzburg had clung to their Evangelical faith where the whole written realm of the Word, of learning and government and law, was ranged against it, where the faith must be wordless or at most a spoken thing, "and so if one looks at the matter from the point of view of reason [Vernunft], it must be impossible" that the Salzburger should have clung to their faith all this time. Their patience and modesty surpassed all understanding or praise, Moser wrote, and made laughable any Catholic claim that these were rebels, unless indeed Christ was one. "Here examine thyself, reader, whether thy spirit stands in so Christ-like and holy a condition."[106] Moser's additional offerings were volumes of documents surrounding the historical and legal positions of the emigrants and the archbishop, and the posture of the other German states and of the emperor toward them. In a preface he wrote that if he had the space and time, and if he were living in Holland, England, Sweden, Denmark, or Switzerland, he would have written a *Raisonnement* over the whole amazing affair, beginning with the question of what it was in the Protestant Evangelical faith that caused it to survive without the Word in these people, that served to unite them, and finally to reassemble them—

105. "Nachricht," p. 35; *Lebensgeschichte*, I, p. 109.
106. *Wohlgemeinte Auffmunterung zur Gutthätigkeit gegen die um der Evangelischen Religion willen vertriebene Saltzburger* (Tübingen, 1732, anon.), pp. 4–6, 19–24.

notably in the Prussia of Frederick William I, where a large proportion of the Salzburg exiles were invited and settled.[107]

By now there could be no doubt in Moser's mind that he truly was a Protestant and that it mattered to him, though he was still in a mere "lawful condition," wherein he pursued a virtuous and religious life but without the gift of Christ's mercy.[108] Thenceforward he wrote and published incessantly on religious matters—a book of fifty simple hymns in 1732, and a journal called "Old News and New from the Kingdom of God, and Other Good and Evil Spirits," devoted to stories of conversion, grace, and salvation, with nineteen issues between 1733 and his departure for Prussia in 1736.[109] Yet he was still at that time the candidate of the Catholic party for a Protestant seat at the Reichskammergericht, had come to public notice as protégé of the now Catholic bishop and imperial vice-chancellor Schönborn, and figured as a member of the entourage of a future Catholic Duke Karl Alexander of Württemberg. It was an eccentric political posture in which Moser had no sure place in any party because he did not fully fit in any, whether by the accidents of politics and faith, or because of a perverse vain quirk in Moser's character that commonly brought him to such a state. However he came to it, he characteristically attacked the problem of his professional and religious identity head-on in that same year, 1732, with a treatise on Article IV of the Treaty of Ryswick.

The problem of the Ryswick Clause did more to polarize German politics on confessional lines and to revive Counter-Reformation anxieties among German Protestants than any other constitutional issue of the early eighteenth century, and it was revitalized whenever some incident like the Salzburg expulsion showed that confessional politics and even religious violence were matters of more than antiquarian concern. When the French had evacuated the Palatinate at the end of the war of 1688–97, they had managed to include in the Ryswick Treaty, which concluded that war, a provision that the Catholic ecclesiastical system introduced by their sponsorship into this largely Calvinist place should be retained. This was almost certainly a breach in the system of confessional guaran-

107. *Derer Saltzburgischen Emigrations-Acten* (Frankfurt/Main, 1732), preface (there may have been a second volume that I have not found); see also *Actenmässiger Bericht von der jeztmaligen schweren Verfolgung derer Evangelischen in dem Ertzbisthum Saltzburg* (Tübingen, 1732, anon.).

108. *Lebensgeschichte*, I, pp. 105–8.

109. *Fünfzig geistliche Lieder* (Tübingen, 1732); *Altes und Neues aus dem Reich Gottes, und der übrigen guten und bösen Geister* (24 parts, Frankfurt/Main, 1733–39). The first nineteen parts, through 1736, seem to be Moser's; only the first bears his name, the rest being anonymous. Most citations to this, including Moser's own, are confused.

tees established by the Peace of Westphalia; most of the Protestant states would not ratify the clause, nor its later reaffirmation in the treaties that ended the Spanish succession war in 1713–14. Thus the matter was unresolved in its German constitutional aspects. Meanwhile in the Palatinate itself the struggle was waged over ecclesiastical supremacy, Kirchenhoheit, between the now Catholic Palatine electors and a determinedly independent Calvinist Kirchenrat or state church council with strong roots in the local communities and parishes. At stake (beside matters of conscience) were not merely tax arrangements to support clergy, and income from ecclesiastical properties, but the whole appointment list that went with ecclesiastical supremacy—more than a hundred members and officials of the Kirchenrat itself, many more other church offices, almost the whole educational establishment, and endowments for social services, down to midwives. (There was in fact a hot debate over whether Protestant women might be obliged to accept the ministrations of Catholic midwives.) Accordingly, to substantiate sentiments of religious allegiance, this was a very real and sensitive issue for the publicists and civil servants like Moser and his colleagues, whose careers were critically affected by the confessional distribution of office and by the dependability of the Westphalia confessional distribution. After the Palatinate it might happen anywhere next—but more especially in a place like Württemberg, Protestant but with a Catholic heir presumptive who had good connections with Vienna.[110]

Moser's professional past and his circumstances made him especially vulnerable in the realm of confessional politics, now stimulated by the Salzburg affair that had strongly affected him personally; and he used the 1732 treatise on the Ryswick Clause to try and define his position. He delivered a tactfully moderate legal argument that defended the Protestant position on the basis of the Peace of Westphalia, and he invoked the interest of German Catholics and Protestants alike in preserving the German constitution against French-inspired violations. His own religious faith, he declared, had nothing to do with his professional views, one way or the other; and he observed further, lest anybody miss the point, that none of the Catholic "Herren" whose favor he had enjoyed were seriously affected by the outcome in the Palatinate. Anyway they surely were too generous and equitable to punish an honest scholar for his position respecting religious rights. On the other hand again, "those

110. For the Ryswick Clause, Pütter, *Staatsverfassung*, II, pp. 316–43, 416–23, goes into great detail about the civil posts and the revenues involved; Hans Schmidt, *Kurfürst Karl Philipp von der Pfalz als Reichsfürst* (Münster, 1963), pp. 114–49; Fritz Wolff, *Corpus Evangelicorum und Corpus Catholicorum auf dem Westfälischen Friedenskongress* (Münster, 1966), pp. 191–98.

who consider me *pro Semi-Catholico* do me injustice in the highest degree." He had, to be sure, written opinions that supported the Catholic side on some issues, but none that endangered the Evangelium; never had he ever accorded Catholics any more than what was their right, *salva Pace Westphalica et bona fide*, saving the Peace of Westphalia and good faith. He could have made his fortune by becoming Catholic, he said, but he had not done so; "and I herewith publicly and joyfully declare myself determined to hold to these views under God's mercy, and to abide by the Evangelium until my mortal end."[111]

All during 1733 Moser seems to have been preoccupied with working out his religious identity and how to behave with it. He was without office or salary, and published only a few perfunctory collections on imperial law. His new religious intimacy with Friderica Rosina brought him, through members of her family, into touch with Württemberg pietist circles; possibly the growth of his children into moral personalities awakened memories and meanings from the religious forms of his own childhood to which he had been insensitive then. And it seems quite likely that his alienation from his secular professional world opened him toward a sphere of spiritual association.

Württemberg pietists never attained or sought the institutional or dogmatic forms of contemporary North German pietist groups. Their association was not ecclesiastical and only barely theological. That makes any general characterization of the Württemberg tendency difficult and dubious; but it seems fair to characterize its members as particularly concerned with an inner quest for salvation and its signs; the intensive biblical studies and mutual testimony in private groups were designed to assist that personal quest, not to provide guidance for behavior in the world. Private religion indifferent to worldly behavior made it possible for people of this persuasion to live with most of the visible ecclesiastical and political systems without much conflict, although a cherishing of their own righteousness (or more nearly, a sense of the greater unrighteousness of others) may have fueled some thunderings against scandal and corruption and power seeking in high places: Württemberg pietists by political tendency had been anti-Grävenitz in her day, and were to be anti-Catholic in Karl Alexander's and anti-Semitic in the Süss Oppenheimer case that lay ahead.[112]

111. *Vollständiger Bericht von der so berühmt- als fatalen Clausula Art. 4 Pacis Ryswicensis* (Frankfurt/Main, 1732), preface.

112. Hartmut Lehmann, *Pietismus und weltliche Ordnung in Württemberg vom 17. bis zum 20. Jahrhundert* (Stuttgart, 1969), passim, but especially the efforts at definition, pp. 12–21; Albrecht Ritschl, *Geschichte des Pietismus*, III (Bonn, 1886), pp. 1–92. Separatism is another matter: see below, §§8 and 12.

Moser himself, however, shared none of these political tendencies, and as far as I know he never called himself a pietist. Indeed, what suited him in the religious tendency was its dissociation from institutions and parties, the thick insulation that it offered between the private religious life of the soul and the public professional life of the world. It could be a moral refuge from failures and disappointments, a balm for the wounds done his vanity by those who disliked and distrusted him; it could provide serenity and integrity of spirit to withstand the consequences of his own choleric worldly temper and the dispersions and frustration of his worldly life. For ultimate justification of one's being, it would be better to avoid depending on peace and position in the world.

Not that religion, pietistic or not, could do this for Moser in 1733: not in the mere "gesetzliche Zustand," the voluntary "lawful condition." It could only really come about by reception of grace; and the Protestant catch there was that grace could not be attained by will, not by wanting it and trying for it, but could only at best be prepared for, so to be recognized when God imparted it. Thus for anyone yearning for peace of spirit and for assurance it was vital to ascertain that conversion and grace were real and not psychological tricks, not illusions fed by one's own worldly will in hoping for them. Above all, ambition and vanity in the world had better be kept away from humility and delight of the spirit. Moser's journal "Old News and New from the Kingdom of God" was composed largely of conversion histories, of persons with a deliberately wide range of worldly backgrounds: "Conversion history of a shepherd boy," even "of a village piper," as well as "of a count's court preacher," of professional men, of noble spinsters. There were religious histories of whole lives, to show, Moser wrote hopefully but a little incautiously, "that the work of conversion is not merely the business of a *raptus* or a *paroxismus*, as spleenish or melancholic persons sometimes imagine all their lives long, but that it also takes effect over a period of many years among people who through all that time do their work decently and wait cheerfully." In these histories there was special attention to the last hours of the pious, on the grounds that the terrible justice and the boundless mercy of God would be most visible at the instant of passage from this world of time to the eternal one: useful evidence might appear there of how the particular person in passage was being received on the other side.[113]

The pseudonymous "Edifying Hours of Death" of 1730, Moser's first religious writing, had been an early symptom of that interest. In the

---

113. *Altes und Neues*, I, pp. 1–15 and passim.

manuscript "Account" written in his old age he described at great length the deathbed scene of one of his sisters in 1736: the ministrations of Pastor Rieger, the announcement by the physician that she could not last the night, the death sweat, the blind and seeing stare, then the joyous "Oh! oh! oh! How beautiful!" and the final hymn around the bed and the flight of consciousness. "The doctor left, saying she would never return, and Pastor Rieger with us saw this to have been a foretaste of blessed eternity, granted to her and to us as a final consolation. But then she came to herself again, lived twelve more years, and finally died in 1748, in grace, of the dropsy." Deathbed narratives of the eighteenth century followed a convention but this one's conclusion is J. J. Moser's own.[114]

---

§8. Favor and Disfavor, 1734–1736

D U K E Eberhard Ludwig died in the fall of 1733; Moser's fifth living child and third daughter was born about the same time; he was thirty-two years old. Moser had assurances in writing from Karl Alexander that he would be brought back to office when Karl Alexander took control of the Württemberg government, and he promptly wrote the new duke to remind him of the promise. Karl Alexander, though, an imperial general of distinction who had been Austrian governor of Serbia, was now engaged in the Polish succession war, commanding the imperial Army of the Rhine; and Moser waited all winter with growing anxiety for a reply. He went to thumbing his Bible again, in the manner that had presaged the fall of the Grävenitzes and the Schüzes; and once it opened, as he remembered, to Isaiah again (it is almost in the exact middle of the Book and Moser's biblical oracles tended to come from there), this time to 13:3: "Therefore with joy shall ye draw water out of the wells of salvation[Heilbrunnen]." On 21 July 1734 came the order from the imperial headquarters at Heilbronn: Moser was to be restored in full honor and dignity to be councillor of state of the duke of Württemberg.[115]

The accession of Karl Alexander set the pattern for the strife that domi-

114. "Nachricht," pp. 40–41.
115. *Lebensgeschichte*, I, p. 112.

nated Württemberg politics for the next sixty years, of which Moser's own imprisonment in the 1750s and 1760s was one consequence. The starting point (compare the Palatinate of the Ryswick Clause) was the confessional difference between the dukes and their subjects and estates. That meant special contention over control of the ecclesiastical establishment and revenues; this in turn developed as a constitutional conflict between ducal government and estates; and all of it was conditioned by the political and judicial events and circumstances of the empire. The traditional and firmly rooted Württemberg political leadership organized as the Landschaft or estates—let us try to speak of the "estates" as a general characterization and distinguish the "diet" as a formally functioning body—now managed, with support from the *corpus evangelicorum* at the imperial diet led by Prussia, England, and Denmark, to remove ecclesiastical revenues from the direct control of the Catholic duke, entrusting them to the privy council, the Geheimrat. This arrangement was formally established in the religious guarantees or Reversalien accepted by Karl Alexander upon his accession at the end of 1733.[116]

The privy council thereby assumed in effect the episcopal authority in Württemberg, meaning not only control over very substantial revenues which supported a large body of prelates, officials, educators, and charitable foundations—about one-third the public revenues and employments of the duchy—but direction of all administrative, economic, and police matters affecting the church and its properties.[117] The privy council was instructed to consult regularly with the estates concerning its exercise of this authority: they were the constituency to which it was responsible in this regard. Moreover, the estates held the purse strings to the other main financial resource of Württemberg government: revenues from taxes imposed and collected by the estates' own fiscal administration and held in their own treasury, from which grants were made ad hoc, after negotiations and bargaining, by the diet to the ducal government.

Only a prince without energy, ambition, or pride could live content with such a situation; and Karl Alexander, who had a special interest in a strong and effective military establishment, was immediately engaged in bitter dispute with the estates over fiscal and political prerogatives. He chose as his chief advisers and executives the Catholic soldier Gen-

---

116. Texts in August L. Reyscher, *Sammlung der württembergischen Gesetze*, II (Stuttgart, 1829), pp. 460–70.

117. Martin Hasselhorn, *Der altwürttembergische Pfarrstand im 18. Jahrhundert* (Stuttgart, 1958), pp. 1–2. Hasselhorn (p. 66) assigns Moser a central role in retaining Protestant control of the Kirchengut in 1733, but he does not document this.

eral von Remchingen, who commanded the army and who undertook
the nastier political and police work, and the Jew Süss Oppenheimer,
who was charged with the coinage and with finding financial ways of
getting around the estates and raising funds to support the duke's and
Remchingen's growing military force.[118]

Moser's autobiographies avoid direct mention of these matters, important though they were for the history of his home duchy and for his own
subsequent fate—and even though he was made rapporteur for religious
affairs on the state council. Nor does he mention that Karl Alexander's
chief political confidant outside Württemberg, in his struggle against
estates' resistance and Protestant hostility, was none other than Friedrich
Karl von Schönborn, prince-bishop of Bamberg and Würzburg, who
finally resigned the imperial vice-chancellorship in 1734—an association
suggesting the reasons for Moser's favor and appointment by Karl Alexander, and for Schönborn's cultivation of Moser at Vienna a dozen years
before.[119]

Instead, Moser's account of his councillorship after his return in 1734
is full of the happy self-important business of being a senior civil servant
in a government small enough for him to have his finger in all sorts of
things: pleasantly routine council meetings in the mornings, special committees in the afternoons, sorting and drafting documents at night. He
boasted of how much paperwork he could get across his desk every day,
and how it amazed his friends and confounded his rivals. He had work
in foreign relations, clearing up the tangled legal residues of disputes
between Württemberg and the governments of Austria, the Palatinate,
Hessen-Darmstadt, and the Knights of St. John. He processed criminal
cases. One raised the problem of judicial torture: Moser opposed torture
on the grounds that evidence extracted by torture was legally worthless if
the defendant withdrew it the next day, which a real villain was sure to
do. Another case examined an accusation of bestiality against a peasant
boy, who claimed that what had happened was that he had gone to uri-
nate while walking along behind his donkey, and the beast had stopped
suddenly and unaccountably. Moser found for the boy on grounds that
the accuser claimed to have seen more than he possibly could have, and
besides was clearly an unpleasant fellow. He dealt with cases on infanti-
cide, and with the factor of prior intent in a conviction for murder.

118. For the constitutional conflicts under Karl Alexander, see Grube, *Stuttgarter Landtag*, pp. 389–97; Francis L. Carsten, *Princes and Parliaments in Germany* (Oxford, 1959),
pp. 123–28.

119. Grube, *Stuttgarter Landtag*, pp. 390–91; Carsten, *Princes and Parliaments*, pp.
124–25.

Moser never could decide in principle whether the deed itself or the intent mattered more, in the deserts of crime.[120]

That is the account of a happy and busy year. Then in the summer of 1735 came an unexplained invitation to visit Schönborn at Bamberg. Duke Karl Alexander promptly gave his permission. Then at Bamberg the bishop, who was suffering from the stone, sent Moser to visit his brother, Damian Hugo Philip Schönborn, cardinal bishop of Speyer, at the Schönborn family seat at Wiesentheid in Franconia. (The manuscript "Account" says of this that Karl Alexander "lent" Moser to the cardinal.)[121] The cardinal set Moser to straightening out the archive, but apparently there was little else for him to do, except gossip with members of the cardinal's entourage and engage in genial religious debate with the widowed Countess Schönborn, née Montfort. Moser always liked associating with the nobility, but he grew uneasy in the casual atmosphere of aristocratic Catholic society and wealth (he had dropped the "von Filseck" from his name in 1733, ostensibly on account of his religious convictions). When the countess took him to see the splendid family palace and garden at Geybach, built by the late Lothar Franz, archbishop of Mainz, Moser crankily remarked at the end of the tour that it was easy to see how much church property had gone into that display. The countess "smiled, and gave me a little rebuke." So wooden a man, she said, had she never seen. Back in Wiesentheid Moser tested the cardinal's religious breadth (Schönborn did regularly employ one Protestant in the chancellery) by gathering Protestant neighbors to sing loud Protestant hymns on Protestant holidays in Moser's room, which adjoined the cardinal's own.

This needling of the mighty may be a symptom that Moser sensed a worm in the apple, or maybe it was just his way and the memory stuck agreeably in his mind. But as the weeks went by, with little work to do, he surely wondered how long he was to stay and what was going on back at Stuttgart. In the fall he fell victim to a "deathly violent fever" that he was convinced could not be cured at Wiesentheid; and despite all remonstrances, still feverish and weak, Moser set out for Stuttgart by post coach.

When he arrived and resumed his duties, conditions had changed. Moser does not say so, but his plain narratives of what he did in late 1735 and early 1736 are foreboding in their selection of detail and in their tone, as if Moser himself was trying to answer the question that

---

120. *Lebensgeschichte*, I, pp. 121–25; Moser, *Abhandlung verschiedener besonderer Rechts-Materien*, XIV (Frankfurt/Main, 1776), pp. 252–59.

121. For the Franconia journey of 1735, "Nachricht," pp. 8, 38–40; *Lebensgeschichte*, I, pp. 125–34.

seems most important for the next turn in his life: what had happened to the relation with Karl Alexander and to the state councillorship so joyously begun in 1734, which would bring the complete break and the move to Prussian service in 1736? The manuscript "Account" compartment on "spiritual life" records that in 1736 he was "plagued by onslaughts of blasphemous [Gottes-lästerlich] thoughts; and the more I struggled against them the worse it was, the way a boiling pot spills over when you stir it; the best thing was to stand quite still under the flood, or to sing a hymn, or say one; and so it went past."[122] Of his public life of 1735 and 1736 Moser tells several particular stories beginning with the Stettenfels affair.

The castle at Stettenfels, which had free imperial status within the Swabian Knighthood (constitutionally separate from the Württemberg duchy) was held by a Catholic Count Fugger, who also held the surrounding tributary Protestant village of Gruppenbach as a fief from Württemberg. Count Fugger had wished to introduce open Catholic religious services in the castle during Eberhard Ludwig's time and had been prevented from doing so; with the accession of Karl Alexander he went ahead, without permission from the authorities designated by the ecclesiastical arrangements of 1733. Not only did he hold services on the castle grounds, he also began to build a Capuchin cloister and church on a hill outside, overshadowing the Protestant village church. In doing this he was encouraged and supported by the "bishop of Bamberg and Würzburg" (who of course was Friedrich Karl von Schönborn) and by other Catholic donors. The Württemberg state ministry and the council found the matter disturbing and ordered a feudal commission to investigate, with President Beulwig of the state council—Moser's immediate superior—as chairman. But, wrote Moser, "the Herr President took no satisfaction in this commission, and so I was appointed first commissioner in his place."

Moser found the cloister half-built and the monks busy laying tiles on the roof. He confronted Count Fugger and warned him to suspend the work. The count made legal arguments and talked about his influence at Vienna, to which Moser retorted in kind and then withdrew to his inn. On the next day Moser went to the building site and threatened the stonemasons he found there with arrest, in the name of the duke of Württemberg, if they did not stop work; learning this the count came raging from the castle brandishing two large pistols, and Moser hastily retreated again to his room at the inn and locked his door. When matters had quieted down a bit, Moser by authority of his ducal commission summoned a force of fifty soldiers from Heilbronn, who arrived silently

122. "Nachricht," p. 40.

in the night—it was All Saints Eve—and took up positions outside the castle, warning the Catholics who arrived for religious services next morning that there would be no services, now or ever, and taking down their names. Then Moser had wagons brought to take away the doors and windows just installed in the cloister, so that the monks got cold and retired to the castle. The ministry at Stuttgart sent approval of these actions and, without mentioning it to the duke, issued Moser an order to raze the cloister and church, for which purpose he collected three hundred artisans (which sounds like a Protestant mob) and put them to work; in a few days "church and cloister were level to the ground; and they still are."

Schönborn among others complained vigorously of this to Karl Alexander, who himself flew into a rage at his officials; he avowed that their purpose was to humiliate him before his fellow Catholics; and he told them that when the emperor ordered construction resumed, he, Karl Alexander, would see that they paid for it from their own pockets. Moser sent Fugger a bill of one thousand gulden for expenses of his commission; when the count refused indignantly to pay, Moser's commission confiscated the harvest that lay in the barns around Stettenfels and sold it, took out their fee, and sent the rest to Count Fugger with a receipt.[123]

That was around the end of 1735. In January of 1736 Moser was sent on a journey to receive oaths of fealty from various places attached to the Württemberg dukeship to which Karl Alexander had legally succeeded, including the districts (Ämter) of Nürtingen, Denkendorf, and Kirchheim unter Teck, all near Moser's old Tübingen haunts. There were in this area and notably at Kirchheim a number of religious groups called separatists, and Moser was warned that they might refuse to take an oath of any kind, out of religious conviction. Württemberg separatism was akin to Württemberg pietism in its communal devotions and absence of formal hierarchy, but more radical in drawing the political and social consequences. It was easy to see separatism as simply a step beyond pietism, but that was a very important step, for it was overtly political. Pietists, as Moser himself distinguished them in two treatises written about that time, did not desert regular church services on account of their own additional private meetings, but remained publicly within the official ecclesiastical system, whereas separatists, by refusing to attend established services, defied the public order; that was what was wrong with separatism.[124] Moser had made an analogous distinction in a state coun-

123. The account of the Stettenfels affair in Tüchle, *Kirchenpolitik*, pp. 100–102, confirms Moser's in all but slight detail; *Lebensgeschichte*, I, pp. 134–43.

124. "Ob der Pietismus durch kayserliche Edikta verworfen seye," analyzed in Fröhlich, *Moser*, pp. 110–12; *Rechtliche Bedencken von privat-Sammlungen der Kinder Gottes* (Tübingen, 1734), analyzed in Ritschl, *Pietismus*, III, p. 13; *Lebensgeschichte*, IV, p. 98.

cil case concerning a separatist couple accused of fornication because they had refused to go through an official marriage ceremony. He had argued (unsuccessfully as it turned out) that the couple, by refusing to marry, had violated the public order and should be punished for that or should leave the duchy; but they might not be punished for the personal delinquency of fornication.[125]

In the case of the Kirchheim separatists, who were described to him by local officials as outstanding citizens, but who would take no religious oaths to secular authority, Moser inquired whether they were ready to obey the duke's authority in all matters not wrongful to God or His Word. When they replied that they were, he asked them to make witness to this by a handshake with him, in place of the religious oath. They agreed and that was done. Moser made a little speech about the good deeds of the present government and departed for Stuttgart.[126]

When Moser returned from his journey, he learned that Karl Alexander was planning a great ball to celebrate the Catholic holiday of Fasching or Karneval, an occasion whose diverting customary observances, erotic and alcoholic, offended some Protestant moral as well as religious sensibilities in that day as in this. The duke had ordered all his officials, with their wives and grown daughters, to attend the affair, on pain of forfeit of a quarter-year's salary. The ball was to be held on the very night after Moser's first appearance at the council after his tour to administer the oaths of fealty; and a colleague in council made a point of telling him about the duke's command to Karneval, in the presence of everybody else, on the record. Moser and Friderica stayed home that night. When their absence was pointed out to Karl Alexander he remarked that if it were any other official he would discipline him, but (in Moser's version) Moser must be absent out of conscience, so official punishment would not avail.[127]

These are Moser's last stories of his Württemberg state councillorship. During his travels he had received intimations from Just Henning Böhmer, jurist at Halle and Prussian privy councillor, that he might be considered for the vacant position of professor and dean (Erster Professor) of law at the Prussian university at Frankfurt on Oder, with additionally the newly created office of director of the university and the rank of Prussian privy councillor. Moser had made a dilatory reply, but now back in Stuttgart he began to make inquiries about that university far to the north. Privy Councillor Schüz, who seems to have recovered from his Grävenitz association and who had once studied there, told Moser that it was a fine post from which to influence Berlin, for Prussian

125. *Lebensgeschichte*, I, pp. 120–21.
126. *Lebensgeschichte*, I, pp. 144–46.
127. "Nachricht," p. 40; *Lebensgeschichte*, I, p. 146.

KARL ALEXANDER OF WÜRTTEMBERG
"He asked me just how it was that I came before him with an odious commission from the King in Prussia." Moser, Lebensgeschichte, *pp. 149–150.*
Württembergische Landesbibliothek, Stuttgart

royal officials often made legal inquiries of the Frankfurt faculty. Moser rather liked that idea. He tried to find out what he could about the faculty but seemed unable to locate any publications of theirs, so he sent away to Leipzig for a catalogue of the lectures they gave. While he was awaiting that another message came from Böhmer, this one including a royal Prussian rescript which accused Moser, in the customary harsh tone of the court of Frederick William I, of using the Prussian offer to bargain with his superiors in Württemberg, and directing him to make up his mind at once.[128]

Bargaining is what Moser then proceeded to do. It is impossible to say how he thought it would turn out, but anyway he was ready to chance it. His position in Württemberg seemed very uncertain again; and just about this time Bishop Schönborn arrived at the palace at Ludwigsburg (the one built for Grävenitz) to help Karl Alexander in his battle with the estates over his army, his revenues, and his advisers Remchingen and Süss Oppenheimer.[129] Moser went to the duke's own quarters to give personal notice of the offer he had from the king in Prussia. He told the chamberlain to inform the duke that he had some letters from the king. The chamberlain, remarking doubtfully that news from Berlin was not Karl Alexander's favorite fare these days, took the message in and returned with his master's reply: How would anybody who posed as the duke's loyal servant come in here on some odious commission from the king in Prussia? Moser now said that what he had was an offer of a position in Prussian service. To this the duke replied that "when this situation is over" Moser could have his release from Württemberg service, but not now.[130]

Moser then made formal written petition for release; Karl Alexander refused on the grounds that Moser knew too much about the affairs of the Württemberg house and state to be allowed to go over to Prussian service. In this position, Moser wrote to Böhmer conditionally accepting the Frankfurt position. Now came the Württemberg response: Johann Theodor Scheffer, a former law professor of Moser's who had come into Karl Alexander's government with him and had risen to considerable prominence there, brought the message that the duke wanted to make him, Scheffer, chief of a reorganized administration with the title of chancellor, and to make Moser vice-chancellor.[131] In reply to this Moser

128. *Lebensgeschichte*, I, pp. 147–49.
129. Schönborn was at Ludwigsburg in May 1736, according to Grube, *Stuttgarter Landtag*, p. 392; this stage in Moser's *Lebensgeschichte* narrative falls at least some weeks after Fasching in late winter but before the end of May.
130. *Lebensgeschichte*, I, pp. 149–50. On the bad relations between Karl Alexander and Frederick William I of Prussia at this time, see Tüchle, *Kirchenpolitik*, pp. 96–97.
131. Schömbs, *Staatsrecht Mosers*, pp. 111–15, doubts that this vice-chancellorship was

asked Karl Alexander to write the king in Prussia asking for Moser's release now from his promise to enter that monarch's service.

That was the end of the game. The outraged Karl Alexander demanded to know what kind of fool Moser was trying to make of him, that he should ask favors of the king in Prussia on the conniving Moser's account. Moser got his dismissal, with some final mutterings from the duke about how Moser would like the master he was getting now. Moser turned his Württemberg papers over to the archives, got himself awarded a doctorate of laws at Tübingen, and departed for the north in May of 1736, not quite clear about what had happened.[132]

Just Henning Böhmer, who had negotiated Moser's appointment at Frankfurt on Oder, was a considerable academic personage. He had published a standard textbook and a number of monographs on Protestant ecclesiastical law, and he also had a reputation as a historian of learning—"Wissenschaftsgeschichte," that genre of intellectual history that gave accounts of learned disciplines through scholarly biographies of those who had constituted them. As professor of law at Halle he had been asked by King Frederick William in 1731 to draft a program to reform and revitalize that leading university of Prussian Protestantism, a commission he performed so well that the king had appointed him director at Halle, the position now offered Moser at the older university at Frankfurt on Oder.[133]

Now, five years later, it was to be Frankfurt's turn. Conditions were bad there, worse than they had ever been at Halle. The faculty had been decimated by deaths of leading members, by official neglect, by resignations of professors who got chances elsewhere; and the government's greater interest in the newer rival university at Halle had even allowed raids on the Frankfurt faculty by Halle. The faculty that was left at Frankfurt had good evidence of their own lack of distinction and they behaved accordingly, doing as little work for their small stipends as they could get away with, slandering one another to superiors and to students, then drawing together for mutual survival when threatened from the outside. There were few students to distract them—or to bring in money. In 1735 the government at Berlin had decided to go outside for a correc-

---

seriously offered, on the grounds that Moser would never have refused it if it had been. Moser did not really claim he had refused it; but still I suspect that Schömbs is partly right—that Karl Alexander hoped to keep Moser safely in Württemberg by shunting him and Scheffer into administrative capacities without political importance. Scheffer fell victim to the Jew Süss purge after Karl Alexander's death and was imprisoned for a time before being allowed to return to his professorship at Tübingen.

132. *Lebensgeschichte*, I, pp. 150–57.

133. On Böhmer: *Allgemeine Deutsche Biographie*, III (Leipzig, 1876), pp. 79–81; Stintzing and Landsberg, *Rechtswissenschaft*, III (1898), pp. 301–4.

tive. It asked the Prussian Academy of Sciences, and Director Böhmer at Halle, to recommend a new law professor who could clean up this situation and make Frankfurt into a serviceable Prussian university, one that could attract and provide skilled administrators and judges for Frederick William's expanding corps of officials. Böhmer had suggested Moser and had been empowered to negotiate with him.[134]

Böhmer apparently did not tell Moser what the conditions were at Frankfurt or what was expected of him, though Moser must have guessed, without knowing much detail. The administrative role must have been uppermost in Böhmer's mind, not Moser's particular scholarly qualities and style. For in the latter respect the appointment seems a remarkably bad one, so bad as to hint at malice or unpardonable inattention on somebody's part, though it is hard to suspect Böhmer himself of conscious ill will. Moser's serious jurisprudence centered on the empire and was decidedly positivist: it relied on existing written law, precedents, and customs whose ultimate sanction was the constitution of the empire. Prussia's jurisprudence was territorial and revisionist, aiming to replace a complexity of vested rights and restraints with a rational system of law and administration that would make the whole of Prussia responsive to the goals and commands of state and crown—an endeavor led by Samuel Cocceji, a natural-law scholar and legislator who was state minister of justice and first curator for universities. Moser's main scholarly specialty was the imperial courts; but traffic with the imperial courts or even judicial mention of them was rigidly prohibited in Prussian law.[135]

These jurisprudential incompatibilities must not have figured seriously in 1736. Moser's rambling dissertations and collections so far had provided no clear scholarly or political configuration, and probably not even Böhmer, let alone the Prussian state curators for university affairs, had read many of them. Anyway, law professors customarily made necessary adjustments to the governments that employed them. Böhmer himself was generally moderate and unimpassioned on the politically sensitive issues of the territorial rights of states, and of historical and of natural law in jurisprudence. He did not know Moser personally. So probably what mainly commended Moser was simply that he was a respectably

134. Conrad Bornhak used Prussian official materials surrounding the Moser appointment for "Johann Jakob Moser als Professor in Frankfurt a. O.," *Forschungen zur Brandenburgischen und Preussischen Geschichte*, XI (1898), pp. 330–39, and in his *Geschichte der preussischen Universitätsverwaltung bis 1810* (Berlin, 1900), pp. 101–24.

135. The unconditional Prussian *privilegium de non appellando*, was formally and fully established only after the Peace of Dresden in 1745, though it is hard to name a specific date; it was a matter of controversy when Moser was at Frankfurt, and he himself never fully accepted it. Wolfgang Rüfner, *Verwaltungsrechtsschutz in Preussen 1749–1842* (Bonn, 1962), pp. 60–61. On Samuel Cocceji's jurisprudence, Stintzing and Landsberg, *Rechtswissenschaft*, III, pp. 215–21.

publishing scholar with a strong practical bent, Protestant, with administrative experience and a reputation for energy and nerve, and that he was remote from the incestuous rivalries of the demoralized Frankfurt jurists. Perhaps the pietist connection helped in some quarters (Halle was pietist and Frankfurt Calvinist in tendency); and just possibly, though I know no evidence, it occurred to somebody that a Protestant jurist who knew as much as Moser did about Catholic and imperial affairs might come in handy, with the issue of the Habsburg succession coming rapidly to a head, as it was then in the late 1730s.

But on the whole it seems likely that the Prussian authorities knew as little about Moser as he knew about the place where he was going. They were thinking about their university more than about Moser; and Moser was not so much going to Prussia as he was leaving Württemberg.

§9. Catastrophe in Prussia, 1736–1737

WHEN Moser set out for Frankfurt on Oder he had with him his wife, six children, a maid, and also a "decent young lady" from Ludwigsburg, the "redliche Jungfrau Schmidlin," "whom God had awakened to accompany us"; she had vague domestic duties, and her brother, a theology student, came along as tutor to the Moser children. It was a long and punishing journey, and they made several stops along the way—at Nürnberg, and, a bit off their route near Bamberg, a visit to the castle and village at Ebersdorf in the county of Reuss in the Vogtland, where there was a religious community Moser had heard about from friends in Tübingen. At Dinkelsbühl, browsing in a bookstore, Moser picked up a copy of Johann Arndt's devotional *Wahres Christenthum*, and saw in the printed list of subscribers a Herr Leidemit of Frankfurt on Oder, a name that stuck in his mind as possibly providential. When he arrived at Frankfurt he inquired about this Leidemit, who turned out to be a godly town councillor married to the burgomaster's daughter, "all fine people." Leidemit willingly provided Moser with information on the state of things in town and university, and suggested what society Moser might wish to seek out and what he should avoid. This, not the university community, made the basis of the quiet social and religious lives of the Mosers at Frankfurt.

Apart from that, Moser wrote in 1763, "the Kingdom of God was dark in Frankfurt." Leading university theologians and preachers were "worldly" Calvinists with whom Moser found no spiritual communion, and the Mosers at Frankfurt held weekly services at home, attended only by their own household, some close friends, and a smattering of Bohemian soldiers from the garrison. "Both in the university and the clergy," Moser wrote his pietist friend Johann Albrecht Bengel back in Württemberg, "they do everything in their power to make sure nothing pietistic crops up here." Faculty wives clustered around Friderica Rosina, especially during yet another confinement in 1737, exclaiming their astonishment at the devotion of the Jungfrau Schmidlin: surely she must really be Moser's sister, or they must be paying her an enormous salary; nobody would travel so far and be so faithful only out of love.[136]

Moser's relations with his faculty colleagues were hostile from the start. They were of course resentful of this young outsider brought in over their heads by the state administration to whip them into shape, and it is hard to doubt Moser's account of their suspicion, jealousy, and balkiness. Nor is there any reason to suppose that he behaved any more tactfully than usual. The new director opened his incumbency with a published lecture, "Frank Thoughts, but Well-Intended and Grounded in Experience, on: How Universities, Especially Their Faculties of Law, May Acquire and Then Maintain Good Reputations, and Be Made Useful and Practical." In it he insisted on public relevancy in university practice; it was more important to impart skills useful for future civil servants than to conduct original scholarship. He followed that statement with printed programs of his own curricular offerings to prospective students, in which he deprecated notions that a university was a place "where we may become learned, as a pleasant way of passing the time or making names for ourselves." He added some remarks about how some of the best professorial minds lacked "the seat-leather, patience, and hard work" required of an academic instructor.[137] And Moser pestered his professors into holding more seminars and lectures, citing financial

---

136. "Nachricht," pp. 41–43; *Lebensgeschichte*, III, pp. 207–9; Rürup, *Moser*, p. 74. On family connections between the Schmidlins and the Mosers, Schmid, *Moser*, p. 7. Two students from Stuttgart followed Moser to Frankfurt: Georg Friedrich Stockmaier and Jacob Friedrich Dann enrolled that year along with Moser's eldest son Friedrich Karl. No other Württemberger came in subsequent years. Publicationen aus den k. Preussischen Staatsarchiven, *Aeltere Universitäts-Matrikeln: Universität Frankfurt a. O.*, II (Leipzig, 1888), p. 344. For Dann's loyalty to Moser in the 1760s, below, §§25 and 27.

137. *Freye, aber wohlgemeynte und auf die Erfahrung gegründete Gedancken: Wie Universitäten, besonders in der Juridischen Facultät, sowohl in einen guten Ruf und Aufnahm zu bringen und darinn zu erhalten, als auch recht nützlich und brauchbar zu machen seyn möchten?* (Frankfurt/Oder, 1736); *Einladung an die Herren Studiosos zu seinen künftig zu haltenden Lectionibus publicis und Collegiis privatis* (Frankfurt/Oder, 1736): both quoted and analyzed in Rürup, *Moser*, pp. 68–78.

cuts and threats from Berlin if they did not teach more students. When the students became aware of the ensuing competition for their attention they stopped paying lecture fees, and the professors lost out both ways. Moser quarreled with faculty over questions of student discipline, and had one professor dismissed for so entertaining students at informal gatherings that they neglected their regular lectures and classes. He himself set a fearful example by offering eight different lecture courses on subjects ranging from canon law to European constitutional law to legal and historical bibliography. He tackled a backlog of cases submitted to the Frankfurt faculty for legal judgment, and wrote forty-five opinions during his first six months.[138]

At New Year 1737 Moser submitted to the curators at Berlin a long and critical report on the university and its academic personnel. He went through the whole list of them, from the head of the theology faculty to the lowliest Dozent, with special attention to the law faculty; name by name, he particularized their indolence, their ignorance, their indifference. On receipt of this report, Minister Cocceji from Berlin promptly sent his aide for university affairs, the second curator and consistory president Friedrich von Reichenbach, to Frankfurt to investigate. Reichenbach summoned the whole faculty together and read out to them Moser's whole memorandum, item by item.

Moser believed then and thirty years later that Reichenbach himself was favorably inclined to him; but "this sort of thing was not his work." An example of Reichenbach's naivety, Moser thought, was that he revealed his intentions to Professor Justus Dithmar as they traveled together from Berlin to Frankfurt, so that the faculty was forewarned and able to prepare a counterattack. The Prussian administrative records used by the historian Bornhak, though, for his account of the affair, show Reichenbach to have been no special admirer or friend of Moser's in state councils. Moreover, it happens that this Professor Dithmar held the newly established Frankfurt chair in cameralism, that science of administrative economy whose practitioners consciously intended to replace traditional jurisprudence like Moser's own as the main university discipline for the training of state officials. So Dithmar was an institutional as well as a professional opponent of Moser's, and may have realized this more clearly than Moser did.

When Reichenbach finished reading out Moser's report the assembly became a nasty scene. The professors struck back at Moser in kind, saying he was incompetent in the private law (he was), that for somebody who expected to raise the level of instruction at Frankfurt he was a markedly dull teacher (he was), that he forced them to vote his way at

138. *Lebensgeschichte*, I, pp. 159–62, 192–93.

faculty meetings (no doubt he did his best), and that his disciplinary measures were stupid (at very least they were imprudent and mostly unenforceable). Moser replied angrily, making special issue of what a state the library was in, with books lying around on benches and floors uncatalogued, and professors taking them home without signing for them. This last charge especially aroused Professor Dithmar's fury. Everybody trooped into the library, where by Moser's account his allegations were borne out, "but Herr Dithmar got sick on account of his violent rage and died." So the curtain falls on that scene.[139]

Reichenbach's report to the state curatorium recorded personal sympathy for Moser, but concluded "that H. Moser is not in a position to do any service for the university or faculty. In truth the good man takes trouble enough, in his writing, and in his reading of documents; he even surpasses all the other professors in that regard; but the question is whether the many books he writes are useful to the *publico* or not, books nobody buys because they are nothing but *Collecteana*."[140] In March an order came down to Moser; it generally accepted his allegations about the other professors, but admonished him to "teach good *Systemata* in both public and private law, and to find a simpler method and clearer propositions so as to attract auditors." This amounted, so Moser believed, to an order that he must lecture on the *Ius publicum* of the present Cocceji's father, Heinrich Cocceji, a systematic jurisprudence that bypassed complications and inconsistencies of positive law by recourse to simple, and quite arbitrary, historical and natural principles, principles that in application turned out to support the aspirations of the Prussian crown and its energetic officials.[141] Two weeks later Moser got a letter from Samuel Cocceji himself about Moser's *Compendium juris publici Germanici*, of which a new edition was just then appearing, saying that Moser's "Systema" was not organized "nach dem *Gout* des heutigen *Seculi*," a criticism best left in its original phrase.[142]

Moser suspected indeed that much of his trouble at Frankfurt came from past criticisms he had made of the elder Cocceji, whose son, now Prussian justice minister and chief curator of universities, was on that account easily turned against Moser, and was easily persuaded not to give Moser the official backing he needed to succeed at Frankfurt. Moser

---

139. *Lebensgeschichte*, I, pp. 163–65; Bornhak, "Moser als Professor," pp. 333–34.

140. Bornhak, "Moser als Professor," p. 334. "Fakultät," which I have translated loosely as "faculty," probably here meant the processing of legal opinions requested by the government.

141. *Lebensgeschichte*, I, p. 166; Bornhak, "Moser als Professor," p. 333; Gross, *Empire and Sovereignty*, pp. 363–67; Stintzing and Landsberg, *Rechtswissenschaft*, II , pp. 112–16.

142. *Lebensgeschichte*, I, p. 163.

had often shown his disdain for Heinrich Cocceji's work, as far back as an impudent review he had written in the *Unpartheyische Urtheile* in 1722: "The author of this book has admirable discernment, and, even when he has only half-grounds for them, profound insights; so that he stimulates in the reader a good many thoughts that otherwise would never have occurred to him his life long."[143] The historian Bornhak from the Prussian state records doubts that loyalty to his father affected Samuel Cocceji's attitude toward Moser, for the reason that the busy and powerful minister did not bother with such trivia.[144] Still, Cocceji was known at the time for his dogmatic and intense loyalty to his father's work. And Frankfurt was his father's university—the father had retired only a few years before Moser's arrival. Above all, Heinrich Cocceji's jurisprudence was calculated to strengthen the orderly authority of the Prussian state, against legally vested interests within, and against imperial constitutional interference from without; this was the goal of the son's career too, so that Samuel's loyalty was political as well as filial.

Probably Cocceji had never read Moser's *Compendium* until early in 1737. At any rate it is clear enough that from that spring onward, the Cocceji ministry and curatorium wanted Moser out of Frankfurt. The remarkable thing is that it took them almost two years to get him out. Moser was stubbornly unwilling to recognize what was going on, failed to behave as he ought, would not resign. In his "natural life," though, he began to suffer from shortness of breath and from blinding headaches, which made it impossible for him to follow the discourse in meetings and seminars; he had to arouse himself repeatedly and ask what had just been said.[145] And Duke Karl Alexander of Württemberg had died suddenly in March 1737.

Late in May Moser sent his superiors in Berlin a defense of his scholarly reputation and his teaching skills. He pointed out, with characteristic impolicy, that enrollments had climbed to a level well above those of Heinrich Cocceji's last years at Frankfurt, and he sent a bundle of notes of scholarly appreciation addressed to him by various German princes and especially old patrons at the imperial court, such as the present prince-bishop of Bamberg and Würzburg. (This publicizing of appreciations he had received was an unpleasant habit of Moser's, especially inasmuch as he got most of them by sending free copies of his books to the courts and chancelleries.) Moser said he would resign if this defense was deemed unsatisfactory. But that was a threat he did not seriously intend to carry out. The ministry at Berlin wished he would. They wrote

143. *Unpartheyische Urtheile*, I (1722), pp. 33–34.
144. Bornhak, "Moser als Professor," pp. 333–34.
145. "Nachricht," p. 4.

desperately to Böhmer at Halle that Moser must resign; Böhmer wrote Moser urging him to look for another post; Moser refused.[146] When Böhmer reported his failure the ministry insisted: "The earlier determination stands: that, inasmuch as it was you who brought said Moser to Frankfurt, it is your problem to see how to get rid of him again."[147] Böhmer then wrote to Moser that he had lost the confidence of the government and must resign. In the fall of 1737 Moser tried to circumvent his enemies by direct appeal to King Frederick William. The king replied that he was not sure why people seemed so annoyed with Moser, but that if he did his duty loyally and energetically he had nothing to fear. Moser triumphantly reported this to Böhmer and stayed on.[148] Never, apparently, did Cocceji or any other superior of Moser's directly ask him to resign or threaten to dismiss him. Probably the reasons had to do with the king, an unpleasant man to make awkward explanations to, whose approval would be needed for forcing Moser out, and who knew very little about the matter. And they may have worried about religious connections too, for these were an important feature of academic politics, and the king had unclear but strong pietist leanings. Then Frederick William I, on a journey through the neighborhood, decided to visit Frankfurt himself and see what the fuss was all about.

Moser was presented to the king by the commander of the Frankfurt garrison, Colonel Camas, a friend of Moser's and a favorite of the king's. Frederick William immediately snapped, before the company: Moser? I thought you wanted to get out of here. Moser replied no, though he believed there were those who wanted him out. The king demanded to know who they were; Moser intimated that that was for His Majesty to say. The king let the matter drop for then. More was coming.[149]

Amongst the entourage of Frederick William I at that time there was one Salomon Jakob Morgenstern, a man of education, intelligence, stunted physique, and a talent for foolishness, who performed as a kind of court buffoon, a Hofnarr, reading aloud the news of the day with satirical comments at mealtimes and evening pipe-and-beer sessions, and staging such affairs as he now planned for the king's visit to Frankfurt on Oder.[150] Morgenstern had composed a parody on learned treatises

146. Bornhak, "Moser als Professor," pp. 334–35; Moser, *Lebensgeschichte*, I, pp. 166–67.

147. Bornhak, *Universitätsverwaltung*, pp. 101–2, and "Moser als Professor," p. 335.

148. *Lebensgeschichte*, I, pp. 167–68; Bornhak, "Moser als Professor," pp. 335–36.

149. *Lebensgeschichte*, I, p. 168. Paul H. T. Camas was on confidential terms with the crown prince, later Frederick II of Prussia, as military tutor and adviser. *Allgemeine Deutsche Biographie*, III (Lepizig, 1876), p. 719; Walter Hubatsch, *Frederick the Great of Prussia* (London, 1975), p. 15.

150. Richard Leineweber, *Salomon Jakob Morgenstern. Ein Biograph Friedrich Wil-

FREDERICK WILLIAM I OF PRUSSIA
"I became so depressed, that I broke out involuntarily: this is an unhappy day for the university!" Moser, Lebensgeschichte, I, p. 171.
"The king shook his head and said: an ounce of mother-wit is worth a hundredweight of university-wit." Moser, Lebensgeschichte, I, p. 174.
Württembergische Landesbibliothek, Stuttgart

entitled *Vernünfftige Gedancken von der Narrheit und Narren*, "Reasoned Thoughts on Folly and Fools,"[151] the title presumably derived from the habit the rationalist philosopher Christian Wolff, formerly of the university at Halle, had of entitling his many books and essays "Reasoned Thoughts . . . " on all manner of subjects. The plan was to set up a formal academic disputation in which the Frankfurt university faculty would solemnly debate this treatise with Morgenstern. When Moser learned of the plan he protested to Colonel Camas, who advised him not to try to prevent the disputation nor to absent himself from it, for the king was eager to see it and expected obedience in all things.

Moser declared he would not attend, but then Morgenstern himself appeared at the director's quarters to make arrangements for the disputation. He was dressed in a costume he had especially designed for it: a long blue velvet coat with huge red lapels and a red vest, and a wig that hung clear to the waist behind; a swarm of silver hares was embroidered on buttonholes, pockets, and hose, the hare signifying a kind of vacuous idiocy; in place of a sword he wore a fox's tail; and on his hat instead of a feather he had a hare's scalp and ears. Moser managed stiffly to tell this apparition that the farcical exercise in prospect would do harm to the university, and the king should not allow it; Morgenstern went off to see the king and came back with the cheerful reply that Frederick William had threatened to put Morgenstern in stocks and have him birched if the disputation did not take place. That evening at supper Moser got a copy of the Morgenstern thesis with a royal command to appear and debate it publicly next day.[152]

In the morning Frederick William arrived early at the auditorium; seeing no Moser he sent soldiers to fetch him, and greeted him jovially when he was brought. Morgenstern was still abed, and while he was being fetched in his turn, the king had a talk with his university director. What did Moser think of Christian Wolff? Moser said he had never read Wolff's work carefully enough to say. The king gave himself to be amazed at this, and Moser explained that when he had been at school Wolff had been only a minor light, and that since that time Moser had been too busy. Where had he studied? At Tübingen. Where else? Nowhere else. No place at all? No place at all; after Tübingen Moser had gone to Vienna, where he had seen a great many things touching His Majesty.

---

helms I (Leipzig, 1899); see also the article on Morgenstern in the *Allgemeine Deutsche Biographie*, XXII (Leipzig, 1885), pp. 233–34.

151. Promptly published at Frankfurt/Oder, 1737. The basic idea is that everybody clings to some particular view or characteristic to the point of folly, but I think it is not cleverly done. Compare Frederick William's similar remark to Moser just below.

152. *Lebensgeschichte*, I, pp. 169–70.

Well . . . what did Moser teach? Mainly the *ius publicum*. The king allowed that public law and philosophy were useful subjects, but the Digests. . . . Did Moser have many students? He had as many as his predecessors.

This colloquy is taken from Moser's own detailed and circumstantial account of the conversation;[153] there is no other except insofar as later writers have modified Moser's story to fit their own sense of what is credible and what the participants must have meant. Christian Wolff, who turned up in the title Morgenstern used for his thesis and again in Frederick William's quizzing of Moser, had been dismissed from Halle by the king some years before as a consequence of conflict with the dominant pietist faction there, but now there was talk of his return. Moreover, Wolff's systematic and naturalistic philosophy was antithetical to Moser's own intellectual style and convictions. Thus Moser had reason to be circumspect about these intimations, though to be sure they need not have signified anything more ominous than that the Wolff case came to Morgenstern's and the king's mind when they came to deal with university affairs and professors' quarrels.[154] Moser in later life took pride in his performance at this most dramatic encounter of his "civic life"; and no doubt he went through what-he-said and what-I-said again and again until he had a triumph of modest eloquence.[155] Still, the account rings true, showing this shrewd and brutal king to be quite aware what he was about as he put Moser through his paces and the faculty through the disputation on folly, and that does credit to Moser's memory of the occasion, or at least to his subtlety as an autobiographer. Moser kept his office for another year and a half while both his superiors and his subordinates—apparently without encouragement from the king—worked for his dismissal. But after this encounter he never recovered genuine active interest in his university duties.

The interview reached its climax and conclusion when Moser, believing he had made a favorable impression and that the king was in a good

153. In *Lebensgeschichte*, I, pp. 170–75; and see n. 155, below. I do not know whether he had notes made at the time.

154. Moser may possibly have had special reason for discretion: the Aletophile Society in Berlin, a clandestine group of intellectuals bearing Wolffian banners, had recently secured a declaration from Crown Prince Frederick that he wished, in his words, "to stand at the head of the party of Wolff and of sound human intelligence." Marcel Thomann, "Christian Wolff," in Michael Stolleis, ed., *Staatsdenker im 17. und 18. Jahrhundert: Reichspublizistik, Politik, Naturrecht* (Frankfurt/Main, 1977), pp. 262–63. On the Wolff case generally, Carl Hinrichs, *Preussentum und Pietismus* (Göttingen, 1971), pp. 388–441; Georges Pariset, *L'État et les églises en Prusse sous Frédéric-Guillaume I*er *(1713–1740)* (Paris, 1896), pp. 651–703.

155. In *Lebensgeschichte*, III, pp. 23–24, Moser remarked on how often he had gone over the conversation in his mind.

mood, asked whether he could "earnestly" debate Morgenstern. He had prepared a panoply of scriptual texts: "The fool hath said in his heart, There is no God," and "The fear of the Lord is the beginning of wisdom, but fools despise wisdom and instruction," and the like. The king lost all patience and shouted, "Oh yes, what a faker; when I don't want the wine I don't make a big fuss about it, I just don't drink it. So what? Everybody's a fool about something. I'm a fool for a soldier, somebody else"— pointing to Moser—"is a fool for pious vanity, somebody else is a fool about something else. It is just a joke and we can have it." Moser was starting a reply on the point of whether good Christians made foolish jokes when Morgenstern arrived in full attire, mounted to the rostrum, and called out the first professor-disputant. Moser left the hall as the burlesque began.

§10. Flight to Egypt

MOSER in the next days fell into a "deathly *Melancholiam hypochondriacam*" that lasted until Easter of 1738. His vital forces were exhausted. He might persuade himself that he had performed well during the royal visit and the disputation; but for a Württemberg civil servant to have bandied arguments and almost to have defied the powerful, violent, clever, and unpredictable Frederick William of Prussia was a shattering experience, and it had come as Moser struggled for survival and everyone's hand seemed turned against him. The king's harsh gibe about religious hypocrisy and vanity (which Moser faithfully reports) surely drove the breath out of his spirit. When the melancholia came he tried to sing a hymn with Friderica Rosina but could produce no sound, only a pale sweat; the doctor came and opened a vein, but no blood would flow. Next day the blood flowed and Moser was terrified at the sight of it. For half a year he was unable to work, unable even to read the newspapers, out of fright at the reports of murder and arson. He dreamed of suicide. He longed for news from home, from the Swabian fatherland, but he was terrified of the postman. The best bodily escape he could find was fast long walks and sawing wood "with a long carpenter's saw, so that one had to draw it far back."[156] This seems

156. "Nachricht," pp. 4–5; *Lebensgeschichte*, I, pp. 175–77.

the place to treat Moser's second great experience at Frankfurt on Oder, his reception into grace and forgiveness of sin.

The most baffling and telling feature of this experience is that one cannot say just when it occurred. Moser describes the experience in great detail, as a specific event in time; but he does not tell just when it happened, except that it was at Frankfurt on Oder and in 1737 or 1738; this vagueness is remarkable in light of his precision with other dates. The most specific dating is in the manuscript "Account," written from memory at Hohentwiel, which says it was on the thirteenth Sunday after Trinity in 1738. That would have been the end of August of that year; but the published Life History, prepared when he had his papers and books and access to the recollections of his family, says merely 1737.[157] Neither account places the redemption in the context of Moser's worldly circumstances, his "civic life," nor of the physical or psychological condition of his "natural life," as we feel compelled to do. Just so. Real grace could not respond to temporal conditions, nor, above all, could a felt need for psychic relief be allowed to engender a false experience of forgiveness. That way lay blasphemy and likely damnation (as any skilled reader would have known). It had to be God's grace, working within, that summoned Jesus into Moser's heart, not the king in Prussia and his minions battering from without.

Moser was an expert and even an addict when it came to conversion histories, and a veteran of many hours of critical soul-searching in community with others similarly concerned, so he knew all this very well. He knew the circles within circles that come with trying to distinguish a false experience of grace, one that comes from conscious or unconscious will, from a true experience, one that comes only to a soul that is passive and hopeless of any fruits from its will or its righteousness, the prostrated soul that can only hope for mercy without claiming any right to it as justice or compensation. The positive evidence would place Moser's forgiveness within a period of a year or so dominated by the crisis in his relations with faculty and curatorium, the disputation of folly and the encounter with the king, and the *melancholia hypochondriaca*. His most detailed account was published anonymously in 1753 in his journal "Monthly Papers on the Furtherance of True Christianity" and reprinted as an appendix to the third volume of the Life History in 1777.[158]

His description there begins with the "lawful condition" in which he

157. "Nachricht," p. 44; *Lebensgeschichte*, I, pp. 197–98.
158. *Monathliche Beyträge zur Förderung des wahren Christenthums*, II (1753), pp. 815–28; *Lebensgeschichte*, III, pp. 247–56. This account minimizes the religious development before 1734, which is clearly evident in other materials, for dramatic focus on 1737–38.

and Friderica Rosina had lived in the early 1730s—following God's ordinances in the belief that this was right and prudent, but without real conviction and even ignorant of the true nature of grace. The first inkling of the nature of grace came around 1735 from a mysterious stranger whom they met on a journey, who asked whether their sins were forgiven; when they piously disclaimed any such "presumption," the stranger accused them of false humility—either one was forgiven or one was not, and why not speak it out; for grace had nothing to do with merit.

The scene then shifts to Frankfurt on Oder (here identified as "another land"), where Moser learned through the agency of the Schmidlins ("two Christians, brother and sister, who came with us"), that there were people who had been forgiven once and for all, forgiven forever, so that nobody could doubt it of them. Some time after that (thus amidst his troubles with university and curatorium), Moser began to lie every day with his face to the floor before the Lord, begging him to see into Moser's heart and let Moser live for God and not for himself or the world. After some weeks of this, on a Sunday afternoon—the morning sermon had been on the Good Samaritan—Moser on the floor found himself before God's Court. He saw all his sins at once, from youth onward, things he hadn't thought of for years. He noticed how far more powerful and vivid they were, in whole timelessness, than mind crippled by temporality could conceive.

Then in his vision "a formal indictment was made against me and what I deserved for my sins; and I was questioned over many articles of it all at once and asked: whether I would concede that I deserved this or that? and in this I came to understand the meaning of God's wrath." Moser conceded everything, and knew that justice must send him to hell; but simultaneously he asked for mercy for Jesus Christ's sake. Hereupon Jesus, not visible before, came forward, and it was just like a familiar verse that had been running through Moser's head this while:[159]

> Mein Sünd sind schwer und übergross
> und reuen mich von Herzen:
> Derselben mach mich quitt und los
> durch deinen Tod und Schmerzen

159. My sins are heavy and too great
   and make my heart repentant:
Rid me of them and make me free
   through thine own death and torment
To Thy father make me known
That Thou for me the measure's done,
So I may drop my load of sin. . . .

> Und zeig Mich deinem Vater an
> Dass Du für mich hast gnug gethan
> So komm ich ab der Sünden Last. . . .

and Moser was overcome with conviction of Christ's intervention with God "and now there came from my inwardest self a command NUN IST ES ZEIT, ZUZUGREIFFEN! now is the time to grasp it! and I did so instantly."[160] Thence matters followed a course presaged by Old Testament histories affirmed by Pauline doctrines of grace.[161] Moser awaited no verdict from the Court, only thanking God for his acceptance of the blood of Jesus in atonement for Moser's sins; and he was flooded with peace as though drowned in it, through body, and mind, and soul.

Now Moser got up, stared around at the world with his new eyes, lay down on his bed and inspected the new Moser, and called his family and domestics to witness. The household expressed some doubt about the veracity of Moser's forgiveness inasmuch as his account differed in some ways from reliable histories they had heard about, but with time and instruction they came to believe in it. Moser himself (incidentally confounding all efforts to date the experience) suffered at least one early relapse into sin and self-reliance, but was brought back on the path by "a member of my household at that time," the awakened Jungfrau Schmidlin. After that, according to all Moser's accounts, he never doubted his state of grace and forgiveness.

The story is told in Moser's usual bald matter-of-fact style, like a quite ordinary experience, without flourishes or apocalyptic monsters. Moser knew throughout what to watch for, and also knew what he must watch out for. When things went along as they were supposed to, when his submission was total and the verse echoed in his ear, then came that extraordinary *Now is the time! seize it now!* as if J. J. Moser could after all manage this Tribunal and its agenda. Did he emphasize this revealing part of the story for the sake of accuracy, which was very important in these matters and which clearly he sought? Or was he after all unable to keep from boasting even here in the telling? Probably both, to be sure; a very common quirk in all of Moser's writing is the revealing slip to show

160. The "Nachricht" version, p. 44, even more remarkably, adds here, "Wann du zugreifest, so hast du es!"

161. 1 Kings 20:32–33; Moser erroneously cites the passage as 2 Kings 20:32–33; and note that the Lutheran is significantly different from the King James version. Zechariah 3:1–7; and there are many references to Pauline grace and conversion, though it is interesting to note that the lawyer Moser never, so far as I know, thoroughly addressed himself to the lawyer Paul's doctrines of law, grace, and justification.

his innocence, with a hint of a wink to show he is not so simple after all. Still it is astonishing to see that trick displayed here: circles in circles.[162]

The literature of conversion, both theological and psychological, matches up neatly enough with Moser's circumstances and his experience of redemption, but this may say as much about his expertness in the matter as about the reality of the experience.[163] Moreover, it might be a mistake to give as much importance to this religious experience in and for itself as, for example, Moser would wish us to do. There is no doubting its value to him as compensation in the spiritual sphere for failures and helplessness in the professional one. Sin and grace, and especially Protestant conceptions of them, may have a particular usefulness for stubborn and vain people: Moser could not or would not see what in temporal fact he had done wrong, to bring humiliation and failure; and while errors or wrongs can be seen, recognized, and corrected, sin can only be passively atoned—and need only be. Natural sin can be acknowledged, and then forgiven, without sacrifice of a sense of worldly righteousness. Sense of guilt shows us we are really better than what we have done, and once forgiven we have conquered life, having it both ways. Knowledge of sin and forgiveness probably preserved Moser's mental and physical health better than any other cure available to him.

But a greater importance of this experience for the life and biography of Moser in the end was that it gave identity, a principle of organization

162. There may be here, though, an echo of the doctrine of terminism, a kind of pietist heresy of the seventeenth century which, in order to deny the efficacy of deathbed repentances, held that only God could choose the time to confer grace. Anybody who did not avail himself of that opportunity might therefore be lost forever; thus his will affected the outcome. This paradoxical notion seems to have been thoroughly discredited by Moser's time, both in orthodox Lutheran and in pietist circles, so in any case the experience is Moser's own. On terminism: *Realencyklopädie für protestantische Theologie und Kirche,* XIX (Leipzig, 1907), pp. 524–27; *Religion in Geschichte und Gegenwart,* VI (Tübingen, 1962), p. 691; Friedrich H. Hesse, *Der terministische Streit* (Giessen, 1877).

163. The main scriptural sources that apply, and that Moser himself most often alluded to, are the letters of Paul to the Romans and to the Galatians, especially their treatment of the relation between grace and the law. See Martin Luther's relevant commentaries on the Pauline letters, but especially his "Lectures on Galatians" in *Works* edited by Jaroslav Pelikan and Walter A. Hansen, vols. 26–27 (St. Louis, 1963–64). William James wrote of a "shift in the center of personal energy," in *The Varieties of Religious Experience* (Modern Library ed., New York, 1936), p. 193, analogous to Moser's strong sense of compartments and a flight from the failed secular to the spiritual one. Sigmund Freud in *Totem and Taboo* described the origins of religion in terms of Oedipal conflict—terror of the child at his defiance of the father, in whose role here it would be hard to miss the king of Prussia. Fröhlich, *Moser,* especially pp. 64–72, discusses Moser's conversion in the context of pietist experience. See also Paul E. Johnson, *Psychology of Religion* (rev. ed., New York, 1959), passim, especially p. 117.

for understanding his life, and thus a form and rhetoric for his auto-biographical writings too—the confusion and despair of the first half of his life, the serenity and security of the latter half.[164] One should be aware of the device, from the beginning. This way of self-knowledge and autobiography succeeded in producing for posterity the composed figure of the elder Moser—honest, pious, benign, unruffled in the face of all adversity to come, simple in his faith, and humbly true to the righteous-ness rendered him by Christ's grace. And although that elder Moser sometimes could fill that personality, especially when that was the best he could do, very often he did not, and behaved as a very ruffled and contentious fellow indeed. Still through it all the twin experiences at Frankfurt in Prussia, professional failure and forgiveness of sin, were the benchmark of his life, hinted at in the beginning paragraphs of his Life History, and coming together at this close of his first life and career.

And there is another level of meaning in these experiences, political but transcending biography. Religious faith as confession in Germany was tied closely to state and episcopacy. By taking God and himself as sole confessors through Christ, Moser could find the stance, free of state and episcopacy and their partisanry, of a true spokesman of the empire itself as a constitutional edifice of public law: a true jurist and public servant of the empire, a member of its general estate, whomever in particular he served. Professor Gabriel Schweder of Tübingen; Friedrich Karl, bishop of Bamberg and Würzburg; Moser's own name-giving father, auditor of the Swabian Circle—all, I conceive, would have understood this.

In March of 1738 Moser again offered to resign his university post at Frankfurt—this time rather more seriously, for his heart had gone out of the job since the disputation and the melancholia. He still had a large household to support, so what he proposed was to keep his salary and earn it by writing a book on the rights of German Protestants. There was no direct reply to this from the ministry, apparently because they were divided on the timing and means of Moser's removal. Colonel Camas of the garrison came and suggested that Moser might have the post of Brandenburg-Prussian representative at the imperial diet at Regensburg if he would promise to follow orders and make all his actions and opin-ions there conform to the king's wishes; Moser declined that. There really was no way for him to stay in Prussian service. By summer, though, the new Moser was hard at work again. What he was writing and pub-lishing was mainly on imperial law, on Reichshofrat procedures, for example; he wrote nothing whatever on Prussian law. Most important, he was working now on his massively conceived *Teutsches Staats-Recht*,

164. See the observations of Fröhlich, *Moser*, pp. 135–56.

a compendium of the imperial law whose introductory volume had appeared the year before. Moser seems to have been faintly hoping for an imperial post, most likely the seat on the Reichshofrat that he was always hoping for and that never came; and such a post was in the gift of the emperor and emphatically not that of the king in Prussia.[165] As for Württemberg, Karl Alexander had died in 1737, Remchingen had been exiled, and Süss Oppenheimer was barely-judicially murdered in 1738; turmoil still ruled in Württemberg, so there was little hope from that quarter. On the execution of Oppenheimer, Moser commented that "there are as many uncut as cut, and most of them worse villains than Süss, still running around as honorable people, free and unpunished."[166]

In the latter part of 1738 King Frederick William himself precipitated the final crisis of Moser's Frankfurt career. He announced a plan to confiscate the corporate properties of the university to the crown, to put them under his fiscal administration, and then to pay the professors directly from his own treasury. There was an immediate uproar at Frankfurt and apparently at Berlin too, and the story was spread that Moser was the author of the idea. He denied this before the academic council, but they did not believe him; the faculty wrote to Frederick William asking that Moser be dismissed or transferred on grounds of ill health and neglect of his duties. Moser wrote a countermemorandum as before, and once more the government appointed a commission to investigate. Colonel Camas warned Moser that the membership of the commission was stacked against him, and so of all people did the royal crony and clown Salomon Morgenstern.

Before the commission's report was ready Moser did some precipitating of his own. He had started a series of treatises on the succession laws of European states, and it occurred to him to work alphabetically, which meant starting with the Kingdom of Bohemia. He plunged thereby directly into the most controversial and dangerous German political question of the time, the Austrian succession issue, which two years later launched a quarter-century of bitter warfare between the present emperor's daughter Maria Theresa and the present Prussian king's son Frederick. Not only did Moser's treatise defend the Pragmatic Sanction, the arrangements which Charles VI had made to assure his daughter's succession rights but which Prussia would deny; Moser even wrote Vienna to tell the emperor's court about a technical defect he thought he saw in their arrangements and to suggest how to correct it. And not only did he "neglect" to ask Prussian crown permission to publish his treatise;

165. Bornhak, "Moser als Professor," p. 337; *Lebensgeschichte*, I, pp. 177–78.

166. *Herzog Karl Eugen von Württemberg und seine Zeit*, published by the Württembergisches Geschichts- und Altertumsverein, I (Esslingen, 1907), p. 363.

his letter to Vienna was "intercepted" and ended up "somewhere else."[167]

Then on the sixth of February, 1739, again without asking royal approval as was customary, Moser gave his Bohemian inheritance treatise publicly. On the twelfth he got his dismissal from the king. Colonel Camas procured a royal rescript saying Moser still stood in the king's grace, and a memorandum to the Frankfurt faculty saying that Moser's industriousness "was cause for shame to many others." Moser had these documents printed and distributed, in a thoughtfully edited version, "to save people the trouble of copying them"; and when the storm broke over that he departed for Ebersdorf in the Vogtland, where, he had learned, the climate and the landscape were raw and the bread was black, but where he would be known as God's acknowledged son. He called it his flight to Egypt.

167. *Specimen Juris publici Europaei novissimi de jure et modo succendi in Regna Europae, speciatim in Regnum Bohemiae* (Frankfurt/Oder, 1739). *Lebensgeschichte*, I, pp. 180–81. Moser liked to believe or to claim that his dismissal was caused by this treatise, and in his old age wrote that his "unpartisan" opinion in the Austrian succession matter had cost him "eine ansehnliche Stelle und mein ganzes Stück Brod." *Lebensgeschichte*, IV, pp. 139–40; *Von der Reichs-Verfassungsmässigen Freyheit, von teutschen Staats-Sachen zu schreiben* (Göttingen, 1772), pp. 101–2.

PART II
The Constitution of the Empire

§11. Ebersdorf

THE village and Schloss Ebersdorf lay in the Vogtland of upper Saxony, a ledged and barren ground with an aspect of isolation, befitting the stories of robber bands and witchery that hung about the region. The manse and territory belonged to a branch of the genealogically intricate family of Reuss, which stemmed from farther east (the name seems to be a cognate of "Russ"). Incumbents then at the Schloss were Count Heinrich XXIX of Reuss-Ebersdorf, about Moser's age, and his sisters: the unmarried elder Benigna Maria and the younger Erdmuth Dorothea, wife of the enterprising pietist leader Nikolaus Count Zinzendorf, of Herrnhuth and of other places that would receive his mission. The parents of these present Reusses had established a Moravian religious community in the village in the 1690s. The villagers met their corporeal needs by forestry, herding, mining, spinning and weaving, and by service to the family and society at the Schloss, where there was constant visiting among neighborhood nobility, many of whom sponsored similar communities.[1]

There was a link to Moser's own past here. The court chaplain and pastor to the village community as well was Friedrich Christoph Steinhofer, Tübingen-educated, and native of that Swabian Alb district around Kirchheim where Moser had encountered the separatists during his service to Karl Alexander of Württemberg. Steinhofer had come as preacher to the Schloss in 1734 by connection with Count Zinzendorf, brother-in-law to Heinrich XXIX, and had obtained ordination in 1738, so as to assume pastoral leadership of the village, through the agency of Moser's old acquaintance the Württemberg pietist leader, Christoph Friedrich Oetinger. There will be more to say about Zinzendorf later, when his influence became critical for the history of the Ebersdorf community and Moser's relation to it; but in 1739 Zinzendorf's presence was remote.[2]

The religious life of the community as Moser found it was relatively simple, peaceful, and comfortable. Moser often declared later on that his first years at Ebersdorf were "the happiest and most blessed" of his

---

1. Friedrich W. Barthold, "Die Erweckten im protestantischen Deutschland während des Ausgangs des 17. und der ersten Hälfte des 18. Jahrhunderts, besonders die Frommen Grafenhöfe," part II, *Historisches Taschenbuch*, 3d series, IV (Leipzig, 1853), pp. 190–98; Marianne Fröhlich, *Johann Jakob Moser in seinem Verhältnis zum Rationalismus und Pietismus* (Vienna, 1925), pp. 72–75.

2. August Schmid, *Das Leben Johann Jakob Mosers, aus seiner Selbstbiographie, den Archiven und Familienpapieren dargestellt* (Stuttgart, 1868), pp. 521–30; Fröhlich, *Moser*, pp. 75–81.

whole life.[3] The community imposed few spiritual restraints. Mutual exchange of religious experience among the awakened was unforced, or perhaps at the time Moser needed no forcing: "The community, or rather the association, at that time was quite free; one could seek out those persons whose hearts and spirits suited best; and nobody was required to reveal more of himself than he himself wished."[4]

Moser's family included now Friderica Rosina, seven children ranging from sixteen to two years old (all there were to be, except for Christian Benjamin, who would be born in 1746 after a nine-year interval), and a converted Pomeranian Jewish girl who had replaced Fräulein Schmidlin in the Moser household and had accompanied them from Frankfurt. The community saw to the schooling and recreation of the children. It applied tests of godliness and conscience in place of parental or schoolmasterly discipline. If a child was naughty he was asked whether the baby Jesus would have behaved so, and the ensuing guilty tears usually sufficed to correct his behavior by the child's own will. Or "if a naughty child came amongst them, he found nobody of his kind, so that he was quickly brought around to be good, else he could not have borne it."[5] That was good for children. The serving class was earnest and loyal. Domestic peace and love prevailed.

Moser himself enjoyed association with the innumerable awakened counts and countesses (often widowed ones) of the comital network of which Reuss-Ebersdorf was a link. The remarkable propensity in that region of persons with the rank of count to be awakened to pious reflections and discourse may have something to do with their situation of noble status without much wealth, political power, or constitutional role. The religious communities they founded and peopled served as their tiny capitals. It was a category of people much given, it appears, to wondering who they were and whether they mattered. Moser could meet and converse with them on an agreeable level of spiritual equivalence.

The religious and social environment at Ebersdorf thus offered important consolation and a sympathetic place to a Moser coming raw from defeat in the world and fresh from spiritual salvation. There was still a problem in his personal spiritual life, however, signified by two theological pamphlets he wrote and published at Ebersdorf in 1741: "Missive on the Perils of Marriage between Awakened or Reborn Persons with Uncon-

3. *Lebensgeschichte Johann Jacob Mosers . . . von ihm selbst beschrieben*, 3d ed., 4 parts (Frankfurt/Main, 1777–83), II, p. 3; Moser, "Nachricht von meinem natürlichen, bürgerlichen und geistl: Leben, Für meine Kinder und Nachkommen" (dated Hohentwiel, 12 September 1763; manuscript in the possession of Helmut Haecker at the Hirsch-Apotheke in Urach/Württemberg), p. 47.

4. "Die Gemeinschaft, oder der Umgang, war damals ganz frey. . . ." "Nachricht," p. 48; see also *Lebensgeschichte*, II, pp. 212–14.

5. "Nachricht," pp. 49, 52–53; *Lebensgeschichte*, IV, pp. 40–44.

verted," and "Theological Thoughts on Marital Cohabitation amongst Unconverted, Awakened, and Reborn Persons."[6] Poor Friderica Rosina had arrived at the Ebersdorf community with her sins still unforgiven, which created a nasty marital problem now that Moser himself had been received in grace. Sexual congress even within marriage, declared Moser in the "Theological Thoughts," could be sinful, especially when one partner was saved and the other was not. Such a relation must inflict great pain upon the saved partner, and laid upon him the duty, before God, to assist the rebirth of the spiritually weaker partner, explaining patiently but firmly the nature of his—the saved partner's—distress.[7]

The Life History mentions only briefly, in an appendix assigned to Friderica Rosina, that she was vouchsafed grace early in the years at Ebersdorf.[8] The link with the theological essays, bespeaking marital tensions and pressures bearing on Friderica Rosina, appears in yet another of those associative anecdotes that pop artlessly into Moser's accounts of other matters. This one, part of a description of the various perils experienced by Moser on his travels, tells of a journey from Stuttgart to Ebersdorf in 1742 in the company of Friderica Rosina. As they approached Ebersdorf they came to a valley so flooded with heavy rains that the coach could not pass laden through a village, so that they had to get out of the coach and carry their baggage on foot over the flood. The path led finally over a single plank, without handrail, fixed high above the water. The coach had disappeared and darkness was falling, and there seemed no hope but to cross. Moser took up the baggage and inched across, one foot after another, and then went back for his wife. In terror she closed her eyes to keep from fainting and let him lead her across to safety despite her mortal fear, telling him on the other side that she had prayed to God only that she might not drag him down with her into the flood and cause him to perish on her account.[9]

Friderica Rosina's submission to grace at Ebersdorf was followed by that of the children, one after another. That freed Moser, whose own spiritual condition was already assured, from further burdensome responsibility for that of his family. If the early Ebersdorf years were "the

6. *Sendschreiben von der Gefahr der Heurathen erweckter oder wiedergebohrene Personen mit Unbekehrten* (Ebersdorf, 1741, anon.); *Theologische Gedancken von der ehlichen Beywohnung unbekehrter, erweckter und wiedergebohrener Personen* (Züllichau, 1741, anon.).

7. *Beywohnung* (I cite the 1900 Leipzig edition), pp. 83–87; Albrecht Ritschl, *Geschichte des Pietismus*, III (Bonn, 1886), pp. 35–36, discusses the problem of sinful sexuality within marriage among pietists. For the sexual and spiritual crisis that developed in Ebersdorf in 1745–46, see below, §17.

8. *Lebensgeschichte*, III, p. 216. This parallels the similarly bald statement in "Nachricht," p. 50.

9. *Lebensgeschichte*, II, pp. 28–29; "Nachricht," p. 19.

happiest and most blessed" of Moser's life, this was not because of an immersion of himself in the religious community but because of his release and freedom from duty and anxiety there. At Ebersdorf Moser had no master; for once in his life he was free—from the choked jungle of court and university intrigue, from the whims of Württemberg dukes, from the goals and discipline of the Prussian state. As for Ebersdorf constraints: Moser's list of his life's changing physical ills notes a certain tightness of the chest, "Engbrüstigkeit," which came and persisted with his time in Ebersdorf, and which he "belatedly" attributed to the closeness of his workroom there, where there was too little ventilation and all the vapors gathered and settled in his chest.[10]

But the truth is that he was barely a part of the community; his main local connections were with the Schloss and with Steinhofer, and he had hardly arrived at Ebersdorf when he began his many visits and legal errands throughout the empire in a private professional capacity. Judging by his itinerary, he probably spent less of his time at home during Ebersdorf years than ever before, or rarely after. He needed a secure place there for his family and a private base for making a living, from which to write his books, draft his opinions, embark upon his commissions. There was even a certain analogy, *multum in parvo*, between the modes of social hierarchy and controls at Ebersdorf and those of the empire at large. But nothing about his being at Ebersdorf gave distinctive shape to Moser's work—not unless we are ready to recognize formlessness by intention to be a distinctive shape.

Moser's scholarly work of that period shows, rather, an absence and even a release from intellectual and professional discipline. This was in some part a conscious denial and a deliberate flight from the intellectual and political world that lay immediately behind him. His most ambitious religious piece—there were ten religious items published in 1740–41—was "Scriptural Thoughts on the Relation of Philosophy, Especially the Wolffian, with Theology." The *Schrifftmässige Gedancken* of Moser's title contrasted with the clown Morgenstern's echo of Christian Wolff's *Vernünfftige Gedancken*; and the *Welt-Weisheit* specified the worldly nature of philosophy as compared with faith. The mark of his recent humiliation and redemption was plain in this work, which he prefaced with a quotation from Luke: "Whoever is ashamed of me or my words, must be ashamed for the son of man when he comes."[11] Here Moser went through the argument that rational metaphysics and analyses might make religion comprehensible in a superficial way to the unawakened, might make it accessible as a theological structure; but he denied that

10. "Nachricht," p. 5; *Lebensgeschichte*, II, p. 5; III, p. 42.
11. *Schrifftmässige Gedancken von der Verbindung der Welt-Weisheit, besonders der Wolfischen, mit der Theologie* ([Saalfeld], 1741); Luke 9:26.

God could or would use human philosophy to bring salvation (the devil is a liar). For of true conversion all the glory was God's alone. If true religion depended on words or reason in any way, it would be child's play to ridicule and refute it. "We, Christ's disciples and pupils, are in your eyes fools indeed; but we rejoice, in that godly folly is wiser than men are."[12] The motif of Christ's fools pervades the religious writing of the early 1740s. Introducing a biographical dictionary of contemporary theologians, for example, Moser wrote how "now that I have resolved myself to the agony of Christ, and have acknowledged what to the wise of this world is the folly of Christ's cross, I care little whether five or ten or a hundred others abuse me or call me fool." Anybody who could write a good catechism, he declared, was more important than an author of "fifty scholarly folios," *50 Folianten scientifice*.[13] Fifty volumes turned out to be the ultimate extent of the huge *Teutsches Staats-Recht* upon which Moser was just getting launched at the time.

As religious views these are unremarkable, but the personal note was strong and distinct. It was a spiritual position, long prepared, to which Moser could readily take refuge out of his professional and psychic crisis of the late thirties. "The more nonsensical the more certain—*je sinnloser, desto gewisser*" is the formulation by one modern psychologist of German pietism: a negative intellectualism of paradox that sees God's presence especially in the otherwise inexplicable and random event or circumstance.[14] For Moser, though he rejected the label of pietist, it was a *credo quia absurdum est* that defended him against the rational strictures and pressures of academy and state. It was an aspect of the freedom and release he found at Ebersdorf; it was part of what he meant when he told colleagues and posterity that he went to Ebersdorf renouncing all thought of being a great man in the world.[15]

Moser's legal scholarship of that time shows a similar renunciation of directed reasoning, of intellectual or political ambition. That did not mean laziness, not exactly, but rather a kind of churning. Moser had reason enough to say all is vanity. But that could not enjoin idleness upon his nervous humors. Almost all the published jurisprudence of

---

12. *Schrifftmässige Gedancken*, p. 64.

13. *Beytrag zu einem Lexico der jeztlebenden Lutherisch- und Reformirten Theologen in und um Deutschland*, I (Züllichau, 1740), preface.

14. Hans R. G. Günther, "Psychologie des deutschen Pietismus," *Deutsche Vierteljahrsschrift für Literaturwissenschaft und Geistesgeschichte*, IV (1926), pp. 158–59. But Moser even during the Ebersdorf years did not call himself a pietist, partly because the name was loosely pejorative, suggesting affected enthusiasm, and partly because the label implied, unacceptably to him, the presence of a doctrine.

15. The Catholic jurist Johann Adam Ickstatt remarked to Moser that had Moser been Catholic, Ickstatt would have said Moser had gone to Ebersdorf to mortify the flesh. "Nachricht," pp. 14, 51a.

1739–41 was particular or territorial public law, *besonderes Staatsrecht*, the constitutional laws of individual states. Moser had for some time had the artless notion of preparing the particular public laws of all the constituent states of the empire; and his Ebersdorf publications start off with Aachen, Augsburg, the monastery at Baindt, and Constance, but lapse into Trier, Zell, Anhalt, Nürnberg. Some of these—notably the quite impressive work on Trier—probably resulted from particular commissions that he had received or that he hoped for. But most were relatively simple and unsystematic compilations of the constitutional materials he had at hand about these places; thus Moser's longstanding legal positivism allowed him to do intellectually undemanding and politically insensitive scholarship.[16]

Even this project ran into trouble, though, which may be one reason why the project broke up early in the alphabet—trouble already with Anhalt and with Brandenburg, the two most significant places that early in the list. When Moser sent his manuscript to the principality of Anhalt for that government's perusal he got a reply that may be paraphrased thus: Thank you for your interest, but do not trouble to publish this; our Dr. Bechmann has already published an adequate constitutional history; and you may be sure, moreover, that we will tolerate no publication of documents disadvantageous to the government of Anhalt; do not risk our displeasure. As for Brandenburg, Moser sent a tentative outline of certain chapters to Berlin and received the following reply: "Inasmuch as We, for various and important reasons, can by no means allow such things to be made known in print: so must you, on pain of Our severe disfavor and unfailing sharp reprisal, totally refrain from this work. Remain you in Grace. Friedrich Wilhelm." Moser refrained in the Brandenburg case, but he went ahead after a pause and published his Anhalt materials ("so as not to have wasted the time") and even sent the Anhalt ministry a batch which he offered them at a reduced price, thereby eliciting outrage from Anhalt: Moser asking pay for what they had prohibited! They warned that if he did not desist, "the Aforesaid Princely House will without fail require the *eclanteste* satisfaction from [Moser], and will seek it in the proper place." Moser was undisturbed by this and proceeded to sell the Anhalt book publicly.[17]

16. The full titles are listed in Reinhard Rürup, *Johann Jacob Moser: Pietismus und Reform* (Wiesbaden, 1965), p. 262. In 1745 they were compiled into a handsome "Erster Band" of *Die heutige besondere Staats-Verfassung des Stände des Teutschen Reichs* (Leipzig), and there the project lapsed. Rürup discusses Moser's *Territorialstaatsrecht*, pp. 103–5.

17. *Von der Reichs-Verfassungsmässigen Freyheit, von teutschen Staats-Sachen zu schreiben* (Göttingen, 1772), pp. 83–88; *Lebensgeschichte*, III, pp. 91–92. Moser repeatedly defended himself against the charge of publishing state secrets: see, in addition to the above,

Such compilations done at Ebersdorf kept the restless, emotionally convalescent Moser busy with work that imposed little moral or intellectual strain. Even those few volumes of the *Teutsches Staats-Recht* that appeared in the early forties were ragged compendia of odd ceremonials, titles, and privileges of the empire. Pastor Steinhofer, contemplating Moser's labors day after day stapling these materials together, declared "with great emotion" that "he had liefer thresh, or split wood, than spend his time that way,"[18] an observation reminiscent of Moser's wood-sawing therapy for the *melancholia hypochondriaca* back in Frankfurt on Oder. But whatever one supposes Moser's inner necessities were, and however these particular works fit his state of mind at Ebersdorf, he wrote after all to bring in money. For again he was without salary and without regular patronage from anybody.

This lack of post or patron, though, gave Moser unusual freedom to write as he saw fit about the law and affairs of the German Empire, freedom of a kind he could never have had as servant or dependent of any powerful government or statesman, or even as resident of any important jurisdiction whose ruler might have serious political ambitions or anxieties—such as were hardly conceivable of Heinrich XXIX Graf Reuss-Ebersdorf. The Ebersdorf sanctuary, moreover, as well as being politically remote, quiet, and inexpensive, was within easy traveling distance of the city of Leipzig, great center of the German book trade. This happy geographical circumstance may have inclined Moser toward settling at Ebersdorf in the first place. Leipzig's masters were markedly easygoing in matters of censorship, for the sake of attracting and keeping the trade, especially away from the rival publishing center at Frankfurt on Main, where the imperial censors sat. Within months after arriving at Ebersdorf Moser had established his own home press, and soon he had his own special permanent agent at the Leipzig book fair, selling for cash. That became the main market for the *Teutsches Staats-Recht*, a quite profitable enterprise written mostly in the middle 1740s.[19] Another geographical peculiarity of Ebersdorf was that it lay almost at the center of a rough circle that might be inscribed through the capitals at Berlin, Prague, Vienna, Frankfurt on Main, Hanover, Munich—and Stuttgart, for that matter. There could hardly be a better situation from which to undertake

---

Moser's *Ihro Römisch-Kayserlichen Majestät Carls des Siebenden Wahl-Capitulation, mit Beylagen und Anmerckungen versehen,* II (Frankfurt/Main, 1742), preface, §9; and *Lebensgeschichte,* III, pp. 112–13.

18. "Nachricht," pp. 51a–52; *Lebensgeschichte,* IV, p. 187.

19. For Moser as publisher, and for some observations on the *Teutsches Staats-Recht* (hereinafter TSR), see below, §13.

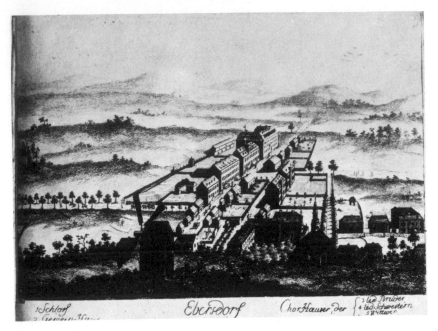

EBERSDORF
"The most contented and blessed years of my life." Moser, Lebensgeschichte, *II*,
*p. 3. "The only problem, and the one that in the end ruined everything, was the
preconceived notion of a commune [Gemeine]."* Moser, *"Nachricht," p. 49.
"The longer I was there the more oppressive it grew to live under that
constitution; so I resolved."* Moser, Lebensgeschichte, *II, p. 48.*
Moravian Archives, Bethlehem, Pennsylvania

free-lance commissions in the political and legal affairs of the empire,
as the political indifference of Moser's awakened territorial counts and
countesses left him quite free to write whatever law he liked.

Imperial politics, and the writing of his huge compilation on the law of
the empire, were the linked themes of Moser's professional career from
the Ebersdorf base, much as civil administration, practical jurisprudence,
and university life had been the theme of the first career that ended with
his Prussian service. Then from Ebersdorf after a decade he would return
to Stuttgart as spokesman for the estates of that duchy to their duke, and
after that he would devote his last major scholarship to the powers of the
territorial states and the constraints laid upon them by the laws of the
empire and by the rights of their subjects.

§12. Whales, Sharks, and Little Fish

IN October of 1740 Emperor Charles VI died. For three centuries past, the house of Habsburg had managed to hold its many and motley dynastic holdings together with the German imperial crown through succession by male heirs; but Charles had none. To compensate for this lack he had, throughout his reign, negotiated agreements whereby all his dynastic lands and titles, of whatever provenance and by whatever right, should descend to his eldest daughter, Maria Theresa, by an arrangement known as the Pragmatic Sanction. This was accepted first by affected members of the house, then by a number of important German princes and European sovereigns, and by the German Reichstag (though not all members assented). The only other possible inheritors were two nieces (daughters of Charles's elder brother, the late emperor Joseph I), both married to important German electoral princes: one to Friedrich August, elector of Saxony and king of Poland, and the other to the elector Karl Albrecht of Bavaria. Maria Theresa's consort—and by virtue of her inheritance the Habsburg candidate to succeed Charles VI—was Francis Stephen of the house of Lorraine, now grand duke of Tuscany. But Francis Stephen had no land or constitutional position in Germany, no "Hausmacht" of his own; and he was held suspect by the French, who had deprived him of his ancestral lands in Lorraine a dozen years before. Maria Theresa had no male heirs but was four months pregnant at the time of her father's death.

In this dynastic situation, the death of Charles VI threw imperial politics into their most precarious and uncertain state since the Thirty Years War; it appeared possible that the empire might collapse altogether.[20] A central and critical constitutional issue for the imperial succession was, as it had been in 1618, who should exercise the electoral right of the Kingdom of Bohemia. Nobody imagined that the college of imperial electors would permit a woman to do so, and Francis Stephen had no standing there. The elector of Saxony admitted the right of Maria Theresa to succeed as queen of Bohemia, but claimed for himself, as nearest male relative, the electoral voice. Karl Albrecht of Bavaria, ranking member of the ever-eager house of Wittelsbach (and who had never

20. That was the judgment of the Hanoverian first minister Gerlach Adolf von Münchhausen. His memoranda of 1740 and 1742 to the British government on the politics of the Austrian succession are as clear and credible analyses as I have seen: Theo König, *Hannover und das Reich 1740–1745* (Bonn, 1938), pp. 4–33; and by the same author, "Eine Denkschrift Gerlach Adolf von Münchhausens über die hannoversche Aussenpolitik der Jahre 1740–42," *Niedersächsisches Jahrbuch für Landesgeschichte*, XIV (1937), pp. 200–232.

agreed to the Pragmatic Sanction), claimed both the Bohemian crown and its electoral voice for himself, in effect declaring thereby his own candidacy for the imperial crown. And if that was not enough, Frederick II of Brandenburg-Prussia, who by mortal coincidence had assumed the late Frederick William I's throne just five months before the emperor's death, invaded and occupied the rich Habsburg duchy of Silesia in December of 1740. In March of 1741 the electoral convocation formally opened at Frankfurt on Main but could not even begin its proceedings, for nobody knew how the Bohemian question would be resolved or whom to vote for.[21]

Johann Jakob Moser had published a dissertation supporting Maria Theresa's right to the Bohemian inheritance at Frankfurt on Oder during his last days there, and he even believed that this had brought about his dismissal by the old king.[22] Then, after the emperor's death, Moser was asked by the cardinal archbishop-elector Franz Georg of Trier—yet another Schönborn brother, whom Moser had met on his Franconian journey of 1735—to prepare another memorandum defending the queen's right to the Bohemian electoral voice, which he did.[23] That summer the elector of Trier invited Moser to join his delegation to the electoral convention at Frankfurt on Main, and Moser readily accepted. He was there for over six months, from September 1741 to March 1742, drafting memoranda and opinions for the electoral negotiations that culminated, to Trier's disappointment, in the election of the Bavarian to be emperor. Then only three years later, after the Wittelsbach emperor's death, Moser was to attend the election of Maria Theresa's consort, the grand duke Francis Stephen, to be emperor, an election that restored the imperial crown to a regrafted Habsburg dynasty.

These two elections of 1742 and 1745 were Moser's most intimate and sustained engagement with imperial politics at the peak, surrounding the imperial crown itself. In between them he worked on his *Teutsches Staats-Recht*, along with other writings and commissions that he owed to his association with imperial elective politics. The elections were, Moser said, an "advanced school" for him in German constitutional law and politics,[24] and indeed they were and are peculiarly instructive. The Austrian succession conflict, by breaking the Habsburg grip on the imperial crown for the first time in centuries, opened up the German constitution

21. Moser, *Von dem Römischen Kayser, Römischen König und denen Reichs-Vicarien* (= NTSR II: Frankfurt/Main, 1767), pp. 49–55, 168–69.

22. See above, part I, n. 167.

23. *Lebensgeschichte*, II, p. 6. This seems not to have been the memorandum on this subject sent to Vienna before the emperor's death: *Lebensgeschichte*, I, p. 181.

24. *Lebensgeschichte*, II, p. 7; IV, p. 194.

to take whatever form the political realities of central Europe might determine.

Subsequent historiography and many contemporary observers have held France mainly responsible for the election of the unfortunate Karl Albrecht of Wittelsbach to be emperor, assuming a foregone conclusion upon which the German maneuvering that intervened had little effect.[25] Moser denied this, both at the time and still in his old age; and although the presence of French influence underlies his account, still the sequence and staging of events as he perceived them focus instead on the German princes themselves and their behavior. To these the French responded. German constitutional politics were for Moser a German responsibility; and whatever the French might wish, the election was by no means rigged from the start. Prussia, for example, was in nobody's pocket.[26]

At the beginning there were in Maria Theresa's corner, by Moser's reckoning, four electorates: Mainz, whose elector, the imperial arch-chancellor, had been receiving a hundred thousand Habsburg gulden a year since 1732 in anticipation of this election; and Bohemia, whose vote according to the Pragmatic Sanction belonged to Maria Theresa; and the Protestant electorate of Braunschweig or Hanover; and the Schönborn electorate of Trier. Behind Karl Albrecht was the solid Wittelsbach electoral block of Bavaria, Cologne, and the Palatinate. Uncommitted were the houses of Brandenburg-Prussia and electoral Saxony-Poland, whose territorial rivalry with one another had been aggravated by Prussia's seizure of Silesia. Frederick of Prussia would gladly have given his vote to Francis of Tuscany in return for formal Habsburg concession of Silesia to him. That would exclude both the Bavarian Wittelsbachs and the Saxon Wettiner from the imperial crown while retaining the edge he had gained over them, in that corner of Germany, by taking Silesia. Frederick's vote would surely have made Francis Stephen emperor; but during 1741 Maria Theresa's government, despite Prussian military victories, stubbornly refused to concede Silesia.

At the end of August, 1741, after a long delay, Prussia announced its vote for Karl Albrecht to be emperor, and in September the Prussia-Wittelsbach block of four, supported by France, declared that the contested Bohemian electoral vote must be suspended for the present elec-

25. Max Braubach, *Versailles und Wien von Ludwig XIV bis Kaunitz* (Bonn, 1952), pp. 340–59; Max Spindler, ed., *Handbuch der Bayerischen Geschichte*, 2d ed., II (Munich, 1974), pp. 466–72.

26. For what follows I summarize Moser's several accounts, consistent in all major points, in *Staats-Historie Teutschlands unter der Regierung Ihro Kayserlichen Majestät Carls des Siebenden*, I (Jena, 1743), pp. 34–39; *Von dem Römischen Kayser* (= NTSR II), pp. 16, 49, 55, 168–79, and passim; TSR *Zusätze*, I (Leipzig, 1744), pp. 185–206; *Lebensgeschichte*, II, pp. 13–14.

tion. That would reduce the college of electors to eight, and thus suffice to block the election of Francis. The other electors protested—Saxony and Braunschweig rather feebly—but then Mainz, Saxony, Braunschweig, and finally even Trier gave way. The decision was left to *force majeur*. In November French and Bavarian forces entered Prague; Karl Albrecht was crowned king of Bohemia; and his formal election as emperor followed in January at Frankfurt.

Charles VII was crowned by his brother, archbishop-elector of Cologne, on the twelfth of February, amidst great pomp. The elector of Cologne and the embassies of France and Spain, Moser observed, exhibited the greatest splendor; the severe handful of Prussian officials who attended "cut no figure." Moser wedged himself into the Trier delegation for the coronation ceremonies to see whether they would follow the forms and language prescribed in the second volume of his *Teutsches Staats-Recht*, but the archbishop rattled it all off so fast that he could not tell.[27]

This account of Moser's leaves undescribed international events such as the rise of the belligerent Belle-Isle over Fleury at Versailles, which reversed a French endorsement of the Pragmatic Sanction made as late as January of 1741; the outbreak of war between France and England; and Spanish and papal support for the Wittelsbachs. These factors underlay features of the crisis that he did remark: the solidarity of the Wittelsbach block, the inconstancy of Saxony and Braunschweig-Hanover. Their relation with German politics was by no means obscure; they were laid out in detail in, for example, the able contemporary analyses sent by the Hanoverian privy council president Baron von Münchhausen to his government in London, which in other respects confirm Moser's.[28] Moser was watching German constitutional politics and how they responded to these contingents of power. What he did perceive and record, arriving as he did in the election city at Frankfurt on Main in mid-September of 1741, was a disruption of legitimate succession procedures before a determined Prussian-Wittelsbach alliance, and a repudiation of the duly ratified Pragmatic Sanction by a college of electors that followed "the law of state convenience," Staats-Convenienz-Recht.[29]

Moser had no trouble adapting his juridical views to the policies of the

27. *Lebensgeschichte*, II, pp. 15–16.

28. See n. 20, §12 above. Probably the election was in doubt, and even favored Francis, until the Prussian victory over Austria at Mollwitz in April of 1741 galvanized French policy and brought Belle-Isle to power at Versailles; Austria's electoral position then deteriorated all that summer, with Trier the last holdout for Francis. Karl T. Heigel, *Der Österreichische Erbfolgestreit und die Kaiserwahl Karls VII* (Nördlingen, 1877), pp. 44–152 and passim; Fritz Wagner, *Kaiser Karl VII. und die grossen Mächte 1740–45* (Stuttgart, 1938), p. 172 and passim.

29. *Von dem Römischen Kayser* (= NTSR II), pp. 49–56.

Trier electorate. He liked and admired the elector Franz Georg, for his industry, his piety (albeit Catholic), and his willingness to be instructed by Moser in legal proprieties. Moser's principal labors at Frankfurt for Trier were directed to the Electoral Capitulation, that constitutional instrument wherein the newly elected emperor agreed to observe rights and privileges pertaining to the imperial estates.[30] There was unusual interest and concern about this in 1741–42, because of the unprecedented political circumstances where the imperial electors had defied the traditional authority of the Habsburg house: they had chosen an emperor who could not, in the degree that Austria might, act independently of them. How much autonomy, then, would the electors demand in the capitulation? So much as to dissolve the empire into a handful of competitive territorial blocks? The goal of the Trier elector Franz Georg, having failed in his effort to reelect the Habsburgs, now became to restrain the ambitions of the powerful electors in the subsequent negotiations over the capitulation. In this effort his natural allies were the lesser, nonelectoral German princes, who were holding their own anxious assembly in nearby Aschaffenburg, then subsequently in Frankfurt itself. Their champion in the electoral college, which by right drafted the capitulation, was Trier, so that Moser as a leading draftsman on the Trier electoral delegation worked in cooperation with them.[31]

These lesser princes, second college of the imperial estates, feared that the electors would exploit the present unsettled situation by making arrangements of their own with the new emperor—an emperor so recently only one of their own electoral number, and by no means the wealthiest or mightiest or cleverest of them. And indeed the electors did prepare a list of provisions favoring themselves. But they introduced them not into the capitulation itself, which they negotiated on behalf of the whole Reich. Rather, they submitted them to the emperor on their own collegial behalf, for him to put forth subsequently as imperial decrees. Meanwhile they stipulated in the capitulation itself that the emperor was bound to promulgate measures agreed to in this way—that is, engagements reached without the foreknowledge or participation of the lesser estates and without the constitutional standing of the capitulation. And there were other constitutional proposals current among the electors in 1742 that would in effect have transferred legislative rights belonging to the whole Reichstag into the capitulation, an agreement reached bilaterally between the emperor and the college of electors.[32]

30. See below, §15.

31. "Nachricht," pp. 10, 53, 81; *Lebensgeschichte*, II, pp. 7–14; III, pp. 65–66; IV, pp. 42–46.

32. A convenient summary is Johann Stephan Pütter, *Historische Entwickelung der heutigen Staatsverfassung des Teutschen Reichs*, 3d ed., III (Göttingen, 1799), pp. 17–31.

The lesser princes, therefore, sought for themselves (as they had before in vain) a right to participate directly in the drafting of the capitulation, and they looked to Trier for help. But Moser, who bore chief responsibility in the Trier delegation for the capitulation draft (and Trier after all was an electorate too), was sharply opposed. He agreed that the electors were trying to slip things into the capitulation that belonged in the Reichstag, but he denied that this trick entitled the lesser princes to a voice in the capitulation draft. He advised them on tactical grounds to desist from their effort to change this constitutional arrangement, for that dispute might cause a crisis that would bring "the greatest benefit to the common enemy," France, while doing "the weaker litigants the greatest harm."[33] Moser instead set to work on the verbal details of the capitulation, in which of course his elector Franz Georg had a voice. Instead of trying directly to defeat provisions brought by other electors that Trier opposed, Moser "got the poison out of them by omitting or inserting a few words, etc." He provided reams of marginalia that became part of subsequent official editions of the capitulation. The document that emerged was similar in pattern and in its main provisions to the capitulations of earlier emperors, but far longer, wreathed with amplifications and addenda. The main changes, Moser remarked later on in his own treatise on the capitulation, lay in recognizing the preeminent importance of the powerful estates by implicit informal ways, rather than by formal changes in imperial institutions: the latter remained intact.[34]

In all these matters Moser was obliged to confront, at second hand at least, the relation between the politics of power and the letter of the law. The experience did not lessen his belief in the law down to the tiniest detail; on the contrary, what he saw of great men and their behavior convinced him all the more that the law in all detail must be preserved

33. Rürup, *Moser*, pp. 132–33; Moser, *Teutsches Staats-Archiv*, VI (1751), p. 140 and passim. Moser's long memorandum on the *Gravamina* of the princes respecting the capitulation is in Württembergisches Hauptstaatsarchiv, Stuttgart (hereinafter WHS) KA III Ls 390.

34. Moser, *Carls des Siebenden Wahl-Capitulation*, II, pp. 251–52 and passim; *Staats-Historie Carls des Siebenden*, I, pp. 62–93. Friedrich Karl von Moser, who shortly after this became closely associated with his father's affairs, claimed twenty years later that the whole elaborated capitulation was aimed not at the piddling Wittelsbach emperor but at an anticipated future Habsburg, but this is not convincing: *Was ist gut Kayserlich und nicht gut Kayserlich* (n.p., 1766), pp. 98–108. Fritz Hartung saw no marked difference from the capitulations of the sixteenth and seventeenth centuries: "Die Wahlcapitulationen der deutschen Kaiser und Könige," *Historische Zeitschrift*, CVII (1911), pp. 340–44. One new provision was that members of the Reichshofrat were to be persons with judicial experience, either in practical negotiations or from a university faculty: Moser, *Carls des Siebenden Wahl-Capitulation*, I, pp. 78–79, and II, pp. 600–601. Moser also inserted a provision respecting the dignity of the imperial courts: *Lebensgeschichte*, IV, pp. 45–46.

and prevail. For in detail lay the best constitutional defenses against political might. But this could not fully solve the problem of relating politics with law in Germany. It was during that convocation at Frankfurt, Moser reminisced later on, that an important imperial personage approached him soliciting support from Trier for "a certain proposal," which Moser found so outrageous that he blurted: "But what you suggest to me here is *contra jus Naturae*, against the law of Nature!" The other replied that whales have no other *jus Naturae* than to eat up little fish. Moser returned (he said) that in the first place, whales don't; only sharks do that, whereas true whales let the little fish swim peacefully about them; "and if it comes to sharks, why, they are *Bruta*; and for such *Bruta* a brutal *jus Naturae* fits well enough; but we are intelligent men and so should deal with one another more sensibly!" The *jus convenientiae*, he warned another person of estate, would one day bring his house down, "and so it did."[35]

Still, this "advanced school in German constitutional law" of 1741–42 was, Moser concluded, a wearisome one, *langwihrig*; but instead of reflecting directly upon its lessons, he ended his account of it with still another story of a journey plagued by floods, this tale the longest and most elaborately told of them all. As he traveled from Frankfurt home to Ebersdorf in March 1742, his open chaise was obliged to take a rough path to avoid the overflowing Saale; and as they set out above it, an old postilion who accompanied them at the start, to show the way, found an ax in the path. At first the postilion thought to take it home with him, but then he gave it to Moser's driver as he left the party to their journey, observing that one could never tell when an ax might be needed on such an expedition. The sunken path being choked with snow, Moser's chaise took to the fields, and found it necessary to drive under a large spreading pear tree. Moser ducked to avoid being struck in the face by a branch; the branch brought the chaise to a stop, and when Moser straightened up his head was caught in a fork behind, with a stiff sharp stub pressing "the so-called Adam's apple" before. Were the chaise to pull back his neck would be broken; if forward, the point would stab him in the throat. After much flurry and consternation among his companions, Moser (who providentially could still move his head and speak) declared, "Now I know why God let us find that ax today; the only way is to chop that branch off"; and it was done. Many people thereafter went out to see that wonderful branch and how Moser had been caught in it; and he often regretted not having taken it away with him.[36]

35. *Lebensgeschichte*, II, pp. 17–18.
36. "Nachricht," pp. 19–20; *Lebensgeschichte*, II, pp. 18–20. The two versions set the same symbolic effect by somewhat different detail.

That summer Moser wrote up his materials on the electoral convocation, including political memoranda that when published brought angry expostulations from various participants (Moser replied that he had come by them honestly and had even paid hard cash for some).[37] By winter he was on the road again, to Stuttgart, Berlin, and Frankfurt again in the interest of the Württemberg estates. He had this commission by virtue of his recent engagement in imperial politics, and here was another lesson about how the doings of the imperial great affected those of lesser estate.

When the Catholic Karl Alexander had succeeded to the Württemberg duchy in 1733, the episcopal authority over ecclesiastical personnel and revenues in that Protestant duchy had been delegated to the privy council, with a voice in their administration allowed to the diet. These religious agreements or Reversalien were guaranteed by the Protestant estates of the empire, led by Prussia, Denmark, and England. Karl Alexander, though obliged to accept this arrangement, had never been content with it; and the ecclesiastical Reversalien issue introduced a religious component to a more general constitutional contest between him and the Protestant diet. Pietist religious leaders and sympathizers were very influential in the diet: there was no noble estate there, but rather an estate of prelates, who had succeeded to the old monastic endowments, and an estate of towns and districts.[38]

The sudden death of Karl Alexander by stroke in 1737 was a great boon for the popular or Protestant party located in the diet, a boon they were not loath to attribute to divine favor. It brought them a great victory over the court party, expressed in the brutal torment and execution of Süss Oppenheimer and the exile of Remchingen, and leading to the establishment of a regency (for the nine-year-old heir Karl Eugen) directed not by Württemberg court figures but by distant relatives, Protestants, of the late duke. The regency had no real interest in sustaining the prerogatives of the ruling line, and even, out of rivalry with the dowager duchess and her Catholic advisers for control of government, tended to support the Protestants of the diet.[39] In 1739 this regency made a formal agreement with the diet that reaffirmed the Reversalien of 1733.[40] The diet's constitutional position, based as it was on the religious and political sentiments of the population and supported by the Protestant estates of the empire, and by the regency, seemed then very strong.

37. *Carls des Siebenden Wahl-Capitulation*, II, preface, §§9, 23–25; *Von der Freyheit zu schreiben*, pp. 27–28; *Lebensgeschichte*, III, pp. 112–14; IV, pp. 171–73.

38. See above, §8.

39. Walter Grube, *Der Stuttgarter Landtag 1457–1957* (Stuttgart, 1957), pp. 389, 409–24.

40. Text of the Landtags-Abschied of 1739 is in August L. Reyscher, *Sammlung der württembergischen Gesetze*, II (Stuttgart, 1829), pp. 517–40.

Complicating the position and compromising the diet, though, were problems created by that same Württemberg religious sectarianism that provided the diet with much of its emotive power and popular support. To summarize these it is probably best here to adopt a main distinction (as Moser had done in 1734) between pietists and separatists.[41] Most pietist leaders, however, faithful to their religious belief in a direct relation between each believer and God, did not object to a strong ecclesiastical establishment, holding it indeed to be a bulwark of their church and confession. Consistent separatists, though, rejected this compromise between the holy and profane realms, and denied the authority of the ecclesiastical establishment over their religious exercises. This divergence reached into diet politics and weakened its leadership. Still, the separatist position was one from which more conservative pietist leaders could not altogether withhold sympathy, because after all it represented only a logical and consistent conclusion from their own religious position, and also because they feared the consequences of a direct and passionate confrontation. Moreover, they were much concerned about the possible effects of a penetration into the quietistic pietism of the Württemberg countryside from the more militant variety led by Count Zinzendorf.[42]

While Württemberg religious authorities in diet and privy council struggled to settle the place of separatism in the ecclesiastical system, the young duke Karl Eugen entered adolescence, and the Wittelsbach elector Karl Albrecht became emperor. The new emperor Charles VII, when the Württembergers asked him to confirm the constitutional rights of the diet and the Reversalien settlement of 1733, was evasive; he replied that he would do so insofar as these rights accorded with compacts made between earlier Württemberg dukes and duchy and which earlier emperors had confirmed, and with the text of the Peace of Westphalia. In this language the diet saw danger for itself and the Reversalien; and in November of 1742 they sent to Ebersdorf for Johann Jakob Moser, just back from his work on the imperial capitulation.[43]

Moser's alienation from the late duke Karl Alexander and from Friedrich Karl von Schönborn—who now seems to have been advising the dowager duchess—commended him to the constitutional party. His timely departure for Prussia in 1736 had, by luck or by calculation, allowed him to escape the obloquy and vengeance wrought upon the former duke's officials following his death. Then from Ebersdorf he had

41. See above, §8.

42. The best treatment of this is Hartmut Lehmann, *Pietismus und weltliche Ordnung in Württemberg vom 17. bis zum 20. Jahrhundert* (Stuttgart, 1969), pp. 61–94; also Ritschl, *Pietismus*, III, pp. 14–15 and passim.

43. *Lebensgeschichte*, II, pp. 20–21.

maintained connections with Württemberg religious leaders; he knew about the separatist problem and was sound there; meanwhile he had become more intimately involved with recent imperial politics than anybody else of sympathetic religious persuasion. And although Moser had doubts about the constitutional position of the Württemberg Protestant leaders, after a summer in Ebersdorf he was willing to undertake a commission to the empire on their behalf. On the journeys and negotiations this commission entailed, Moser got an impression of the consequences for Germany of recent constitutional events, and the costs his land and countrymen bore for the doings of politicians who relied on military power.

As he traveled through Franconia, he found it traversed by French soldiery and officials on their way east to support the Wittelsbach emperor against Maria Theresa. Moser had to explain to spokesmen of an embittered and hostile country populace that he was only an honest German on his way to his Württemberg homeland, on a mission to set the French and the emperor straight. At Stuttgart a dubious privy council tried to dissuade him from pursuing the Reversalien matter further, so it is not clear just who Moser thought he represented; but finally they allowed him to go on to the imperial court at Frankfurt at least to sound out the situation there. Inasmuch as the Theresan forces under Prince Carl of Lorraine were now driving the French back on the Rhine, Moser equipped himself with a personal pass from the regent, and set out through the combat zone. He reached Heidelberg just as the French evacuated it in face of an advance by a column of Hungarian hussars; but half a day past Heidelberg Moser was stopped by a troop of French chasseurs: to these he explained that he was a Prussian privy councillor (which technically he still was). Destruction, the dying, and the dead lay all about Charles VII's Frankfurt as Moser approached it; and now he again had to explain himself as an honest German. He thought about the absurdity of abolishing judicial torture while politicians made war.[44]

At Frankfurt nobody would pay any attention to him. The Danish Baron Bernsdorff told him that although the government at Copenhagen had indeed once guaranteed the Reversalien, they had just written to ask again what the Reversalien might all be about; that hardly sounded like convinced support. The Swedes at Frankfurt told him their government was not interested in German affairs. Moser hovered about. From the lesser personages ready to talk with him, he picked up a collection of gossip about the emperor's incompetence, his weakness, the repeated humiliations he was obliged to swallow. Once the emperor found a scurrilous squib had been put in his hat, in his private quarters; when he

44. *Lebensgeschichte*, II, pp. 22–24.

offered a thousand ducats for the identity of the author, next day another squib appeared saying the author would gladly turn himself in for the reward if the emperor could only show where he would get the thousand ducats. The emperor had an "immoderate taste for the female sex"; and one of Moser's confidante countesses told him that the empress had shown her a box full of hairs that the emperor had plucked out of the empress's head. So the talk went at Frankfurt. The closest Moser came to the emperor was a conversation with the Bavarian court chancellor Bratenlohn, son of a Freising butcher and unhappy with his master's new role. Bratenlohn said nothing could be done about the Württemberg Reversalien unless Frederick himself of Prussia pressed the matter upon the emperor. Moser had had enough of Frankfurt now and headed back for Stuttgart.[45]

There it was decided that he should go on to Berlin. Moser went by way of Ebersdorf so as to drop off his wife, who had been visiting in Stuttgart,[46] and to pick up young Friedrich Karl, whom Moser was beginning to initiate into his affairs. But nobody would listen to him at the Prussian court either: they told him not to expect Frederick—now precariously at peace with both Habsburg and Wittelsbach and in military possession of Silesia—to undertake vain gestures in so trivial a matter. Moser complained to the Prussian privy councillor for imperial affairs that a new failure here would leave Moser looking like a fool. Grudgingly then an order was drafted for the Prussian ambassador at Frankfurt that he ought on balance to support the position of the Württemberg diet, but not if that should hamper his other duties, in which case he should ignore the question. Moser then returned to Stuttgart. By that time the regular counsel to the Württemberg diet was in Frankfurt negotiating the Reversalien, to Moser's apparent chagrin. For when "the diet" (Moser does not say specifically who or how) asked him to return to Frankfurt himself, he went "with such extraordinary swiftness" that the bemused Prussian ambassador refused to believe he was already there again until he saw him.[47]

The emperor now inspected the documents himself, took advice from the papal nuncio and from the president of the Reichshofrat, and finally approved the Württemberg petition because he had been advised that it was "in substance conformable with the Peace of Westphalia and previous compacts of the Württemberg House and State." This wording was a gain over what had been offered before, but it was no ringing vindica-

---

45. *Lebensgeschichte*, II, pp. 25–27; IV, pp. 46–50.

46. This journey from Stuttgart to Ebersdorf was probably the scene of Friderica Rosina's salvation from the flood by Moser: see above, §11.

47. "Nachricht," p. 54; *Lebensgeschichte*, II, pp. 30–32.

tion of the rights of Württemberg Protestants and diet. The main gainer was probably the Reichshofrat, whose advice, here given in support of the Württemberg estates, thereby was officially acknowledged by the new emperor.[48] At any rate there was no more to be done. Before Moser departed from Frankfurt, one of the emperor's court suggested that Moser might be made an imperial court councillor—not actually to sit on the Reichshofrat as a full deliberating member, to be sure, but to work for the imperial cabinet with that rank. While Moser was always full of stories telling how he turned down important posts, this one sounds plausible enough.[49]

The reign of Charles VII in Moser's description was that of an emperor without experience, diligence, or confidence, ill equipped with either military power or competent domestic advisers, whose consequent dependence on force that he could not control, and counsel that sought its own ends, brought war, fear, hatred, and confusion to the empire and its people. This view does not derive from any national chauvinism on Moser's part, it seems clear, but from sober observation of constitutional politics and their consequences. If Moser himself had hoped for an important role in the new regime, based on the contacts and experience he had accumulated, that hope was not fulfilled, and this may have colored his view of the regime. But there was no reason why Charles's ministers should have shown favor to this firm Protestant who had served Trier's effort to block their emperor's election. Allowing all this, Moser seems to have been convinced in 1743, by his traveling commissions and his experience with Charles's court, that the Wittelsbach imperial experiment was a failure.

Back in Württemberg later that year, the religious question reached a settlement that, it was hoped, forfended the institutional perils of religious enthusiasm while allowing free expression of the religious convictions and practices of the awakened. The "Pietist Rescript" of October 1743 allowed voluntary religious meetings apart from regular services, provided that the regularly appointed local pastor was informed of them, that husband or wife should attend only with the consent of the other, and that meetings should not be held in remote places or at night or when

48. Albert E. Adam, *Johann Jakob Moser als Württembergischer Landschaftskonsulent, 1751–1771* (Stuttgart, 1887), pp. 5–6. The text of the imperial affirmation, dated 23 March 1744, including the Reversalien of 1733, is in Reyscher, *Sammlung*, II, pp. 537–40. Lehmann, *Pietismus*, p. 89, and Rürup, *Moser*, pp. 130–31, credit Moser with greater influence and success with the Reversalien than he himself claimed; this would mean uncharacteristic modesty on his part or some obscure prudence, so there is room for doubt.

49. *Lebensgeschichte*, II, pp. 32–33. Many of the offers Moser recounts were probably efforts to curry his favor, or perhaps even fishing for bribes; and this seems most plausible in this Frankfurt incident.

there was work to be done. Strangers might not be admitted to such meetings, nor was any "unnecessary rooting after [Grübeln nach] strange doctrines" to be allowed. This accorded with Moser's own views, with those of his old teacher and adversary Chancellor Pfaff of Tübingen, and of leading Württemberg pastors and theologians; and this had been the actual practice of preceding decades.[50] Shortly after the settlement was achieved, Karl Eugen, aged sixteen, fully assumed his dukedom.

Moser went back to Ebersdorf, and remained there most of the time for about two years, until he set out for another imperial election in 1745. Around and between these two imperial elections, Moser worked day after day on his *Teutsches Staats-Recht*, of which twenty-five massive volumes appeared between 1743 and his final departure from Ebersdorf in 1747. Here is the place to look at what Moser conceived the empire and its law fundamentally to be. The conditions of his trade, the way his mind worked, and the institutions he undertook to describe, all came together in Moser's imperial jurisprudence.

---

§13. Writing the German Public Law

T HE factors that gave the imperial jurisprudence especially of Moser's middle years its particular character may be labeled his market, his methods, and his materials. These factors were processed through Moser's personal style, by now firmly established and distinctive to him. Moser's disposition to see himself as a practical official, and his deprecation of intellectual flourishes and academic preciosity, were traits already apparent at Tübingen and strengthened by the events of his life since then. To this came his religious experience and belief, justifying this sober, industrious, and unadorned Moser in face of his failure to dazzle the eyes and minds of men. Now he wrote without any patron, regular official position, or even academic post. The latter situation meant three important things: that he must address himself to a very various and uncertain market, to earn his family's bread and butter; that he was free politically and pedagogically to write as he chose; and also that this freedom and variety exempted him from the shaping influence of controls outside himself and his materials.

50. Lehmann, *Pietismus*, pp. 89–94.

The market to which Moser now addressed himself was the whole range of German officialdom, particularly of the lesser principalities and estates of the empire, for to them—and there were very many of them—the imperial jurisprudence was particularly important. This diffuse public put a premium on his vaunted nonpartisanship. But its diversity also tended to suppress clear themes to his work or criteria for inclusion and emphasis, thus reinforcing Moser's own intellectual and juridical tendencies. As was the empire, so was its law. A jurist patronized by a powerful state or personality might select and order his materials to suit the interests of his patron or employer, and indeed was expected to do so; but the greater market for the imperial law was precisely among those who, in their infinite variety, looked to it for protection against the powerful. They looked to it for detail, not sweeping principle or active theme; and Moser's method of composition yielded no juridical fact to aesthetic symmetry or rational orders of will or causation. He put together tomes of reference, where officials could find readily whatever particular thing might be useful for them to know in dealing with their counterparts. These materials, so grouped, were the body of the Holy Roman Empire: the endless settlements, reservations, and procedures which stifled political will and power and which, guarded and applied by those who lived by it, were a constitutional substitute for ordering will and power. The *Teutsches Staats-Recht*, as Moser entitled his vast compendium, "German Public Law," was a constitutional peculiarity of early modern Germany. Governments of England and France, growing from Tudor and from Valois and Bourbon monarchies, could assert general laws by royal authority or by common authority of the realm. But no German ruler could, so Germany required—or at least Germany developed—a body of jurisprudence to define severally the relations of the empire with its many parts, and the parts with one another, for the sake of adjudication and negotiation, which nobody could dominate, but which had to get done. At least some tolerable equilibrium or suspension of conflict had to be attained.

In critical situations and at the initiative of the mighty, German states ignored or violated the public law, and these were the capital events of political history. But in the day-to-day administration of everyday matters, managed by lesser men, the public law was needed, sought, and applied.[51] The law of the empire was the law of the everyday and the

51. Ferdinand Frensdorff, "Das Wiedererstehen des deutschen Rechts. Zum hundert-jährigen Jubiläum K. F. Eichhorns Rechtsgeschichte," *Zeitschrift der Savigny-Stiftung für Rechtsgeschichte, Germanische Abteilung*, XXIX (1908), p. 37; see also Johann Stephan Pütter, *Entwurf einer juristischen Encyklopädie und Methodologie* (Göttingen, 1757), pp. 80–84; and Hanns Gross, *Empire and Sovereignty: A History of the Public Law Literature of the Holy Roman Empire* (Chicago, 1973), pp. 293–310 and passim.

lesser. Moser had begun his *Teutsches Staats-Recht* in Prussian employ at Frankfurt on Oder, and his opening volumes may have helped his superiors to the conclusion that here was no devoted servant of the Prussian crown. His sortie then into particular state constitutions around 1740 had aroused more hostility than support, and he found only minute specialized markets. Now he went ahead, consistently with his professional and personal independence in politically remote Ebersdorf, to collect and publish the whole law of the empire itself.

In Ebersdorf Moser began to publish the successive volumes of the work on his own, without a commercial publisher. One reason was that the Nürnberg publisher who had handled the first few volumes died, and his successors in the firm were reluctant to continue with this seemingly limitless work, inasmuch as potential buyers were inclined to wait for a complete set before they bought. But there were a number of apparent advantages in acting as one's own publisher. One could escape the cash deposits commonly demanded by publishers and booksellers who were unwilling to tie up capital of their own in early volumes of multivolume sets, and try instead to finance successive volumes oneself from the sale of preceding ones. Moreover, commercial publishers were obliged to be careful lest the new work compete with some title of theirs for which they had already established a market, or whose author or publisher they wished not to offend. An author ready to do his own editing and proofreading could save costs and control the finished product better. Moser had no finicky objections to this kind of labor; and besides, if his dealings with publishers were like his other professional encounters, doing this work himself no doubt saved him a great deal of bickering and annoyance.[52]

Probably the most important attraction Moser saw in being his own publisher was the thought of greater profit. Whatever his aspirations to produce the first full and definitive compendium of the German public law, he was after all a free-lance jurist who depended on his work to bring in money; and let us try to work out the economics of it. Supporting his family at Ebersdorf cost Moser around 1000 fl (gulden) a year.[53] If Moser by one kind of publishing arrangement was able to sell his manuscripts to a publisher, as he had been accustomed to do, at the rate of 50–75 fl per printed "alphabet" (each of twenty-three signatures quarto),

52. On this general topic see Gunter Berg, "Die Selbstverlagidee bei deutschen Autoren im 18. Jahrhundert," *Archiv für Geschichte des Buchwesens*, VI (1964–66), pp. 1371–95; and Hans Haferkorn, "Der freie Schriftsteller. Eine literatur-soziologische Studie über seine Entstehung und Lage in Deutschland zwischen 1750 and 1800," *Archiv für Geschichte des Buchwesens*, V (1962–64), pp. 523–712. Moser discussed the problems of self-publication in *Lebensgeschichte*, IV, pp. 155–70; and "Nachricht," pp. 23, 51–52.

53. Rürup, *Moser*, p. 141.

he would then earn 150–225 fl from each *Teutsches Staats-Recht* volume of some 550 pages (three alphabets), however many copies were sold; profits or losses went to the publisher. In this way, Moser could support his family for eight or ten weeks from the writing of one such volume.

If by another option he advanced printing costs himself (including the usual cost overruns) and gave books to dealers on commission, the dealers required about a one-third discount from the retail price, and another one-third for handling costs, yielding Moser about 40 kr (kreuzer) for each copy sold at 2 fl each—if the whole printing was sold—to meet his own costs and from which to eke out a profit. That would be some 700 fl on a press run of a thousand copies, the sale volume he aimed for, optimistically, in the *Teutsches Staats-Recht*. Any gain over the first arrangement would have to be squeezed out of the 500 fl left for printing costs—some gain but probably very little, judging by the margins in a regular publisher's contract.

But if he printed and published himself, and sold his books retail at 40 kr per alphabet (2 fl per volume), then his gross income from sales would be some 1300 fl higher than the 700 fl gross he might get from commission sales, and about 1800 fl—almost ten times—higher than the price he could ask for his manuscripts. That must have seemed a great figure to conjure with, even assuming printing costs at a full 500 fl for a thousand copies. As nearly as I can construct an estimate from Moser's fragmentary figures, then, the break-even point in quantity of sales, beyond which it profited him to act as his own publisher and dealer, would be in the neighborhood of three or four hundred copies of each volume. Every copy beyond that brought in an extra 2 fl. He anticipated sales of a thousand copies per volume; then each volume could support his family for more than a year, if printing and distribution costs were reasonably controlled; and he was composing five or six volumes of the *Teutsches Staats-Recht* per year in the middle 1740s.[54]

As his own publisher, of course, Moser depended not only on his reputation and the merit of his work but also on his own enterprise to sell his books. He began with one employee, who kept the Moser stall at the annual book fair at Leipzig and processed orders that came to Ebersdorf: this was a certain "awakened" Vollrath, whom Friderica Rosina had met providentially at the miller's, where she was waiting to have barley ground. Vollrath knew nothing of bookselling, but he was poor; between these two qualities he made a compliant and inexpensive agent. His instructions at Leipzig were to sell only for cash and carry: he gave no credit, nor did he offer the discounts other dealers expected on sales

54. *Lebensgeschichte*, III, pp. 118–20; IV, pp. 159, 168. An alphabet treated the letters *I* and *J* as one letter, *U* and *V* as another, and omitted *W*: thus 184 pages quarto.

made to them, nor did he join in the Leipzig practice of swapping items of his inventory for those of other dealers to minimize the need for cash exchange. Moser needed the cash, not promises nor other people's books. At first sales were slow, perhaps because of hostility in principle within the trade against an author's acting as his own publisher and dealer, but especially no doubt because of Moser's unwillingness to follow the customary ways of the trade. After two or three fairs, though, as Moser records with satisfaction, dealers who at first had rejected his cash terms and boycotted his stall found themselves embarrassed by their inability to supply Moser's books to their customers, and Moser's sales improved. He soon acquired his own private printer, a penniless journeyman whom he lent the money to set up a press in Ebersdorf to turn out Moser's works.[55]

The *Teutsches Staats-Recht* was really a substantial publishing enterprise and eventually a quite profitable one. Where Moser got the capital to begin it, though, is a puzzle. Moser does not say, apart from observing that he relied on Providence to guard the risk he was taking. It cannot have financed itself at the beginning; the investment required was many thousands of gulden before there could be substantial returns. Savings from his salary at Frankfurt on Oder surely cannot account for it, even discounting his protestations of poverty at the time he arrived in Ebersdorf. A loan or subsidy from the Reuss family is more likely; Moser mentions none, but he was never inclined to declare an obligation. Another guess is that the money came from retainers or gifts connected with his work at the imperial convocation and election, where a great deal of cash was passed about in informal ways. There is no evidence for this dark speculation either, except negatives: Moser notably omits to proclaim his moral probity on that occasion, and mentions no rewards; he wrote over a hundred opinions there, for a variety of imperial and foreign officials there as well as for the elector of Trier, and these were often done hastily and without reference works so that as legal opinions many were surely worthless.[56] Then he omits to explain his sudden capacity for large investment after his return, while his account is at pains to describe how much income his publishing enterprise brought to the village of Ebersdorf. By 1747 he had reached volume XXXIII, on the rights and procedures of the imperial electors.

Moser's scholarly method in the *Teutsches Staats-Recht* was similar to most of his jurisprudence, but here at its most characteristic reach. The strategy of this work, consistent with the market for which it was intended, was to provide the most complete treatment of German public

55. *Lebensgeschichte*, III, pp. 118–20; IV, pp. 158–71.
56. *Lebensgeschichte*, II, p. 7.

law in existence, more thoroughgoing than teaching manuals like Moser's own, and encompassing the many sources and issues, theretofore treated in separate works, within a single vast topical arrangement. Thus anybody who wanted to seek out any point of law touching the empire, whether the inheritance laws of comital families, or the constitutional perquisites of electoral status, or the proper ceremonials for opening the diet of an imperial circle, would look first in Moser's big work, because he would surely find it there if it was to be found anywhere. So everybody concerned with imperial affairs would want to have it. Everything in it was to be "useful," *brauchbar*, in that sense. The slag heaps of ancient and forgotten controversies were discarded, along with the academic musings and disputes of the professors. Moser was not attracted by the problematical. Nothing was to be included on account of its novelty, and nothing omitted just because everybody knew about it: no shrinking from the obvious, no itch for originality. Nothing was to be omitted or slighted because it had been treated exhaustively elsewhere, by Moser or anybody else: he printed whole excerpts of works by others (carefully noting his source) when he considered them definitive. Where others had preceded him, wrote Moser in his preface, and where he had found their work sound, he preferred to use their own words, rather than give the matter some little twist or phrasing of his own so as to make it appear his own devising; and generally he abided by that rule, to the degree that whole long sections consisted of strung-together quotations from the work of other scholars. Indeed, "if we only had all the many separate subjects well worked out, I should gladly have put forth my work itself as nothing more than a mosaic, and the result would have been important and useful enough, just as the most costly of palaces are built of stones brought together and set together from hither and yon."[57]

Moser's ordering of materials shows no interest in chains of causality in the law, either logical or historical. There is no hierarchy of truths or principles. No sense of a transcendent order, metaphysical or natural or moral, controlled the materials as it had for natural lawyers like Pufendorf or deductive jurists like Wolff, nor any hint that the very act of ordering rights was a creative act, as with the great contemporary Bavarian codifier Wiguläus Kreittmayr, or the Prussian code then being launched by Frederick II.[58] It was a storehouse, more on the pattern of the Library of Congress cataloguing system, say, than an analytic

57. TSR I (Nürnberg, 1737), preface; TSR *Zusätze*, I, preface; *Lebensgeschichte*, III, p. 80; IV, pp. 167–68.

58. On eighteenth-century codification projects as normative legislation, see Wilhelm Ebel, *Geschichte der Gesetzgebung in Deutschland*, 2d ed. (Göttingen, 1958), pp. 73–77; Hermann Conrad, *Deutsche Rechtsgeschichte*, 2d ed., II (Karlsruhe, 1966), pp. 384–405.

encyclopedia or even a thesaurus, let alone a code. Moser's ordering was almost entirely a matter of working convenience, for the efficient identification and sound transaction of existing right—"nicht nach dem *Gout*," Cocceji had observed, "des heutigen *Seculi*."

For Moser found unnecessary and irrelevant to jurisprudence such questions as: Where does sovereignty lie? What kind of state is this? What laws lie in man's nature to observe, or in God's to ordain? Law was cumulative artifact, a collection of imperfect, incomplete, piecemeal, sometimes arbitrary arrangements and procedures reached by men to get out of the difficulties they were prone to get themselves into, to regulate affairs of theirs in detail that God was really not seriously interested in—nor were reason or logic either. Things that got along together well enough in the world of facts, Landsberg once remarked, got along well enough in Moser's head too.[59] It was not a matter of geometry or design, or if it was, they were beyond men's scope or power of recapitulation and Moser did not trouble about them. That stance freed him of worry about ultimates of right, much as divine grace had freed him of anxiety about his soul's justification. This does not mean at all that Moser thought illogically or had no historical sense or sense of injustice; on specific points his reasoning was acute, his sense of context in political time was shrewd, his moral judgments emphatic. A particular feature of the political culture of the German Empire was that the relations among rulers, estates, and subjects were legal relations, and that is what gave lawyers their central role. So Moser's job as jurist was to put reliable materials together in such a way that other German officials who needed them could find them.

Every working day Moser sat down before an array of boxes, each a foot square and four inches high, and each filled with rows of four-by-six slips separated into rubrics by labeled upright cards. His learning was keyed there in compartments. Whatever he found in his reading that seemed valuable was abstracted or copied and its source identified, placed upon the slips, and filed under the appropriate rubric. When he came to write a book, he thought out what headings it ought to include, and in what order, and arranged the rubrics accordingly. Then he went through his slips chapter by chapter, paragraph by paragraph, writing his text on fresh slips as he went, labeled and filed by paragraph, no more than one topic to a slip, so as to keep the topics separate, making excerpts from his sourcebooks or other documents where he had them. Finally he looked through all his new slips, numbered them in serial order, and sent them to the printer.

59. Roderich Stintzing and Ernst Landsberg, *Geschichte der Deutschen Rechtswissenschaft*, III (Munich, 1910), p. 324.

This system, Moser claimed, was a remarkably efficient one, without which he could have written only a fraction as many books as he did. It was flexible: if he decided in the middle of a book or even after it was finished that he wanted to order it differently, all he had to do was reshuffle his wads of slips; he could reorganize a book completely in less than a quarter of an hour—"put the last part first, make the fifth chapter into the second, or the seventh into the eleventh, etc., and as soon as it is done, nobody can tell that it was in some other order before or what the order had been." Or if he felt doubts about some part or was obliged to delete it for some reason (perhaps censorship or exclusion from some market), he could take out whole paragraphs or chapters and the rest stayed complete and unaffected. Similarly he could add sections without needing to modify what he already had. Afterthoughts required no messy balloons or asterisks or confused numberings or sequences in his manuscript; at most he would have to rewrite a slip or two and file them under their rubrics. He needed no more than one book before him at a time; he need think about no more than one subject at a time. There was no ambiguity or disorder. And so he filled and filed his slips, day after day, from nine in the morning to seven in the evening, with fifteen-minute breaks every hour so as to pace his room thinking about something else. He never read at table or worked at night. His study and desk were always neat.[60]

This quite extraordinary but superficial orderliness of composition, of course, is what made Moser's books themselves seem to others so disorderly. He escaped thereby literary problems of transition from one topic to another, where he might have had to think out or show how they were related: when one set of slips was exhausted he simply went on to another. Once he had his labels and his filing done he never had to, and almost never chose to, think about intrinsic or tangential relations among his facts, or how the bits might fit dependently into a whole. The order was in the labeling. For anybody reading the work sequentially, though, page after page—especially anybody seeking some theory or theme to Moser's jurisprudence—the abrupt incongruity of paragraphs is often so absurd and the sequence so preposterous as to make it seem often that underneath it, some secret Moser must be choking with laughter at the German public law, while the sober jurist was writing it all down. Indeed I suspect there was, but far down and perhaps consciously suppressed, surfacing only in a wry phrase here and there. Late in life he remarked that to write wittily was not one of his mortal sins; in his youth he had had a certain tendency to the *ridendo veritatem dicere*, telling truth in laughter, but in maturity he had left that talent, or whatever it was, under-

60. *Lebensgeschichte*, III, pp. 17, 102–5.

developed. More often his later work, even the *Neues Teutsches Staats-Recht*, written after his release from imprisonment at the Hohentwiel, shows a sardonic relish at some of the inconsistencies and incongruities in the law; assuredly Moser was clever enough to detect these, though during the Ebersdorf years he appeared not to notice them. For Moser was not humorless; rather, he had all the gifts of humor save laughter. Laughter would not suit his enterprise. Laughter might have dealt as rudely and impatiently with the German public law as logic would have done. (And in a Life History anecdote of his university years Moser related how, on a cold night's journey between Tübingen and Stuttgart, he and his companions found their faces so frozen that they could not laugh at their plight even when they tried.)[61] Neither laughter nor logic could abide rubrics without relations, or sequence *non sequitur*. The German constitution was vulnerable to either. Put more positively, its necessary genius was to survive the corrosion of rights by either one, and that constitution of rights was important, seriously so, to Moser and to many others. Laughter or logic might dissolve belief and observance, which, for the empire to work, had to be voluntary.

The form of the *Teutsches Staats-Recht*, then, was ruled by its material and not by the kind of conscious art of composition that disciplines content with form in the manner of a sonnet or a monograph. The untruthfulness that tempts art and scholarship was apparent enough to Moser. After some preliminaries about sources and method Moser launched upon a description of the emperor, whatever valid law had to say about him, listing all his attributes, activities, and the procedures surrounding the exercise of his authority; then he worked down through the other members and elements of the imperial legal structure. He wrote on each successive topic until he thought he had everything in, without troubling whether a topic's intrinsic importance warranted as much space as he gave it, or whether the whole would end up as a balanced representation of the empire. If there was a lot of law about something, it got a lot of space. He fed slips to his printer as he went along. Whenever he had filled the three alphabets required for a volume he had them paged, printed, and bound and sold as a volume, whether he had concluded the topic or not; then when he had three more alphabets filled he had another volume. Thus not even technical considerations of length or topical balance forced him to think critically about what might be cut from his text and what might be expanded, and thus about what mattered most, or least, or why.

So it appears as one moves from topic to topic, volume to volume.

61. *Lebensgeschichte*, I, pp. 20–21; IV, p. 131. Horace's *ridentem dicere verum* is in *Satires*, I, 1, 24.

Here, though, is a summary topical analysis of the *Teutsches Staats-Recht* of the 1740s, as a preliminary picture of how Moser came at the imperial structure:

Sources	about 2 volumes
The head—emperor, king, vice-regency	6
Imperial estates:	
Their identity, inheritance, groupings	18
Imperial circles	7
Electors	1
Princes	2
Prelates	1
Counts	2
Towns	4
Diet	7

That is as far as Moser had got when, after his appointment as counsel to the Württemberg diet, he dropped the work at fifty volumes. The outline followed conventional notions of hierarchy, but not in any necessary way, not in any sense of a logical or political descent of authority. Some very important legal topics were scarcely mentioned in those fifty volumes: for example, the imperial courts, the territorial authority of the imperial estates, the rights of lesser estates and of subjects. These matters became central to the *Neues Teutsches Staats-Recht* of the 1770s, which was to be much more thematically conceived and which, as it turned out, more directly reflected Moser's own political experience and constitutional concerns at that time. Still, if these matters do not appear in the work of the 1740s, the main reason may be that working in his fashion, he simply did not get to them.

Consequently it is best not to seek out a thorough scheme or theory of the Holy Roman Empire of the German Nation in the body of Moser's *Teutsches Staats-Recht*.[62] For such a purpose the work lacks intellectual

---

62. Erwin Schömbs's analysis of Moser's imperial jurisprudence, *Das Staatsrecht Johann Jakob Mosers (1701–1785)* (Berlin, 1968), pp. 222–72 and passim, relies mainly on the earlier, more brief and systematic *Compendium juris publici Germanici, oder Grundriss der heutigen Staats-Verfassung des Teutschen Reichs* (Tübingen, 1731), and on the theoretical observations in the later *Neues Teutsches Staats-Recht* of the sixties and seventies. The same is generally true of the section on Moser in Stintzing and Landsberg, *Rechtswissenschaft*, III, pp. 315–30. The standard modern analytical survey of the German public law of Moser's time is Emilio Bussi, *Il diritto pubblico del sacro romano impero alla fine del XVIII secolo*, vol. I, 2d ed. (Milan, 1970), vol. II (Milan, 1959). Pütter's historical treatment in *Staatsverfassung* is clear and straightforward; its contemporaneity more than compensates for its Protestant and Hanoverian bias. Stintzing and Landsberg, *Rechts-*

vitality and political credibility. To avoid quagmires of constitutional controversy, for example, Moser would make his definitions with studied neutrality or ambiguity, and then go on to a catalog of attributes without clear characterization of them. Thus the emperor was Oberhaupt or "head" of the empire (not "sovereign" or "lord"); he was chosen by such-and-such procedures; and he might do these particular things and he might be constrained in those particular respects, for six volumes. Germany had Glieder, "members," who all together were a *corpus,* "body," apparently meaning only that they were all, each its own way, parts of one thing. Some members were imperial estates, Reichsstände, and might sit on the imperial diet, the Reichstag; the categorical definition of an imperial estate was that it *did* sit on the diet; and then the particular documentation of each estate's right to sit there was examined in detail. But their historical origins were irrelevant and obscure; Moser refused to engage in "Coccejian and Ludewician whimsies" about that.[63] And they were described by complexes of particular rights, not by functions in a constitutional system. The empire described in Moser's *Teutsches Staats-Recht* was a maze of particularities ranged under tautological labels; this was not false to its nature, but for analysis we must try another way.

---

§14. Sources of the German Public Law

THE part of the *Teutsches Staats-Recht* that merits attention now is a part which Moser himself deemed trivial and only prefatory to the substantive particularities that made up the mass of the whole work: the analysis of sources. Here he had to make explicit decisions, about validity, priority, and flow of rights. He was careful to call them "Quellen," sources, and not "Urkunden," documents; for though they ordinarily appeared in valid documents, they were not immutable like documents; they were subject to change by voluntary agreement or by concession to force. The documents themselves were not sources; rather, they recorded sources; and the distinctions mattered. The sources of law,

---

wissenschaft, remains an excellent description organized in traditional fashion as a series of scholarly biographies.

63. TSR II (Frankfurt/?, 1738), p. 279; VIII (Leipzig, 1743), pp. 473–89; IX (Leipzig, 1743), p. 6; and TSR, passim.

documentary or not, were conceived as valid known transactions or procedures, not as permanent rights. Written law itself, even constitutional law, could not be eternal, even though written preambles proclaimed them to be; for posterity had as much right to change laws as anybody had to make them. Moser divided sources into three kinds or ranks: "Haupt-Quellen" or chief sources, "Neben-Quellen" or supplemental sources, and finally "Hülffs-Mittel" or aids, auxiliary means. The first category included those sources upon which the German constitution was directly and unmistakably founded; the second included those materials that could be invoked to the German public law where the chief sources were insufficient; the final category included information and methods that might on occasion serve usefully to clarify the sources themselves.[64]

Chief sources in turn were divided into five categories, ranked roughly by priority or importance. First were the basic laws, the "Grund-Gesetze," appearing in written public documents like the Golden Bull or the Peace of Westphalia, to which I shall give more particular attention shortly. Second were formal agreements reached between some part or member of the empire with the emperor, or with the empire as a whole, affecting all members in a categorically consistent way, as for example the agreed rights of electors. Third were treaties between the empire and foreign powers, affecting the borders or internal constitution of the empire. The treaties of Nijmwegen and of Ryswick, incorporating the territorial and confessional arrangements with Louis XIV's France, would be examples, or the subsequent treaties of Rastatt and Baden that concluded the Spanish succession war. The fourth chief sources were particular rights and privileges of individual estates and members of the empire "insofar as these bear on the present constitution [Staats-Verfassung] of the whole German Empire." This category included a multitude of provisions involving imperial jurisdictions where the rights of estates differed, mainly privileges like the operation of a mint, or exemption of an estate's courts from appeal to imperial courts, and extended down to the edge of the so-called "Urkunden-Kram," or privilege-peddling of certain emperors to individual members. It was hard to tell just where the imperial public law left off and the rights of particular estates began.[65]

Moser's fifth chief source, imperial tradition or "Reichs-Herkommen," gave him the most trouble and embarrassment. "This material is by its

---

64. TSR I, pp. 30–36; *Lebensgeschichte*, IV, p. 189. For comparative perspective on Moser's analysis of sources: Bussi's categorization of *fonti* in his eighteenth-century survey is 1) einheimische Quellen, 2) auswärtige Quellen, 3) geschriebene Gesetze und Verträge, and 4) Observanzen or Reichsherkommen. *Diritto pubblico*, I, p. 17.

65. TSR I, pp. 31–32; II, pp. 130–39.

nature as a proposition, *in thesi*, doubtful, uncertain, and obscure," for nobody was sure what legitimized it; and it was even more difficult in practice, *in applicatione*. The problem was not the purported antiquity of tradition, not that ancient Teutons put little in writing—let the school-men palpitate about that irrelevancy. The trouble was that much of the public business of the German Empire in fact followed procedures, and implicitly accepted rights, for which there were no direct or explicit sanctions. Insofar as that was the fact (or facts), Moser had reluctantly to admit tradition as a valid category of source. "For something to be an imperial tradition in Germany is and means this much: that in some matter affecting the state constitution of the German Empire, nothing is expressly contained in imperial agreements or laws, but it can be shown that in earlier like cases, by the wills of the affected parties, it has been done in this way." Similarly, sometimes explicit laws were in fact consistently ignored; and these, by this same force of tradition, were not valid.[66]

Thus whereas prevalent German scholarship habitually looked to antiquity or priority to validate tradition or custom, Moser characteristically inverted that sanction, using tradition, as usage, to *overrule* priority in time. Tradition so understood was on the side of innovation. The more ancient a custom's purported legal origin, the less likely modern jurists were, in Moser's mind, to understand it and follow its original intent anyway. Repetition, to be sure, gave a tradition validity, and that took time—the oftener it happened, of course, the less time it took. In any event it was not time-out-of-mind, not *unfürdenckliche Zeit*, that established tradition; the time needed was only time enough for any affected party to see what was going on, to raise objections, to deny or accept the validity of the practice. By that same token, no tradition could be unilaterally established or invoked: by its nature tradition could not be created by force alone, not even repeated force. Its qualifications were acceptance, and practice. Moser in fact was quite unhappy about proposing any criteria at all for validating tradition; it was too slippery and hard to verify; tradition came and went more readily than any other source of positive law. He had to admit there was such a thing, but when he came to cite examples of valid tradition, none was constitutionally important, and none dated earlier than the mid-seventeenth century. Tradition occupied a very dubious and last place among the chief sources of the German public law.[67]

The "Neben-Quellen" or supplemental sources contained some more marked demotions of juridical sources from the status many of Moser's predecessors and colleagues had given them. Indeed, Moser intended, by

66. TSR II, pp. 142–43.
67. TSR II, pp. 139–67.

placing them in this category, to deny them the independent validity that characterized the main sources. Some were driven out of the category of sources altogether by Moser and became "Hülffs-Mittel" or aids. Before turning to these, though, there was one notable promotion: first place among Moser's supplemental sources went to Holy Scripture, which most imperial jurists left out of consideration.[68] Moser felt awkward and defensive about including this. It had not appeared in his 1731 summary textbook on the public law, before his reception into grace; "and I know very well in advance what most of those who read this will think and say." Where did Scripture apply to the German public law? The public law, Moser replied, was there to tell every member of the Reich, whether emperor, estate, or subject, what postures they were to adopt toward one another; and Scripture—particularly the New Testament—was what bound Christians to their mutual obligations under the law. Its principles, though general in nature, were acknowledged by everybody—a juridical rarity actually. Moreover, it could be shown that powerful men sometimes really did act according to scriptural tenets—thus Moser protested, rather lamely, so as to validate Scripture by usage. He conceded that "in Germany, as in the whole of so-called Christendom," Christianity appeared "more in tongue and title than in hearts," so that it was not a very practical legal source. Still, how Christians ought in principle to act merited "some brief mention."[69] It was brief and cautious, and out of character for Moser the jurist, compromising as it did the separation of compartments. Scripture for Moser had some part of the role natural law had for others, but he restricted it to the behavioral sphere of Christendom. And although he listed it among sources, he never cited it in his compilations of positive law. Scripture was a source of right, but anybody could quote it to his own ends.

A second supplemental source was the "allgemeines Staats-Recht," the general public law. This too Moser treated only cautiously and briefly, inasmuch as it was tainted by the natural-law theories that to his mind opened the way to subjective lawlessness. The general public law was "that portion of the natural law that concerns those rights and duties which, according to natural equity and sound sense, all empires, rulers, and members of a state ought to observe toward one another, or toward other empires, rulers, and members of foreign states, where sometimes by agreement, tradition, or in another valid way, something peculiar and

68. Catholics had theological reasons to exclude it; Protestant jurists, especially those like Thomasius who had substituted a form of natural law, had dropped it in their struggle against scholastic literalism: Stintzing and Landsberg, *Rechtswissenschaft*, III, pp. 93–94. Schömbs discusses Moser's "Neben-Quellen" in *Staatsrecht Mosers*, pp. 244–51.

69. TSR II, pp. 168, 186–91.

deviant from these general rules may have been established." Here Moser seems implicitly to have acknowledged that natural equity and sound sense might override positive law, at least positive law clearly aberrant in its nature; but he was unwilling to say it directly, so that his language was confused and his meaning obscure. I am not sure my translation has got it straight, if indeed it is to be got straight.[70] Moser's examples came from interstate relations covered by no formal agreements: the case of a government which, having effectively dissolved its bonds of allegiance with another, must be treated as separate even though the parent state has not acknowledged its independence; or the problem of what repressive measures a state may adopt toward the subjects of another state with which it is at war. The most important area where the general public law was applied, however, was in the *Landeshoheit*, the territorial supremacy of imperial estates over their subjects, of which little was to be found in imperial law or tradition but which unquestionably existed. And notice that Moser might have got out of his difficulty here if he had been willing to adopt a principle of sovereign rights; but he was not. Landeshoheit—again the weakness of any translation reflects an unresolved conception—was a topic which Moser disliked and which he managed to avoid almost completely throughout the body of the *Teutsches Staats-Recht*. He concluded this inescapable allusion to it with: "There is a very serious difficulty here, in that this very general public law rests on no written statutes, but flatly on each person's own insight [Einsicht]"; and obviously anybody could have his own "insight," so all was very various. And the worst of that was that particular "insights," oddly, had a particular disposition to dive into very basic questions, into first principles. Give "insight" legal standing and one person will talk about something like the authority of rulers, and another about the freedom of subjects; then somebody will say that one is just as right as the other, and nobody will agree.[71]

Moser treated the related subject of international law, the European "Völcker-Recht" (his third supplemental source), in a similarly brief and reserved way, though it interested him. This included certain customary forms with which the government or subjects of one "European Christian

70. "Dasjenige Stück des Natur-Rechts, welches von denen Gerechtsamen und Pflichten handlet, die, nach der natürlichen Billichkeit und gesunden Vernunfft, von Rechtswegen, alle Reiche, Regenten und Glider eines Staats, gegen einen der selbsten, und gegen andere Reiche, Regenten und Glider fremder Staaten, haben und beobachten sollen, es wäre dann, dass hier oder da durch Verträge, das Herkommen, oder auf eine andere erlaubte Art, etwas besonderes und von disen allgemeinen Reglen abweichendes eingeführet worden wäre." TSR II, p. 168. Schömbs, *Staatsrecht Mosers*, p. 251, also seems uncertain about this passage.

71. TSR II, pp. 192–94.

nation" dealt with the governments or subjects of another, or sometimes by analogy a rule with his own estates or subjects. These forms were sometimes invoked in matters internal to the German Empire, even relations within the territories of estates. But that Moser thought dangerous; for whereas by contrast the general public law had been too loose a proposition to be useful in particular instances, the precedents of international law were too particular to their situations. Scholars had tried to give them a generalized flavor by examples out of the distant histories of Romans, Greeks, Persians, and such; but these hardly pertained in modern times. Modern examples, usually touching the rights and credentials of ambassadors, delegates, or representatives, were tied closely to the particular constitutions of the different European states, so that to transpose them by analogy from one to another "could have evil consequences," as for example a recent attempt to apply rules governing members of the English Parliament to those of the German imperial college of princes.[72]

Moser placed Roman or Justinian law firmly among supplemental sources only, no more, and he did not trouble to discuss the old argument about its reception *in toto* by the Reich, which he properly considered to have been settled by Conring and his successors.[73] More surprisingly, though, he did not dismiss it here on grounds that an ancient Mediterranean code was inapplicable to the modern German Empire. Nor did he even limit its effect to those specific provisions which had been explicitly accepted in German practice, as he, in company with others, had done in the past (and which made German law out of those provisions anyway).[74] Indeed now he turned that argument over, declaring that Roman law as a *whole* was a *supplemental* source because the Reichshofratordnung, the Regulation of the Imperial Court Council, itself a basic constitutional law of the empire, implicitly held Roman law as such to be an auxiliary source. It said this through its provision that in the absence of explicit

---

72. TSR II, pp. 169, 194–96; Schömbs, *Staatsrecht Mosers*, p. 245. Moser seems to skip confusingly between positive international law as concerned with interstate relations, and something nearer the *ius gentium*, a difficulty I find with much German jurisprudence of the time; the term *Völcker-Recht* often did include both. The Völkerrecht problem fascinated Moser all his life, increasingly with time toward the latter part of the century; and his last major work, which some commentators consider his most original and important, was the *Versuch des neuesten europäischen Völkerrechts in Friedens- und Kriegszeiten . . . seit dem Tode Kayser Karls VI . . .* , 10 vols. (Frankfurt/Main, 1777–80), followed at the very end of his life by *Nord-America nach den Friedensschlüssen vom Jahre 1783*, 3 vols. (Leipzig, 1784–85). See Stintzing and Landsberg, *Rechtswissenschaft*, III, p. 327; and below, §32.

73. See above, §2.

74. As in the *Compendium juris publici* of 1731; on Moser's changing treatment of Roman law generally, see Schömbs, *Staatsrecht Mosers*, pp. 255–63.

provisions of acknowledged imperial law, the high courts should observe "imperial rights, and legitimate observations and usages"; and Moser said these would include Roman law as an element of what he called "common written imperial rights." Thus any element of Roman law might be applied in any matter where the imperial courts had jurisdiction, on points to which positive German sources did not speak. Territorial princes, Moser added, might make good use of it in settling quarrels with their own subjects.[75]

This last remark throws the role of Roman law into some confusion. To begin his argument Moser let in the Roman law, with its implications of sovereignty, as a tool of the imperial courts; now he proffered it to the political and constitutional rivals of the courts, a political point of some importance that can have escaped nobody. Moser offered no resolution to this anomaly, glaring though it appears in his own description. Nor did he address the complications that seem to arise when Roman law is conceived as a kind of imperial common law. Erwin Schömbs has concluded from this that Moser had not thought it through, and criticizes him for offering no examples to help clear the matter up.[76] Yet if there is a resolution, it would seem to be Moser's meaning that territorial princes could avail themselves of the Roman law to exercise their internal authority only in ways subject to review by the imperial courts. To develop the Landeshoheit in this fashion would not be at the cost of imperial authority; on the contrary, it would bring the whole matter of the territorial authority more directly under the imperial courts. To say this was Moser's conscious intent might be unduly to strain a casual inconsistency so as to produce a positive point; but it fits, and Moser's more obvious inconsistencies are always worth thinking about. He did not offer this resolution, so that it remains speculative; but as to why he did not, remember that these opening sections of the *Teutsches Staats-Recht* were written while he was still in Prussia struggling to keep his post at the university, and a principal goal of Prussian politics and jurisprudence was to exclude imperial interference, especially by the Reichshofrat, from the development of the Prussian king's (and his servants') independent internal authority.[77]

Moreover, it was not at all clear, at that particular moment in German constitutional history, who stood to gain most from the application of Roman legal principles: whether the emperor and his instruments, who had advanced and used Roman law in the past to assert their authority

75. TSR II, pp. 169, 197–217.
76. *Staatsrecht Mosers*, pp. 257–60.
77. Wolfgang Rüfner, *Verwaltungsrechtsschutz in Preussen 1749–1842* (Bonn, 1962), pp. 60–61.

over the estates, or the territorial governments or princes, just then striving to convert their particular powers formally into something like undivided sovereignty over all inhabitants of their territories.[78] Perhaps Moser had a glimpse here of how strong and flexible government on an imperial scale might be made consistent with the rule of law, thus gaining more respect for Roman law than he had felt in the past; if so he had neither the turn of mind nor the patience to develop the point.[79]

The two remaining supplemental sources were canon law and Lombard law. Moser treated both of these with skepticism, and limited them severely, with more assurance and firmness than he had the preceding four. Neither was valid on its own, but only insofar as specific points had been taken up in valid German public law, or were authoritatively applied where German law was silent. Moser could not in conscience leave canon law out altogether, for almost half the imperial estates were ecclesiastical officials, and canon law guided them in such matters as ecclesiastical elections and episcopal jurisdictions. But it was the German practice, not the papal origins, that gave them force. Incidentally the whole *Teutsches Staats-Recht*, though Moser claimed confessional impartiality, was unrelievedly antipapal in tone, if not quite anti-Catholic. He opined that it was all right to call the pope the Antichrist, inasmuch as this was not a slander but a theological judgment.[80]

Elements of the Lombard feudal law, Moser said, had "sneaked into" the Roman law and thence to some German usage, and so might be invoked in matters which came before the imperial courts and for which other rules, written or customary, were absent. To include the category at

78. Imperial officials during the eighteenth century found themselves making common cause with small princes and nobility against the emerging greater Landesherren; as they did so their jurists dropped their previous claim of imperial sovereignty, and with it their liking for Roman law, and turned to German customary and historical law. Conversely, the princes, who previously had developed German customary and historical rights to combat imperial claims, were turning to notions of sovereignty, contained or implied in Roman law, by way of natural law. In this slow and uneven reversal, the 1730s and 1740s—the period of the Austrian succession war and the reign of Charles VII, and the time of Moser's *Teutsches Staats-Recht*—would be as good a place as any to date the turn. See Schömbs, *Staatsrecht Mosers*, pp. 178–96; and Stintzing and Landsberg, *Rechtswissenschaft*, III, pp. 245–71 and passim, especially the specific conjuncture identified (p. 258) between the defense of *ständische Freiheit* on behalf of small or mediate nobility, and the posture adopted by the imperial jurists.

79. Schömbs, *Staatsrecht Mosers*, pp. 257–58, suggests that Moser's growing acknowledgment of Roman law resulted from his juridical experience in Prussia. For Moser's own jocular comment on an encounter with Cocceji over this issue, *Von Teutschland und dessen Staats-Verfassung überhaupt* (= NTSR I: Stuttgart, 1766), p. 533.

80. The latter issue arose on the point of whether a Roman Catholic prince could punish a Protestant subject for doing so: TSR VIII, pp. 258–64. On canon law as a *Nebenquelle*, see TSR II, pp. 169–70, 218–25.

all was a perfunctory concession to the fact of occasional citation and usage, and, again, brought the matter under the jurisdiction and control of the presently sitting imperial courts. Antiquarian medievalism had no place in Moser's conception of the Holy Roman Empire. He warned German scholars against their fascination with "the oldest, most abstruse Germanic antiquities, useful to nobody, good only as quaint curiosities." Carolingian capitularies and statutes were "as remote to our public law as Old-Frankish dress is to our costume now"; and he altogether banished the famed medieval Sachsen- and Schwabenspiegel, beloved by contemporary constitutional researchers and commentators, from amongst the sources of public law.[81]

Moser's use of history distinguished him sharply from his immediate predecessors—like the "whimsical" Heinrich Cocceji of Frankfurt on Oder and Johann Peter Ludewig of Halle, in their use of German antiquity to validate law—and from eminent successors like Pütter and Savigny of Göttingen and Marburg too. Moser placed political history among "aids," along with such studies as geography and diplomatics, without status as a source of law. That did not make history unimportant. It was needed "to understand and to explain, more easily, clearly, and thoroughly, the main sources of the German Empire [*sic*]." For getting at the meaning of a law, history was a better means than logic (logic does not appear as an aid at all, let alone a source). "Often somebody reasons [*raisonirt*] far and wide over an obscure place in an imperial statute, and writes whole books and treatises about it, pro and con, and still misses the real meaning, where history would place that law easily, clearly, and indisputably in the light of day."[82] History showed the context of documentary materials and of traditions, making sources out of documents; it showed the particular interests and prejudices that went into their formation, and how to sift them for valid law. But that same objective—the use of history to put a document or tradition in critical context and show its true meaning—forbade the use of written history as itself a source of law. The reason was the way historians worked, especially those who thought history gave law. Such historians, however good their intentions might be, "ordered their histories more according to *Ideen und Systematibus* they had got fixed in their heads, and how they would have wished and preferred history to be, than they have ordered their doctrines according to history; and thus they have presented us with a configuration of old Germany which is quite unlike history; and yet we are still supposed to conduct ourselves according to it even now!" And

81. TSR II, pp. 170–86, 225–32, 241.
82. TSR II, pp. 237–38.

Moser complained particularly of the modern scholars' neglect of recent history for the sake of rummaging in ancient times.[83]

His rejection of history as a source of law has exposed Moser to the criticism, from one side, that he lacked any historical sense, that he was unhistorical or antihistorical in his thought. That was probably the most general complaint against the *Teutsches Staats-Recht* when it appeared, and it has persisted.[84] Conversely others have hailed Moser's "emancipation" of the public law from history, an achievement that Daniel Nettelbladt, Christian Wolff's follower at Halle, as early as 1756 announced to be a watershed in the history of German academic jurisprudence.[85] A better label than unhistorical, though, would be unantiquarian. Moser's methodological principle of reducing history from "source" to "aid" meant excluding infinite reams of old privileges, charters, and capitularies, which had been dredged out by researchers for two centuries past in their hunt for priority of right, from the status of valid law—unless there was present practice based on a true understanding of them. His apparently pedestrian pragmatic proposition, that only useful and currently observed law should be respected, dismissed a whole tangled and controversial mass of the published jurisprudence of his time. Of course that brought another kind of disorder, the kind that permeates the *Teutsches Staats-Recht*. But in Moser's view this simply reflected a disorderly objective world, and it did not trouble him.

Past and present, though, were not to be confused. History was to stay in the past where it belonged, and to be adduced to the present only so as to winnow out and illuminate those artifacts of the past for which the present had present use. Paradoxically perhaps, Moser's strong sense of historicity, of change over time and the difference between other times and his own, made his turn of mind (even to himself I suspect) seem then unhistorical. The real point, though, is not that Moser preferred new law to old. His emancipation of the public law from history meant that any positive legal statement was specific to its situation—a verbal action, a linguistic artifact within a political order. Moser conceived it the jurist's trade to know that situation and language well enough to understand the statement as it was meant, so as to know what, if any, its present import was. It was the duty of the legislator, and not the jurist, to make a new

---

83. TSR II, pp. 240–41; *Von Teutschland und dessen Staats-Verfassung überhaupt* (= NTSR I), pp. 186–89.

84. TSR *Zusätze*, I (1744), preface; also the citations in Schömbs, *Staatsrecht Mosers*, p. 206; and in this book below, §31.

85. Stintzing and Landsberg, *Rechtswissenschaft*, III, pp. 325–26. This phrase is the chapter title of Erwin Schömbs's good treatment of the subject, *Staatsrecht Mosers*, pp. 196–221, upon which I draw here. Nettelbladt's review is in *Hallische Beyträge*, V (1756), pp. 66–69.

law if situation and language had changed enough to invalidate the old one.[86] So the legal documents he called "Quellen" were not immortal sources of right in the sense of "Urkunden"; they were written testimony of transactions and of agreed procedures and must be understood as such. Moser the pragmatic jurist was true to Moser the public official, the civil servant of the empire in all its parts.

---

§15. The Basic Laws of the Empire

NOW we may come to consider what Moser called the "Grund-Gesetze," the written basic laws of the empire. They seem an oddly uneven collection, if we come to them expecting a summary general constitution, timeless and resonant in every phrase. Though Moser's list follows a roughly chronological sequence, he avoided assigning specific dates to them, or even identifying specific texts. He listed the Golden Bull, the Public Peace (Land-Friden), the Religious Peace, the Execution Ordinance (Executions-Ordnung), the current Imperial Cameral Court Regulation, the current Imperial Court Council Regulation, the most recent Electoral Capitulation, and, with reservations, the Peace of Westphalia. As constitutional documents none of these were pure; all contained matter that did not qualify as basic law. The Peace of Westphalia raised particular problems on that account, because the French and Swedish crowns were party to it and because of the series of international agreements that followed in its train over the next century. On these grounds Moser placed the document in the category of state treaties, but he left no doubt that he considered it a preeminent source for the basic law of the empire.[87]

86. For an introduction to the modern application of linguistic structuralism to the history of political ideas by J. G. A. Pocock, Q. Skinner, and J. Dunn, see Charles D. Tarleton, "Historicity, Meaning, and Revisionism in the Study of Political Thought," *History and Theory*, XII (1973), pp. 307–28.

87. TSR I, pp. 45–83. For Emilio Bussi's list of basic laws, summarizing the eighteenth-century literature, see below, n. 100. If Moser had chosen to do so, he might easily have included the Peace of Westphalia under basic laws by virtue of its imperial ratification in the Reichsabschied of 1654: see *Von Teutschland und dessen Staats-Verfassung überhaupt* (= NTSR I), p. 204; for the Reichsabschied provision, Johann Jacob Schmauss, *Corpus Juris Publici, enthaltend des Heil. Röm. Reichs deutscher Nation Grund-Gesetze*, rev. ed. (Leipzig, 1794), pp. 957–60.

Nobody doubted that the Golden Bull was basic law; there had been more written about it surely than about any other German constitutional document. This agreement among German emperor and princes had formally established the principle, in 1356, that the office of emperor was an elective one, and it specified those princes entitled to cast votes—at that time the archibishops of Mainz, Trier, and Cologne, the king of Bohemia, and the electors of Saxony, Brandenburg, and the Rhenish Palatinate. In subsequent centuries it had been cited again and again as a basic constitutional source; but it had been modified too, notably by the subsequent inclusion of the dukes of Bavaria and of Braunschweig-Hanover among the ranks of electors. Such modifications were acceptable and inevitable, Moser said, inasmuch as nobody could tell what good sense and experience might require in the future. But changes could come only by assent of the emperor and of all three colleges of the imperial estates—electors, princes, and towns—and not, say, by the decision of the emperor, or of the emperor and incumbent electors. Thus Bavaria had legally achieved electoral status only with the ratification of the Peace of Westphalia in 1648, and Hanover with a formal Conclusion of the Diet in 1708.[88]

The Public Peace was "an agreement and law [Vertrag und Gesetz] between the emperor and the imperial estates, that nobody in the German Empire shall use force against the other, but rather the course of law; and other matters affecting the inner peace and security of the empire." It had been developed to suppress the Faust-Recht, the law of the fist, that primitive condition which once had subjected Germany to "continual disorder, where nobody could be sure of what was his for so long as that did not satisfy some unruly neighbor greedy for what belonged to others." Public peace was an ancient aim particularly of the weak, but it had been impossible to achieve for so long as the administration of justice was too primitive and insecure to provide firm and effective procedures for settling disputes. The great formal step of the empire in this direction had been the "eternal public peace" proclaimed in 1495, establishing on behalf of emperor and estates the two chief imperial courts. This had been followed by a series of actions to amplify and extend the rules of the peace. The Public Peace to be sure was very far from perfect: long delays, outside meddling, or plain defiance weakened its force; but "still Germany is, praise God! much the more peaceful on account of it."[89]

The Religious Peace was "an aspect and a part" of the Public Peace, whereby the Catholic and Protestant parties in the German Empire were

88. TSR I, pp. 83–105; II, p. 313.
89. TSR I, pp. 105–19.

bound to carry out their confessional rivalries without resort to violence —according to rules. The rules, laid out generally at Augsburg in 1555 after a series of preliminaries, and amplified thereafter, forbade the emperor or any estate of the empire to deprive any other estate of free exercise of the Roman Catholic or Protestant faith. No imperial estate might interfere in the religious lives of the subjects of another, so that each was left the authority to direct religious activity within his territory according to the particular rules that prevailed there (Moser noticeably did not quote the famous tag *cuius regio, eius religio*). Long controversy and protests over particular provisions of the Religious Peace could not invalidate it in principle; most were settled in the Peace of Westphalia. Changes might be made at an imperial diet, or uncertain points resolved in the imperial courts, but only by consent of both religious parties in diet or courts.[90]

The Execution Ordinance was that basic law which described how the Peace was to be enforced and administered. It was "an agreement between the empire and estates of the Reich, partly on how the force and effect of the Public Peace shall be maintained, and the judgments of the high imperial courts carried out; and partly on how one shall behave when the Reich is attacked from without, in a hostile way, or otherwise distressed." Its history began with the Public Peace of 1495, and it had been repeatedly modified and amplified.[91] The proper instrumentalities for maintaining the peace and carrying out imperial judgments were the imperial Kreise, circles or districts, each of which had its own constitution and its own public peace, some antedating the empire's own. Along with their imperial execution powers they had nomination rights to the imperial courts, minting rights, taxing powers. Moser conceded that there were limits to the circles' usefulness and reliability, from the point of view of "Staats-Klugheit" or politics. Their geographical structure was awkward; they were subject to confessional quarrels; their inequality of power and size and their mixed internal character, containing as they did both mighty and feeble estates in one circle—all these were drawbacks and sometimes incapacitated the circles altogether. People who sat by the stove with Plato's *Republic* before their eyes, wrote Moser a bit unreasonably, might find the circles useless and unnecessary political shells. Yet he thought it certain that without these institutions, the Public Peace and the administration of imperial justice would have no structure, and all would fall into "Barbarey." The most effective circles were those made up entirely of lesser estates and personages, especially in areas bordering on foreign states, where they organized mutual protection against outside

90. TSR I, pp. 119–78.
91. TSR I, pp. 178–98.

pressures. Without the circle constitutions and mutual obligations, moreover, there was no peaceable way to keep the judicial and budgetary functioning of the petty states in order; and without internal order and solvency, they were sure to be seized upon and swallowed up by their neighbors.[92]

It was not customary among Moser's contemporaries to list the regulations of the two chief imperial courts as basic laws of the empire. These ordinances were procedural in nature; the extent of the courts' respective jurisdictions was controversial; and the impartiality and effectiveness of their judgments were dubious, to say the least. And yet, Moser argued, what could be more important for the German public law than "when, where, and how one imperial estate may accuse another, or a private person, an estate, or a subject appeal a judgment of his prince? or how judges be appointed?"[93] Moser did not address himself directly to the shortcomings of imperial courts in the *Teutsches Staats-Recht*, though certainly he was as aware of them as anybody else.[94] He included their procedures as basic law because he thought them fundamental to the judicial constitution of the empire, whatever their shortcomings in practice or politics. For Moser the many small decisions and routine business they did accomplish, or where their presence was felt, weighed as much as the great political decisions and business they could not do. Their procedures, not their powers, were the basis of their usefulness.

He had no doubts about including the "latest" Electoral Capitulation among the basic laws. The capitulation was the way in which a newly elected emperor bound himself to observe the other basic laws, and promised to modify none, nor introduce new ones, without the assent of the electors, princes, and other imperial estates. It set limits on the authority of the emperor as "head" of the Reich, and described his duties toward the empire and its estates and subjects; his authority was void wherever he violated it. The capitulation from which eighteenth-century

92. To include these political judgments I have left Moser's catalog of basic laws to pursue his remarks on the Kreise in TSR XXVI (Leipzig, 1746), pp. 284–329. He devoted the following six volumes of the TSR to them.

93. TSR I, pp. 53–54.

94. Among Moser's papers seized in 1759 is an essay on the malfunction of justice on the part of the Reichshofrat, undated but most likely, from internal evidence, written in the early 1740s (see Rürup, *Moser*, p. 132): WHS KA III Ls 390. Where Moser asserts the right of subjects to appeal from the judgments of their territorial lords in TSR V, 2d ed. (Frankfurt/?, 1752), pp. 484–85, he describes appeals to the emperor himself, not the imperial courts. The electoral capitulation of 1742 enjoined visitations of both the great imperial courts: Hans E. Feine, "Zur Verfassungsentwicklung des Heil. Röm. Reichs seit dem Westfälischen Frieden," *Zeitschrift der Savigny-Stiftung für Rechtsgeschichte, Germanische Abteilung*, LII (1932), pp. 94–97.

forms descended had been extracted from Charles V in 1519, not precisely as a condition of election, but as a price of ongoing support from
the German electors; subsequent emperors had all issued capitulations
with much the same language, immediately after their election and before
their coronation. That gave the capitulation a contractual quality, and
tied that quality to the elective nature of the imperial office; the new
emperor moreover guaranteed in the capitulation the elective rights of
the electors, as set forth in the Golden Bull.[95] Efforts had been made in
the seventeenth century to draft a permanent capitulation, but these had
failed on account of disagreement between electors and other estates over
how a capitulation was to be negotiated and who was party to it (recall
the quarrel between electors and princes at the election of 1742). Consequently, though the language remained much the same, the capitulation was not an immutable statement distributing and limiting sovereign
rights—this is what caught Moser's attention—but an agreement transacted between the incumbent emperor and the electors (who elected
by their own right but negotiated the capitulation on behalf of all the
imperial estates), on how that "head" should conduct his office.[96]

The Peace of Westphalia, as an agreement between the emperor and
the estates of the Reich, was basic law and one of the most important of
them, and Moser repeatedly described it so, while explicitly excluding all
other treaties from that status (recall here the matter of the Ryswick
Clause).[97] For the Peace of Westphalia incorporated all the other basic
laws into one statement. It named them all—Golden Bull, court ordinances, imperial capitulations, and the rest; it had been solemnly sub-
scribed by all members of the empire, and it had been cited in nearly
every major constitutional document thereafter. "Indeed the greatest
part of the German *juris publici* of today may rightly be said to be
contained in it, and not only can but should be built from that as well as
from the original sources."[98] This was the grand transaction that had
concluded the Thirty Years War, that fearful mesh of religious, political,
and constitutional strife that had laid open and raw the peculiar dangers
and problems of German public life. The terms of the Peace had become
the foundation of the German Empire of Moser's time. He expounded it

95. TSR I, pp. 47, 182; II, pp. 279–280, 444–45. Gross, *Empire and Sovereignty*, pp.
42ff.

96. On this point see Schömbs, *Staatsrecht Mosers*, p. 233; Moser, TSR I, pp. 237–82,
especially pp. 242, 282. On the capitulation generally see Hartung, "Wahlkapitulationen,"
which dismisses it as having on the one hand little restraining effect on the behavior of
emperors, but on the other hand as marking the weakening of the empire at the hands of
the princes.

97. TSR I, pp. 51, 55, 397; see above, §7.

98. TSR I, p. 466.

through a political history of that war and of the negotiations at Münster and Osnabrück that had ended it.[99] They were basic sources of the German public law.

The main descriptive body of the *Teutsches Staats-Recht* that follows is a running compilation of the materials contained in Moser's card files, subjected to no theoretical and scarcely any systematic form except in crude topical outline. That is why we must seek his sense of the imperial constitution in these opening discussions of methods and of sources— bearing in mind, surely, the formlessness of ensuing detail, for that was part of his sense of it too. Inasmuch as jurists of his time were not at all agreed on what the basic laws of the empire were and what made them valid, Moser's chosen list shows clearly enough what he in particular thought the empire was about.[100] Summing them up here: the Golden Bull told how imperial authority was imparted and by whom; the Electoral Capitulation showed conditions constraining and directing it; the Public and the Religious Peace were to keep the Germans from one another's throats; the procedural laws of the courts and executive agencies served to replace "the dagger in the fist"; the Peace of Westphalia finally set forth the relations of all estates of the empire with one another, with the emperor, and with foreign authorities. And although Moser looked to present usage to sustain their validity, still his rough chronological sequence for their written historical origins suggests that he perceived them as successive steps from a "natural" condition, of barbarity and violence, to a civilized one, based on rules and procedures. That must explain why he included, despite his proclaimed pragmatism, laws and institutions that he knew were regularly violated and ignored: he did so when they were indispensable parts of the empire as he conceived it, as he understood and justified his work within it.

Some later apologists and students of the empire, seeing its lack of executive power but the persistence of its institutions, have explained it as a sovereign idea and a sentiment, because (thus, for example, Hans Feine in 1932) "it bore an idea a millennium old, because it had for centuries embodied a living form in which the German found both his humane and his national ideals fulfilled."[101] Moser, in his way the most

99. TSR I, pp. 390–503.

100. Bussi, *Diritto pubblico*, I, pp. 17–36, summarizing the eighteenth-century literature, categorizes the following as *"leggi fondamentali dell'Impero"*: 1) Golden Bull; 2) Concordat (between Pope Nicholas V and Emperor Frederick III) of 1448; 3) Public Peace; 4) Imperial Matriculation of 1521 (apportioning imperial fiscal obligations among the imperial estates); 5) Execution Ordinances; 6) Imperial Court Ordinances; 7) Electoral Capitulations; 8) Peace of Westphalia; 9) other imperial treaties having constitutional effects; 10) imperial recesses. Thus he would add the Concordat, the Matriculation, and the treaties and recesses to Moser's list, and omit the Religious Peace.

101. Feine, "Verfassungsentwicklung," p. 66.

eminent Reich patriot of his century, was closer to the matter, and he never talked about sentiments or ideals when it came to the law. For him the Reich existed in operative laws and procedures, agreements and negotiations, that bore the sanction and regulated the relations of its members. Moreover, the laws emanated from and were to be sustained not by a single source or sovereign power, not even the emperor's, but by submission to known agreements and regular procedures—one is tempted to say, by submission to the learning and management of legal scholars and juridically trained civil servants. If Moser had identified any "sovereign" in the realm of German politics, he might have got himself into that sovereign's employ (that is more likely than the converse: that he would have attributed sovereignty to an employer). But he would never name such a person or thing. He refused any notion of personal mastery, in his jurisprudence or over his own life and career. The basic laws are "those agreements and laws [Verträge und Gesetze] which have hitherto been arrived at by the head of the Reich and its collective imme-diate estates, or their representatives, at imperial diets or elections, and established and brought to paper. . . . An agreement means consent by two or more parties in a matter where neither party has a legal right to oblige another." Such "agreements" by imperial sanction were laws as well, binding upon individual estates that may have opposed them, and upon mediate subjects who had no voice in them, so long as they were properly arrived at, and properly drafted, recorded, and endorsed.[102]

It was not an inspirational vision. Along with renouncing worldly masters, Moser had disallowed any guidelines from natural or divine law that might have given form and direction to his thoughts and labors; he tried hard—compartments—to exclude even himself; and so, for the forty-odd volumes of the *Teutsches Staats-Recht* that followed the dis-cussion of sources and methods I have just tried to analyze, Moser was left with his mindless card files. What Pastor Steinhofer said at Ebersdorf, watching Moser as he sorted the German public law out of his boxes—that he'd liefer thresh wheat or split wood than spend his time that way—stuck in Moser's mind, and many years later he remembered him-self as replying: "As long as God allows this constitution of the world, and there is an emperor, pope, electors, princes, imperial estates, diets, subjects, and so on, so long too must there be someone to tell what their rights and duties are."[103] That was the law of the empire, and it was the realm of the jurist and not the prince.

And here, shuffling those same endless card files at Ebersdorf, Moser got a training in the German public law that he might not have got if he had approached it with a predetermined pattern, or had created one, or

102. TSR I, pp. 46–47.
103. "Nachricht," pp. 51–52; *Lebensgeschichte*, IV, p. 187.

even if he had sought a principled system in it by inductive means. There was or came to be a quality of scope and truth in his perception that not only survived the dispersed triviality of his mode, but even required it. *Credo quia absurdum* is not at all a bad posture from which to study the German constitution of the Old Law; and it was a constitution with important merits, qualities that were positively related to its disregard for simplicity and form. In this way Moser accumulated vast learning in the agreements whereby people arranged their affairs and their relations with one another—how and why these agreements were reached, sustained, modified, abolished. Perhaps this was a better way to learn such things than, for example, to winnow and treat his materials in terms of authority, subjection, and order, as other jurists were trying to do, which sat ill with the particular nature of the German constitution. Moser achieved his preeminence as a German constitutional lawyer in the 1740s with his *Teutsches Staats-Recht* and his work with the two critical imperial elections of that decade.

§16. Imperial Politics in 1745

IN January of 1745 the emperor Charles VII died, an event for which no lamentations are recorded, bringing to an end that brief and curious reign. Moser from Ebersdorf had issued those parts of the *Teutsches Staats-Recht* that dealt exhaustively with the rights and duties of the emperor, and was launched into the particularities of the imperial estates, when a call came to attend the impending election. This invitation did not come from Trier, as in 1741. That Schönborn elector, Franz Georg, was boycotting the electoral proceedings in an effort to force Maria Theresa to dismiss her chief minister, Bartenstein, whose intransigence the elector blamed for all the recent failures of Austrian policy.[104]

104. *Lebensgeschichte*, II, p. 45; IV, p. 363. Johann Christoph von Bartenstein (1689–1767) had been a principal adviser to Charles VI and a rival of Friedrich Karl von Schönborn, whom he was believed to have driven from imperial office. Despite general unpopularity he was retained in office in 1740 by Maria Theresa, who felt unable to cope with her difficulties without drawing on his experience, and whose passionate hatred toward Prussia he encouraged. His unyielding hostility toward Frederick II of Prussia and unwillingness to make concessions to him was considered a major bar to peaceful relations between the two great German states and by 1742 led to hostility between Bartenstein and England-Hanover. *Allgemeine Deutsche Biographie*, II (Berlin, 1875), pp. 87–93; Alfred

This time Moser's principal was Gerlach Adolph Baron von Münchhausen, privy councillor and effective head of King George II's ministry in the electorate of Hanover, and leader of his government's delegation to the election in Frankfurt on Main.

Münchhausen was probably the ablest politician Moser ever knew, alongside Friedrich Karl von Schönborn and Frederick William of Prussia; and Münchhausen's grasp of imperial politics in their European context probably exceeded theirs. His role at the 1745 election was an eminent one, befitting the representative of the British crown, both in its Hanoverian electoral capacity and as main supporter and subsidizer of the "Pragmatic" Austrian party. Moser's work for Münchhausen at Frankfurt was distinctly political in nature, by comparison with the formally juridical labors he was engaged with at Ebersdorf. But it was addressed to like problems of imperial authority, allowing comparison between Moser's constitutional perception of the empire and his political perception. The substantive issues were alike but the working format and method were different. This was a recognized difference of disciplines of which Moser was particularly conscious. Moser's jurisprudence was, to be sure, substantially a collection of political records, but the forms of the *ius publicum* or Staats-Recht were very different from the *politica* or Staats-Klugheit that framed Moser's political memoranda for Münchhausen in 1745.

Still, the political views underlying this political work affirm the constitutional views that underlay Moser's jurisprudence. They cannot be taken as pure and direct statements of Moser's personal opinions; Münchhausen repeatedly sent Moser's drafts back for revision, until he got what he wanted.[105] But Moser thought of himself as something far worthier than a hired hand, and almost certainly would not have drafted opinions with which he privately disagreed. More important, there is every reason to believe that Moser in his way thought about the empire much as Münchhausen did in his—Moser the exponent of the webby complex of conditioned rights that muffled violence, and Münchhausen the subtle maneuverer among them, leader of a second-rank North German Protestant state that must forfend the aggressive territorial power of Prussia as well as any renewed threat of Catholic hegemony from Vienna. As Hanoverian statesman and servant to His Britannic Majesty, Münchhausen wanted the Reich preserved, that Reich perceived by Moser as

---

von Arneth, "Johann Christoph von Bartenstein und seine Zeit," *Archiv für Österreichische Geschichte*, XLVI (1871), pp. 1–214.

105. *Lebensgeschichte*, II, pp. 39–40; Rürup, *Moser*, p. 136, n. 147.

imperial jurist and now as consultant at the imperial election. It was an appropriate appointment.[106]

Münchhausen had solicited Moser's opinions on a variety of matters before inviting him to Frankfurt, some ceremonial and technical but some politically sensitive.[107] He seems to have seen in Moser a ready pen, combined with an extraordinary grasp of the constitutional detail and language through which imperial politics operated, and, I am persuaded, with a shrewder grasp of political realities than often appeared in the formal jurisprudence. Probably the most important task Münchhausen gave to Moser—at least the most interesting—was the memorandum "Reflections on the present high candidates for the Roman Emperorship," written probably in the early spring of 1745, and followed that summer by "Thoughts on the eligibility of the Grand Duke of Tuscany to be Roman Emperor." These were designed to bring together the most convincing arguments and most prudent terms for returning the imperial crown to Austria, and to refute arguments raised by Prussia against the candidacy of Maria Theresa's consort.[108] The other candidates were the electors of Bavaria and Saxony.

The root problem that imperial politics had to confront, Moser wrote, was the thoughtless greed of certain powerful German princes, and their sacrifice of the common weal to their private interests. Greed brought these princes into the service of the French crown, which remained fixed in its competition with the Habsburgs; and he warned against any "cleverly thought-out *Systemata*" based on the theory (as in 1742) that French power could be used by German states to check the ambitions of the Austrian house without destroying the empire, and particularly its weaker and middling members. The empire and its members being what they

106. An appreciation of Münchhausen's statecraft on a European as well as German stage in the 1740s and 1750s runs through Walther Mediger, *Moskaus Weg nach Europa* (Braunschweig, 1952).

107. *Lebensgeschichte*, II, p. 33; Rürup, *Moser*, p. 133. I rely for this and for much that follows on Rürup's researches in the Hanover state archives.

108. *Von dem Römischen Kayser* (= NTSR II), pp. 32–33; Rürup, *Moser*, pp. 134–38. Rürup discusses these memoranda at length and prints the "Reflexiones," pp. 215–33. The manuscript in WHS KA III Ls 390 is dated 30 September 1743, but Rürup dates the memorandum between January and April 1745, which seems more plausible. The versions I have used, in Moser's hand, differ in some detail and bear a different archival identity (probably because they were among Moser's own papers later seized by Württemberg). Moser does not mention them in the *Lebensgeschichte* (there were prudential reasons not to in the 1760s and 1770s), unless one is the unspecified document alluded to in II, pp. 39–40, in which case he may have drafted it at Ebersdorf. The chapter in *Von dem Römischen Kayser* (= NTSR II), pp. 20–336, on "Kayser-Wahl und Crönung," has scattered through it a great many political observations made by Moser in 1745.

were, France was "a far more dangerous born enemy for the Germans than the Turk is for Christendom." That was why the election of another Bavarian prince would be the worst option of any. Recent experience had shown how that worked. The Wittelsbach would be totally dependent upon France; and how then would he repay the French—and at whose cost—for their vast investment in his imperial crown? Bavarian resources would not suffice. Bavaria was not able to meet even the ordinary domestic costs of bearing the imperial dignity on its own, nor was its government equipped for the task, technically or politically, as the late emperor Charles VII himself had finally conceded. "The whole pattern of the last imperial reign, fatal from beginning to end, should remove any German's inclination to retrace these steps that run with blood and misfortune." There was reason to believe that most of the Bavarian ministers themselves now repudiated their own policies of the preceding years, realizing that these imperial adventures did more harm to the dignity and safety of Bavaria than the imperial Habsburgs ever had or could.

Saxony would be a rather less perilous choice; but Saxony too lacked the fiscal and governmental resources to sustain the imperial office adequately "without outside help eventually, and where would that come from?" Also, Saxony was generally distrusted for its ambiguous role in the 1742 election, for its persistent failure to observe treaties, and for its tendency to bully small neighbors (for example, the counts Reuss). As Catholic king in Poland ruling a Protestant German principality, the Saxon elector was suspect to both religious parties. And even if, for the moment, Prussia and Austria should be agreeable on allowing a Saxon on the imperial throne, it could not be long before a crisis of interests developed which "might cost the king his life; his land its last drop of blood; his house its allies and other real assets and who knows what else; with bad luck, his advisers their heads; but the poor Reich, still more now and future misery." The rhetoric shows that Moser's memorandum was aimed at more than the private delectation of Münchhausen, who cannot have been very concerned for the Saxon elector's advisers' heads.

And it was important too, thinking about these candidacies (Moser went on), that the imperial office ought not to move frequently from one house to another. Here emerged a curious political theory in which Moser apparently saw no contradiction: a theory that continuing possession of the crown made the possessing house less overbearing. "The less *ambulatorisch* the imperial dignity is, the better it is for Germany: the experience of all elective monarchies shows this; the old and the newest German history teach it; and it is easy to understand; because any newly elected house, and its ministers, think only of cutting pipes while they are sitting in the reeds, which never happens without harm to the whole Reich and many of its members—not to mention the problems respecting the imperial archives, etc."

All these defects in the candidacies of Bavaria and Saxony pointed to the grand duke of Tuscany, husband of the queen of Hungary who bore the Habsburg line. Even here there were doubts and difficulties, to be sure. The Austrian government had not always behaved well; the selection of Francis Stephen might involve the empire in particular quarrels of his; he was little known in Germany and had no lands there; there was some indignity in his being pensionary of his wife; and the succession problem might turn out to be complicated. Still, most of these objections applied as much or more to the other candidates, and the defects of the other candidacies—their weak resources, their perilous ambitions, their rivalries with other German princes—were less marked in the Austrian case. The Habsburg family situation and the succession could be worked out and agreed upon. Austria could sustain the imperial office without oppressing or betraying the estates and would more nearly be trusted with it than anybody else. "In that way the matter would come back to the old *Systema*, by which the Reich has in fact so far been preserved such-and-so, *taliter qualiter conservirt*, and has been much better off than has happened under the new *Systematibus*." Surely—Moser inserted—the queen must dismiss Baron von Bartenstein, with his penchant for "unjust, unfortunate, and unpolitical" war with the Turks, his intransigent posture toward Prussia, and his manifest failures at the last election.

One problem still remained: how the college of electors could be brought to support Francis Stephen's candidacy in spite of the flat opposition of France and Prussia. Now Moser laid out the political landscape and undertook to say how this might be done, in terms very political indeed. As in 1741, he developed his argument from the electoral situation.

Bavaria again could count on the dynastically related electorates of Cologne and the Palatinate, and probably on Prussia if Saxony had no chance or withdrew. That would be four out of nine; it could be improved to four out of eight if the nasty fight over the validity of the Bohemian vote were reopened and, as was probable, met stalemate; but even then at best Bavaria would have only parity, not majority, and parity would not suffice. Quite possibly France would try to force the vote of Mainz or Trier for its Bavarian client by military means, though both were inclined to Francis Stephen. In that case it must be hoped that these electors would hold out against French pressure, or that the other electors would "thereby be awakened from their deathly sleep." Should they succumb to force, and the others still not awaken to their peril, "then indeed there is nothing to be done for us Germans."

Saxony had only its own vote, and probably Prussia's if the Saxons forswore any hostilities toward Prussia—that is, accepted Prussia's aggrandizement in Saxony's neighborhood by the seizure of Silesia—and if Saxony promised to help fend off Russian pressure against Prussia in that region. Frederick of Prussia might expect to find comfort in the bitter antagonism that inevitably would exist between Saxony and Austria should Saxony, by itself not very *formidabel*, assume the imperial crown. But all the Catholic electors were sure to reject Saxony on religious grounds, and so would the others on account of the interminable and indiscriminate Saxon efforts to pick up bits of territory from its neighbors—a constant irritant now, and one that might prove a seriously dangerous trait in an emperor. So Saxony really had no chance. Moser did not even raise the possibility that Prussia might.

Francis Stephen could count to begin with on Mainz, Trier, and Hanover, and probably Saxony once it recognized its own position and interests. That would be the same total of four projected for Bavaria, and so still no majority unless the wrenching Bohemian issue was brought up, a step Moser warned would lead to a renewed bloodbath and would cost Austria the support of Mainz and Trier anyway. Consequently the best hope was somehow to win the support either of Prussia or of Bavaria. That was what it came down to, and there was a problem to think about.

Frederick of Prussia, Moser thought, would grow sick of war soon enough when he no longer could wage it on other people's territory, with still other people's money. But he would insist on keeping Silesia, he would require credible assurances that Austria would not promptly reopen hostilities, and he would demand a change of ministries at Vienna —Bartenstein must go. Maria Theresa no doubt had good reason and grounds for wanting Silesia back, but political realism dictated that she should "adjust to circumstances"; she must not expect England and the Netherlands to bear the burden of getting it back for her. Prussia should be guaranteed Silesia, both in Francis Stephen's electoral capitulation and in a formal undertaking of the Reich as a whole.

Of course Prussia would be easier to deal with if Bavaria was brought to terms first. That would require the clearing away of some bitter rivalries and disputes, some of long standing but most resulting from the abnormalities wrought by the Wittelsbach emperorship. Bavaria would have to be given back the home territories seized by Austria in recent military campaigns, and also—however undeserving of it—be allowed further satisfaction in Italy, say, or Austrian Swabia. In return, Bavaria would have to renounce any imperial ambitions and promise to stay clear of the French connection. As for the Saxons, they by this stage should be glad to save whatever they could. Moser thought they could be paid off adequately by a prior arrangement, wherein the sea powers would promise that after full peace was attained, they would ask Austria what compensation she would offer the Saxon elector "in proportion to the services he has done and sacrifices he has made to [Austria's] favor."

In these proposals Moser showed no qualms, moral or legal, about pressing Austria to make whatever territorial concessions were needed to recover the imperial crown; and that included renouncing Silesia, the Habsburgs' former strong arm into the north of Germany. This surely represented the political purposes of England more than those of Austria; but it serves too as a reminder of what Moser's advocacy of a Habsburg emperorship meant. He was an imperial advocate, not an Austrian one. This was political counsel of realism that followed Moser's constitutional belief that the empire, by its proper nature, worked best in the absence of any hegemonial force or threat of it, headed by an emperor with enough political and financial resources to carry out his proper duties effectively, but not enough to be tempted into aggressive enterprises; and to trim Austria to that role, this might be the occasion to clip the Habsburg wings a bit while restoring their imperial office. "Neither an all-too-powerful nor an all-too-powerless emperor suits for Germany" was a phrase he came to use, citing the war-ridden years of Charles V and Ferdinand II for the first evil extreme of power, and those of Charles VII for the second of debility. "But who can put such things on a scale once and for all, or adjust them?" Nobody, and no formula. Usually one had to take things as they came and live as conditions allowed; but when there is a free choice, a "Wahl," Moser said, then do not lose sight of this principle.[109]

The immediate steps Moser proposed then were these. First, Hanover or England must put the above proposals to Maria Theresa, to the elector of Saxony, and to the Netherlands. If Maria Theresa balked, the sea powers were to use her dependence upon them to force her into line; if Saxony balked, he should be invited to invoke the mercies of Frederick of Prussia. All circles and estates of the empire were to be rallied to support a free election, held in the absence of either contending army (the French, or the allied "Pragmatic" army that supported Maria Theresa); and they were to take no thought of subsidies, "for England cannot be cashier for all Europe." Indeed, they were to be warned that the maritime allies, being unable to uphold the Reich alone, might be obliged to take compensation of their own in Germany if the estates did not cooperate. These

109. *Von dem Römischen Kayser* (= NTSR II), pp. 39–40.

last threats were to be addressed particularly to the ecclesiastical electors, above all the Wittelsbach of Cologne. England should then approach Bavaria and Prussia secretly; if either agreed to the plan, then Maria Theresa could be brought around so much more easily. But if all these maneuvers failed, and lest all fall to pieces, Moser said, then in the name of God, claim the disputed Bohemian vote so as to make an electoral majority, and try to get enough support from the nonelectoral princes and circles to make it stick.

In the event, Maria Theresa under pressure from her allies did come to terms with Bavaria, returning to its new young elector the Bavarian lands lost to Austria in the imperial adventure, receiving in return Bavarian support at the Frankfurt election.[110] While a French army remained encamped around the city, the electoral delegations there, by Moser's description, retired to the local sour springs where they promenaded casually every day and discussed "one thing and another." Finally in June, combined forces of Austria, Hungary, Great Britain, and the Netherlands forced the French to retire. The Austrian party was clearly in control. Then the Bohemian vote was certified to be Maria Theresa's as queen of Bohemia. The Prussian and Palatine electors protested this but were overridden, and Francis Stephen was elected on 13 September and crowned as Francis I three weeks later.[111]

Moser attended the election ceremony. The dean of Mainz, he reported, read out the results in a voice so weak that nobody could hear what he was saying. Then the keeper of the keys (being long at breakfast) could not be found to let the sequestered dignitaries proceed out of the cathedral, so that people climbed out the windows and cried to the crowd, "The Queen in Hungary's husband has become Emperor!" which unleashed a popular jubilation Moser had found quite absent in 1742. He watched wigs being thrown into the air, drums beat till they split. An "ordinary Tyrolean" who stood beside him announced, "Today I'm going to get so drunk that I won't be able to tell whether I'm a boy or a girl," then after a pause, "If that be God's will," by which he meant, Moser regretfully concluded, if he found money enough.

It had been military power and decisions made far from Frankfurt that settled the election there in the end, so that it is easy to dismiss all Moser's headcounting, and the political maneuvering he proposed, as irrelevant to the outcome—too easy, in fact. For headcounting was the way of getting at the political configuration; and military power was not independent of the political configuration Moser outlined through his

110. Treaty of Füssen, 22 April 1745.
111. Pütter, *Staatsverfassung*, III, pp. 37–38; Moser, *Von dem Römischen Kayser* (= NTSR II), pp. 201–13.

electoral analysis—more nearly it followed it. The means and terms by which Francis Stephen assumed the imperial throne turned out to be very close to Moser's negotiating proposals. If anything, Moser was prepared to sacrifice more Habsburg interests, territorial and electoral, than turned out to be necessary for their election. The dispirited Bavarians succumbed to considerably less enticement than Moser would have offered them. Then Prussia did not receive quite the formal guarantees that Moser had contemplated; but Prussia kept Silesia, and (after the election) acknowledged Francis Stephen to be emperor in return.[112] The unfortunate Saxons had to pay the Prussians a million Reichsthaler for their sins. Baron von Bartenstein was not dismissed from his place in the Austrian government, but as the price of staying he was obliged, under pressure especially from Trier and Hanover, to accept a settlement far less favorable to Austria than he had insisted upon.

Moser's depiction of imperial constitutional procedures was not alien to its politics or its conditioning of power. The survival of the empire was a near thing in the 1740s, and Moser knew it very well. The French monarchy he feared most of all, writing of that power in a tone unwontedly shrill: the France that "has sought to build its fortunes on the ruins of Germany."[113] But it was not so much France the outside aggressor that he feared and denounced as it was the persistent French policy of encouraging "particular interests" of the German states to defy the principles, and the details, of the constitution of the empire as he conceived it, and so cooperatively to destroy it. That is just what happened only a few years after Moser's death; his diagnosis of 1745 foretold the way to the empire's dissolution in 1803.

How to reconcile "particular interests" with the German imperial constitution, without the presence of a dominant imperial power—this was to be the underlying concern of Moser's second massive work on imperial jurisprudence, the *Neues Teutsches Staats-Recht* of the 1760s and 1770s.[114] It was already a theme of Moser's final political composition for Münchhausen at Frankfurt on Main: some "Preliminary Thoughts" on how the new emperor ought to conduct his government to make it succeed.[115] The German Empire, Moser began, "must be ruled lovingly." The phrase in English sounds rather more sentimental than Moser's *mit*

---

112. Treaty of Dresden, 25 December 1745.

113. "Bedencken über die Eligibilität des Gross-Herzogs von Toscana zum Röm. Kayser," WHS KA III Ls 390.

114. See below, §§28–29.

115. *Lebensgeschichte*, II, pp. 42–44; Rürup, *Moser*, pp. 136–38; Walter Buff, *Gerlach Adolph Freiherr von Münchhausen als Gründer der Universität Göttingen* (Göttingen, 1937), pp. 9–10.

Liebe beherrscht werden muss, but still there is no reason to doubt that Moser meant this seriously and literally: that the Reich, as Moser understood its constitution and as political experience affirmed, could not function without generous personal relationships and confidence among its leading members and uncompromised devotion on the emperor's part —not at all a banal observation (though hardly sufficient, to be sure). Along with this, wrote Moser, the emperor must always be aware of the limits of his power. With the goodwill and confidence of the estates he could achieve much, and do much to maintain harmony among them. But he should never undertake any project or policy that powerful estates would and could thwart: better never to have started something than to suffer the double liability of trying and failing. Also he must avoid vain juridical quarrels over the nature of imperial majesty and the like, those functionally irrelevant *quaestiones juris publici de potestate Caesaris* that exercised so many of Moser's fellow jurists to the empire's hurt; and he must loosen any court ceremonial that aroused needless jealousy and friction. Imperial justice must be impartially administered: favoritism and corruption were ready political expedients, but in the end they could only weaken his government. And religion: religious divisions were a growing threat, not a declining one, to the peace and unity of the empire. The emperor would have to stay on good terms with the Protestants lest he throw them into the arms of France; or if he undertook to suppress the Protestants, he could only do this by joining forces with France and thus becoming himself hostage to the French. (This in a way presaged the confessional realignment of European politics that unleashed the Seven Years War ten years later.) Measures against the German Protestants would block the reconciliation between Prussia and the emperor, which was now indispensable for the peace and security of the Reich.

These observations, along with some particular advice about the importance of good relations with Hanover, England, and the Netherlands (apparently incorporated at Münchhausen's special instance), were sent to Francis Stephen shortly after his coronation in October 1745. It is hard to suppose the new emperor found them really helpful, let alone adequate; and the painful part of that is that they were probably as good advice as the Holy Roman Emperor of the German Nation could get. Nor can Moser have written them and the other political memoranda without experiencing serious doubts about the political future of the empire.

During this second imperial election Moser received new intimations that he might have a place on the Reichshofrat or the Reichskammergericht. How substantial they were may be questioned; such proposals seem to have drifted about whenever Moser was connected with large

events but tended to evaporate thereafter. He was able to use the Münchhausen connection to get a promise, in advance of the election, that
a brother of Friderica Rosina would have an advocate's post at the
Reichshofrat if Francis Stephen became emperor; and the promise was
honored after the election, though only after considerable difficulty and
bureaucratic maneuver.[116] These signs of patronage and favor marked
his professional and political standing, no doubt; they were grounds for
personal confidence. So was a suggestion from Münchhausen that Moser
might set up a private academy for public administration in Göttingen.
Moser turned aside suggestions of office for himself in 1745 on the
grounds, he said, of the "tightness in the chest" that had afflicted him
since coming to Ebersdorf. But, he added for posterity, telling of these
passed opportunities, he probably would have accepted one of them if he
had known what had been going on at Ebersdorf while he was in Frankfurt for the election.[117]

---

§17. Break with Ebersdorf

THE communal intimacy at Ebersdorf had suited Moser very well
at the beginning of the 1740s. It had provided congenial shelter
while he licked his wounds from the failure in Prussia; then it
had seen to the elementary education and pious rearing of his children,
freeing him for his scholarly labors and professional travels. In that
insular place he had written most of his *Teutsches Staats-Recht*; from
that secure base he had journeyed to Frankfurt and elsewhere. It provided
an awakened Frau Moser with a circle of close women friends, the dearest
she ever had. Moser had no professional rivals there. Friedrich Christoph
Steinhofer, preacher to the Schloss and village pastor, was five years
Moser's junior, an earnest and a decent man who was Moser's most
nearly confidential friend.

Steinhofer was native to the hilly region around Kirchheim unter Teck,
where Moser had encountered the separatist communities in 1736, when
he had allowed them to make a secular affirmation of loyalty to the new

116. "Nachricht," p. 55; *Lebensgeschichte*, II, pp. 44–45; IV, pp. 57–60.
117. "Nachricht," pp. 55, 59; *Lebensgeschichte*, II, pp. 46–47; Götz von Selle, *Die
Georg-August-Universität zu Göttingen* (Göttingen, 1937), pp. 107–8. For the plan for an
academy see below, §18.

duke of Württemberg in place of the usual religious oath. As a theology student at Tübingen, Steinhofer had worked out and set forth some firm opinions, based on his reading of the New Testament, on the nature of Christian community in its visible expression. The early Christian communities, he believed, consisted entirely of pure souls redeemed in grace. Such communities were the whole intention of Christ for his visible Church, and they existed wherever groups of such souls gathered together under their elders and other spiritual guides. Each community stood immediate to Christ, embodied his spirit, and so might regulate its affairs freely of any intervening authority, ecclesiastical or secular. For each was itself a totality and a Christian universe, a perfect model of the bride of Christ, expressing every particular of the universal and eternal Church.

Moser had decided doubts about all this, beginning with Steinhofer's reading of Scripture and extending into the whole matter of communal wholeness, ubiquity, and spirituality. His historical skepticism about primeval states of purity and their recapture, important for his jurisprudence, underlay his reading of Scripture too. Moser read the Acts of the Apostles with the eye of an experienced committee man, and the Pauline letters as somebody who had conducted many a circuit visitation. He and Steinhofer argued good-humoredly about the matter; they disagreed on it as they disagreed on whether the writing of Moser's compendia on the German public law was any better than sawing wood. Moser claimed that early Christian communities, like latter-day ones, had included all sorts of people who might confess the faith for any number of reasons, including pragmatic and hypocritical purposes as well as error. Thus the visible Church was a human contrivance of convenience; and thus the faithful were obliged to bear the admittedly imperfect constitution of the organized Lutheran Evangelical church, or else risk a new popery, a perverse union of flesh and the spirit in communal form that was more dangerous and insidious than Rome's. Even among the primitive Christians there had appeared the false apostle Simon the Magician.[118] Up until 1744, to the eve of Moser's second imperial election, the disagreement over the visible community of the faithful seems not to have disturbed his relationship with Steinhofer and Ebersdorf. Then Count Nikolaus

118. "Nachricht," p. 50; Martin Schmidt, *Pietismus* (Stuttgart, 1972), pp. 86–88; Moser, *Hanauische Berichte für Religions-Sachen*, I (1750), p. 718; and II (1751), pp. 62–63. A specific context for this debate was the current problem of regulating the Württemberg church, from which both Moser and Steinhofer had come. The *Pietistenreskript* of 1743, following principles Moser had long favored, allowed private devotional meetings but forbade full Separatism particularly of outside (Herrnhuth) persuasion. See above, §§8 and 12; Lehmann, *Pietismus*, especially pp. 82–94. There is a biographical sketch of Steinhofer in *Allgemeine Deutsche Biographie*, XXXV (Leipzig, 1893), pp. 726–27.

Ludwig von Zinzendorf, the very visible and energetic organizer of the German pietist movement, arrived upon the scene.

Moser had known Zinzendorf slightly for a good many years. In 1733 the count had visited Tübingen, to witness the migration of the Salzburg refugees but also to ask the theological faculty of the university whether pietist preachers in Zinzendorf's Moravian movement could be regularly ordained in the Evangelical church. On that occasion Moser, professionally at loose ends and just developing his own religious interests, had paid Zinzendorf a call and asked for spiritual advice, but came away dissatisfied. Then after Moser had moved to Stuttgart in 1734 Zinzendorf came there, staying at Moser's house, in quest of a Württemberg prelacy for himself, not so much for the sake of its revenues—indeed he offered to restore the crumbling cloister of St. Georg from his own funds if it were bestowed upon him—but for the sake of the ecclesiastical ordination it entailed, from which he hoped to gain certain official and political advantages. The request was denied by Duke Karl Alexander on stated grounds that this would offend his own coreligionists. The episode cannot have helped Moser's standing with his duke or privy councillors, nor have made his house guest quite welcome. On that same visit to Württemberg Zinzendorf asked the Tübingen faculty for a doctorate in theology; it was not granted but he was allowed, despite some serious doctrinal reservations on the part of ecclesiastical authorities, to preach a sermon in the Stiftskirche, which he delivered "with his embroidered star upon a black velvet suit," further nourishing the doubts of the Württemberger.[119]

During Moser's years at Frankfurt on Oder, Zinzendorf continued his efforts to get official recognition for his movement and ecclesiastical office for himself. In 1737, preparing a petition to King Frederick William of Prussia for an appointment as Moravian "bishop," Zinzendorf wrote Moser to ask what Prussian endowments might be vacant and available to support that office—secularized monasteries or the like. While this exchange was going on, documents arrived for the perusal of Moser's law faculty complaining of conditions at Zinzendorf's Herrnhuth community. When Zinzendorf learned of this he asked Moser to remove a complaint submitted by a community member from the file and send it to him. Moser had found this proposal not only irregular and embarrassing but altogether suspect, and there was a disagreeable exchange between them. One reason Moser gave later for having chosen Ebersdorf over Herrnhuth as his refuge after Frankfurt on Oder was

119. Ritschl, *Pietismus*, III, pp. 272–79; Moser in *Hanauische Berichte*, I (1750), pp. 559–62; see also above, §7. The quoted report on Zinzendorf's sermon at the Stiftskirche is in George F. Jones, ed., *Henry Newman's Salzburger Letters* (Athens, Georgia, 1966), p. 526.

Ebersdorf's remoteness from Zinzendorf. The count spent most of the early 1740s attending conferences and inspecting missions and daughter communities in Europe and America, including more than a year in Pennsylvania.[120]

The ties between Zinzendorf and Ebersdorf were nevertheless close, albeit inactive during Moser's early years there. Heinrich XXIX Reuss and Zinzendorf had met in Paris as young men and had even got vaguely engaged to marry the same young lady, a cousin of Zinzendorf's whom he relinquished to Reuss, marrying instead that count's younger sister, Erdmuth Dorothea.[121] It was Zinzendorf who, after one of his Württemberg visits, had brought Steinhofer to Ebersdorf. And in 1743, immediately after his return from Philadelphia, Zinzendorf began a campaign to bring the Ebersdorf community into conformity with the strict Herrnhuth rule and directly into the Herrnhuth orbit, as though one community with one rule and hierarchy. He announced that communal religious observances were altogether too slack at Ebersdorf—a critical matter because in Zinzendorf's view, community or Gemeinschaft, which commanded the spirits of its mortal members, was where salvation resided, the community itself being a perpetual socioreligious totality transcending individuals. "The Church of Christ, though invisible, can be made visible through bonded members," wrote Zinzendorf. "I recognize no Christianity without Community."[122]

The authority of the community, Zinzendorf declared, must be extended and perfected at Ebersdorf. Steinhofer was troubled. Had he been failing in his duty to his flock? Had his spirit grown brittle and wordly and vain? Zinzendorf's notions about community struck a chord with his own, the thoughts from his youth recurrent in his debates with Moser. Steinhofer wavered. But Moser was a loner for whom Ebersdorf had been a retreat and not a commune; that was how it had matched his spiritual and professional needs; and he was not yet ready to give it up. He struck back with an acid personal and theological attack on Zinzendorf and on the Herrnhuth system.

Moser knew that Countess Benigna Maria Reuss, spinster elder sister of Heinrich XXIX and chief patroness of the community (though living now some distance apart) had been scandalized by rumors of certain views and activities of Zinzendorf. Zinzendorf's long interest in the sexu-

120. "Nachricht," p. 46; *Hanauische Berichte*, I (1750), pp. 563–65; Ritschl, *Pietismus*, III, pp. 320–32.

121. Ritschl, *Pietismus*, III, pp. 205–21.

122. "Ich statuire kein Christentum ohne Gemeinschaft," quoted in Schmidt, *Pietismus*, p. 100. For Zinzendorf on community see also Ritschl, *Pietismus*, III, passim, especially pp. 197–99, 378–83.

M Friederich Christoph
Steinhofer
Superintendent u. Stadt Pfarrer in Weinsperg
geb: 1706. 16 Jan: gest: 1761. 11 Febr:

FRIEDRICH CHRISTOPH STEINHOFER
"He put aside his office as preacher, but still wanted to be teacher to the community." Moser, Lebensgeschichte, II, p. 48.
Württembergische Landesbibliothek, Stuttgart

ality of Christ was taking on some explicit features; it was producing remarkable doctrines for the communities of his redeemed and a body of erotic religious symbolism elaborated around Christ's wounds, the spear, the flow of holy lamb's blood.[123] Moser knew too that Zinzendorf's authoritarian efforts to impose his views had caused disaffection at Herrnhuth itself and elsewhere. And he knew that many of the pillars of German pietism were, as was he, offended theologically that Zinzendorf aimed at a concrete social order of religious redemption on earth among mortals, a blurring of compartments and a doctrinal deviance that imperiled souls. A secular counterpart of this was that Zinzendorf was all too energetic in his organizational activities, too pushy and too proud for a simple vessel of Christ. Moser consulted with Count Reuss and with the new Moravian bishop Polycarpus Müller (who had assumed a leading role in the movement during Zinzendorf's absence), and at Müller's suggestion (according to Moser) put down his doubts and complaints in the form of fifty questions addressed to Zinzendorf. Then he sent them off—not to Zinzendorf, but to Countess Benigna Maria, to the Württemberg pietist theologians Bengel and Oetinger, to the educator and prelate Johann Adam Steinmetz at Berg, and to other such eminents.[124] He collected a number of replies hostile to Zinzendorf, incorporated them into his queries, and sent the whole, now a broad manifesto, to the count himself. He got back a confused and angry reply signed by two of Zinzendorf's lieutenants, which spoke of Judas kisses and the friends of Job, concluding: if Polycarpus Müller had put Moser up to this, let Moser send it to him; Zinzendorf had no time for it.[125]

Moser did so; Müller now recoiled and refused any further part in the matter; Steinhofer continued to waver; and that was the position at the beginning of 1745 as Moser prepared for the imperial election at Frankfurt on Main. Meanwhile he drafted a history of the Christian Church emphasizing the distinctions among the realms of the visible Church, of doctrine, and of the spirit: a "Threefold Outline of the History of the Reich of Jesus Christ on Earth," which seems to me a quite interesting and unusual historical composition (Moser wrote almost no other histories). Its three compartments were: I, a chronological history of the visible Church from the incarnation to the present, emphasizing very

123. Gottfried Beyreuther, *Sexualtheorie im Pietismus* (Munich, 1963), pp. 30–68; Ritschl, *Pietismus*, III, pp. 378–403; Schmidt, *Pietismus*, pp. 103–7.
124. *Lebensgeschichte*, II, pp. 34–35; "Nachricht," pp. 55–56; Rürup, *Moser*, pp. 41–42.
125. "Nachricht," pp. 55–56; *Lebensgeschichte*, II, pp. 35–38; IV, pp. 51–57; *Hanauische Berichte*, I (1750), pp. 569–72; Fröhlich, *Moser*, pp. 88–89; Schmid, *Moser*, pp. 175–81.

recent times; II, a systematic description of the written sources for the knowledge of Christ; and III, an analysis of the inner manifestations of the Spirit.[126] Then Moser turned his attention to the Reich of the Germans. But while he was preoccupied with imperial politics at Frankfurt that autumn, Pastor Steinhofer attended a synod of the Moravian Brethren at Marienborn, which was dominated by the Herrnhuth party. He returned full of news about blood and wounds; he lay down his office as court preacher at the Schloss and rededicated himself, as "teacher of the community," to the establishment of the purer Herrnhuth pattern at Ebersdorf. But by the beginning of 1746 a movement of religious enthusiasm was sweeping over Ebersdorf which Steinhofer had not anticipated, which Moser was unable to share and which in the end would have none of him.

The emotional wave that inundated German pietist communities at that time may have owed something to the Great Awakening in America, which Zinzendorf had journeyed to observe and which had been analyzed and described in the press by the prelate Steinmetz over a period of several years.[127] It had begun from an elaborate division of the community into exclusive groups defined by sex, marital status, and maturity: eight Chöre, "choirs," one each for widows, married men and widowers, married women, bachelors, spinsters, boys, girls, and small children; and each had its own spiritual leader or Arbeiter, "worker." This Moser at Ebersdorf had found, at first and on the face of it, not an unreasonable or impractical way to organize community affairs, which after all had to be ordered and categorized somehow. He did note certain tensions that he attributed to rigid sexual segregation: a housemaid of his, for example, was frightened to visit a physician because he was an unmarried male, from another choir.[128]

But as the system elaborated, rigidified, and developed strong hierarchical features, a confused countermovement set in, most pronounced

126. *Dreyfacher Entwurff einer Historie des Reichs Jesu Christi auf Erden, besonders von des seel. Herrn D. Speners Zeiten an, bis jezo* ([Ebersdorf], 1745). Moser reprinted it by installments in expanded form in *Hanauische Berichte für Religions-Sachen*, I–II (1750–51).

127. Johann A. Steinmetz, *Nachricht von dem herrlichen Werke Gottes in der Bekehrung vieler 100 Seelen zu Nordhampton und an anderen Orten in Neuengland . . .* (Magdeburg, 1738–45); *Hanauische Berichte*, I, p. 575.

128. "Nachricht," pp. 57–58; *Lebensgeschichte*, II, pp. 48–52. See Beyreuther, *Sexualtheorie*, pp. 42–68; and Gillian Gollin, *Moravians in Two Worlds* (New York, 1967), for a comparison of Herrnhuth with Bethlehem, Pennsylvania, emphasizing community as religious sacrament and as substitute for family. On the apostolic term "Arbeiter," see the Lutheran versions of Matthew 9:37–38 and Luke 10:2–3. "Chöre" probably reflected the separate seating and separate worship of the several groups; but see also 1 Samuel 19:20.

among young unmarried members of both sexes, who complained that the community was ruled coldly by oppression and fear, and who called for self-revelation, for the opening of hearts to one another, so as to free true spirits from these ranks and files of age and sex. As this counter-movement spread through the community, biblical inquiry was replaced by simple emotional questions: Do you love the Lamb? Have you felt the blood of Jesus in your heart? If you did, you were admitted to "Lammesgeschwister" status: sisters and brothers of the Lamb. Men put on red caps, and women the special Moravian bonnets with ribbons announcing their married or unwedded state—ribbons that became more costly and coquettish as matters proceeded.

The countermovement (though never quite distinct from what it opposed) was directed against communal discipline of the Herrnhuth tradition; but as the struggle for control over the Ebersdorf community went on amidst these emotional manifestations in both places, the party of the Lamb in Ebersdorf became associated with the effort from Herrnhuth to replace, at Ebersdorf, the domination of the Reuss family, and of people like Moser, who by this time was thoroughly alienated from Zinzendorf. In the spring of 1746, the organization of the Ebersdorf community was taken over altogether by the "heated" young members of the pro-Zinzendorf Lamb party. They became workers over all the choirs. There were celebrations of the victory and processions, and new holidays were proclaimed; the sisters and brothers of the Lamb invented whimsical pet names for one another, denoting birds and animals with human appetites and features, ("more childish than childlike," Moser complained to Steinhofer). Around March 1746 the religious eroticism of the movement reached a high pitch. The young folk fell to their knees and kissed one another's feet, took one another's heads under their arms, and spent their time with what Moser called "dallying and moonshine," Lappereyen und Tandeleyen, leaving all else. (It happens, though, that Moser's son Christian Benjamin, his first child in nine years and the last he was to have, was born in December 1746.) And there were other visible manifestations. A weaver with a velvet vest claimed a seat in the church that denoted his spiritual superiority to Heinrich XXIX Reuss. For even this new commune could not after all do without hierarchy. It devised a new one, of three ranks based on spiritual estate: first, those who had truly received the blood of the Lamb in their hearts; second, those for whom there was some hope that eventually they might; and third, the hopeless. When the list was read out before the congregation, Johann Jakob Moser's name was at the very bottom of category two.[129]

129. "Nachricht," pp. 58–60; *Lebensgeschichte*, II, pp. 58–60; *Hanauische Berichte*, I, pp. 575–85.

That cleared the matter up satisfactorily for Moser. It relieved his anxiety lest a true spirit might really be at work here. This showed that the whole business was nonsense, got altogether out of hand. He had genuinely tried, he said, to find out about this experience of the blood of the Lamb in the heart and how it differed from the grace and forgiveness in which condition he had been these nine years. Now he would try no longer. On Judgment Day, he allowed, there would be another classification. He forbade his family to wear the caps and ribbons enjoined by the community, for these began to look to him remarkably like the crowns of blasphemy, the mark of the Beast described in the fourteenth chapter of the Revelation of St. John, a book he had been studying of late. He wrote and traveled to consult Steinmetz and others about what was going on and what was to be done, and they generally agreed that the whole affair did look like the work of the Beast. Moser then argued the point with Steinhofer, who gently urged that Moser had the wrong apocalyptic animal: the Zinzendorf party spoke for the Lamb. Moser denied it, for by now he was ready to identify Zinzendorf himself with that terrible false apostle of the Revelation, or at least a main limb of him.[130]

At the end of 1746 Zinzendorf came to Ebersdorf in person. Moser confronted him and demanded that Zinzendorf clear up the confusion of the community, but got no satisfaction: Zinzendorf denounced his detractors—Moser's allies—and went on to deliver sermons and hold private meetings whose content, particularly in those meetings restricted to married persons, Moser found shocking, "abominable." Zinzendorf claimed, for example, that Judas was redeemed at the Last Supper, by the efficacy of communion: apparently one could sin infinitely if he only took a little blood of the Lamb afterwards. New popery. Then, after celebrating the total unity of Ebersdorf with Herrnhuth in an elaborate ceremony complete with a hymn of jubilation composed for the occasion, Zinzendorf departed.[131]

Moser's position at Ebersdorf was now all but impossible; he had denied the community and rejected its right and authority over him. Now it excluded him. Once at communion a number of men pressed around him, threatening, he thought, physical humiliation and "lewd mishandling," so that he struck out at them and cried for help. In January of 1747 Steinhofer came to him to say that the hearts of the community

130. "Nachricht," pp. 59–60; *Lebensgeschichte,* II, pp. 53–56; *Hanauische Berichte,* I, 580–81.

131. *Denk- und Dank-Lied des Hauses Ebersdorf bey seinem am* 10ten *Dec. einfallenden Kirchen-Iubilaco* (Ebersdorf, n.d.), of which there is a copy at the Historical Society of Pennsylvania in Philadelphia; "Nachricht," p. 61; *Lebensgeschichte,* II, pp. 56–60; *Hanauische Berichte,* I, pp. 582–84.

NIKOLAUS LUDWIG VON ZINZENDORF
"This Count had an extraordinarily vivid imagination, which sometimes led him to suppose merely possible things to be actual facts. Then when he had described them a few times, he became quite adamant about them." Moser, Lebensgeschichte, *IV, p. 97.*
"Carnal purpose and swagger; pride, lies, and the arts of attracting money . . . new popery. . . . Even among the primitive Christians came such as Simon the Magician." Moser, "Nachricht," *pp. 50, 55–56.*
Württembergische Landesbibliothek, Stuttgart

were so oppressed to see Moser at communion that he must not come any more. The pastor tried to be merciful and gentle: Moser might still attend lesser exercises, those open to anybody; for though he was stubborn in his error the reason perhaps was his condition of confusion: that he was *in statu perplexitatis*. Moser at this replied cheerfully, "Cut is the tie and we are free!" and when Steinhofer asked what he meant by this jingle he jingled it again: *Strick ist entzwey und wir seynd frey!* Then he recalled without trouble the verse in the ninth chapter of the Gospel according to John, about the blind man given sight by Christ, and then expelled by the Pharisees on account of it: "Jesus learned that they had cast him out."[132] That chapter concludes, I find, with the verse: "Jesus said unto them, If ye were blind, ye should have no sin; but now ye say, We see; therefore your sin remaineth." Moser's account does not mention this concluding judgment, an omission that seems at first to show unwonted restraint on his part toward the Ebersdorf community; but then, he expected us to know how that chapter ends.

---

§18. Hessen-Homburg and Hanau, but never Göttingen

AFTER his break with the Ebersdorf community Moser's health improved immediately, as his "tightness in the chest" subsided. This was a more confident and a prouder Moser now than the defeated university director who had fled to the community eight years before. In truth he was not "perplexed," and his spiritual recovery had a professional dimension. Ebersdorf had been a kind of microcosm or analogy to the empire itself, where Moser might hope to exercise his piety, and his profession, in ways individual to himself and yet within spheres of association that transcended political and social specifics. Then it came to seem a stifling place, where the freedom he had sought in the wider empire and in his faith had funneled down into an oppressive opposite.

132. *Lebensgeschichte*, II, p. 60; *Hanauische Berichte*, I, pp. 567–87; "Nachricht," p. 61, says it was Moser's old Tübingen acquaintance Günther Albrecht Rentz who carried the message excluding him from communion, but in this instance the published version appears more reliable; perhaps both Steinhofer and Rentz told him of it. Steinhofer himself left Ebersdorf in the following year, broke with the movement in 1748, and spent the rest of his days in a series of minor Württemberg pastorates, dying at Weinsberg in 1761.

Moser's attention began to turn now from empire and community toward princely states. He grew bored with the *Teutsches Staats-Recht*, which had just passed its thirtieth volume of imperial law, and was eager for new work that would take him out of Ebersdorf village altogether—so eager that he took the first chance that came along that spring (to be sure, there was no flood of offers), to be privy councillor and chief of chancellery to the tiny landgravate of Hessen-Homburg, just outside the city of Frankfurt on Main. It was a position of far lesser importance than Moser thought his talents and eminence qualified him for; he insisted on his own terms in negotiating the post with the landgrave, and would abide no opposition while he was there.[133]

The Homburg principality was in dubious condition. Its tiny population and its scant revenues could hardly sustain the landgrave's position as a reigning prince of the empire, and nobody knew for sure how bad the financial situation actually was. Moreover, the landgrave was caught in a dynastic dispute with his stronger cousins of Hessen-Darmstadt, from whom his branch had separated only a century before, over revenues and resources without which his independent principality might not survive at all.[134] Moser's predecessor had in effect abdicated the dual job of establishing internal solvency and settling with Hessen-Darmstadt. Moser arrived out of Ebersdorf full of newfound energy, brandishing a new broom.

Moser began by flatly rejecting the financial plan handed him by the landgrave at their first meeting. It was too optimistic and too loose, he said. It overestimated income, and it allowed no room for unforeseen expenses that were bound to arise. He would not work by it. In its place he drafted a double-entry annual budget organized for quarterly review, whereby debits and credits could be understood in detail at any point and be controlled. He insisted that no new debt should be assumed on one budget column without cross-reference to anticipated new income on the other; that the public payroll and the scheduled debt (especially that owed Hessen-Darmstadt) be met promptly; and that everything possible be done to establish the credit of Hessen-Homburg as a thrifty and orderly government. He called upon the landgrave to make personal economies "in the right place: namely unnecessary servants, stables, clothing, building, furniture, table, travels, music, and hospitality."[135]

133. For Moser's experiences at Homburg, I rely, except where otherwise indicated, on my reading of his account in *Lebensgeschichte*, II, pp. 65–79.

134. Friedrich Karl Moser printed Homburg's documentation of the dispute in *Sammlung der neuesten und wichtigsten Deductionen in Teutschen Staats- und Rechts-Sachen*, III, (Frankfurt/Main, 1752), pp. 74ff; see also [J. J. Moser], *Factum, in Sachen: Hessen-Homburg contra Hessen-Darmstadt* (Homburg, 1748, anon.).

135. *Lebensgeschichte*, II, p. 70.

Moser installed his son Friedrich Karl, now well into his twenties, to be his confidential aide for administering the affairs of the landgravate, and he mounted an assault upon the casual habits of the existing chancellery. The clerical staff, he reports, customarily came and went as they pleased; they lounged about the council chamber, where they had no business, accompanied by nosy wives who found nothing better to do; they were given to reading newspapers, and were inclined to desultory debate over instructions he gave them. Moser promptly drafted a body of strict administrative regulations to govern chancellery procedures, had it endorsed by the landgrave, and had it printed for everybody's instruction.[136] He himself set a brisk example by arriving early in the morning and sending out lackeys to fetch tardy clerks and councillors. He maintained careful running registries of how documents came and went, who was responsible for processing which, who had them at a given time, and how long he had had them. Nothing was to be shuffled out of sight. It is not hard to imagine the kind of muttering that went around the Homburg offices and court about this new chief of chancellery.

Probably Moser had been hired for the main purpose of conducting Hessen-Homburg's case against Hessen-Darmstadt; here his juridical learning and experience and his connections with the judicial world of the empire came into account. But if the landgrave had expected an unconditional advocate, he had failed to reckon with Moser himself, whose duty to his sense of himself and of office, and to a larger constituency of formal justice, exceeded his devotion to the landgrave's particular interests. Indeed, there is reason to suspect that the "unpartisan" Moser had been pressed upon the landgrave by outside personages whose interest in straightening out the principality's affairs were not quite the landgrave's either. The theme of Moser's negotiations with Darmstadt was that Homburg should claim no more in this contest than it could prove unmistakably its right, so as to settle the matter in stable and definitive legal terms. But this strategy, if it was a strategy, had no visibly softening effect on his negotiating counterparts of Darmstadt. Moser tried unsuccessfully to invoke mediation by the electors of Mainz and Brandenburg, and he scoured the Homburg archives for missing records of how the Hessian dynasty had distributed its rights in 1622–23 at the time of the separation of Homburg—records apparently available to the Darmstadt negotiators but not to him. Repeated conferences with Darmstadt and memoranda brought no conclusion to the matter. Moser made a jocular observation to the landgrave: one way to settle the dispute would be to give the chief Darmstadt negotiator a substantial cash

136. *Fürstlich-Hessen-Homburgische provisionale Canzley-Ordnung* (Homburg v. d. H., 1747).

gift and an annual pension, but inasmuch as the landgrave might not like Moser to be tempted by a similar offer from Darmstadt, Moser would not recommend this step. After a time the landgrave began to hear talk that Moser was not doing his utmost for Homburg in the Darmstadt negotiations. Moser retorted that his position in law was quite unassailable.[137]

Moser's righteously bureaucratic and legalistic style surely aggravated everybody with whom he dealt, and his haughtily deaf ear to the landgrave's private interests and pleasures left him vulnerable on that flank. The Life History recounts in detail intrigues launched against him by his rivals for the landgrave's confidence. Moser's budget of expenditures was overrun in the very first quarter, and deficits rose thereafter. One rival (who ultimately became Moser's successor) persuaded the landgrave that any prince who lived parsimoniously lost credit thereby in the eyes of possible lenders, not to mention his compeers—very possibly this was true—and started him on a program to raise quick cash by the sale and lease of capital in the form of agricultural land, cattle, and the like. When Moser learned of this—from the newspapers, he claimed—he sent the landgrave a written ultimatum, reminded him of the conditions under which he had assumed the post, and complained of the hearing the landgrave gave to his rivals. What was happening here, Moser declared, destroyed his own good name. People who observed the landgravate's affairs must believe either that Moser was not the honest man he was reputed to be, or else that he had no influence with the landgrave; and either, Moser wrote, was intolerable. Here were, clearly enough, contradicting notions of "credit."

Moser got back a euphonious but plain reply in the landgrave's own hand. The landgrave regretted that Moser, being the honest man he was, could not remain in his service under existing conditions. There were, alas, so many different opinions about how the principality's affairs should be conducted. He had full confidence in Moser's skill and honesty, but it was not possible for him to abide by Moser's budgetary principles. Inasmuch, then, as he could not expect the honest Moser to change his own posture just to please the landgrave, it seemed their ways must part. He hoped Moser would finish out the present quarter. And perhaps some day, some more prosperous day, the landgrave might find it possible to give Moser some testimony of his esteem.

No separation pay. Moser had lasted some fifteen months in Homburg service. Now where was he to go?

His first choice was to settle in nearby Frankfurt on Main, a publishing center where he had friends; but the Frankfurt town council rejected his

137. *Lebensgeschichte,* II, p. 62.

application. The grounds they gave were that Moser wished to settle as an "uncharacterized person," without becoming a citizen and outside the civic constitution, which would have allowed him to come and go without paying citizens' admission and demission fees. There is reason to think that Moser asked or hoped to combine unencumbered residence at Frankfurt with freedom from city censorship: he was particularly concerned about problems of censorship as he contemplated returning to writing for his livelihood. Frankfurt was seat of the imperial censors, though, and this arrangement might have created problems for the city government.[138]

Another reason Moser was unwelcome in Frankfurt may have been his controversial religious associations. These surely would have made him a discomfiting figure in the eyes of the Frankfurt burghers, for whom religious differences were a serious civic problem. The noisy scandals and religious quarrels surrounding the Zinzendorf communities at Herrnhuth, Ebersdorf, and elsewhere were at a high pitch of notoriety just then. Moser had tried to stay clear of it all while at Homburg (where he was *ex officio* head of the Lutheran consistory).[139] But his pietist connections were well known, and his dramatic break with Ebersdorf made them all the more controversial. When Moser tried then to settle in nearby Usingen he was warned that if he did he must be silent on any religious matter, to preserve the peace; Moser stayed away. When he tried Friedberg the pastor there warned his flock to repel any pietist infection, and Moser was warned in turn that he and his family might not be safe there from the frolicsome attentions of the native "Pöbel," the crowd.[140] His family was miserably unhappy at Homburg meanwhile; they regretted leaving Ebersdorf, and this was a reproach to him. He himself had nothing to hold him in Homburg—quite the contrary. As he usually did in such circumstances, Moser undertook varied commissions and wrote legal tracts that might commend him to potential employers— Kurland, Worms, imperial towns—and sent a proposal for the reform of the university at Mainz, where the elector Johann Friedrich Karl was an

138. "Nachricht," p. 63; *Lebensgeschichte*, II, pp. 85–87. The Frankfurt city records offer no further detail, for which information I am indebted to Gerald L. Soliday.

139. "Nachricht," pp. 62–63; *Lebensgeschichte*, II, p. 85. Moser's closest friend and ally at Homburg was the Reformed court preacher Rexrath. On the background of the confessional problem in Frankfurt politics, Gerald L. Soliday, *A Community in Conflict: Frankfurt Society in the Seventeenth and Early Eighteenth Centuries* (Hanover, N.H., 1974). See also Moser's subsequent quarrels with the Frankfurt town council over religious matters in *Lebensgeschichte*, II, pp. 92–93.

140. "Nachricht," p. 63; *Lebensgeschichte*, II, pp. 61–62, 86.

old acquaintance from the days with Schönborn.[141] All in vain. But his greatest opportunity, perhaps the truly most important lost chance of his life, came when Baron von Münchhausen initiated a correspondence with him about the future of his favorite enterprise, the flourishing new university at Göttingen.

Münchhausen had been favorably impressed by a memorandum Moser had prepared for him in 1745 on "How young persons of rank may be attracted to Göttingen and there, among other things, be better prepared for political and administrative affairs than anyplace else in Europe." Here Moser had proposed a curriculum of practical training for budding jurists and officials. There had been some thought then that Moser himself might set up such a program at Göttingen, but apparently no serious negotiation; Moser then was still taken up with Ebersdorf affairs.[142] In the following year Münchhausen had appointed the able young jurist Johann Stephan Pütter to his law faculty. Pütter persuaded him also to install a close friend of Pütter's from their student days, Gottfried Achenwall; and together the two young men set about carving a place for themselves in the Göttingen faculty of jurisprudence. In 1748 Pütter wrote for Münchhausen an outline of a plan for organizing his own work at the university.[143] Münchhausen sent a copy of Pütter's curricular plan to Moser among others (he was at loose ends now at Homburg) for his evaluation and comments.

Moser's first comments on Pütter's plan were put as advice to the young jurist. Pütter should stay away from history, to begin with. Know where the history is in case it should be needed, but do not become a historian. Anyway, "perhaps I do not err when I judge by his writings that he has no aptitude for it." History almost never influenced actual decisions. Neither did natural law. Natural law might be sprinkled into the discourse to spice it up, "for recreation and to show one's *force d'esprit*," but there was no conclusive effect to it; "in the end it remains mere *Raisonnemens*, and to make *Raisonneurs* is not Professor Pütter's destiny." Pütter should write his own teaching texts, and should write them in German (few working officials could manage Latin), although

---

141. *Lebensgeschichte*, II, pp. 78–80; see the polemical tracts listed in Rürup's bibliography to *Moser*, pp. 260–61, most of which however are related to Homburg affairs.

142. See above, §16. Moser had published his plan as *Entwurff einiger Anstalten zum Dienst junger Standes-Personen, so sich denen Staats-Sachen widmen wollen, dem Publico zur Prüfung vorgelegt* ([Ebersdorf], 1745).

143. Wilhelm Ebel, *Der Göttinger Professor Johann Stephan Pütter aus Iserlohn* (Göttingen, 1975), pp. 14–27, with the text of Pütter's proposal on pp. 26–27; also Ferdinand Frensdorff, *Die ersten Jahrzehnte des staatsrechtlichen Studiums in Göttingen* (Göttingen, 1887), pp. 13–14.

ILLUSTRIS = SIMO VIRO
GERLACO ADOLPHO
A MÜNCHAUSEN
DYNASTAE IN STRAUSSFURT
REG. M. BRIT. ET ELECT. BRUNSVICO LVNEB.
A CONSIL. INTIMIS ET IN DUCAT. CELL.
MAGNO ADVOCATO

GERLACH ADOLPH VON MÜNCHHAUSEN
"I see no special promise in Privy Councillor Moser's plan. He would like to build a statum in statu, academiam in academia, *which is quite dubious and dangerous." Münchhausen to Pütter,* 1749.
Württembergische Landesbibliothek, Stuttgart

again he should make it clear in his work that he could use Latin if he chose. He should make careful notes of everything he learned on small filing slips for future use, "by which others will be amazed at where he got it all."[144]

Pütter assented generally to Moser's advice, which does seem frank and generous, even to this revelation of Moser's own favorite professional secrets. But then a week later another long memorandum arrived at Göttingen from Homburg. Moser had been thinking. Now he proposed a political academy at the university, to be taught by three professors, each meeting the class for one lecture a day. Pütter would handle German state affairs: "Staats-Klugheit" or policy, imperial public law, judicial procedures, the political circumstances of the major German courts, and the like. Achenwall would do recent European political history, comparative constitutions, European (not universal) international law. A third professor, unnamed, would teach chancellery practice, the written and oral management of public affairs.[145]

Possibly Moser had his eldest son Friedrich Karl in mind for that third professorial post.[146] It would have been an excellent situation for Karl, who at twenty-five was near Pütter's and Achenwall's age, and Moser was ambitious for him. But it seems just as possible, in view of Moser's own current desperate circumstances at Homburg, that he had himself in mind. In any case Pütter and Achenwall promptly acted together to head off any such possibility, replying to Münchhausen that there was a good deal to be said for Moser's plan, but only if it could be adapted to "conditions as they exist here." A separate academy would be *quasi corpus in corpore*, like one body within another, and impinge on the proper sphere of university administration. All the topics listed by Moser could be made available by personnel already at the university, they argued; and to prove it they submitted new curricular proposals whereby they themselves undertook to teach nearly all of them, giving a practical twist to their courses so as to make that expensive unnamed third professor and special program unnecessary. Münchhausen agreed: "I see no special promise in Privy Councillor Moser's plan. He would like to build a *statum in statu, academiam in academia*, which is quite dubious and dangerous."[147]

144. 7 March 1749. Frensdorff, *Die ersten Jahrzehnte*, prints the text on pp. 14–16; Ebel, *Pütter*, pp. 28–29.

145. 14 March 1749. Frensdorff, *Die ersten Jahrzehnte*, pp. 19–21; Ebel, *Pütter*, pp. 29–31; Rürup, *Moser*, pp. 81–82.

146. Thus Frensdorff, *Die ersten Jahrzehnte*, p. 20; and Ebel, *Pütter*, p. 29.

147. 27 March 1749. Ebel, *Pütter*, pp. 30–34; Frensdorff, *Die ersten Jahrzehnte*, p. 21; Rürup, *Moser*, pp. 82–83.

Moser's response to the new Pütter-Achenwall proposal, passed on to him by Münchhausen, was combative but partly resigned. "So what I'm getting here, with these two good *Professoribus*, is what I have got so often before with the ablest *academicis*: they have no sense of (so to say) the practical theory, the immediate approach to extrajudicial and public practice, nor do they go deep enough into pragmatic *Idéen*: so that in such matters more could be accomplished by somebody else of even moderate capacity." Professors Pütter and Achenwall both clearly possessed the admirable quality of being able to hear criticism, but Moser must now say that they had not yet grasped his meaning, that their proposals did not accomplish what he recommended, and that they would not achieve the good for the university that was Moser's purpose. Perhaps, Moser added, the kind of institution he had in mind ought to be set up in a capital—Hanover, say—rather than in a university town. At universities the "Jalousie" against anybody who stepped off the beaten track was too much to overcome, whereas in a state capital the students and the teachers would have better contact with people who worked in the real world.[148]

Münchhausen told Pütter that although Moser's proposal was "impractical for the university," still there ought to be regular instruction in the everyday practice of the public law. Pütter prepared such a program for the coming year, which went then to Moser, who replied in July—now quite resigned but still wistful—that of course he could not expect so able a man as Pütter to pattern himself precisely on Moser's thinking. "Moreover I wish Professor Pütter the best of luck with his program; we do not stand in one another's way and the good God has bread for us both and for others besides. With Your Excellency's kindly and continuing guidance this man will be an ornament to the university at Göttingen and a more useful teacher there than a hundred others."[149]

That seemed to end Moser's immediate prospects at Göttingen, although it is possible to read Moser's July letter as saying: Pütter has come now as close to my thinking as is reasonable to expect; I do admire him, we could get along; he has nothing to fear from me. The senior scholar, outmaneuvered or not, could hardly go further. At any rate, Moser's generous predictions about the young Pütter's future achievement were accurate. Pütter went on to lead the superb law faculty at Göttingen for more than fifty years. He himself became Moser's chief rival for the reputation of grand master of the German public law in the

148. 7 April 1749. Frensdorff, *Die ersten Jahrzehnte*, pp. 22–25; Ebel, *Pütter*, pp. 33–34; Rürup, *Moser*, prints the memorandum on pp. 206–14.

149. 5 July 1749. Frensdorff, *Die ersten Jahrzehnte*, p. 28; Ebel, *Pütter*, p. 34; Rürup, *Moser*, p. 84.

eighteenth century, a career marked by scarcely less energy than Moser's and by rather greater originality and flexibility of mind, albeit less independence of spirit and person. Moser was always generous in writing to Pütter or about him. The younger man for his part was proper and careful in his treatment of Moser, at least until his own position was securely established and perhaps a bit longer than that; and in Moser's old age he was generous in his praise.[150] Moser was given to sighing, in after years, about "how I might have shone [brillirt] if I had come to a place like Göttingen or Halle" instead of places like Tübingen and Frankfurt on Oder, and if he had used the years given over to politics and administration for intellectual pursuits.[151] He maintained his connection with Münchhausen, and his eldest daughter Wilhelmina married Gottfried Achenwall in 1755, and on several occasions a call to Göttingen seemed in the offing; but it never quite happened.

In June of 1749, with the chance at Göttingen fading, Moser published a "Plan for a State and Chancellery Academy, or a More Thorough Introduction and Preparation of Young Princes, Counts, Chevaliers, and Other Persons Coming from Universities or Travels, to European and Especially German Politics [Staats-Klugheit]; to the Now Usual International Law in Time of Peace and of War; to the Most Recent European and Especially the German Comitial, Judicial, and Extrajudicial State Affairs and Controversies; to All Manner of State and Chancellery Written Materials [Aufsätze]; and to the Usual Procedures of a Well-Ordered Chancellery; also Congresses, Conferences, etc."—a look at which title, even on a bookseller's list, was enough to tell anybody what Moser was advertising. The proposed academy embodied ideas developed in the interchange with Münchhausen and before. University instruction was well and good, Moser set forth, but it left both potential rulers and their servants without any sense of what actually happened in the process of governing, and how and why, "in *puncto juris* and of *raison d'Etat.*" There were to be included the three main groups of topics Moser had proposed for Göttingen, and eventually two more, on military and on commercial or cameral administration. Fees were scaled according to the

150. For the rivalry of Moser's and Pütter's reputations see Ebel, *Pütter*, pp. 1–6, 200–201 (hostile to Moser), and the literature there cited; Pütter's discussion of Moser in his *Litteratur des teutschen Staatsrechts*, I (Göttingen, 1776), pp. 408–30, includes (p. 417) the often-quoted judgment (but not first made by Pütter) that Moser's massive contributions to the Staatsrecht were an "immortal" service—"In der Geschichte dieser Litteratur wird er allemal Epoche machen." Some years earlier Moser had expressed his admiration for Pütter in *Neueste Geschichte der teutschen Staats-Rechts-Lehre und deren Lehrer* (Frankfurt/Main, 1770), pp. 47, 125–26.

151. See, for example, *Lebensgeschichte*, I, p. 161; IV, p. 111.

IOANNES STEPHANUS PÜTTER

JOHANN STEPHAN PÜTTER
"*I wish Professor Pütter the best of luck . . . and the good God has bread for us both . . . this man will be an ornament to the University at Göttingen.*" Moser to Münchhausen, 1749.

IOANNES STEPHANVS PÜTTER
Magnae Britanniae regi
a consiliis iustitiae intimis
et iuris publici professor ordinarius
in academia Georgia Augusta.
nat. d. 25. Jun. 1725.

"How I might have shone, if I had come to a place like Göttingen or Halle."
Moser, Lebensgeschichte, I, p. 161.
Germanisches Nationalmuseum, Nürnberg
Württembergische Landesbibliothek, Stuttgart

184 | *The Constitution of the Empire*

student's rank, from five gulden for commoners, through nobles, barons, and counts, to twenty-five gulden for princes.[152]

This project got Moser away from Homburg, finally; the landgrave of Hessen-Hanau welcomed the enterprise to his little capital and put a substantial building at Moser's disposal. From there Moser published four more booklets explaining in detail his program and his own qualifications. The academy opened in November of 1749 with ten students. Friedrich Karl taught along with his father, and so for a few months did a young Professor Kahle, on his way out of Göttingen to an Ordinarius post at Marburg. Moser attended all class exercises himself. It is hard to judge the merits or success of the Hanau academy, for it operated for only two years, until Moser went home to Stuttgart to serve the diet there. He hoped for great success, but as far as I can learn there were never more than a dozen students, and finances were precarious.[153] Innovative it may have been, but it did not flourish.

Meanwhile Münchhausen had not altogether dismissed Moser from his mind: perhaps something might yet be done with Moser if in the end he should show himself amenable and useful to Göttingen's circumstances. He watched Moser's Hanau academy as he watched Pütter's program in practical jurisprudence, simultaneously launched; and he warned Pütter that he must not offend Moser. He sounded Moser out on the possibility of moving the academy to Göttingen but as a private operation, separate from the university. Moser refused; he was fully committed now, he said, to Hanau. The exasperated Münchhausen lost his patience. "The worst thing about this man," he wrote to Pütter at the end of January, 1750, "is his unsettled disposition and dissatisfaction and his more-than-pietist disposition in religious things, in which he goes farther than is sensible. *Est et datur nimium in pietate*—he is and is known to be immoderate in his piety."[154]

Here was a curious summary. Moser's religious beliefs had played no visible part in his relations with Münchhausen or the interchange about Göttingen. But Münchhausen was a skillful recruiter of talent and a prudent judge of personalities. And this remark of his about Moser's character strikes the relation between Moser's religion and his professional behavior: Moser is changeable and prickly and unreliable and overly pietistic. To be sure, Moser at Hanau had revived his religious

152. *Entwurff einer Staats- und Canzley-Academie* . . . (Hanau, 1749). Rürup analyzes it in *Moser*, pp. 85–87.

153. *Lebensgeschichte*, II, pp. 87–92; Rürup, *Moser*, pp. 85–95, 265, describes the academy and lists Moser's brochures; see also Wilhelm Stieda, *Die Nationalökonomie als Universitätswissenschaft* (Leipzig, 1906), pp. 42–45.

154. Frensdorff, *Die ersten Jahrzehnte*, pp. 26–31; Ebel, *Pütter*, p. 35, n. 57.

activities and his feud with Zinzendorf,[155] and that may have been on Münchhausen's mind; but his juxtaposition of Moser's piety with undependability bears thinking about. The point is not that Moser's religious views tied him to some sectarian loyalty that might compromise or conflict with an employer's secular aims or program, and as far as I know that never happened. They did not oblige him to take any particular political or institutional position. Neither did his pious emotions. Rather, they absolved him of any obligation, and that was the trouble. Moser's cultivation by his pietist moral logic of his own uprightness, honor, and energy made him changeable and unreliable and even uncooperative in pursuit of any general aim. His piety was not programmatic. It was a Christ- and self-centered faith, raveling strands of Christian humility and proud self-satisfaction that released vital energy but gave little direction.[156]

It can be argued here that pietistic religious views, far from turning Moser in upon his unworldly self (as some traditional interpretations of pietism might suggest), instead urged him directly outward to change his world. This is a capital theme of Reinhold Rürup's good book about Moser, with its subtitle "Pietism and Reform"; and it follows upon judgments of pietism made by Carl Hinrichs about its relation to a Prussian moral and political style in general and to Frederick William I in particular.[157] Where the theologians Spener and Francke had reformed theology, goes the argument from pietist pattern, Moser turned with similar spirit to the public law and the state. Moser's pedagogical plans make a case for this, though the argument extends to his jurisprudence and his politics. But even there it is hard to see a thing called pietism behind his programs, or even reform as a general conception. It is not hard to see Moser in them, though: his failure and rejection at two universities and his inability to find a place at another; his insistence on his own practicality as a working jurist; his contempt for high-flown

155. *Lebensgeschichte*, II, pp. 92–94; *Hanauische Berichte*, I (1750), pp. 559–93 and passim; Gottfried Mälzer, "Johann Jacob Moser als Journalist," *Archiv für Geschichte des Buchwesens*, VIII (1967), pp. 1395–1403.

156. See on this point generally Günther, "Psychologie des deutschen Pietismus," especially pp. 151–53. But Ritschl, *Pietismus*, III, pp. 28–29, finds Moser for this reason a "möglichst entgegengesetzte Erscheinung" in German pietism: that Moser's *Bekehrung* had no effect on his worldly activities.

157. Rürup makes the point most explicitly in *Moser*, pp. 46–50; Hinrichs, *Friedrich Wilhelm I, König in Preussen* (Hamburg, 1941), and *Preussentum und Pietismus* (Göttingen, 1971). This argument seems often affected by an implicit effort to link German pietism with English puritanism and French jansenism. See also Horst Schlechte, "Pietismus und Staatsreform 1762/63 in Kursachsen," *Archivar und Historiker: Festschrift H. O. Meisner* (Berlin, 1956), pp. 364–82; and Eduard Winter, *Der Josephinismus und seine Geschichte* (Brünn, 1943), which associates josephinism with jansenism.

ideas and fancy phrases. He had himself in mind, and exercising himself by making things work; and his piety indeed related to these. But his justification lay between him alone and God, with Jesus to mediate; and neither God nor Jesus told him how to find a law or run an office, and they had better not.

Moser could never give allegiance to a whole community or a whole system of thought, nor wholly submit himself to a goal shared with others—that is the salient fact of his career. For that disposition, as Münchhausen seemed to say, his private justification in faith was an indispensable, or inescapable, foundation. What was missing in the *Teutsches Staats-Recht* was commitment to a positive whole idea; there was no affective principle of a kind to urge and guide his knowledge and thought into a mutuality. That lies partly in the nature of the empire that was his subject, and in his market and his method; but still Moser by his own nature resisted any such domination by commitment. He rejected and rebelled against that even as he rejected and rebelled against the ties of pietist religious community at Ebersdorf. One may labor too hard for resolution of a character so resolutely divided, but perhaps too that is why Moser so insisted upon his compartments. It appears that the same absence of affective principle that left his jurisprudence in truth, and deliberately, a kind of *collecteana*, also left him unwilling to bear the constraints of membership in any community, or devotion to any master. Johann Jakob Moser was not an organization man, and that was part of his identification with the Old Law of the empire.

The student enrollment at the Hanau academy at the start of its second year, 1750–51, was down to nine. Pütter's enrollment at Göttingen was growing. The two exchanged notes that autumn. Pütter expressed gratitude for all Moser had done for him, and hoped that nothing he was doing caused Moser discomfort. Moser in reply told how he had said in a lecture that Pütter would one day surpass the giants Conring, Thomasius, and Treuer; and would Pütter here and there make mention of a new book of Moser's, and recommend a Göttingen bookseller to handle it? At the end of 1751 Moser received the call to be counsel to the Württemberg estates at Stuttgart, and promptly accepted; the Hanau academy disappeared. The Göttingen program in practical jurisprudence organized to preempt Moser there faded from the catalog about 1753, when Pütter was appointed full Ordinarius.[158]

158. Frensdorff, *Die ersten Jahrzehnte*, pp. 31–35; Stieda, *Nationalökonomie*, p. 45. But according to Ebel, *Pütter*, p. 37, Pütter continued successfully to teach an *Anleitung zur juristischen Praxis*. Gottlieb Samuel Treuer, senior jurist at Göttingen, had died in 1743.

PART III

State Politics and the Constitutional Conflict in Württemberg

§19. Counsel to the Estates of Württemberg, 1751–1752

MOSER'S years as counsel to the estates of Württemberg, an office he held from 1751 to 1770, make a story in the politics of German principalities that is both peculiar and exemplary. The particularity of Württemberg was that the constitutional balance there, roughly even between prince and estates, brought out the issues and processes of dualist state politics in an unusually clear way. The particularity of Moser was his own righteous vehemence and indiscretion, his unwillingness to give full personal allegiance to anybody, and his compartmentalizing of roles. These allowed him to serve first one side, then another, or both at the same time—a behavior he conceived as a mediating or nonpartisan position but which, pursued in his partisan style, seemed to others more like inconsistency and disloyalty. Combining the particularities of Württemberg and of Moser the story becomes exemplary: a parable or fable of German state constitutional politics where the facts are true to type and visible, even accentuated to the edge of parody. The events brought Moser successively to long imprisonment by his duke, then to angry dismissal from his office by the estates. The imprisonment is the more notorious, but it was easier for Moser to accept and to bear than the dismissal was. One may deem the story in perspective to be a tragedy played at a crisis point of dualist politics, where Moser was caught in a constitutional chasm between the representatives of the duchy and its ruler; or it may be a tragedy of Moser's person, where in characteristic fashion he chose to antagonize and to defy both parties to a bitter dispute. Both are true, and in the sequence of events they are inseparable.

The Moser of those years emerged as the Moser of popular account and most biographies, including the one about himself he first published in 1768. The lonely old prisoner atop the Hohentwiel took shape as a patient martyr in the name of the Good Old Law, chosen victim of arbitrary and despotic wrong, yet firm in the right and serene in his faith, beloved of those who held the right.[1] There is a good deal of truth in that sentimental picture after all; this story is not disposed to refute it nor, on

---

1. Two examples designed for timely popular appeal bespeak the political resilience and versatility of the legend: Christian F. Hermann, *Johann Jakob Moser, der württembergische Patriot als Gefangener auf Hohentwiel* (Stuttgart, 1869), in verse, and Alo Münch, *Johann Jakob Moser, der Gefangene vom Hohentwiel* (Giessen, 1937), calling upon Christian readers to follow Moser's steadfast example.

the other hand, to gainsay altogether the enlightened reformist Moser of another telling.[2] To insist on either would be to demand retrospectively a political consistency and a location in the currents of history and of ideas that even Moser himself never really attained, admitted to, or accepted. Still, Moser's successive and willful failures as counsel to the estates of Württemberg became his life's triumph, in a way (quite suspiciously and not really accidentally) almost biblical. A goal of this chronicle is to put one thing after another as nearly as may be—above all, and to start, not to let the Moser that emerged a martyr to dominate the Moser who arrived in Stuttgart in October to take up his new post.

Domestic circumstances in the Moser household there were unpleasant from the start. The family was in transition. The two grown sons had left—Friedrich Karl was engaged at Frankfurt on Main in the apparently interminable Hessian negotiations, and Wilhelm Gottfried was a forestry official in Stollberg-Wernigerode—and there were five unmarried daughters and the tardily born Benjamin at home. Friderica Rosina, forty-eight, was unhappy and cranky at yet another move, and at this one in particular. There was less household money than there had been, partly because Moser had not held out for all the pay he might have got from the estates, a sign perhaps that he was reluctant to be altogether beholden to them. The Mosers were quartered in the estates' building at Stuttgart. They had fewer servants than before; Frau Moser quarreled with those, and there were constant changes. The girl who had been a poor relation in Stuttgart thirty years before missed triumph in return at middle age, and she naturally enough blamed her husband. When Moser remonstrated with her "lovingly" about her ill temper and her spats with the servants, she turned on him with a verse from Corinthians implying that Moser was a pious hypocrite who preached his homilies to benefit his vain and selfish ends, but she refused to detail or debate her meaning; so it stuck in his

2. See above, §18. The most thorough studies of this phase of Moser's career are Albert E. Adam, *Johann Jakob Moser als Württembergischer Landschaftskonsulent, 1751–1771* (Stuttgart, 1887); and Reinhard Rürup, *Johann Jacob Moser: Pietismus und Reform* (Wiesbaden, 1965), pp. 153–205. Adam knew the Württemberg politics of that time in great detail, but his account lacks historical breadth and biographical depth, and suffers from his exasperation at the fecklessness of his protagonists; Rürup's more thematic and sympathetic treatment is shaded by a monochromatic and I think misleading preoccupation with the theme of reform. On this issue Hartmut Lehmann, *Pietismus und weltliche Ordnung in Württemberg vom 17. bis zum 20. Jahrhundert* (Stuttgart, 1969), p. 104, insists that the Moser of the 1750s was no representative of pietism. Ursula A. J. Becher, *Politische Gesellschaft: Studien zur Genese bürgerlicher Öffentlichkeit in Deutschland* (Göttingen, 1978), presses Rürup's argument still further. Pursuit of her own theme leads her to overlook Moser's skepticism about the political rights and capacities of estates, Reich or Land, and so to miss an important reason for his insistence on the positive law.

mind.[3] Then she refused to pray in his company, a serious injury to his spirit. Moreover, that meant she prayed quite alone, and so did Moser; for they were partially ostracized by the Stuttgart religious community, even by surviving members of Moser's old family there. The Herrnhuth scandal had tainted the Mosers. Any emotional quality in religious exercise was particularly suspect, and religious exercise was Moser's emotional sphere, especially now: it was the only place he deeply sought himself or opened himself to others. But in his company the Stuttgarter preferred academically to discuss biblical texts.[4]

The religious situation in Württemberg was still sensitive and still politically and even constitutionally important. Confessional politics were at the bottom of the strong constitutional position that Protestant leaders of the estates and of the privy council had achieved against the ducal administration during Karl Eugen's minority. But to maintain that position depended on the suppression or tempering of pietistic passions and differences.[5] To understand Moser's behavior as counsel it is important to have in mind that when he arrived in 1751 the estates dominated a politically quiescent, Catholic, young Duke Karl Eugen. To understand estates' leaders it is important to remember the unstable base and the confessional nature of their predominance. Their champion in the administration was the state councillor Friedrich August von Hardenberg, who had been in and out of Württemberg state service since 1725, and who now in 1751 was the most influential figure in the government of the duchy. Hardenberg during the 1740s and early 1750s seems to have performed remarkably well in providing the kind of leadership the circumstances called for. It was he who had arranged a long sojourn by the adolescent Karl Eugen at the most powerful German Protestant court, at Berlin, during the last days of the Württemberg regency (and amidst the Austrian succession wars) in 1742–44. He had helped arrange Karl Eugen's marriage in 1748 to Princess Elisabeth Frederike Sophie of Brandenburg-Bayreuth, a favorite niece of Frederick II, so that Württemberg had a Protestant duchess with a powerful Prussian uncle. And it

3. 2 Corinthians 5:11. "Dieweil wir denn wissen, dass der Herr zu fürchten ist, fahren wir schön mit den Leuten; aber Gott sind wir offenbar. Ich hoffe aber, dass wir auch in eurem Gewissen offenbar sind."

4. Moser, "Nachricht von meinem natürlichen, bürgerlichen und geistl: Leben, Für meine Kinder und Nachkommen" (dated Hohentwiel, 12 September 1763; manuscript in the possession of Helmut Haecker at the Hirsch-Apotheke in Urach/Württemberg), pp. 64–65; *Lebensgeschichte Johann Jacob Mosers . . . von ihm selbst beschrieben*, 3d ed., 4 parts (Frankfurt/Main, 1777–83), II, pp. 219–21; Lehmann, *Pietismus*, p. 104; Albrecht Ritschl, *Geschichte des Pietismus*, III (Bonn, 1886), pp. 39–40.

5. See above, §12.

seems to have been Hardenberg who particularly commended Moser as counsel to the Württemberg estates.[6] Here already was an irony or a dissonance, in this association of the estates of Württemberg, through confession and dynastic marriage, with the autocratic Prussian monarchy. That kind of alliance was common enough in German politics, but for Counsel Moser the irony here got an imponderable twist from his own experience with the Prussian autocracy and his sentiments toward it.

The estates or Landschaft of Württemberg were understood to represent the interests of the country in matters affecting all its parts, for which purpose they might meet as an organized diet, also called Landschaft or Landstände.[7] The diet, in one house, was composed of two elements, neither of which was noble, for the knights of that region had left the Württemberg estates in the sixteenth century. First there were fourteen prelates, administrators by title of monastic properties incorporated into the duchy mainly during the Reformation; these posts were customarily held by Protestant theologians or ecclesiastics, some of them able men and administrators but more commonly indolent or at least politically inactive. Each prelate was legally accountable, for his action as an estate of the duchy, only to himself. Then there were some seventy deputies of the towns and districts, of which Stuttgart and Tübingen were recognized as preeminent. These deputies, unlike the prelates, were elected and instructed delegates; but as leaders of the groups that deputized them—town councils and district assemblies—they had a good deal to say about their own nomination and instruction. The customary political role and posture of the estates was to resist, guide, or at least make complaint about administrative initiatives that came from the duke's person or officials. They sustained their role by control over a large proportion of the duchy's fiscal resources, and also through political weight based on their regular and intimate relations with Württemberg society at large, and their familiarity with its structure and patterns of influence.[8] Moser's own general definition of German Landstände (set

6. *Allgemeine deutsche Biographie*, X (Leipzig, 1879), pp. 560–62; Walter Grube, *Der Stuttgarter Landtag, 1457–1957* (Stuttgart, 1957), pp. 425, 429; Adam, *Moser*, p. 5. On the boy Karl Eugen at the Prussian court, Eugen Schneider, "Herzog Karls Erziehung, Jugend und Persönlichkeit," in *Herzog Karl Eugen von Württemberg und seine Zeit*, I (Esslingen, 1907), pp. 29–40. Regarding the long memorial Miroir des Princes that Frederick of Prussia addressed to Karl Eugen when he attained majority in 1744: recall that the emperor whom Karl Eugen was urged to honor was Charles VII of Wittelsbach. *Oeuvres de Frédéric le Grand*, IX (Berlin, 1848), pp. 1–7. Frederick had urged the proclamation of Karl Eugen's majority upon the emperor in 1744 as a move against the dowager duchess of Württemberg and her adviser, the now bishop Friedrich Karl von Schönborn.

7. See above, §8.

8. Alfred Dehlinger, *Württembergs Staatswesen*, I (Stuttgart, 1951), pp. 79–87; Rürup,

down in 1731 and repeated almost verbatim in 1769) was "the body [*Corpus*] of those subjects who, by force of the freedoms or traditions of a land, must be consulted in certain concerns affecting the welfare of the land."⁹

The Württemberg diet, though, had not met in plenary session since 1739, when it had dissolved after the session addressed to crushing the remnants of the late Karl Alexander's rule. This was not an unusually long recess; before 1736 there had been no plenary diet since 1700. When no diet was in session (thus the usual situation) the estates' business was directed by the Small Committee (Engere Ausschuss), composed of two prelates and six deputies, always including the deputies of Stuttgart and Tübingen. The committee administered the estates' treasury and other affairs, notably including continual intercourse and negotiations with the duke and his officials, with the privy council, and with others who might have business with the estates. In the estates' offices at Stuttgart was a permanent appointive staff, which advised the committee and did the actual work of drafting memoranda, petitions, statements of position, and the like—one or more juridically trained counsels, plus an advocate, a secretary or two, messengers, and so on. It was not specified whether the counsels were responsible to the estates as a whole or to the committee, because the committee was deemed to speak for the estates when the diet was not sitting; but it was the committee that appointed counsels and other staff.¹⁰ At the time of Moser's appointment there were already three counsels: two were aged and inactive, and the other was Johann Friedrich Stockmayer, about Moser's age, a hard-bitten and experienced chancellery warrior, devoted to committee interests, who was simultaneously secretary and advocate as well. But Moser got the title of senior or first counsel.

Neither is it certain just how Moser conceived his place as counsel to

---

Moser, pp. 13–17. Moser himself prepared a "Kurze Einleitung in die Württembergische Staats- und Landes-Verfassung" in 1752, whose subsequent history was sketched by a commentator in 1785: LBS Cod jur 4° 239. It was so criticized and modified by censors that Moser refused to acknowledge it as his own work, and it was never published: *Lebensgeschichte*, III, p. 117. Subsequent drafts, whole or in part, abound: UBT Mh 202, 253, 712; LBS Cod his fol 557b. These documents, still mainly Moser's work, constitute a fascinating overview of constitutional dualism, but they cannot be used here to represent Moser's own views at any particular time. The existence of the Moser constitutions aroused great annoyance and suspicion especially in 1758 and in 1770.

9. *Compendium juris publici Germanici, oder Grundriss des heutigen Staats-Verfassung des Teutschen Reichs* (Tübingen, 1731), p. 564; *Von der Teutschen Reichs-Stände Landen, deren Landständen, Unterthanen, Landes-Freyheiten, Beschwerden, Schulden und Zusammenkünften* (= NTSR XIII: Frankfurt/Main, 1769), p. 322.

10. See above, n. 8.

the estates of Württemberg when he arrived—to whom or what body he thought himself ultimately responsible (besides of course himself). He set right to work as usual, straightening out the files and archives; he made abstracts with cross-references by date and topic for all modern negotiations between duke and estates, and for the deliberations of recent diets; he organized and indexed all actions taken by diets since the sixteenth century. This kind of administrative spirit was unusual at the Estates House. The committee was bemused but seemed pleased as long as this served their administrative and deliberative labors, and marshaled their own legal arsenal. Yet Moser clearly intended from the beginning to be something much more than an office manager and draftsman, if only because he conceived such a role to be beneath his dignity and deserts (to be sure, he had thought this about nearly every post he had ever taken, and this time at least Friderica Rosina concurred). In his explanation of why he took so low a post as counsel, written in the Life History of the 1760s, Moser to dignify it listed a series of predecessors in that office who had gone on from it to important positions of political authority, all, notably, as real privy councillors; so there it sounds almost as though Moser thought of the counselship as a stepping-stone to higher governmental office.[11] But this was written at a time when Moser was anxious especially to show that it was not inconsistent or disloyal for a counsel of the estates to serve other agencies of government as well, and that his true duty was not to the committee but to the duchy as a whole. What rings true in it is Moser's sense that it would demean him to be no more than an agent of the Small Committee.

The language of the appointment he had from the committee considered him entirely the estates' man: by its terms Moser was to be fully acquainted with all the affairs of the Landschaft, to attend all sessions of diet and committee, to make himself useful to them in every way, and finally, "concerning whatever is said or considered in council, or secretly in general diet, he shall be silent, and keep secret to himself unto death, and make it known to nobody."[12] By taking the office Moser at least implicitly assented to this description of it; and he always took pains to deny ever having betrayed any secrets that came to him by that office. But he never assented to being no more than the committee or even the estates made of him, or to doing no more than they asked of him. He had left Hanau and taken the post, he later wrote, because "if an estates counselor is up to his office, and if he has credit enough with the estates, then in many situations he can do more good and prevent more harm

11. *Lebensgeschichte*, II, pp. 94–95.
12. This is from a copy of the formal appointment dated 4 November 1741, retroactive to 27 July: UBT Mh 253.

JOHANN JAKOB MOSER, AGE FIFTY-ONE
*"In 1751 I answered a call to my Fatherland as counsel to the estates. Prelate
Bengel said to me: I had worked and endured all my life; now God had bestowed
this place on me so that I might live out my days in peace. I, however, saw the
matter then with quite other eyes." Moser, "Nachricht," p. 64.*
Württembergische Landesbibliothek, Stuttgart

than a privy councillor, more in fact than the whole college of privy councillors; and the court itself normally confides the conduct of estates matters to the counsel. Of course I knew," he added, "that this position could not be compared with some I had refused. But I knew what my fatherland was needing."[13]

Doing much good as well as preventing much harm, and what the fatherland needed—this was the language of active ambition and positive achievement. Moser was only a few years past the hothouse confines of Ebersdorf and the weary frustrations of imperial elections; he was bored with the *Teutsches Staats-Recht* (which had now reached forty-five tedious volumes with no end logically in sight); he had been balked as chancellor at Homburg; and his school at Hanau and his negotiations with Göttingen had brought no successes. Now Moser, his sons departing, had passed his fiftieth year, perhaps uncertain of his remaining powers, surely afflicted by frustrated energies and ambitions unachieved: and as counsel to the estates, Moser meant to take an active role in guiding the government of the duchy.

But the estates and committee were, by their institutional principle, their political ethic, and historical experience, hostile to any administrative ambition, energy, or innovation, for these forceful qualities in the nature of things were the tools of their constitutional rivals, the duke's own officers and entourage. Recall again, though, that the government of Karl Eugen so far had been quite passive; the young duke himself showed interest in little beyond his private needs and satisfactions. Indications are that Privy Councillor Hardenberg had brought Moser from Hanau with just this situation in mind, hoping, by injecting some initiative and energy into the estates, to forfend recourse to active and arbitrary government by the Catholic duke. Hardenberg barely appears in Moser's account; Moser was oddly reluctant to write about him, and I cannot guess how much he relied upon him in his relations with the committee.[14] Anyway Moser hardly needed a cue. He began by lecturing the committee, in meetings and in writing, about their customarily fuzzy procedures when confronted with a government demand: the invariable dragging of feet, the wrangling and bargaining, the compromise or concession at the end. One should go immediately to the correct final position, Moser said, and there stand on it. One should not antagonize a ruler unnecessarily,

13. *Lebensgeschichte*, II, p. 95.

14. Hardenberg may be the "otherwise stalwart privy councillor" who warned the busy Moser against the posture of "Reformator." *Lebensgeschichte*, II, pp. 98–99. Probably one reason Moser did not like to mention Hardenberg was that he did not help him and may have turned against him, hoping even to replace him, when Hardenberg was dismissed by Karl Eugen in 1755. See below, §21.

but neither should one ever give way on a position once taken; so take only the ones you mean properly to stand by. Moreover, even though a government's demands might seem oppressive (on this particular occasion only some minor forest and military obligations were at stake), that was less harmful to the country than governmental neglect.[15]

Having instructed the committee and its staff on how to carry out the business of the estates, Moser then set about telling them what needed to be done. Late in 1752, the issue was a special grant of thirty thousand gulden Karl Eugen wanted from the estates toward the construction of the new residential palace at Stuttgart. There is every reason to believe that estates leaders were inclined to support construction of this new residence, despite the expense, in the hope that the duke thereby might be induced to forsake the exclusively court-oriented society at Ludwigsburg in favor of the sphere of their own predominance centered at Stuttgart. This is a political estimation, appropriate to the estates' way of thinking. Moser's thoughts on the matter were fiscal and administrative, and he took the occasion for a disquisition on money and political economy: the preservation and increase of the sources of public finance and public activity, based on the general prosperity of the duchy.[16]

Württemberg suffered from a serious shortage of money, Moser said (so far so good; estates always said that). Crops stayed in the barns, artisans could neither buy nor sell. Moreover, there was an unfavorable balance of trade or of payments: of some five million gulden circulating, Moser claimed, about two hundred thousand left the duchy every year, which meant, inasmuch as Württemberg had no gold or silver mines to replenish the supply, that at this rate there would be no cash left in twenty-five years and all would stagnate and starve. Borrowing money at interest from outside the duchy (a point aimed at the government) made the situation worse. If the monetary supply was not stabilized and taxes were not held down, no merchant or manufacturer would settle in Württemberg, and her sons would go to America to be free from eternal tax burdens and economic restraints.

Moser went on to particularize the complaints and conditions that should be put before the government before any consent to the palace construction grant. Taxes should be lowered, to reduce the volume of private debt and allow prices to rise; if the duke replied with increased military appropriations so as to inflate his own budget, the estates should

15. *Lebensgeschichte*, II, pp. 99–101, quoting from a manuscript memorandum whose original I have not seen; see also Rürup, *Moser*, p. 158.

16. Memorandum reprinted by Albert E. Adam as "Württemberg vor dem siebenjährigen Krieg, geschildert in einem Gutachten Johann Jakob Mosers vom 9. November 1752," *Württembergische Vierteljahrshefte für Landesgeschichte*, NF XII (1903), pp. 205–26.

refuse assent even to ordinary levies, and should call for a plenary diet. Soldiers whose enlistment terms were over should be released, and cavalry should not be quartered on the country. Boar and deer damaged the rural economy, and peasants should be allowed to hunt them without being prosecuted by the forest administration, however noisily the duke and his cronies might lament the ruination of the hunt.

Now, a particularity of this memorandum of Moser's (and of a similar one that followed)[17] is the way it moved back and forth between two themes: for one part, the general poverty of the country and its inability to pay, a routine complaint on the part of the estates, and for the other part, the means for improving the supply of money and the vitality of the economy, a customary ambition of governments.[18] Moser put both brands of political rhetoric together. He even proposed that ducal officials should sit right down with officials of the estates, collect accurate information, and put it together to see just what the resources of the countryside were! This was behavior more than odd on the part of a counsel to the estates, one who thought that post in itself rather beneath him, and who had taken little interest in how much they would pay him. For now, as counsel to the Württemberg estates, of all things, the jurist Moser was becoming captivated by the sciences of innovative political economy and administrative efficiency, the police and cameral sciences, which by their nature and through their sponsors were almost antithetical to the constitutional and political positions of estates, and even to the Old Law of conditioned rights upon which the rights and powers of estates were based.[19]

On one matter (before turning to that large issue) Moser stood firmer indeed than the committee found comfortable; and this may be what precipitated Moser's memoranda on political economy. At the end of 1752 Karl Eugen, looking about for a way to exceed the financial limits and escape the controls laid upon him by the regency settlement of 1739,

17. Summarized in Rürup, *Moser*, pp. 175–76; see also Albert E. Adam, "Herzog Karl und die Landschaft," in *Herzog Karl Eugen von Württemberg und seine Zeit*, I, p. 201. Testifying to Württemberg concern over the emigration to America: the rescript of 5 May 1750 in August L. Reyscher, *Sammlung der Württembergischen Gesetze*, XIV (Tübingen, 1843), pp. 348–49.

18. Possibly a tenth of the cash money in Württemberg passed through the hands of the government every year in peacetime, if Moser's total figure of five million is accurate. Compare here the figure for the 1730s in Karl O. Müller, "Die Finanzwirtschaft in Württemberg unter Herzog Karl Alexander (1733–1737)," *Württembergische Vierteljahrshefte für Landesgeschichte*, NF XXXVIII (1932), pp. 276–317.

19. On the divergence of cameralistic from jurisprudential thinking, see my article, "Rights and Functions: The Social Categories of Eighteenth-Century German Jurists and Cameralists," *Journal of Modern History*, L (1978), pp. 234–51.

negotiated a military assistance agreement with the French government, whereby in return for a regular cash annuity he undertook to provide several regiments of infantry on demand, and thus in effect placed his foreign policy in French service. This was no proper business of the estates, he argued, for it would cost them nothing—indeed, it would relieve the financial obligations laid upon them. Moser drafted a sharp memorandum for the committee denouncing the project. To the question of the estates' proper business, Moser warned that if Württemberg subjects were sent into the service of a foreign prince, there might be a general popular rising that the estates could not control, nor themselves escape.[20] Cameral political scientist he would become, despite his office with the estates; but that did not make him a partisan of princely glory either. He seems not to have seen the political contradiction, or if he saw it he did not let it distract him.

§20. Counsel as Cameralist, 1753–1754

PARTLY at least it was the state of Moser's own temper that made him unwilling to be a simple servant of the estates, let alone of the committee. Reordering their archives and clarifying their procedures he did reflexively, after his fashion at Hessen-Homburg, causing similar irritations among the administrative staff. Drafting the committee's documents gave him a considerable voice, and he was indefatigable at that. He wrote clear and forceful statements, unlike his own previous jurisprudence and quite unlike the tone that customarily ruled documents emanating from the estates, with their plaintive grumbling, riddled with pious exclamations and smothered with constitutional jargon. Moser's ways made the second counsel and secretary Stockmayer in particular uneasy; Stockmayer had served the committee and often dominated it for twenty years, and these were not his habitual ways of managing their affairs.[21] Moser was legal adviser to the estates, but even his established role and profession as jurist had come to seem stuffy and dull and insuf-

20. Adam, "Herzog Karl," pp. 200–201; Eugen Schneider, "Regierung," in *Herzog Karl Eugen von Württemberg und seine Zeit*, I, pp. 149–50; Grube, *Stuttgarter Landtag*, p. 428.

21. On the Stockmayer dynasty and on the character of this Johann Friedrich Stockmayer: Adam, *Moser*, pp. 4–5, 16–18; and below, §23.

ficient to him. For thirteen years as counsel he published almost no jurisprudence except for some perfunctory last volumes of the *Teutsches Staats-Recht*, which he let lapse in 1753, and some particular tracts and documents addressed to current issues. This was the time when, by his testimony, "cameral, provisioning, and police sciences were my favorites, and I burned with eagerness to serve my fatherland with them."[22] And he did not contain his eagerness within the confines of his post as estates counsel.

As soon as Moser came to Stuttgart he tried to reestablish there his Hanau academy, which had included in its curriculum the subject of "Teutsche Staats-Klugheit," an approximation in Moser's German of *raison d'état*. Staats-Klugheit was altogether secular and political, and it stood apart from questions of particular vested rights. Its sources, in contrast with jurisprudence, were "natural wit, theoretical knowledge of the German constitution, and experience," wrote Moser; and it dealt with what governments could do by virtue of their Landeshoheit, the territorial authority of imperial princes.[23] But reestablishment of his academy in Württemburg was blocked by fears that it might compete with the university in Tübingen; and opposition was all the more vocal when he tried later to set it up in the ducal town of Ludwigsburg. Moser also proposed a "Patriotic Society" for the Duchy of Württemberg, to study its politics and organization, its agriculture, manufactures, commerce, and economic regulation (Polizey). The society was meant to stimulate and to guide public interest and to prepare specific proposals for improvement; but it smacked of "reform" and came to nothing.[24] Suggestions like these quickly identified Moser with a political type marked at the time with epithets like "project makers," "coin clippers," "plus makers," "wind puffers": political impresarios who came tempting governments with fanciful schemes for increasing their wealth and power, schemes of government which, said their critics, ended with collapse and with economic and political harm to their subjects. Bodies like the estates of Württemberg had a sharp eye out for projectors, especially when they made open appeal to public opinion or spurred the avarice of

---

22. *Lebensgeschichte*, IV, p. 114.

23. *Nähere Anzeige derer Teutschen Staats-Sachen, welche in der Moserischen Staats- und Cantzley-Academie Ersten Class abgehandelt werden* (Hanau, 1749), pp. 14–61. In 1739 Moser had distinguished *Staats-Klugheit*, as "general-Politic," from *Staats-Raison*, as "special-Politic," in his *Allgemeine Einleitung in die Lehre des besonderen Staats-Rechts aller einzelnen Stände des heil. Röm. Reichs* (Frankfurt/Main, 1739), p. 5.

24. *Lebensgeschichte*, II, pp. 98–99, 108–9; Rürup, *Moser*, p. 179; the proposal for the patriotic society was printed in Friedrich Karl Moser's *Wöchentliche Franckfurtische Abhandlungen*, XX (1755), pp. 305–20.

princes.[25] The estates thought there was enough government going on in Württemberg already.

Moser tried to persuade them with a discourse entitled "Principles of a Reasoned Art of Government." The *vernünftige Regierungs-Kunst* of the title already had a rationalist and systematic ring to it, even beyond the Staats-Klugheit of the Hanau academy curriculum; and the rather startling favorable use of *vernünftig* echoes in odd contrast the encounter with Morgenstern in Prussia, and the aftermath in Ebersdorf—a separation in time, or roles, or both.[26] Moser laid his discourse before members of the committee. One old prelate read away at Moser's manuscript for a time and then said to Moser in grumpy sarcasm, this is so fine that it aches my teeth to think how nothing will come of it: a remark that Moser quoted in Swabian dialect, something he used nowhere else in the Life History but in this passage. Another prelate declared to Moser, "I've told the duke time and again: Your Grace! *nuh nex nuis!* just nothing new!" Moser retorted that the prelate was wearing a periwig after all, and once periwigs had been something *nuis*. "Aha," returned the prelate, "but I wouldn't have worn a wig when that was *nuis*."[27]

Moser published this "Reasoned Art of Government" early in 1753 at Stuttgart without putting him name on it, but the text made his identity, counsel to the Württemberg estates, clear to anybody who knew anything about the affairs of Württemberg. Introducing it he invoked the memory of the late Frederick William I of Prussia, who by bringing cameral and police science to bear on his administration had succeeded in raising his house "to a position respected by all Europe." The art of government was no secret lore, claimed Moser (that distinguished it from what he heard and did as counsel). It had been a public science since the time of Aristotle, and nobody, "of high or low estate, in or outside the land," would find any breach of confidence or cause for annoyance in what he had to say about it. Anyway he would stick to fundamentals here and avoid specifics; it was his duty to lay these correct principles before his ruler, the ministers, the estates, and the whole public.[28]

25. For definitions and examples of *Plus-Macher*, Johann Gottlieb Justi, *System des Finanzwesens* (Halle, 1766), pp. 83–94. The term seems generally equivalent, though perhaps more strongly pejorative, to the terms "projector" and *projecteur* elsewhere in early modern Europe. John Elliott, "Self-perception and Decline in Early Seventeenth-Century Spain," *Past and Present*, no. 74 (1977), pp. 41–61, identifies a Spanish variant, *arbitristas*, as serious critics of old-regime finance, on the way to modern political economy.

26. See above, §§9, 11.

27. *Lebensgeschichte*, II, pp. 102–3.

28. *Einige Grund-Saetze einer Vernünftigen Regierungs-Kunst, nach der jetzigen*

The main principles of "reasoned government" Moser found in police and cameral science, whose main objects were the natural produce of the land, the population, and money. Respecting the first: every government must learn as much as it can about the productive capacity of the country—a) animal, b) vegetable, c) mineral—and do everything possible to scout out new resources and raise the productivity of existing ones. Then respecting population: the basic principle was that no country should have fewer inhabitants than its productive capacity would support, but no more either. No member of the state or inhabitant of the land should be left unuseful to the common weal, and "where their goodwill fails, then institutions must be so made as to oblige them." Government should see that not too many people took up their time with studying, or with writing (this from Moser); rather, the sort of people who tended toward these often sterile occupations should be encouraged to enter "wholesale commerce, exchange, factories, and the like," instead of reproducing their kind "in heaps." The bedrock of the common weal was the "middling man," who provided more support to the common weal and imposed less burden "than the capitalist is inclined to do, or than the poor man can."[29]

Money was the main instrument of political economy, and the three principles of managing money were these: 1) keep as much as possible of a country's money supply from leaving it; 2) attract as much as possible from outside; and 3) maximize the internal circulation of money, so that each party to the economy will through monetary exchange provide steady livelihood to the others. Unnecessary imports should be located and prohibited, with special attention to goods that were or could be produced at home. Natural produce in excess of what was needed at home should be sold abroad. But the best source of money from outside was not natural produce but a country's industry and commerce, developed by the "art and energy" of its inhabitants. Transportation and post facilities, exchanges, prompt justice, and good schools were the underpinning for industry and commerce and thus a primary responsibility of government.

Moser was fascinated by the notion of the velocity of money circulation (he used the term *Circulation*, and no direct cognate for velocity, nor the later German term *Umlauf*). This seemed a magical way of increasing money and wealth. Without movement, on the other hand, a country could be full of money and still be poor; the value of the money depended

---

Gedenckens-Art und Handels-Weise verständiger Regenten, Ministers und Land-Stände (Stuttgart, 1753), pp. 3–7.

29. *Einige Grund-Saetze*, pp. 9–11.

on how frequently it changed hands. So money was an economic commodity, but a peculiar one in this respect. It was circulation that converted the hoards of the "capitalists"—hoards actually a public liability if they were inactive—into a productive element of the common weal. What made money move was trade and exchange, "Handel und Wandel," and manufacture. These in turn called for capital. Often commercial undertakings or factories were only feasible as joint enterprises or "societies." Great personages and other "capitalists" should be encouraged to participate in such societies, but not to dominate them nor to speculate in them: they should neither throw their weight about in the conduct of business, nor put their money in and out capriciously to take profit. A large enterprise required careful and sober planning, and without it no personage should invest. For a factory to develop a successful export trade—that was its essential place in the state economy—it must offer a new invention, or else especially high quality, or else especially low prices.[30]

All the foregoing was a rather unremarkable distillation of German cameralist wisdom of a century past (partly excepting the doctrine of money velocity, which I have not found common).[31] Moser followed it with a series of reflections or exclamations that seem more particularly addressed to his own customary ways of thinking as a jurist, compared with what he was thinking now about Württemberg. He noticed for one thing that "in trade and exchange and police there is something systematic and coherent [systematisches und zusammenhangendes]. One particular meets the other; one natural gift, one transaction, manufacture, or establishment must reach its hand to the other." That quality seemed to give governments a particular role, and suggested in turn what government ought to be like and to be about. Both rulers and estates should assist economic enterprises with advice and financial support—only practical and feasible enterprises to be sure, but they must not be frightened away by "the hated name of project making [Projectenmacherey]," or by the "groans and cries" emitted by people who had "an inordinate fear of anything new." First responsibility in this lies with the ruler. Where he does not understand such matters, then, he must have ministers who do.

30. *Einige Grund-Saetze*, pp. 11–18.

31. Wilhelm Roscher first observes the doctrine of velocity in German political economy with Johann Georg Büsch's *Abhandlung von dem Geldumlauf* (Hamburg, 1788): Roscher, *Geschichte der National-Oekonomik in Deutschland* (Munich, 1874), pp. 559–76. Justi paid it no attention in *System des Finanzwesens*, but it appears in Johann August Schlettwein, *Grundfeste der Staaten oder die Politische Ökonomie* (Giessen, 1779), pp. 327–52. It reaches back further in English and French traditions: M. W. Holtrop, "Theories of the Velocity of Money in Earlier Economic Literature," *Economic History*, I (1929), pp. 503–24.

If he does not have them . . . but Moser did not go on to assign any active function to estates or diets for economic regulation or enterprise. To be sure, it was the duty of estates to support and not to block government economic measures of this nature, and it was their right to be heard where legitimate rights were at stake; but they could not plan or act without the ruler or ministry. Moser the cameralist could never attribute to estates or their organs a power of legislative or administrative initiative in political economy. That was the work of responsible administrative officials with a rational grasp of the systematic whole.[32]

A second thing that struck Moser about cameralism and police, along with their systematic and coordinate nature, was their universal applicability. These were rules that worked anywhere—anywhere in Germany, anywhere in the world, he said; they were, thus, no "school-whimsies" or fantasies; he proposed no Platonic republic. "And if our ancestors did not think in this way, and yet a country prospered: now we no longer live in the times of our ancestors." It was true that there were imperfections in the observed conduct of cameralistics and police, as in all human activities; "but for that very reason we need something complete as a model [Muster]"; for in political economy if we allow principles to be obscured by particular phenomena, nothing complete or solid can be achieved.[33]

Moser's reasoning here was about as different from that underlying the *Teutsches Staats-Recht* as the mind can imagine. Again these "principles," though philosophically unconventional in spots, were not new or original with him. What they show is that Moser was well versed in what contemporary police and cameral scientists had been saying and writing during the years he had devoted to jurisprudence and chancellery practice. As far as I can tell, he himself had never before published a word on the subject of political economy, just as now his work in jurisprudence had almost wholly lapsed. The other surprising thing is the systematic, rationalist cast and rhetoric of the essay itself. Not only was it more systematic in sense and form than anything Moser the jurist himself had written. It was also more systematic, or rather more imbued with a sense of the harmonic relation of economic activity with police administration, than most other, full-time writers on the subject had then attained; the work of Johann Justi, great systematizer of these sciences, had scarcely begun to appear. The point is not that Moser was clever about this, nor that he had been reading a lot, but that at this place in his life and career he seemed to fall in love with dynamic system; and political economy remained his "favorite subject" until he went to the Hohentwiel. A biog-

32. *Einige Grund-Saetze*, pp. 18–23.
33. *Einige Grund-Saetze*, pp. 23–24.

rapher is unprepared for this sudden turn of mental style and interest; unquestionably the Small Committee of the Württemberg estates was too; and Moser's own language for the "Principles" of 1753 reveal this particular jurist's naive intellectual giddiness and wonder: here was a discipline of human relations that was essentially systematic, integral, and coherent, *zusammenhangend,* one moreover which, quite unlike the law as he had professed it, could be applied anywhere. It was a different thing altogether from the law.

He continued to study it while he was active counsel to the estates. He founded and edited a journal called "Swabian News on Economic, Cameral, Police, Commerce, Manufacture, Mechanical, and Mining Matters" that ran 1756–57; in 1758 he published a bibliography on political economy that is still useful.[34] His favorite authors seem to have been Georg Heinrich Zincke, whose best work had begun to appear in the 1740s, and Justi, whose career was just beginning. It is worth remarking here that Zincke, as court councillor and favorite at Weimar, had a decade before been accused, convicted, and imprisoned for three years for having "harmed the interests of the land," and that Justi was to die in the Prussian fortress at Küstrin in 1771.[35] The political issues were not trivial.

Moser's own aggressive temperament, and his drive for activity and achievement and its frustration over recent years, fired his avid interest in these matters during the early 1750s. So too, no doubt, did his intellectual fascination; and so too perhaps (as the committee probably suspected) did an unspoken hope for high administrative office or academic position. But this was no whole commitment to a program of constitutional reform; for alongside Moser the political economist still lived Moser the partisan of established right; and the constitutionalist, when invoked, was as energetic and uncompromising as the economist. And Karl Eugen grew more and more restive, trying to break through or around the dual domination of privy council and estates. The French subsidy nego-

34. *Schwäbische Nachrichten von Oeconomie- Cameral- Policey- Handlungs-Manufactur- Mechanischen und Bergwercks-Sachen,* 10 parts (Stuttgart, 1756–1757); *Gesammelte und zu gemeinnützigem Gebrauch eingerichtete Bibliothec von oeconomischen, Cameral- Policey- Nahrungs- Manufactur- Mechanischen und Bergwercks-Gesetzen, Schrifften und kleinen Abhandlungen* (Ulm, 1758).

35. Summarily on Zincke (1692–1768), Erhard Dittrich, *Die deutschen und österreichischen Kameralisten* (Darmstadt, 1974), pp. 90–93; and *Allgemeine Deutsche Biographie,* XLV (Leipzig, 1900), pp. 313–15. On Justi (1720–71), Dittrich, *Kameralisten,* pp. 103–10; *Allgemeine Deutsche Biographie,* XIV (Leipzig, 1881), pp. 747–57. Johann Friedrich Pfeiffer (1718–87) spent time in Spandau in the 1750s under an apparently false accusation of peculation—Dittrich, *Kameralisten,* p. 80; and *Allgemeine Deutsche Biographie,* XXV (Leipzig, 1887), pp. 641–42.

tiations, to take one example of this, presented the committee with a dilemma. For if they were parsimonious with the money they delivered to the duke, that might make him turn to outside resources like these which they could not control and which thus posed serious political dangers to them. Indeed, Karl Eugen seems deliberately to have used this threat of turning to outside sources (here the French) as a means of extorting money grants and other concessions from the estates. On the other hand, if they readily gave him what he asked, their ability to influence and restrict his government through control of the purse strings was undercut and discredited. And whatever the politics of it, hard money was involved. Their chosen as well as customary way was to bargain, to temporize, to compromise. Early in 1753 the committee proposed to Karl Eugen that the privy council should mediate their fiscal differences; the duke refused and rode contemptuously off to Venice for Carnival. From there, apparently, he sent a demand directly to the estates—pointedly bypassing the constitutional mediacy of the privy council—for the large sum of one hundred thousand gulden, to cover his treasury deficits and meet his military requirements. The committee refused and Karl Eugen in irritation returned home personally to press his demand.[36] He would have his money.

What position ought the committee now take? Moser gave adamant counsel: where Karl Eugen behaved unconstitutionally the estates had no obligation to him whatever and need say no more than their refusal. What, refuse and say no more? That would risk everything, and gain nothing out of the situation. It was not the style of the counsel-secretary Stockmayer, nor of the senior prelate Wilhelm Gottlieb Tafinger, who was joined with Stockmayer into a kind of copresidium in the committee. Stockmayer, old hand at the Estates House, strongly opposed the intransigent posture Moser wanted, and argued heatedly for the tactics of delay and bargaining, so as to extract every possible concession from the duke over a long course of negotiations—and then see what to do. That was the tested way, and not at all an unreasonable or unfruitful way. The committee was divided but finally chose Stockmayer's way. At first Moser said he would conform to the tactical decision. But after another disquisition on the indignity and futility of saying no, no, again no, and finally yes, and after discovering a legal argument that by this tactic the committee would be exceeding the powers accorded it by the diet plenum now in recess, Moser declared he would have nothing more to do with the matter and asked to be excused from participating further. His challenge to Stockmayer thus oddly included a slur on the legitimacy of a committee decision. Stockmayer promptly called it an attack upon his own

36. Adam, "Herzog Karl," pp. 202–3; Grube, *Stuttgarter Landtag*, pp. 428–29.

integrity and asked to resign his office rather than put up with it. The committee managed to calm him and for a time to smother this test of strength between counsels.[37]

In September of 1753 the issue between duke and committee was compromised: the committee provided fifty thousand gulden in return for promises from Karl Eugen that he would ameliorate his objectionable military and forest practices. But tension remained alive: the duke commenced to make inroads on ecclesiastical properties, which by the agreements of 1733 and 1739 were to be controlled by the privy council with the estates' oversight and approval. Again Moser called for intransigence, to bring the fight into the open. Ever since the first confrontation with Karl Eugen a year before he had urged convocation of a diet; and now the introduction of ecclesiastical matters and the bypassing of the privy council raised, to Moser's thinking, serious constitutional issues. But the committee viewed the prospect of a plenary diet without enthusiasm. That very victory of the 1737–39 diet over the dowager duchess, the Austrian party, and Schönborn, which had established the political predominance of the estates and privy council, had freed the committee from dependency on the diet in their dealings with the regency and then the duke. In this position the committee had begun to think of reactivated estates as a potential limitation on its power, not a support for it. Again it preferred to delay and to bargain—what Moser called *lavieren*, tacking across the wind. There may have been more on their minds; for there was more in the situation. Perhaps, with the international scene threatening and French money in the offing, the committee was reluctant to drive the Catholic Karl Eugen into a corner particularly over ecclesiastical issues, afraid of an open constitutional showdown that would invoke religious alignments—as ultimately happened. If Moser shared such anxieties his response was quite opposite: right was right. But maybe Stockmayer in his way was right too.[38]

Surely Moser by 1754 was a difficult figure for the committee to comprehend. That is not because they were obtuse, but because Moser's own position was politically ambiguous, and the committee in fact thought far more politically than did he. The forthrightness of Moser's opinions may have disguised the ambiguity of his position from himself; almost certainly it did. But consider: Here on the one hand was Moser the fiery defender of the inviolate rights of the estates against illegal princely initiatives, whose very intransigence in this role discomfited the committee and threatened not only to imperil their position but even to shatter the political equilibrium of the duchy. Here on the other was the earnest

37. Adam, *Moser*, pp. 18–19.
38. Grube, *Stuttgarter Landtag*, p. 429; Adam, "Herzog Karl," pp. 204–7.

impatient new Moser of cameralism and police, proclaimer of new efficient ways, economic theorist and improver. This was a sphere of governmental action that by Moser's own analysis belonged to energetic and
ambitious princes and their servants, who themselves hoped by calculated
economic and fiscal innovation to escape dependency on the estates and
attain political hegemony over them. The institutions of estates were not
expected nor equipped to govern political economy; that was an attribute
of the Landeshoheit, the territorial superiority of princes that estates
habitually and constitutionally restrained and opposed. Moser accepted
and understood the dualist constitution in this way, and stood firmly on
both sides of it—unless he thought he stood above it.[39]

Summarily: a prince's own fiscal interests were intertwined with the
general prosperity of his subjects, and there was "something systematic
and coordinated" in the art and nature of political economy. But that
something was alien and threatening to the art and nature of constitutional estates. The prince, Moser thought, must not violate the weal
of the land; and the estates must not obstruct it. But who in the end
was to say what the land's weal was? For that question was political,
and there the walls between economic and constitutional compartments,
between wealth and right, would not hold. Why, Grimmelshausen's Swabian peasants had asked, in the novel of the 1640s, when the Adventur-
ous Simplicius had offered them a magic spring that would bring wealth
and splendor to the land—why should we provide our master the stick to
beat us with?[40] *Nuh nex nuis*, said Moser's finger-wagging prelate.

§21. The Duke's Committeeman, 1755–1756

AROUND the middle of 1755, Duke Karl Eugen decided to break
out thoroughly of the political inactivity to which the estates'
victory of 1737–39 had assigned him. Up to that time his
demands of privy council and estates' committee had been of a semi-
private nature—funds for his court and household, for travel, for his new

39. Moser himself in 1731 had attributed to any imperial estate (as was Karl Eugen), by
virtue of the Landeshoheit, authority to issue laws on cameral, police, and artisanal subjects,
to establish factories and control foreign trade: *Compendium juris publici*, pp. 491–92.
40. In book V, chap. 18.

residence, for small ornamental military units, hunting privileges. These were normal everyday matters that the committee and council could absorb or bargain over; they were the expected price of his quiescence. Such were the customary irritants that sustained the desultory internal politics, the "Landespolitik," of small German states in the eighteenth century.

But Karl Eugen's naturally violent and domineering temperament had chafed in his passive and private role, and his duchy was not quite pretty enough to immunize it against princely ambitions. Twenty-seven years old, finally he would be a boy no more. Great events seemed impending in a retrial of strength between the great houses of Habsburg and Hohenzollern, summoning him to show his princely mettle and make his mark as a German ruler. Moreover, this German confrontation had been revitalized and altered by changes in the European scene that go down in diplomatic history as the "Diplomatic Revolution," which for the first time since the religious wars aligned Catholic France beside Catholic Austria against Protestant England and Protestant Prussia respectively.[41] This alignment of major powers underlined and evoked the confessional party alignments of the politics of the German empire. The conjuncture offered unusual and challenging opportunities to a Catholic duke of Württemberg, not only on the European and imperial scene but in his own duchy, whose constitutional poise was based on the confessional settlement. Thus did events at Vienna and Versailles, at Potsdam and Westminster, penetrate and arouse the politics of the Württemberg duchy.

So Karl Eugen set upon a vigorous political activity that grew rapidly into a full confrontation over who should rule in the Duchy of Württemberg. It was a struggle over mastery, for the realization of sovereignty. Johann Jakob Moser's imperial jurisprudence, to which all polar notions of sovereignty were alien, nowhere equipped him with ways to determine who was master, nor was his spirit so formed as to acknowledge the existence of any. He was counsel to the estates. Yet his temperament too, not unlike the duke's, had chafed under the ragged restraints of estates politics. Moser was pleased and excited when Karl Eugen summoned him to consult about how to bring new life and order to the administration of the duchy. The prospect interested Moser enough, it appears, so that at the same time he turned away tentatives from Baron Münchhausen in Hanover that Moser might come to Göttingen after all, to the administrative post of university chancellor. It is likely that Münchhausen with his usual acumen had thought out the situation developing

41. Max Braubach, *Versailles und Wien von Ludwig XIV bis Kaunitz* (Bonn, 1952).

KARL EUGEN OF WÜRTTEMBERG
"In the year 1755 His Grace the Duke began to manage many government affairs himself." Moser, Lebensgeschichte, *II, p. 103.*
Landesbildstelle Württemberg, Stuttgart

in Württemberg and the empire, and out of goodwill or out of policy hoped to extract Moser from one of its vortices.[42] Administrative craft was at work in Hanover as well as Ludwigsburg.

Karl Eugen's first step to show the scope of his intentions was to dismiss Privy Councillor Hardenberg, on 24 June 1755—an event Moser's Life History noticeably does not mention. Only days thereafter, apparently on the advice of the "Vienna *banquier*" Kühner, the duke brought Moser to his cabinet at Ludwigsburg.[43] There and at a series of private audiences that followed, he talked with Moser about the welfare of the land and questioned Moser at flattering length about his "Principles of a Reasoned Art of Government." On 29 June, Karl Eugen appointed a new "Deputation for Commerce," a body of experts set apart from the regular administrative structure and answerable only to him. It was headed by a privy councillor and included several other officials, three private businessmen, and "on behalf of the Estates, Counselor Moser." The deputation was ordered to produce a general rescript "which would encourage [Württemberg] subjects to take more thought of what can bring real benefit to themselves and the whole fatherland," and to institute rewards for anybody who would "work out and submit projects actually useful and profitable to the duchy."[44]

There was that word, *Projecta*, with its political and economic taint; Moser was prompt to caution Karl Eugen against "stupid or wicked project makers, who start off too grand and so ruin themselves and others at the start." He warned against "chimeric and Spanish castles in the air." Real improvements could not be "shaken out of the sleeve."[45] But proposals of every kind flowed in to the deputation, by the scores upon scores. Moser himself drafted at least twenty-seven memoranda (probably closer to forty) for Karl Eugen in late 1755 and early 1756, on every imaginable administrative topic: economics, politics, education,

42. The offer, if it was a real one, was relayed through F. K. Moser: Götz v. Selle, *Die Georg-August-Universität zu Göttingen* (Göttingen, 1937), p. 353; WHS KA III Ls 390 (Moser's papers seized in 1759 that were not subsequently returned).

43. Adam, *Moser*, p. 23. Moser in *Lebensgeschichte*, II, p. 103, wrote "Kiener"; although he makes no mention of Hardenberg's dismissal, on p. 104 he says defensively and abruptly that he was not party to any alienation between Karl Eugen and the privy council.

44. Gerhard Krauter, "Die Manufakturen im Herzogtum Wirtemberg und ihre Förderung durch die Wirtembergische Regierung in der zweiten Hälfte des 18. Jahrhunderts" (Ms. diss., Tübingen, 1951), pp. 242, 276. On the general history of the deputations, Wilhelm Söll, *Die staatliche Wirtschaftspolitik in Württemberg im 17. und 18. Jahrhundert* (Tübingen, 1934), pp. 99–116; Friedrich Wintterlin, "Zur Geschichte des herzoglichen Kommerzienrats," *Württembergische Vierteljahrshefte für Landesgeschichte*, N. F. XX (1911), pp. 310–27.

45. Three memoranda of July 1755, as cited in Rürup, *Moser*, p. 181.

finance—and a very considerable number about the selection of personnel for the duke's service. Most were directed to the business of more
than a half-dozen other special deputations to which Moser was also
appointed, on taxation, justice, charities, currency exchange, fire insurance, a mortgage bank.[46] Moser proposed a voluntary fund to support
widows and orphans, for example. This was a life insurance scheme
which, Moser claimed, would avoid the actuarial miscalculations and
frequent bankruptcies that had plagued such enterprises, by basing flexible payments to survivors on shares in a mutual investment trust, rather
than on fixed return to premiums paid.[47] This scheme was established in
law and survived. Another project, one dating back to Hardenberg's
initiative some years before, was for a fire insurance fund. Because the
estates had refused to underwrite fire insurance in the past, Moser's plan
was based on private funding received at interest; but nobody trusted it
enough to invest, and the project got nowhere. So then Moser proposed
an array of small mutual fire insurance societies without capital, to
which, he argued, "one might belong for fifty or a hundred years without
paying anything at all."[48] That scheme too came to nothing; nobody was
willing to operate it. No more effect, surely, had Moser's plan for a
reorganization of the university at Tübingen, which would have recruited
additional junior faculty, especially in the field of political economy, to
relieve the labors of tenured professors. Nor did a new plan for "the
advancement of the town of Ludwigsburg" by the establishment of a
political academy there on Moser's own Hanau model with himself as
director. More seriously, neither did the mortgage bank Moser proposed.
When the estates refused to support it or even commend it to private
investors, there was no money and no bank.[49] In Württemberg's political
circumstances, capital was hard to come by for public purposes, especially where public purposes meant the government of Karl Eugen and
where the estates would not pledge their credit. To the mind of the Small
Committee of estates, financial operations to generate money or credit
for public purposes meant money passing into and through the hands of
the duke's government, rival sphere to their own. Moser's chief legislative
achievement of those years was a vast community ordinance, compiled
from more than a thousand rescripts and privileges, which guaranteed

46. *Lebensgeschichte*, II, pp. 109–10; WHS KA III Ls 390; WHS KA III 1, 66–71.
Several of these are discussed in Rürup, *Moser*, pp. 182–88.
47. *Herzoglich-Würtembergische Ordnung für die allgemeine freywillige Wittwen- und
Waysen-Cassa* (Stuttgart, 1756); *Lebensgeschichte*, II, pp. 105–6.
48. *Lebensgeschichte*, II, p. 107; for the titles of four fire insurance proposals, see the
bibliography in Rürup, *Moser*, p. 266.
49. Rürup, *Moser*, pp. 185–86; *Lebensgeschichte*, II, pp. 106–9.

the local selection of communal officials and raised their emoluments; it was accepted by the committee and then published in 1758.[50]

"Would God," Karl Eugen wrote to Moser in July of 1756, after a year of this, "that everybody thought in such patriotic ways as do the Herr Counsel and myself; it would be to the good of lord and land." But those were not the committee's ways of thinking at all, though patriotism was a quality they considered peculiarly and properly an attribute of the estates. They were annoyed from the first moment their counsel lent himself to Karl Eugen's projects and insisted on knowing precisely everything that went on between him and the duke. Moser replied that he betrayed no estates secrets or interests in any of the services or advice he rendered Karl Eugen; and was it not better for the duke to be consulting an honest Protestant, a Württemberger, an estates counsel, rather than a Catholic, maybe, a soldier, a foreigner?[51]

But committee distrust and vexation grew as Moser gave more and more attention to the deputations and to his plans and memoranda for the ducal government. By drawing Moser into his sphere, Karl Eugen was using the estates' own counsel to bypass their right to advise and consent to legislative action: that was the committee's quite credible view, and they had explicit grounds. Special deputations or committees for specific purposes were not unprecedented, but by custom dukes had appointed to them some members chosen by the committee of the estates, from among their number, and answerable to them all. Moser was not of their number, nor had they chosen him to represent them (that was the flaw in his later claim to have been a bridge between parties). The committee informed Moser in meeting that he could not be construed, by themselves or by the government, to be their representative in anything he did without receiving or following their direct instruction.[52] But to receive or follow their instruction was exactly what Moser refused to do in his work for Karl Eugen, though he seems conscientiously to have reported to the committee those matters that he deemed their proper concern. The committee was incensed to learn that Moser had recommended to Karl Eugen that a single ducal minister (a title alien to Württemberg, with an ominous executive ring to it) should be appointed

50. *Lebensgeschichte*, II, pp. 110–12; text in Reyscher, *Sammlung der württembergischen Gesetze*, XIV, pp. 537–777. This ordinance remained in force until the young Friedrich List was assigned to revise it in 1817: List's *Schriften, Reden, Briefe*, I (Berlin, 1932), pp. 7–8, 12, and indexed notes passim.

51. WHS KA III Ls 390; *Lebensgeschichte*, II, pp. 103–4.

52. Moser's report of 10 June 1756 on a meeting of the committee, quoted in Hartmut Lehmann, "Die württembergischen Landstände im 17. und 18. Jahrhundert," in Dietrich Gerhard, ed., *Ständische Vertretungen in Europa im 17. und 18. Jahrhundert* (Göttingen, 1969), pp. 197–98.

to coordinate the whole program of commerce and political economy or Polizey, and indeed that the whole government should be organized systematically into departments for efficient rational administration.[53] Moser thought that was no business of the committee. The committee was sure it threatened their position and interests. They were quite unable to grasp Moser's proposition that he could do loyal duty in two compartments at once without being untrue to either. Stockmayer in particular was furious. The committee of the estates was his life's work and his whole being, and his working style and strategy of delay and compromise conflicted head-on with the direct procedures and speed of execution that attracted Moser to the duke's administration and to the sciences of administration. Chief Prelate Tafinger in meeting denounced Moser as *intrusus et obtrusus*: by intruding himself into the duke's councils, charged Tafinger, Moser had enabled Karl Eugen to obtrude upon the estates. Moser replied to this, he reports, "as it deserved."[54]

That was the position in Württemberg when war began between France and England in June of 1756. In August Frederick of Prussia invaded Saxony; and the Seven Years War, whose serious nature and wide ramifications for German politics were recognized there from the beginning, was under way. A French officer arrived in Stuttgart to inspect the regiments his government had been paying for these last four years. They simply were not there, for Karl Eugen had spent the money on other things; now the French insisted that he set about producing the troops he had contracted for. Frederick's niece, the duchess of Württemberg, departed the duchy for the Hohenzollern principality of Bayreuth: Karl Eugen was an ally of the French and of the emperor against her royal uncle, leader of the German Protestant party.[55] To the estates of Württemberg, the European events meant that they could no longer hope to rely on imperial justice to uphold their constitutional rights against their duke. For Johann Jakob Moser, counsel to the estates and busily engaged in Karl Eugen's administrative plans, supporter of the duke's aggressive fiscal and economic policies and constitutional adviser to the center of resistance to them—for Moser the position became difficult indeed. His separated compartments had become an excruciating bifurcation of roles.

53. Adam, *Moser*, p. 26; Rürup, *Moser*, p. 182, invokes this as an example of Moser's experience and clarity of vision.

54. *Lebensgeschichte*, II, p. 102; Adam, *Moser*, pp. 29–30.

55. P. Stälin, "Karl Eugen, Herzog von Württemberg," in *Allgemeine Deutsche Biographie*, XV (Leipzig, 1882), p. 379. For Karl Eugen's trouble in finding soldiers to fulfill the French treaty, A. von Pfister, "Militärwesen," in *Herzog Karl Eugen von Württemberg und seine Zeit*, I, pp. 121–27.

It is conceivable in principle that in some circumstances a dualist constitution like Württemberg's might have been well served by the presence of an official of the estates in the councils of the administration.[56] But any political situation that strained and polarized the two sides made it very difficult. Moser thought he could serve both by keeping their respective spheres clearly delineated, yet with his own person as bridge or pivot between them; and this makes an interesting analytical problem. One may even fairly claim on Moser's behalf that in this location he tried to make public purpose and progress, that theme and sphere of rational cameral administration, compatible with the rule of known law, the theme and sphere of a legally constituted society of estates. That in perspective is the fascination of this stage of his career, as an exposition of the crisis of the Old Law. These are large terms and issues to discern in the awkward situation of one cantankerous official. But when all the personal quirks and the accidents that had got Moser there are taken into account—the vanity of character, the proud religiosity and "unpartisan" independence, the pedantic ordering of roles and rights—what they did was place him at an intersection of political forces where nearly everybody, proportionally to the strains imposed by circumstances, was obliged to be partisan of one side or another.

Sometimes Moser seemed to perceive as time went on that the only moral ground upon which he could stand was that of general spokesman for the whole Württemberg state and people, an advocate and servant neither of the duke's government nor of the committee of the estates, a full-blown ethic of civil service.[57] But of course he never had the political authority or security to make such a pose real. Instead in practice he became advocate for both and tried to keep them apart by dividing himself.[58] Thus Moser tried to distinguish clearly between *Polizey* and *Recht*, between administrative purpose and constitutional right—a distinction that stands in contrast for example with the principles of natural law, which tended to equate law with purpose (as does twentieth-century totalitarian legality). But to insist on this distinction left Moser for one part with little save procedural norms for his jurisprudence, and, for

56. Compare Reinhard Renger on the case of Justus Möser in Osnabrück: *Landesherr und Landstände im Hochstift Osnabrück in der Mitte des 18. Jahrhunderts* (Göttingen, 1968), pp. 96–97.

57. See definitions of the modern civil servant in this sense in Hans Rosenberg, *Bureaucracy, Aristocracy and Autocracy; the Prussian Experience, 1660–1815* (Cambridge, 1958), p. 14.

58. Years later he observed that "alle Menschen können, wann sie verschidene Eigenschaften haben, auch verschidene moralische oder politische Personen vorstellen." *Versuch des neuesten Europäischen Völker-Rechts in Friedens- und Kriegs-Zeiten*, I (Frankfurt/ Main, 1777), pp. 10–11.

the other part, with few internal safeguards on the administration of power save personal morality and beneficence. That was a place where Moser and Württemberg, and the empire and the Europe in which they participated, were constitutionally vulnerable.

The duality between power and rights, here (returning to the case) between duke and estates, might in some circumstances be bridged and absorbed in Moser's terms of "what the fatherland needed," but only with great difficulty or violence in time of war—particularly for Württemberg then and in that war. Not merely was the confessional nature of Württemberg's political duality aggravated by the new confessional alignments of 1756, pitting Catholic against Protestant in Europe and in the German Empire. Any war to which the emperor was a party undermined those legal procedures and political mechanisms, the essence of the Holy Roman Empire, which Moser, and the Old Law of his *Teutsches Staats-Recht*, relied upon to maintain the distinctions and respective rights of constitutional spheres. And finally for this war, the turn of political gears had made the emperor himself an ally of Moser's master, Karl Eugen, against the estates he served as counsel. The restraining weight of imperial justice and imperial jealousy, normally working against German princes and part of the political calculus of any middling German state, was lifted from Karl Eugen of Württemberg.

During the next three years, from the beginning of the war until his arrest, Moser struggled painfully to sort out his position. His mind turned to the problem in whatever he wrote and said, no matter what the topic. (But it is odd that with all his penchant for biblical quotation, there is no sign he ever mentioned "No man may serve two masters," something he must have read a thousand times.) In an article published anonymously in Friedrich Karl's new "Weekly Frankfurt Commentaries," Moser examined the problem of finding a *raison d'état*, a rational political wisdom or science, for the German Empire itself. Could the principle live with the institution? The essay seemed a broad political analogy to the position in which he found his own person. "For as our Reich now is like a palace shaken terribly by earthquake, where nothing holds together any more, and collapse threatens first here, then there: so the Staats-Klugheit is needed more than ever before." Maybe all was up with the empire now, and with the law.

Still he held to the crucial distinction: "The Staats-Klugheit is an altogether different thing from the public law; for the latter teaches only the constitution of the state, the rights and duties of rulers, of estates, etc., without considering the strengths and weaknesses of states, their preservation or destruction, or providing rules on how actually to achieve what is right, where by contrast the Staats-Klugheit is concerned with just these subjects, but not with what is right."[59] Since 1755, when he had begun his work with Karl Eugen and had married off two daughters, Moser had been troubled by an illness he called "heaviness of spirit," *Schwermuth*, which he attributed to too much coffee and too little exercise. Along with this malady he grew fat. In 1756 as the war began, he began to be plagued with "hip-and-joint misery," *Hüft- und Glieder-Weh*, apparently a form of gout, which he blamed in turn on the violent exercise that had been prescribed to him to correct the depression and obesity—bodily exercise he hated. He now kept a close watch on his urine: it had been Moser's practice, since discovering symptoms of stone on official travels some years before, to save urine every morning and inspect it later. If it was dark or cloudy, or especially if it seethed, he knew his system was in trouble. He called this daily flask of urine his weatherglass, foretelling storms.[60]

Into late 1756 and early 1757 Moser maintained his campaign for active economic policies. He argued for them publicly in his "Swabian News on Economic Matters." That journal opened with an anonymous attack on the behavior of the estates, at the same time identifying their counsel to be its author. It was his own first duty and that of the estates, declared this hardly veiled Moser, to further the interests of the country and its inhabitants; and this meant not only to preserve the constitution, but also to support effective administration, economic activity—good Polizey. The duke had shown his confidence in these policies by putting Moser on the commerce deputation. But certain other "dear fellow countrymen" had such "curious perverse notions about wholly beneficial police institutions as to make you laugh yourself to death," and they took pride in blocking these good measures and institutions "just as though these put the fatherland in great danger, and this were a mighty victory." Moser discerned not only ignorance but positive malevolence at the root of this stubborn perversity. We don't refuse to build fires in stoves because sometimes houses burn down, he wrote, we make reasoned calculations. But then Moser went on to denounce "deductive cameralists" in turn for their fantastic use of the demonstrative methods of "modern worldly wisdom"—folk who proceeded rationally from general principles on down to how to milk a cow.[61] In a 1757 review he quoted with special

59. "Einige Sätze von der Teutschen Staats-Klugheit und deren Lehre," *Wöchentliche Franckfurtische Abhandlungen*, II (1756), pp. 491–92 and elsewhere. For the German distinction between politics and jurisprudence, established by Conring and here resumed by Moser, see Dietmar Willoweit, "Hermann Conring," in Michael Stolleis, ed. *Staatsdenker im 17. und 18. Jahrhundert: Reichspublizistik, Politik, Naturrecht* (Frankfurt/Main, 1977), pp. 132–46. For other connections between Conring's views and Moser's, above, §2.

60. "Nachricht," pp. 2, 5–6, 65; *Lebensgeschichte*, III, p. 17.

61. *Schwäbische Nachrichten*, 1756, preface and pp. 3–25.

approval Johann Justi's opinion (in Justi's *Staats-Wirthschaft*, which had appeared in 1755) that "the times when juridical learning sufficed for all state service are over." He himself did not think things out or order his material just the way Justi did, Moser admitted. Possibly the ordering of material was mainly a matter of taste.[62] However that might be, there was one word of caution about Justi: Justi's book seemed, Moser thought, to have been written for states "where everything goes by the *tel est notre plaisir*," and so might not properly apply where there were constitutional estates. "Things have not yet gone so far in Germany that nobody may ask: Pope! What are you up to?"[63]

The last article to appear in the "Swabian News" was a legal essay, where Moser tried to sort out the respective rights of rulers, estates, and officials in police affairs. Since the goal of police was the weal of subjects, by either natural or divine law it fell to rulers, and by German imperial law, to the territorial lord. Lower officials could not obstruct his will. Where there were estates the prince was bound to respect their rights; but the estates would be foolish and irresponsible to cling to antiquated privileges that stood in the way of clear benefits to the country. And the benefits should be clear to anybody endowed with sense and goodwill— especially anybody "who has had a certain amount of experience, or who has got out beyond the borders of the fatherland."[64] This provocative remark concluded the "Swabian News on Economic, Cameral, Police, Commerce, Manufacture, Mechanical, and Mining Matters." Moser's next journalistic outlet was a series called "Occasional Pieces on German Affairs of State," which began to appear in February 1757. These were articles mainly about constitutional transactions, and they rapidly developed a different tone.[65] For by the time they appeared Moser had still more to sort out.

---

62. For a comparison of the ways in which topics were ordered and emphasized in the writings of Justi and Moser, see my article "Rights and Functions."

63. *Schwäbische Nachrichten*, 1757, pp. 569–75, 675–88.

64. *Schwäbische Nachrichten*, 1757, pp. 934–51.

65. *Neben-Stunden von Teutschen Staats-Sachen*, 6 vols. (Frankfurt/Main, 1757–58).

§22. Constitutional Crisis for the Empire, the Duchy, and Moser, 1756-1757

A T the beginning of 1757, war was declared in the name of the German Empire against Frederick of Prussia. This "war of execution" was based legally on a declaration by the Reichshofrat at Vienna that Frederick had broken the peace by his invasion of Saxony. However, the Protestant party at the Reichstag, the *corpus evangelicorum*, managed to block formal imposition of the imperial ban against him there, so that the constitutionality of the war and its binding effect on imperial princes were questionable.[66] For constitutional lawyers the problem was not so much whether powerful princes would govern their behavior according to constitutional forms—there were few illusions about that—but whether the constitutional system itself could survive the strains put upon it by the behavior of these powerful princes.

Duke Karl Eugen, although Württemberg had not voted against Prussia at Regensburg, made ready for full engagement in the war, as a prince of the empire and ally of the emperor and the French. Moser dreaded this war and warned the duke against it in sharp language. If Karl Eugen sought a military command he "might well destroy his reputation, but never gain one." This was no war for Württemberg, Moser argued. Religion would be an important factor, and "many officers and troops will fight Prussia only against their will, and Prussia will learn about all military decisions and plans soon enough."[67] Talk like this could not please Karl Eugen, who hungered for martial glory and who had his eye on electoral status for himself and his duchy, something he might well achieve in a victorious war against Prussia, and who therefore looked more kindly upon those subordinates who had an eye on becoming the servants of a great warlord and imperial elector.

Karl Eugen's military expectations made Moser's position quite untenable, though still he clung to it. He was still fully committed to his projects for economic and financial development, projects that only the duke could or would carry out. But a major military effort would make a mockery of these programs, and make Moser himself out to be the coin-

66. For constitutional histories of these imperial proceedings, *Von denen Teutschen Reichs-Tags-Geschäften* (= NTSR VI: Frankfurt/Main, 1768), pp. 206–20 (see n. 168 below); and Johann Stephan Pütter, *Historische Entwickelung der heutigen Staatsverfassung des Teutschen Reichs*, 3d ed., III (Göttingen, 1799), pp. 87–113.

67. Lehmann, *Pietismus*, pp. 102–3.

clipping, plus-making, government projector his enemies held him to be. His dual position between government and estates must fly apart. The estates were reflexively, almost constitutionally, hostile to any war, because of the cost and the recruitments, and because of the power that war gave the ruler as military commander. This was immeasurably more the particular case in a war to be waged against two of the northern Protestant guarantors, Prussia and Brunswick-Hanover, of the constitutional position and ecclesiastical control the estates had gained in 1739. Karl Eugen for his part was just as determined, and probably he welcomed this conjuncture of European and Württemberg politics. There were constitutional gains to be had from military exigencies, in Württemberg as well as the empire. As warlord he had to find the six thousand soldiers he owed the French, and beyond that still had to find the contingent he owed the Swabian Circle for the imperial war, for these troops did not exist either.[68] His resource would have to be the public resources of the duchy, a large proportion of them tied into ecclesiastical properties and the revenues of the estates. This was not politically distasteful to Karl Eugen. Where was Moser to stand? Who was he after all?

During that winter of 1756–57, until Easter, Moser's gouty condition grew worse, and for most of the time this incapacitated him altogether. The pain was so great that he could lie neither on his back nor on his right side. He had crutches and a stick, but even so it took several people, and great trouble and agony, to get him even to the chamber pot. To aggravate the pain in his joints, which flared up with every movement, there came chills, presumably malarial, that shook his racked body. This vicious combination of maladies was "like hell, or at least torture," and his skin was covered with cold sweat "like peas." Nobody could help him much, although "his people" stood about unhappily and tried. He spent his nights in tears, and "I cried out many hundreds and thousands of times, until I could no more: o! o! o! o!"[69] These passages in the manuscript "Account" (in both the "natural" and the "spiritual" parts) are an affecting and convincing relation of the brute physical pain that enforced the memory. One thing that does not appear in Moser's account of his 1756–57 agony, though, is any mention of Friderica Rosina.

In January—while Moser lay ill in his apartments—Karl Eugen began his war measures in earnest. At this time the committee was not in formal session. The "interim" group at the Estates House, consisting of appointive staff, the mayor of Stuttgart, and the chief prelate, had no power to act alone where constitutional issues were at stake. Tafinger and the secretary-counsel Stockmayer therefore called for a meeting of the full

68. Adam, "Herzog Karl," pp. 209–10; and Adam, *Moser*, p. 30.
69. "Nachricht," pp. 5, 66; *Lebensgeschichte*, III, p. 9.

committee to take formal position against the duke. But their right to do so without the duke's approval and initiative was constitutionally tangled and unclear, and Karl Eugen surely had no mind to order invocation. Stockmayer, supported by most committee members, claimed on grounds of Württemberg law that in these circumstances they could meet on their own initiative. Moser from his sickbed issued his opinion that they could not, on grounds taken from imperial law. The provision of the Imperial Electoral Capitulation on which Moser based his argument did sound a bit that way, but it actually had been designed to keep the emperor from encouraging estates to meet where princes did not wish them to. Moser also cited a clause of the Last Imperial Recess of 1654 that bound all subjects of any prince to support imperial action taken in the name of the Public Peace (here the military execution against Prussia).[70] Moser declared, moreover, that the subsidy treaty with France was binding on the estates, thus: that a constitutional provision giving the estates a voice in foreign treaties applied only during a ruler's minority; when he achieved his full capacity as ruler, as Karl Eugen had in 1744, the duke assumed full responsibility for foreign affairs.[71]

These legal opinions of Moser are so doubtful on the merits that they seem perverse and pettifogging, gratuitous provocations of the committee —unless they were extreme results of a desperate effort by Moser to keep constitutional divisions of authority absolutely distinct and literally defined, which suggests not altogether a different motive. When Moser partially retreated from them later in 1757 he made the excuse that in January he had been very ill, without access to the necessary materials.[72] But Stockmayer and the committee had no trouble fetching opinions contrary to Moser's from Tübingen and elsewhere; and it is hard to believe that Moser, who boasted total recall in such cases, was not affected by

70. Article XV of the Wahlcapitulation is in Moser's *Wahlkapitulation Ihro Römisch-Kayserlichen Majestät Frantz des Ersten*, I (Frankfurt/Main, 1745), pp. 55–58. Moser had analyzed this provision at length, designed to restrain the emperor from conspiring with estates against their princes, in *Ihro Römisch-Kayserlichen Carls des Siebenden Wahl-Capitulation*, I, pp. 51–53; II, pp. 438–67 (both at Frankfurt/Main, 1742); and see Moser's later thorough discussion in his anonymous *Abhandlung von der Teutschen Land-Stände Conventen ohne Landesherrliche Bewilligung* (n.p., 1765). Section 180 of the Reichsabschied: texts in Johann Jacob Schmauss, *Corpus Juris Publici S. R. Imperii Academicum, enthaltend des Heil. Röm. Reichs deutscher Nation Grund-Gesetze*, rev. ed. (Leipzig, 1745), pp. 1018–19, and appendix, pp. 36–38.

71. Adam, *Moser*, pp. 30–32; *Lebensgeschichte*, II, p. 113; Moser's explanatory memorandum in UBT Mh 267; Moser's "Von der Collision widriger neuerer Reichs-Gesetze mit älteren Landes-Compacten und Privilegien," *Neben-Stunden*, 1757, pp. 506–68; and "Von der Teutschen Land-Stände Conventen ohne Landes-Herrlichen Bewilligung," *Neben-Stunden*, 1758, pp. 876–902; and see below, §29.

72. Memorandum of November 1757 in UBT Mh 267.

his annoyance with the committee and perhaps a wish to retain or regain his standing with Karl Eugen. At any rate, the Tafinger-Stockmayer party was predictably outraged, and the committee—which by now was in fact assembled, whether legally or not—ordered Moser to keep his views private, to say no more about them, and they adjured upon him his duty as counsel to defend legal positions taken by the committee whether he personally agreed with them or not. In April Moser replied that in his view the committee, by exceeding its constitutional powers, threatened to destroy the constitution, and they were bound to lose out politically anyway. As for his professional opinions, they belonged to him and he had never hidden any of them. He had defied a king of Prussia once and never had retracted; and this Small Committee was no master of his voice and conscience.[73]

Early in May Moser's health improved somewhat, a recovery he attributed to God's grace and two weeks at the baths, and he presented himself to the committee, ready to resume his duties with them. At this, however, Stockmayer declared that he would participate in no more deliberations nor offer any opinions where Moser was present. He would give his views privately to committee members if they asked for them, but only on condition that these views be kept secret from Moser. This move succeeded in the main, and his party prevailed through a procedural decision: on 11 May the committee majority resolved that inasmuch as Moser had been absent from the discussions leading up to that day's business, they would continue without him. Thus Moser, though not dismissed, was effectively excluded from the committee's deliberations, and remained excluded until December.[74]

The story of Karl Eugen's violent and illegal measures to make himself a warrior prince at his duchy's cost—the ruthless impressment of soldiers, the seizure of church property, the bullying of officials—is part of Württemberg's historical mythology, beginning with a collection of documents published by the committee of estates in its own defense in 1758, which included ducal correspondence, appeals from unwilling soldiers, lamentations from citizens, and the like.[75] It would be a callous error to disregard this, and there can be no doubting the great discontent

73. Adam, *Moser*, pp. 32–33; Moser's memorandum of 22 April 1757 in UBT Mh 267.
74. "Nachricht," p. 5; *Lebensgeschichte*, II, p. 113; III, p. 9; Adam, *Moser*, pp. 32–33.
75. *Verhandlungen zwischen des regierenden Herr Herzogens zu Württemberg Hoch-Fürstl. Durchlaucht und dero treu-gehorsamsten Prälaten und Landschafft in denen Jahren 1757 und 1758* (n.p., 1758). Editorship of this was attributed to Moser by his great-grandson Robert von Mohl, who may well have known: *Das Staatsrecht des Königreiches Württemberg*, I (Tübingen, 1829), p. 73. But the university library catalogue at Tübingen does not attribute it to Moser, nor does Rürup include it in his thorough bibliography of Moser's work, nor is Moser's hand anywhere obvious in it. This collection, whoever put it

and even public unrest and disturbances in the country. But much popular hostility was directed at the estates, authorities the countryside knew best, and who were deemed to be, if not traitorous accomplices to the duke's iniquities, then remiss or impotent to stop them. A share of the outrage, moreover, was directed at Moser himself, of whom it was said that inasmuch as he defended the duke's right to make foreign treaties, he was responsible for the seizure of Württemberg lads into the service of the papist French. Moser's prior association with Karl Eugen was well known, and the duke seems to have tried to revive it in the summer of 1757 after Moser's exclusion from the committee. Late in June the soldiers in the Rotenbildthor barracks in Stuttgart mutinied and broke out of the compound, throwing the town into turmoil; there were threats to storm and burn the estates buildings, where the counsels lived with their families. Stockmayer sensibly left to spend that night elsewhere, but Moser, "trusting in God and my good conscience," stayed and sat up awake in the dark all night with his family. Next morning early Moser came in person, unasked, to put himself at the disposal of the committee; but they recoiled at this and refused to have anything to do with him. The Stockmayer party began steps to dismiss him from his post altogether and find a replacement. But then on 23 July 1757 Chief Prelate Tafinger died unexpectedly. At this Moser again asked for reinstatement, but now on his terms, adorning his request with complaints about the way the committee had behaved toward him. There was no reconciliation and the committee dissolved for the rest of the summer.[76]

Meanwhile Moser kept trying to sort out his position and explain it publicly in the series of "Occasional Pieces on German Affairs of State" that appeared through 1757 and into 1758. He dug up and published materials having to do with his relations with King Frederick William I and with Count Schönborn, probably less to clarify his relations with Prussia or the empire (there were stories going round) than to assert his own dignity and incorruptibility. He exhumed the story of the failed appointment from the Lower Saxon Circle to the Imperial Cameral Court.[77] He tried to work through the dual role he had been playing, the relation between constitutional rights and police administration, in an essay on the respective spheres of cameral and judicial officials; here he studied and cited in particular the jurisdictional arrangements for this in

---

together, is probably the one printed by Friedrich Karl Moser at the committee's instance: see below, §23.

76. 20 June 1757. "Nachricht," p. 66; *Lebensgeschichte*, II, pp. 113–14; Adam, *Moser*, pp. 34–37.

77. See above, §7.

Prussia.[78] He wrote about whether German estates could convene without their ruler's consent, and on how previous rights of estates were affected by new state or imperial laws, and on whether the imperial constitution (the Last Recess of 1654) obliged estates and subjects to support the military establishments of their lands. Few of these essays seemed conclusively to answer the questions they posed, and in many of them Moser's argument fell into tangles of contradiction or was broken off incomplete.

The prevailing theme of these "Occasional Pieces" of 1757–58, whatever their particular topics, was Moser's effort to delineate the relations between politics and law. An especially interesting one of these (though it too was left unfinished) was a "preliminary" essay on the breach of the Public Peace, the doctrine that Moser in the *Teutsches Staats-Recht* had held to be a basic law of the imperial constitution. This now had been invoked by the empire against Frederick II of Prussia, and upon it, therefore, rested Karl Eugen's right and obligation to put his duchy into war against Frederick.[79] Events had shown, Moser wrote, that the old laws of imperial procedure concerning this were now outdated, insufficient, and inappropriate to the times; they did not take modern military and political circumstances into account. Such a condition of the imperial law was critical just now, for the Public Peace was at the heart of the German constitution and must be made to respond accurately to true conditions revealed in the present crisis. The law consisted of machinery to punish peacebreakers; but what if there was reasonable disagreement (the way wars started now) about who it was that really broke the peace? It was law of the empire; but what if the emperor himself or a member of his family was directly involved, or if one or more parties denied or was exempt from the jurisdiction of the imperial courts, or if foreign powers were involved? The law put the burden of military execution upon the Kreise, the imperial circles; but the Kreise were not capable militarily, nor were they politically constituted to manage that role under present conditions. The business of warfare had so changed in recent years that the whole country could be laid waste before this cumbersome machinery could work. It should have been streamlined and repaired long ago;

78. "Wie weit sich die Landesherrliche Gewalt erstrecke, denen Cammer-*Collegiis* zugleich auch Justiz-Sachen anzuvertrauen?" *Neben-Stunden*, 1757, pp. 434–74. Moser concluded there was no imperial law applicable here; it was part of the Landeshoheit, conditioned by particular agreements and privileges; the spheres were separate but a single official might operate independently in either; but, significantly for the way Moser's mind was turning, appeal could be made from cameral administrative decisions to judicial courts.

79. *Neben-Stunden*, 1757, pp. 223–45; for Moser on the Landfrieden as a basic imperial law, above, §15; Pütter treats the application of the Landfrieden in this instance in *Staatsverfassung*, III, pp. 87–113.

could it possibly be done at a time of crisis, "with the inner condition of Germany such as now, alas! it is? . . . when public and private enmities threaten our whole imperial constitution with total collapse, making Germany the battlefield [Tümmel-Platz] for all Europe?" The aim of the Public Peace was after all to suppress violence and establish the rule of law; for this, courts and procedures had been established. But what if the Peace itself was made into a pretext for war, and the imperial courts were made "a mousetrap"?

Here Moser had in mind Frederick II's claim that his invasion of Saxony had been a preventive campaign, undertaken only because the Kaunitz coalition of France, Austria, and Russia, along with Saxony, had been preparing war against him (which they were, with some justification as well as avarice). Moser was bruiting the proposition that here the Public Peace was used perversely by Austria as a device to draw the imperial estates, and Württemberg, into a continental and world war among great powers over interests to which they, imperial estates or no, were not party. There must be cases, he argued, where all juridical and political sense excluded true invocation of the imperial Public Peace and the constitutional involvement of all the empire. Such a case arose where, in a quarrel between parties, peacekeeping procedures designed to suppress a disruptive member were blown up instead to engage whole bodies of ecclesiastical and secular estates, "so that it becomes a political affair" rather than a judicial action. In light of the confessional confrontation in the developing conflict, in Europe, at the Reichstag, and in Württemberg itself, Moser feared a German civil war on confessional lines, with foreign abetment on the pattern of the Thirty Years War but with France this time on the Catholic and imperial side. He thought there had to be a constitutional way to restrict the Austro-Prussian war, to keep it out of the imperial system and out of Württemberg—not because of any innately pacifistic temper of his, but because of what the crisis was doing to his professional roles and aims and to himself. Above all (he went back to the argument), we have to know who really broke the peace, and the law offers frail guides to this. To be sure, imperial law requires us to punish peacebreakers. He meant to offer them no escape hatch . . . he would write more later. . . . And there the essay was broken off, and not resumed.

Inconclusive though it was, and easy to read as taking Prussia's part, this was as deft and thoughtful a blend of juridical with political analysis as one is likely to see from Moser's pen. His political exegesis of precedent, his identification of changes that had taken place since a law's formulation, his analysis of present politics, all followed and vindicated a position that Moser the jurist had always taken: that history is there to help understand old rules and so to help in modifying them for present needs. On the political side, one may read it as a justification and also a revelation of Moser's own changing views, as he drew away from the war policies of his duke. As this took place, his thought was beginning to turn away from administration and back toward the law. If it gave aid to Prussia's contention that the imperial war against it was unlawful, that was inseparable from Moser's purpose; but he was not at all happy to be cast as Prussia's defender. What Moser meant was that Württemberg, as in wise policy so in true law, had no business in this war; the Public Peace could not be shown to apply and probably did not apply; as went the empire so went Württemberg, and vice versa.

Still, Moser at about the same time thoughtfully sent to the Prussian resident at Frankfurt on Main an opinion sharply challenging the procedures of the Reichshofrat in its action against Prussia, an opinion that the Prussian foreign ministry in Berlin, however, refused "on various grounds" to use in public.[80]

---

§23. Road to Banishment, 1757–1759

IN the summer of 1757 the mutinous Württemberg soldiers were got under enough control, and brought to sufficient strength and training, that Karl Eugen's officers were able to herd them eastward to confront the Prussians. There were spattering mutinies along the way, but the leaders of them were identified and executed and the march continued. The duke's most useful servant in the recruiting and financing of these troops was Phillip Friedrich Rieger, a Württemberg-born jurist who had been brought from Prussian service to Karl Eugen's in 1755, and who by 1757 was his chief military adviser with the title of privy war councillor (Geheimer Kriegsrath). Rieger, black sheep of a family of proper Stuttgart pastors, was a man of intelligence and energy, personable and cheerful, apparently uncorruptible, professionally ruthless and ambitious. And Rieger was not only a born Württemberger of family and a former Prussian official, but also son-in-law to the chief court preacher, Oberhofprediger Ludwig Eberhard Fischer—Protestant of course, and mark now the name. Most likely Karl Eugen had had the problem of deal-

80. Reinhold Koser, "Brandenburg-Preussen in dem Kampfe zwischen Imperialismus und reichsständischer Libertät," *Historische Zeitschrift*, XCVI (1906), p. 241, n. 1.

ing with the Württemberg Protestant leadership and estates in mind when he had brought Rieger into his service. But the war councillor's activities as organizer of the duke's war soon made his name hated in the countryside. Abroad Karl Eugen commanded Württemberg and Bavarian troops at the successful siege of Schweidnitz in November, and his soldiers went on to share the Austrian victory at Breslau. But Karl Eugen himself gained no glory in the latter, for the day after the fall of Schweidnitz on 11 November, the duke hurried back to Stuttgart. The Small Committee of the estates had reconvened.[81]

There plots were thickening, and the story will be wrong if we make no effort to work them out. The late chief prelate Tafinger, once duumvir with the secretary-counsel Stockmayer and Moser's most important enemy on the committee, had been succeeded by none other than the aforesaid court preacher Fischer. Fischer had been sympathetic to Moser's economic and administrative enterprises and was in no apparent way beholden to Stockmayer, and he was Rieger's father-in-law; still, he was nobody's puppet, surely not Moser's. But his succession to Tafinger as chief prelate had thrown open the disposition of forces in the committee; and Moser's own attitude toward Karl Eugen's policies had changed as war superseded internal affairs as the duchy's main concern. On 7 November, while Karl Eugen was still before Schweidnitz, Moser applied to the committee once more for full active reinstatement as counsel. He said it was his right. He had never received any special favors from the duke; he had never supported any violation of the constitution; he had had nothing to do with the French subsidy treaty. As for the opinion he had given about the binding effect of ducal treaties on the estates—well, that opinion had been given casually, abstractly, to a hypothetical case, delivered from a bed of pain without knowledge of the particular circumstances or the detail of the legal sources. Now having seen the documents he was ready to concede that that opinion might not apply to the case at hand. Moser was even ready now to admit the committee's right to convene itself, under certain circumstances; but the committee must be careful not to exceed its clear rights and get into a dubious position that would throw all constitutionality into confusion.[82]

Alarmed by this un-Moser-like contrition, Stockmayer expanded his perimeter promptly, to rebuild his position in the newly reconstituted committee. He insisted that Moser must do more than explain or adjust the heretical views he had expressed in the past; Moser must fully and explicitly retract them. Only complete recantation and humiliation would do. Moser must not only take back any doubts about rights claimed by

81. Stälin, "Karl Eugen," pp. 379–80; Lehmann, *Pietismus*, p. 107.
82. Memorandum of 7 November 1757, in UBT Mh 267.

the committee that he had ever expressed, he must in future place his mind and pen exclusively at the committee's command, and he must publish no more. The committee itself was a little more cautious or forgiving than Stockmayer wanted. After addressing some peevish reprimands to Moser for past behavior, it resolved that he might now return if henceforth he would indulge no opinions publicly that questioned rights claimed by the committee, and would faithfully support all committee positions; he was not to publish any constitutional or religious opinions without prior consent of the committee; and finally he must recognize that the committee was his lawful employer and superior. Stockmayer protested that this was not enough; Moser must admit error. Sooner than agree to Moser's readmission on these terms he himself would resign. The committee replied to Stockmayer that if he really felt so strongly about it, he might resign—next year, if he should still want to resign then. Stockmayer choked this down and stayed on. Moser returned to his duties on 2 December 1757, apparently without giving the formal assurances specified by the committee, at least not for the record.[83] The committee and its staff attained thereby a precarious solidarity against the demands of the duke's government; for though Stockmayer continued to chafe and to sulk, his loyalty to the committee and the estates was absolute, as Moser himself always acknowledged. That gave Moser an advantage in this clash of counsels where his own loyalty was in doubt; for the danger to the committee in this quarrel was not the loss of their services, nor even so much the political scandal if one of them resigned in a huff, but rather that a disaffected counsel might carry his views and his knowledge of the committee's activities to a hostile quarter. This Stockmayer would never do, but Moser conceivably might. The committee needed concealment to confound force.

In February of 1758 one of the great villains of Württemberg tradition arrived in Stuttgart, the notorious Count Friedrich Samuel von Montmartin. Montmartin had formerly served in Bayreuth, then as emissary of Sachsen-Gotha to the imperial diet at Regensburg. As a result of unusual services rendered these Protestant courts,[84] Montmartin had only recently been raised to the rank of imperial count by the emperor and had been commended by him to the service of the duke of Württemberg.

83. Committee protocol of 18 November 1757, in UBT Mh 267; Adam, *Moser*, pp. 37–39.

84. From Bayreuth service Montmartin (b. 1712) had become Reichshofrat under Karl VII, in which capacity he had helped arrange the declaration of Karl Eugen of Württemberg's majority in 1744. In the next imperial regime he left the Reichshofrat; but as Gotha representative to the Reichstag in 1756 he had then, contrary to instructions, voted for the Reichsexecution against Prussia. Eugen Schneider, "Montmartin," in *Allgemeine Deutsche Biographie*, XXII (Leipzig, 1885), p. 204.

Karl Eugen and Montmartin now reorganized the Württemberg government "on the pattern of other most eminent courts," and erected a new "State and Cabinet Ministry" which effectively supplanted the old privy council, with Montmartin at its head.[85] That meant open war with the estates, who had traditional close ties with the old council and had enjoyed some protection from the duke's government by the council's intermediacy. Montmartin as prime minister showed no deference at all for the fussy forms of Württemberg constitutional politics; what he wanted from the estates was money, all that could be squeezed out of them, by whatever means. The committee's whole duty, he told them, was "unconditional obedience" to Karl Eugen's "absolute command."[86]

To confront this situation the committee (first doubling their number into a "Greater Committee") now requested the summoning of a plenary diet; or, failing that, they would themselves collect instructions from the towns and districts to support them against the government. The duke refused to convene the diet and forbade any collection of instructions. In reply the committee refused to consider his demands for money. At impasse nerves grew taut; committee and staff began to remove their cash and their records from their Stuttgart offices and hid them in various secret places. Moser, obsessed with premonitions of disaster, imprisonment, or death (verses from Jeremiah and Daniel were running through his head), gave his books to his sons. Karl Eugen and Montmartin made sure of full support from Vienna; and the committee for its part appointed Friedrich Karl Moser, relatively safe at Frankfurt on Main, to be their extraordinary representative to the guarantor powers. Johann Jakob Moser pressed the committee to invoke the direct protection of governments friendly to the estates; but the committee was not willing to do this. During the spring and summer of 1758 Karl Eugen sent demand after demand to the committee, citing the "imminent onslaught of the Prussians." Montmartin appeared repeatedly before them and excoriated them with violent tongue.[87]

The committee submitted a long list of grievances, in acerbic language, drafted by Moser; to this Montmartin replied that only Karl Eugen's "inborn mildness and grace" had preserved them so far from his wrath, and demanded to know at once who had drafted the grievances. The committee—honorably, consistently, and probably wisely—refused to name Moser and refused their counsel's offer to resign. They prepared to call for instructions from the constituencies, and had documentation of

85. Dehlinger, *Württembergs Staatswesen*, I, p. 107.
86. Stälin, "Karl Eugen," pp. 378–79; Adam, *Moser*, pp. 39–40.
87. "Nachricht," pp. 3, 6, 67; *Lebensgeschichte*, III, p. 78; IV, p. 65; WHS A34 B86 passim; Adam, *Moser*, pp. 41–42; Grube, *Stuttgarter Landtag*, pp. 429–30.

their position printed secretly by Friedrich Karl Moser in a village near Offenbach in Hessen.[88] Karl Eugen summoned the committee before him personally, and in the presence of his ministers he denounced it and dissolved it; he would collect the money he required on his own. That was on 26 June 1758. On 15 July, Karl Eugen ordered Montmartin to make ready to seize the estates' treasury by force of arms, and to incorporate their funds into the duke's own war chest.[89]

Now the position of the estates' representation was a peculiar one. With the committee dissolved, the affairs of the estates were conducted "in interim" by the group consisting of the mayor of Stuttgart, Chief Prelate Fischer, and the counsels and secretaries; the staff members "in interim" were entitled to vote, for this was considered to be an administrative body. Inasmuch as this group had little constitutional authority, let alone sure political footing, the question promptly arose that had divided and excluded Moser from the committee in the spring of 1757: whether the whole committee could be assembled without ducal summons and approval. Stockmayer again insisted that it could, and must; Moser doubted whether it could, or should. The interim group decided that it would in fact summon a meeting of the committee.

Moser's doubts about the legality and the wisdom of this were well known. His last essay in the "Occasional Pieces" had been about this question; and where it had been broken off (probably because of the committee's insistence), just before he came to discuss the Württemberg case, he had finished with a Mecklenburg precedent considered unfavorable to the committee's position.[90] Consequently the government's obloquy fell on Stockmayer, who in turn blamed Moser for publicly undermining the committee's solidarity and giving aid to its enemies. Then, while Moser was away at the baths, Stockmayer drafted a strong opinion to be volleyed at the ministry in support of the committee's right to reassemble; Moser, when he returned, criticized parts of it and advised Fischer not to submit it. Stockmayer, furious, sent in a new letter of resignation—a long, shapeless, apoplectic tirade against Moser's *conduite* and his *principia*, his behavior and his doctrines. Stockmayer could not serve with the traitorous Moser; he had stood by when Moser had been readmitted but Moser had become only more impudent, espe-

88. Adam, *Moser*, pp. 42–44; and see above, n. 75.

89. WHS A34 B86 nr. 23; for a legal opinion by Moser about this, ibid., nr. 42.

90. *Neben-Stunden*, 1758, pp. 876–902; see above, §22. The final *Neben-Stunden* fragment seems to have appeared very shortly after Moser's return to the committee, and so violated the rule of silence laid upon him; thus it reaped Stockmayer's special fury. Probably it had been written and possibly it was in press before then; but that is not to say Moser could not have suppressed it if he had chosen to; from the tone of the dispute, he could have and did not.

cially with that talk about Mecklenburg. "Is this just, loyal, patriotic, collegial, Christian, upright, or in any way according to his duty?" The committee must eradicate this constant sedition, this divider of counsels, this scourge of mutuality and confidence.[91]

The duel between Moser and Stockmayer was charged with personal rivalry, couched in legal technicalities, draped with chancellery jargon. Both were honorable and, alas, earnest men—Stockmayer a single-minded advocate of his office, a literal spokesman for the estates of Württemberg embodied in the committee and its permanent staff; Moser an advocate of his own views, and virtual spokesman for that complex of partial and defined rights, in Württemberg and behind that the German Empire, upon which the Württemberg constitution ultimately depended. Their intransigence sent Stockmayer into retirement and Moser to the solitude of the Hohentwiel.

Stockmayer was the first to go. He had resigned once too often. The committee asked Moser whether he could frame a reply to Stockmayer that would mollify him and leave room for him to stay on. Moser, feeling at this that he had the upper hand, replied that he should not be asked to answer personal attacks, and he asked the committee instead to appoint a new second counsel, right away. He said the times were too critical to let the post remain unoccupied. If the committee would replace Stockmayer promptly, Moser promised to profess no *principia* contrary to the estates' constitutional rights; and as to conduct, Moser would publish nothing on Württemberg affairs for a term of two years—"if he remained in his present office and in the country for that long."[92] Stockmayer now tried another attack on Moser's insolence, but he was out of range and outdone; the committee declared itself satisfied with Moser's statement and appointed a new second counsel, Johann Friedrich Eisenbach, a former secretary to the duke and a *Dozent* at Tübingen.[93] Stockmayer continued to give unofficial advice to committee members friendly to him; and moreover his son, Friedrich Amandus, had recently got the post of second secretary and retained it, while a brother, the prelate Christof Friedrich Stockmayer, was a committee member.[94] But with Johann Friedrich Stockmayer out of the Estates House, Moser was the

91. UBT Mh 267; Adam, *Moser*, pp. 49–50. Here I have combined two letters of resignation from Stockmayer: one of 15 September and one of 3 November 1758, the latter in reply to a committee resolution which sought to quiet Stockmayer and dissuade him from resigning.

92. Oral committee protocol of 1 December 1758, in UBT Mh 267; Adam, *Moser*, pp. 50–51.

93. Committee conclusion of 2 December 1758, and Stockmayer memorandum of 6 December 1758, both in UBT Mh 267; Adam, *Moser*, pp. 50–51.

94. Adam, *Moser*, p. 4, n. 6, and p. 51.

undoubted, and the visible, chief legal spokesman and adviser to the committee of estates.

Karl Eugen's threats and demands continued to mount. Chief Prelate Fischer was inclined to give way; he argued that it would be better to leave matters of constitutional form for peacetime. Moser disagreed, characteristically: "We won't get through this without taking a beating anyway, and the more concessions we make the worse it will get." As a result the committee granted some of the duke's more regular demands but refused any extraordinary military levy for the war against Prussia. With Prussian troops next door in Franconia, they declared, the policy of the estates must be peace, not war; and in truth, if they had cooperated in the war and Prussian troops had entered, the dangers for the duchy, not only material but civil and social, were incalculable. But the Prussian threat was the government's very grounds for the emergency military assessment. Karl Eugen, assured of support from Vienna, ordered the assessment on the duchy by his own authority. He forbade communication between the committee (whose legal presence of course he denied) and the constituencies, and he imposed fines on the estates' receivers of revenue for their recalcitrance. On 30 January 1759 he sent the Stuttgart garrison on what he called "a local maneuver against the estates," surrounded their buildings, and did not end the maneuver until treasurers there delivered thirty thousand gulden in cash.[95] Through the spring and early summer the government, having shown its willingness to use force, continued to seize estates' revenues by threat of force. The committee and its receivers paid what they had to pay and could pay, still complaining and arguing and calling in vain for a diet.

Moser was now, by his victory over Stockmayer, the most exposed member of the estates party. As senior counsel he was responsible for drafting the committee's resolutions and remonstrances; it was he who repeatedly faced and debated the fire-breathing Montmartin when the minister scourged and bullied the committee. On the other hand, he could not be altogether sure of his position with committee and estates. He had not really recanted his earlier unpredictable *conduite* or *principia*; and there were those other Stockmayers still with their eyes upon him; and Moser and Chief Prelate Fischer, though generally allied, seem not to have had full confidence in one another.[96] Friedrich Karl Moser by this

95. Adam, "Herzog Karl," pp. 220–21; Adam, *Moser*, p. 52; Grube, *Stuttgarter Landtag*, p. 430. A side effect of this *Kassensturz* was that the estates' outside creditors called their loans and it became very difficult to borrow more—which inconvenienced and frustrated the government as well.

96. Adam, *Moser*, pp. 55, 61. Recall also that Fischer was father-in-law to the war councillor Rieger, whose own position with Karl Eugen, to complicate the matter further,

time was busy trying to rally support from the guarantor courts. Two of these were already at war with Austria. The third, Denmark, would not risk direct intervention but in April appointed Johann Jakob Moser to be a royal Danish state councillor, "with all the rights, immunities, and prerogatives" pertaining thereto—that was the title Moser set behind his name for the rest of his life, though it was to do him little good in the year 1759.[97]

Summer drew near and it was time for war. On the tenth of June Moser was called out of morning chapel by an estates messenger to attend a meeting of the privy council called by Montmartin. The minister lectured Moser and told him there was real trouble coming now; the committee must learn to behave or take any consequences. Moser replied that he as an appointed official could only follow instructions; but he warned Montmartin that the whole country was against him. The committee was not responsible for these troubles nor was he; but they were quite aware what was at stake. There might be private efforts at reconciliation, he allowed, but "publicly the Collegium and I can take no other position than the one we have taken, lest we be false to our oath." After long bargaining over amounts of money, Montmartin remarked that the committee could after all legitimately yield to force without betraying their mandate, thereby conceding implicitly that to make the grants willingly would violate it; this was a point that stuck in Moser's mind and that he was to exhume six years later. Now he answered provocatively that he for his part would have to see palpable force; he would sacrifice his own gray head, he said theatrically, before yielding his honor, false to his oath. Montmartin assured him that force was ready to hand.[98]

Next day the government issued a decree blaming the committee's "treasonous machinations, taken under cover of patriotic sentiments and affected hypocritical ardor," calculated to ruin the credit of the country and "to undermine and to thwart all measures by His Grace the Duke for the protection and the weal of his most tenderly beloved subjects." The government demanded to see all the financial records: revenues and

---

was increasingly threatened by the energetic Montmartin and who ultimately was driven from office by him; see below, §§23–24. The Stockmayers, though, seem to have played no role in Moser's arrest; and even Moser, though darkly suspicious, never dared claim directly and openly that they had: Adam, *Moser*, pp. 57–59.

97. *Lebensgeschichte*, II, pp. 116–17; Adam, *Moser*, p. 56.

98. See the memorandum in Moser's hand in WHS LA 2 41 5. I do not know for whom it was prepared or to whom submitted—probably the committee, though Moser may have written it for his own use. See also Adam, "Herzog Karl," p. 223. Neither am I quite sure that this was the meeting at which the talk of Moser's gray head occurred, but it fits all other evidence circumstantially. *Lebensgeschichte*, II, pp. 142–43; WHS KA III Ls 389.

expenditures, debts and receipts in prospect, lists of officials and employees.[99] Later in June the committee made reply, mostly in its sprawling legalistic way but including a particular attack upon Montmartin that stood out clear on the page: "The undersigned cannot believe that these harsh and undeserved thoughts and accusations have grown out of Your Ducal Grace's own heart"; they must presume "that they have had the misfortune to have been painted black falsely before Your Grace's eyes," and prayed that such persons "would repent and reveal their sins," and that Karl Eugen "would give no ear to these evil calumnies," but rather would "expel such persons from his presence."[100]

Montmartin vowed, to the junior counsel Eisenbach, that he would have the author of this language to earth if he had to go down there after him. In fact, the particular passage attacking Montmartin had been written by Eisenbach himself and inserted in a late draft at the instructions of the chief prelate Fischer, father-in-law to the war councillor Rieger, who by this time was beginning to feel the ambitious Montmartin's breath at the nape of his own neck.[101] But Moser was chief draftsman for the committee, had drafted most of the document himself, and in his recent debate with Montmartin had shown himself to be immovable and defiant —almost suicidally so, it seems now—in defense of the estates. It may even be that Montmartin took this attack and Moser's defiance to be part of a direct and serious challenge to his position with Karl Eugen: after all, Moser had been a favorite of the duke's quite recently, and then there were Fischer and Rieger. The military and political situation in Europe and the empire was uncertain, and Karl Eugen had shown, and would show again, that the distribution of favor he gave subordinates was adaptable to the times. But Karl Eugen and Montmartin stood firmly together now. On 1 July 1759 Moser's second son, Wilhelm Gottfried, since 1757 a ducal official in ecclesiastical affairs, was abruptly dismissed from his post and forbidden to leave the duchy to seek another.[102] That was a signal.

On 12 July 1759 Moser was awakened at dawn by Privy Secretary Knab of the duke's cabinet and brought to Ludwigsburg. As Moser

99. Adam, *Moser*, pp. 53–55; Adam, "Herzog Karl," p. 224.

100. WHS LA 2 41 5; WHS KA III Ls 389; Adam, *Moser*, p. 60.

101. Adam, *Moser*, p. 60. Moser at every subsequent opportunity denied that he had written the attack on Montmartin: see, for example, his letter of 23 November 1765 to Karl Eugen printed in Rürup, *Moser*, p. 245, and the protocol of 18 September 1764 in WHS KA III Ls 389. But he did not name Eisenbach either.

102. *Lebensgeschichte*, II, pp. 115–16; "Nachricht," p. 67; Adam, *Moser*, p. 55. Wilhelm three years later was able to leave Württemberg for Hessen-Darmstadt service and there made an important name for himself as a founder of German state forestry: *Allgemeine Deutsche Biographie*, XXII (Leipzig, 1885), pp. 384–85.

waited in the anteroom there he thought of a hymn, a seventeenth-century verse by Paul Gerhardt, "Why Then Should I Grieve?" When he was summoned he spoke a line or two to a secretary there, beginning *Unverzagt und ohne Grauen*: "Free from dread, without despair, Shall a Christian, no matter where, Let himself be known."[103] When Moser entered the inner cabinet Karl Eugen informed him that inasmuch as the duke's addresses to the estates had brought none but disrespectful and libelous replies, he found it necessary to take custody of Moser's person as author of them, and to hold him at the mountain fortress at Hohentwiel. The whole matter would be thoroughly investigated. Moser replied that His Grace would find him an honest man, and was escorted out to a coach, waving cheerfully as he went to a crowd that had gathered there.[104] He was delivered to an adjutant, who bore an order to the commander at Hohentwiel written in Karl Eugen's own hand. Moser was to be held in close confinement. Colonel Kommerstätt "would answer for it with his head that said Moser speak with no one and be allowed no pen or paper, except to write me or the colonel, in which case the latter shall be present, as also when he eats at noon and at night. *ich bin mein cher Collonell sein affectionirter Carl.*"[105]

Karl Eugen could have thought of no remoter spot. Hohentwiel was a Württemberg exclave, a tiny patch of territory far to the south separated from the duchy proper by a smattering of small principalities and Austrian territories. Its whole extent was an eccentric volcanic outcropping, where the fortress stood, that reared high and lonely over Lake Constance. It was two days' ride across the Swabian Alp and the forest to the Hohentwiel heights, accompanied by soldiers with fixed bayonets who, Moser thought, spoke only Roman tongues, French or Italian. The sun was hot, and they gave him only a cotton cap to wear and almost nothing to drink. When they had climbed the summit at the end of the journey, Moser had to be carried from the vehicle. His urine, he saw, was the color of blood.[106]

Later on the day of Moser's arrest, Karl sent the committee a brusque

103. *Evangelische Kirchengesangbuch für die evangelisch-lutherische Kirchen Niedersachsens* (Hanover, 1962), pp. 384–85. This is not a remarkable hymn, but the rhythm and melody as I have heard it sung—at the Zion Lutheran Church in Baltimore in 1976— have a distinctive pattern of tension and release: after a drawn and lugubrious verse, the refrain lines *Soll ein Christ, Wo er ist* break the stress with an unburdened sound of tra-la-la, tra-la-la.

104. *Lebensgeschichte*, II, pp. 117–18; WHS KA III Ls 389. August Schmid, *Das Leben Johann Jakob Mosers* (Stuttgart, 1868), pp. 278–80, prints Wilhelm Gottfried's letter to Friedrich Karl reporting these events.

105. Adam, *Moser*, p. 57, n. 39.

106. *Lebensgeschichte*, II, pp. 120–21.

demand for two hundred thousand gulden; the language reads like Montmartin's. His Grace would now for the present suspend the question of whether the obstinacy of the estates had resulted "out of an exaggerated and fanatical zeal, or some other, criminal motives." He had placed Moser in solitary arrest, he announced, pending further action to be taken "against him, and against all who share his opinions, persons who are not unknown to His Supreme Self."[107] On 17 July the weekly newspaper *Stuttgarter Wöchentliche Nachrichten* carried an entry in large type announcing Moser's arrest. "This man, who has played so many peculiar roles, now has, by his unruly behavior and his unconstrained ill judgment, made himself notorious in all Germany, so that he nowhere finds an abiding place." Moser in Württemberg, said the announcement, had sought to sever "the sacred bonds between head and members." In the present emergency it was a ruler's duty to exercise "the supreme law of the common weal, and to deprive so dangerous a member of civil society of opportunity to instigate further harm."[108] From Vienna came a letter signed by the emperor Francis (whom Moser fourteen years before had instructed on how to be an emperor) congratulating Karl Eugen on the detection and seizure of the "mainspring" of the machinations and slanders of the estates, this "tool of the rebellious King in Prussia, Elector of Brandenburg."[109]

Later that summer and autumn the committee made several petitions for Moser's release. There is no reason to doubt these were meant in earnest, but they were imbedded amongst the whole panoply of constitutional and fiscal grievances regularly addressed to the government. Karl Eugen had linked Moser's arrest to the two hundred thousand extra gulden which he wanted from the estates that summer and which the committee refused to provide; the committee accepted the link, and thus the imprisoned Moser became another regular item in the interminable list of *gravamina*.[110] In December the unemployed Wilhelm Gottfried Moser told the committee that with ten thousand gulden to spend in Vienna in unspecified ways, or maybe only two or three thousand, his father could be freed; but the committee found this proposition "most questionable." Friderica Rosina appealed in vain to Karl Eugen in public

107. WHS LA 2 41 5; WHS A34 B87 nr. 45.

108. WHS KA III Ls 389; *Lebensgeschichte*, II, pp. 118–20. Much the same language had already been used in the message to the estates on Moser's arrest.

109. Dated 20 August 1759, in reply to a message of 12 July 1759 from Karl Eugen: WHS LA 2 41 5; see also Adam, *Moser*, pp. 62–63.

110. For example, WHS A34 B87 nr. 45a, "betr. Arretierung des Landschafts-Consulenten Joh. Jak. Moser und die angesonnenen weiteren 200,000 fl," 21 July 1759, and other items in B87; also WHS LA 2 41 5; and UBT Mh 268.

audience; she was deliberately humiliated and turned away.[111] Moser himself for the first few months at Hohentwiel seems to have hoped for an early release. But in Stuttgart the committee did not yield, and in Ludwigsburg the duke did not relent, and in the fortress Moser remained. There in his room high on the Hohentwiel Moser entered his place as one of eighteenth-century Germany's, and Europe's, few martyrs for the right and for the law against despotism; and that he was, however he came to it.

§24. Hohentwiel, 1759–1763

F O R more than five years, nearly always alone, Moser sat in the Hohentwiel. He had one stroke of luck: the commandant Colonel Kommerstätt, ordered to keep this prisoner in total isolation or answer with his head, put Moser in the most secluded room in the fortress. This happened to be the chamber that the duchess had occupied during the ducal family's visits to Lake Constance; she would not be using it now. From here Moser could view the town of Constance some twenty kilometers distant, the lake, and the Swiss and Tyrolean Alps beyond. Windows facing a neighboring building were boarded up. Even Moser's usually blind eye for scenery saw this to be a "peaceful" vista for his second "flight to Egypt," while war seethed in Germany and the cacophony continued between duke and estates in Württemberg.[112]

It was something like Ebersdorf, a refuge not unwelcome after crisis, impasse, and rejection; but here Moser was undisturbed by family, community, or even prospect of employment. He had almost nobody to deal with. For the first four years he never left that room. He saw the commandant at mealtimes twice a day, and he saw the servants or prisoners who brought food and fuel and who infrequently, under guard and forbidden to speak with him, took away his slops. Food was plentiful though ill prepared—Moser retained his small salary from the estates—and there was fuel enough in winter until the commandant learned to pare the government allowance. There were a few other political prisoners in the fortress: the court concertmaster Franz Pircker with his musician wife Marianne, she a favorite of the estranged duchess, and the hairdresser

111. WHS LA 2 41 5; Adam, *Moser*, p. 67.
112. *Lebensgeschichte*, II, pp. 121–24; III, p. 21; "Nachricht," p. 5.

HOHENTWIEL
"For four years I never got out of that room." Moser, Lebensgeschichte, *II, p. 1*
  Württembergische Landesbibliothek, Stuttgart

Twiel.

A. Das Fürstlich Hauße.
B. Das Zeughauße.
C. Die Hochwacht.
D. Handt und Roßmühlen.
E. Cantzley.
F. Marstall.
G. Der Vorhoff.

Reich, also formerly of the duchess's service. Late in 1762, when the war was being lost, Montmartin achieved Rieger's fall and disgrace, and the former war councillor entered solitary confinement in the darkest dungeons of the fortress below. Moser's account makes no mention of the other prisoners and very likely he did not know about them when he was there.[113] He saw no pastor, attended no chapel, received no communion. He got a Bible and eventually a few hymnals and a book of his old friend Steinhofer's sermons; but he was forbidden any professional books or journals or writing materials. He was not altogether ignorant of what went on in the world: his ears grew sharp in confinement and soldiers on the battlements chattered aloud about current events, perhaps for his benefit as he stood silent at his window; but the world was far away and seemed not to change.[114]

Colonel Kommerstätt was a disagreeable man, and he had reason—being stuck with this ignominious assignment as jailkeeper, watching jailbirds eat while glory and promotion were being won in the field. He also had a disagreeable dog, which for some reason, though, adopted a benevolent attitude toward the prisoner, allowing Moser some homiletic remarks to Kommerstätt about the holy Lazarus. Kommerstätt in his boredom and malice teased Moser about such things as possible poison in the food ("Here is some wine with something in it that will take away your headache for good!"). Moser baited him back by commenting on the news of the day that he had heard illicitly from his window, and once by analyzing in detail the organization of the fortress and garrison, as he had learned about it from a paper that came wrapped around a bundle of tinder.[115]

But despite the peace and these small triumphs it was prison all the same, and it went on and on. There is a bitter cold mist that lies in the valley and creeps over the slopes below the Hohentwiel, and sometimes from the summit there is nothing else to see. Moser's chamber pot leaked, and in summer the place stank; in winter the frost made him close his shutters and sit in the cold shadows. Kommerstätt began to arrive at mealtimes drunk, stumbling and falling to his own great annoyance, complaining that this was no job for a soldier, not this sitting in the stink and cold, watching so mean a personage as Moser eat his dinner. Would the duke ever give him real duty and get him out of this place? Moser finally asked his keeper whether it had occurred to him that he, Kommerstätt, was in precisely the same situation as Moser? There was a

113. WHS KA III 1 161; Stälin, "Karl Eugen," p. 381; Stälin, "Die beiden Ehen des Herzogs," in *Herzog Karl Eugen von Württemberg und seine Zeit*, I, p. 70.
114. "Nachricht," p. 68; *Lebensgeschichte*, II, pp. 123–24, 127–28, 144–45; IV, p. 66.
115. *Lebensgeschichte*, II, pp. 123–28.

great victory! In 1761 Kommerstätt resigned his commission and disappeared. The new commandant, a General von Roman, arrived on the scene with grim talk (like many a demoted officer) about doing things right, now, talk of putting bars on Moser's windows and chaining him to the wall. But soon he got over it and became more amiable and more lenient with Moser than Kommerstätt had been.[116]

From the time when Moser realized, after some months, that his stay at Hohentwiel was to be indefinite, he determined to devote his hours to his soul's weal. He partitioned his time among praying, reading the Bible, and singing hymns. As the months went by, his zest for composition returned and he thought of composing religious verses and hymns himself. He could think them up fast enough, but where was he to write them down? For the first time in his life he was without his good companions, the sheaves of paper and quills, the flasks of ink and sand; the spirit in his fingers twitched. One day some medicine arrived wrapped in stiff paper; Moser pricked out some words on the paper with a pin, but that was slow and did not go far. Then came a small tablet as a gift from Friderica Rosina, but though Kommerstätt let him keep the gift there was still nothing to write with. Moser found he could press letters onto the blank pages with the tongue of a shoebuckle, then the handle of a spoon, but not very clearly. The wall was better: he learned to scratch words into the plaster with his candlewick trimmer, and soon covered the whole wall, as high as he could reach, with pious verse. Now the wall was used up; and anyway how could he take these verses with him when he left the place? He found that if he laid a soft sheet between the pages of Steinhofer's sermons he now could press and scratch words in the margin that were legible from close up, held in the right angle to the light; and from there he went on to his other books, even the thin pages of his Bible as he gained skill, then to the letters he was allowed to receive from his wife, and after her death from his sons; and to the printed scraps, old newspapers and the like, he had for toilet paper. His tools grew dull too quickly and he tried to sharpen them on the stove; that made them too sharp and they tore the paper, so he learned to sharpen them on an oaken chair. "Now I could scratch again—write, that is, after my fashion, white on white!"[117]

He copied down onto paper scraps all the verses from the wall, and he composed more, enough to fill several volumes that he published after his release.[118] Then he went on to write paragraphs on theological

116. *Lebensgeschichte*, II, pp. 128–29; "Nachricht," p. 68.

117. *Lebensgeschichte*, II, pp. 144–48.

118. These are listed in the bibliography in Rürup, *Moser*, p. 268. The verses—several hundred hymns, with twenty-odd stanzas apiece—are as poetry unmetrical, cursory, and

subjects, and then to the legal problems (writing from memory) that had brought him to Hohentwiel—a treatment of the taxation rights of imperial princes, a history of recent European politics. He prepared a plan for "An Economic Commission, to be established in every significant province of the German Empire," which would organize and disseminate information concerning earth sciences, agriculture, manufacture, and commerce.[119] For amusement he wrote nineteen fables that he called "An old man's lighter hours during close fortress arrest," among them "The beloved, unusable [unbrauchbare], and hated honest man"; and "On those persons who do the state its most important service"—musicians and mistresses; and "Political and philosophical thoughts at the feeding of hens," a satire on European politics inspired by the daily sight of poultry scrabbling in the courtyard below. The fable of the hens was an anecdotal allegory for which Moser gave the apology that his arrest had made him a kind of "par-force Philosophen." It tells how the hens came running when Moser threw them the scraps from the window, but were driven away by a goose. Although the hens united might have resisted the goose, their republic did not comprehend their mutual interest; and when they complained severally of the tyrannical behavior of the goose, the latter replied with 1) natural law and modern worldly philosophy, 2) Roman law, and 3) international law, including something called neighbor law, and the law of convenience. Moser wanted to help the hens, but he was shut up and could not. Among them was one hen, he noticed ruefully, that tried to crow like a rooster. The actual rooster was outraged and attacked that hen, and the flock scattered. Another fable, which Moser favored or at least which he later printed in the Life History, was "The unfortunate patriotic carter." This was about the teamster Shortsight (Kurzgesicht), who prospered so well that he was made a town councilman, where in alliance with his fellows and the mayor (a member of the estates of Gutland) he stood fast against the creation of anything new. When a new paved chausée was built outside the town by the government of Gutland, Shortsight still insisted on taking his wagon

---

clumsy, largely addressed to God's power to overcome spiritual depression and doubts and to provide composure and integrity of soul. A review in the *Allgemeine Deutsche Bibliothek*, VI (1768), part 2, pp. 221–23, which appears to have been written by Friedrich Nicolai himself, called them "diese höchst schlechten und undeutschen Lieder . . . keine elenderen Gesänge als diese." The old Moser replied that they were "mehr für das Herz, als den Kopf," and he had not written them so as to make a name for himself as a poet; and if they were "undeutsch," then so was "meine ganze liebe Schwäbische Nation." *Lebensgeschichte*, III, p. 51; IV, pp. 129–30. See also the preface to Moser's *Gesammelte Lieder*, 2 vols. (Stuttgart, 1766–67).

119. *Lebensgeschichte*, II, p. 149; III, pp. 196–200; see below, §26.

over the winding hilly path even when it crumbled and washed away
with time and weather. One day the horses fell and the wagon collapsed
on top of Shortsight, but "he died still a patriot, who had never yielded to
these innovations." Moser added a parenthetical paragraph to explain
the political moral to readers of the Life History.[120]

On 3 September 1762 Friderica Rosina Moser died in Stuttgart, *mit
vor Gram*, Moser put it oddly and laconically in its place in the Life
History: acquainted with grief. Moser had a long letter from Wilhelm
Gottfried describing her agony and terror, hour by hour, as death approached, her struggle to compose herself for it, her protestations of love
for all her family—"ALL?" "Yes! all! near *and* far!" A few weeks later
Moser's daughter Wilhelmina Achenwall died, and shortly after that his
eldest sister.[121] That winter Moser's own health began to suffer, as the
war was ending; and by the summer of 1763 he was very ill again.

It is hard to say how Friderica Rosina's death affected Moser. He had
not seen her for more than three years, and there had been some distance
and failing of confidence between them in Stuttgart during his time with
the estates. She had written him faithfully during his imprisonment, letters full of pious exclamations and exhortations of a conventional kind;
but they were all, except one written at the very end that rings loving and
clear, oddly opaque and barren of personal intimacy, hard to read now
with sympathy and interest.[122] Her health had always been frail, and her
death had been expected for several months when she died. But if her
marriage had really been an unhappy one—so Moser at Hohentwiel
scratched out on his scraps of paper after her death—she could not have
lived so long. There had been little gaiety in their marriage. Indeed,
Moser admitted, often he had wished she had been more affectionate,
flirtatious, *tandelhaft*, toward him. But then he reflected that if she had
been, the consequences, given his own disposition, might have proved
injurious to his own health and shortened his life. Then he thought about
the passage in 2 Samuel 12, where David grieved and fasted while his son
lay ill, but arose when the child was dead and went to Bathsheba.[123]

During the years of arrest Moser had often had to struggle against
religious doubt and against "Kleinglauben," the limited faith of the
"natural" man. Now after his wife's death he began to be plagued with
"sacrilegious thoughts." He combed his mind to find where they had
come from and how he deserved them: it must be the devil. To add to

120. *Lebensgeschichte*, II, pp. 150–53; Schmid, *Moser*, pp. 318–29.
121. *Lebensgeschichte*, II, p. 131; III, pp. 231–35; "Nachricht," p. 69.
122. I mean the letters published by Moser in *Lebensgeschichte*, III, pp. 230–31, 240–45.
123. "Nachricht," pp. 22, 26, 69.

the stink of his slops bucket he developed flatulence, and remembered, appalled, how Jesus had called evil spirits unclean spirits; but he consoled himself that if God could put up with the devil, he could. It is hard to be sure about the chronology of Moser's illness because of his auto-biographical compartments, but I think I have it right. His gout, the hip-and-limb pains, came back in the winter of 1762–63. On 15 February 1763 the Treaty of Hubertusburg ended the war between Austria and Prussia that had precipitated the crisis between Karl Eugen and his es-tates and had delivered Moser to the fortress. At Hohentwiel Moser's peace was ending. By spring he had cramps in his lower back as well, "Kreuzschmerzen," and was all but crippled, hobbling about on crutches or lying painfully in bed. He thought how if he ever did get out of prison, then at certain times—dressing and undressing, going to the privy, getting in and out of bed—he would have to have help, maybe female help. He scratched out an "Instruction on Chastity and Modesty"; but the devil inflamed his fantasy as had not happened since his and Friderica Rosina's awakening, thirty years before. He lay awake at night, and prayed in the mornings to be released from sinful images.[124]

In May 1763 Moser wrote a letter taking leave of his children, with the practical thought that although he still might be released before he died, this letter would not make him die the sooner.[125] In August he sent an appeal to Karl Eugen, about his young son Benjamin: the boy's mother was dead and his brothers were away; he was falling behind at the Stutt-gart Gymnasium and soon must enter the university. Might not Benjamin come stay with his father, so that Moser could teach him? What good did it do Karl Eugen to keep Moser in this severe isolation? Might he not at least talk with somebody, a pastor, an officer, "only about indifferent things?"[126] Then in mid-September Moser began to scratch out the "Ac-count of my natural, civil, and spiritual life," which has provided (parts later transcribed in Moser's hand, the original scratchings having long since faded or been lost) much of the personal detail of his life so far recorded here.

As soon as he began the "Account" Moser promptly had a renewed attack of gout, and lay crippled with it for a week. Then he read through the story in Matthew 9 about the man sick with palsy—*gichtbrüchig* is the term Luther used, and *Gicht* usually means gout—who was forgiven

124. "Nachricht," pp. 5, 69, 71, 73; *Lebensgeschichte*, III, pp. 9–10.
125. It was printed by Friedrich Karl von Moser in *Patriotisches Archiv für Deutschland*, V (1786), pp. 466–78, and reprinted in Rürup, *Moser*, pp. 249–54.
126. Moser to Karl Eugen, 31 August 1763, in WHS KA III Ls 389. His concern for Benjamin was real, and justified: letter from Wilhelm Gottfried in Schmid, *Moser*, pp. 342–45; to Friedrich Karl in *Patriotisches Archiv*, V (1786), pp. 371–73.

his sins and so arose and walked; and he read of the two blind men healed through Jesus by their faith. Moser prayed for the faith of his sons. The gout went away and Moser set to work steadily on his "Account." Meanwhile his sons had indeed been working on his behalf, and on 12 December Frederick the Great of Prussia informed Friedrich Karl Moser that he had ordered steps at Vienna, Stuttgart, Hanover, and Copenhagen to bring about his father's release.[127] On 13 December the Austrian court confirmed titles of nobility to Friedrich Karl, Wilhelm Gottfried, and Christian Benjamin Moser von Filseck und Weilerberg, reviving the lapsed titles of a sixteenth-century Moser. The patent spoke praise for their father's "learning in the German public law." The arms displayed a gray goat on a red field, tongue extended, rampant.[128]

---

§25. Politics of Release and Return, 1763–1765

MOSER'S staged release and his stormy effort to reenter public life engaged the intertwined imperial, state, and confessional politics of the time. Most parties to it thought of Moser as a political and moral symbol in the engagement, an inanimate secondary piece to be thrust forward when that was useful, and to be silenced and immobilized when it was not. Moser was old and now long out of sight, a figure from the past; the past gave his name symbolic meaning. But Moser himself was not cut out to be an inanimate piece and the name of martyrdom was not enough. He would not accept the role assigned him by others. The symptoms were already there in his growing uneasiness, his renewed mental activity, and his illness at Hohentwiel from late 1762 onward.

The Württemberg estates had no trouble perceiving the changed political constellation after the Peace of Hubertusburg, even before that treaty was complete. With peace they were ready to rejoin battle. Duke Karl Eugen himself anticipated a renewed confrontation after the constitu-

---

127. *Lebensgeschichte*, II, pp. 132–33; III, pp. 10–11; "Nachricht," pp. 1, 70, 72.

128. UBT Ml 1; *Lebensgeschichte*, I, pp. 1–2. But Johann Jakob Moser had already used that seal on his August letter to Karl Eugen, and Wilhelm as early as August 1760. WHS KA III Ls 389.

tional stalemate of the war years. When the tide of war had turned in Prussia's favor in 1762, he had begun a reorganization of the constituencies, the local communities and district assemblies. This was designed to replace these social and political foundations of the estates with new electoral districts managed by his own officials. If he was not to be an imperial elector, at least he would be master in his own house. It was a direct threat to the existing estates; for if these organizational reforms took hold, they would find themselves politically undermined and constitutionally superseded. Moreover, the indefatigable Karl Eugen, after the French withdrew from the war at the end of 1762 and his military subsidies ended, demanded as compensation from the committee a sufficient sum (over a million and a half gulden) to support a standing army of ten thousand men, about four times the amount stipulated for peacetime by the 1739 settlement with the diet. When the committee refused to comply, the government set about collecting the revenues itself, on the wartime pattern. But now the emperor no longer needed Karl Eugen, who in some ways had become a political liability to him, or at best a bargaining counter; and even Frederick of Prussia was demobilizing, so that the duke could hardly claim any military emergency. The committee therefore, on 11 March 1763, reiterated its position that only a plenary diet could consider such a grant, and it even felt bold enough to threaten that if the duke did not summon one it would take its constitutional case to the emperor himself and his courts. At the same time it made representations to the guarantor states, who were now at peace and in a position to resume their sponsorship of the Württemberg estates.[129]

Within two weeks—and scarcely more than a month after Hubertusburg—the Württemberg emissary to the imperial diet at Regensburg, Johann Lorenz von Seefrid, reported to Karl Eugen and to Montmartin that Brandenburg and Denmark had asked for the release from arrest of Johann Jakob Moser (who, we know, now lay crippled with gout and obsessed with sexual fantasies at the Hohentwiel). In April Seefrid reported strong representations from Baron Münchhausen, in the name of his master, George III of England, to the same purpose; he added anxiously that like pressure was coming from all sides and from high places. The *corpus evangelicorum* was becoming actively interested. But the Prussians were the most important. Seefrid begged Montmartin to

---

129. Grube, *Stuttgarter Landtag*, p. 431; Adam, "Herzog Karl," pp. 234–42; Adam, *Moser*, pp. 69–72. The reorganization of districts and relocation of officials was an item of the estates' *Beschwerden* of 1764: *Von der Landeshoheit in Regierungssachen überhaupt* (= NTSR XVI, part 1: Frankfurt/Main, 1772), p. 182; and see below, §27.

persuade Karl Eugen to yield on this; the duke's delegation at Regensburg needed all the help it could get.[130]

Karl Eugen agreed to call a plenary diet for that summer, partly responding to outside pressure, but partly with the thought that he might do better with a newly chosen and instructed full diet than he could with the entrenched committee eminents. With the war over he might reasonably hope to get better support from the countryside than the committee would; moreover he seems to have been encouraged to believe that he could still count on Austria in a pinch. But his effort to collect the military assessment with his own officials made the constituencies unruly. Karl Eugen brandished threats and military force. The committee appealed to Vienna for imperial protection and asked the guarantor courts to exert themselves to bring it about. The emperor did not grant his protection, but he did not openly support the duke either. Nobody had a clear upper hand when the diet finally met on 19 September 1763. When it was assembled and began its deliberations, however, the diet proved to be solidly behind its committee, reelecting them all without dissent, and also behind its counsels—Eisenbach, Johann Wolfgang Hauff, who had replaced Moser in 1759, and the ex-counsel Stockmayer, who was prompting from the wings. It set forth a long list of Karl Eugen's iniquities and of formal grievances and demands, beginning with the unconstitutional treatment of its servant Moser and insisting on his prompt release and regular trial. An angered Karl Eugen, vigorously seconded by Montmartin, denounced the diet for its "criminal, foolhardy, malicious, and frivolous undertakings" and dissolved it early in November. And the diet went home, first nailing its flag to the mast in the form of a new demand for Moser's release. The next straw in the wind for Moser's own case was that patent of imperial nobility for his sons in December 1763.[131]

Now the government announced a new revenue plan: a regular general property tax to be administered by its officials, to replace the present unequal (and inequitable) assessments collected by the estates and passing through their treasury. Whether this plan would have reduced many people's taxes substantially is not clear. But it would have raised levies on the traditionally influential and the wealthy, and it laid assessments on the charitable endowments and funds which were a part of the network of patronage that sustained the estates and which theretofore had been

130. Seefrid's reports of 25 March and 19 April in WHS KA III Ls 389; see also Rürup, *Moser*, p. 166.

131. See above, §24; Adam, *Moser*, pp. 72–74; Adam, "Herzog Karl," pp. 234–44; Grube, *Stuttgarter Landtag*, pp. 432–35.

immune from government attachment. In March 1764, Karl Eugen ordered a general referendum on this plan, through his new organization of districts and towns. He threatened his officials with disciplinary action if they did not provide majorities, and in many districts they did. But the resistance of the older structures and forces was strong, led by the town of Stuttgart and by the Tübingen district director, Johann Ludwig Huber (who for his pains got an honorary doctorate of laws from the university and a term in the Hohenasberg fortress from the duke). In the countryside the estates held fast.[132]

In Vienna too the tide was turning against Karl Eugen and Montmartin. In March Montmartin was there for the election of the young imperial heir Joseph to be King of the Romans. Joseph was friendly with Friedrich Karl von Moser and would be emperor next year; at Vienna Montmartin found himself constrained to promise that the elder Moser would soon be released. At the Hohentwiel Moser's regimen softened: he was allowed for the first time to leave his high room and move about on the battlements, accompanied by an officer. Still very ill, he was allowed a doctor, but he could not speak with anyone else nor receive any other visitors.[133] In June the committee, having sent the counsel Hauff on a mission to test the weather at Vienna, decided to make a formal complaint against their duke before the Reichshofrat, seeking there an imperial order for Karl Eugen to release Moser, to reconvene the diet, and to meet their legitimate grievances. In July representatives of the Protestant guarantor powers arrived in Stuttgart—expenses and fees paid by the estates—to take up the estates' cause. Karl Eugen refused to receive these envoys and complained to the emperor about them. The emperor said he surely sympathized, but that was all he said.[134]

Formal court action against the ruling duke of Württemberg was filed at Vienna on 30 July 1764. It was supported by public dispatches from the guarantor kings to the emperor. Frederick of Prussia took the lead. A strong Württemberg estates beholden to him was a valuable, almost unique asset to Frederick in that corner of Germany, especially when this body served to curb and punish the military ambitions of a prince who had just made common cause with Frederick's near-mortal enemies; and not least important, Frederick resented Karl Eugen's treatment of Frederick's niece the duchess. His message recited the duke's repeated illegal extortions and violations of the estates' constitutional rights, rights that had been confirmed by the empire and the *corpus evangelicorum.* He grounded his own intervention, and that of England and Denmark,

132. Grube, *Stuttgarter Landtag,* pp. 436–38; Adam, *Moser,* pp. 74–75.

133. "Nachricht," p. 68; *Lebensgeschichte,* II, pp. 130, 133–34; Adam, *Moser,* p. 77.

134. *Lebensgeschichte,* II, pp. 134–36; Grube, *Stuttgarter Landtag,* p. 438; Adam, *Moser,* p. 75.

on their capacities as guarantors of the religious settlement, especially inasmuch as that settlement was an integral part of the political and constitutional issue. Karl Eugen's raids on ecclesiastical rights and properties, said the Prussian brief, violated the diet settlement of 1739, the Reversalien agreement of 1733, and even the 1555 Peace of Augsburg. Württemberg stood "on the border of chaos," Potsdam declared, and it was the emperor's clear duty to defend the rights of its estates. George of England said his grandfather had guaranteed the constitution of Württemberg and that he, George III, stood by that pledge. He had already told Karl Eugen this in a fraternal way, he said; now in his capacity as a prince of the empire he insisted on imperial action. And so said Denmark as well. The emperor Francis replied (to Frederick) that he was planning to look into the matter, this being his responsibility as sole judge of it.[135]

Moser's name did not appear in these royal declarations of late summer 1764, as it had in the remonstrances of the estates. Karl Eugen himself, though, casting about him for some reply, decided it was time now to do something about Moser. On 18 August he sent a message to General von Roman at Hohentwiel saying that he now felt inclined, despite Moser's heavy crimes, to release him from his arrest—on condition that Moser formally acknowledged that his release was "an act of grace that he did not deserve," and would petition in writing to be let free "repenting his great errors and offenses." Such a document from the hand of Johann Jakob Moser would have been a useful thing to the duke just then; and Moser on his side would be free. But a week later Moser replied (saying that he had only learned of the offer that day) that he would write nothing of the kind. "I have now in this sixth year had time enough to examine myself to see whether I am guilty of any offense against Your Grace; and if my conscience told me so I should not have waited this long to repent and ask forgiveness," wrote Moser. He was quite sure that he had always been true to his duty to the duke, and to the land of Württemberg, and that he had tried to erase frictions between them (no mention here of committee or estates). As an old man on the edge of his grave he would not purchase his freedom at the cost of his hard-won honor. Moser's righteousness shaded into impudence. If the duke wished it, Moser wrote, he would be glad to "offer his hand in any way that did not sully his honor," and would try to forget the past; otherwise he was ready for whatever might happen. Moser drafted a kind of treaty he was prepared to strike with the duke, specifying his terms: inasmuch as the duke had now decided to release him, Moser wrote, he was ready to

135. For the Prussian statement Robert von Mohl, *Beiträge zur Geschichte Württembergs*, I (Tübingen, 1828), pp. 38–42; for the others Moser, *Abhandlung verschiedener besonderer Rechts-Materien*, IV (Frankfurt/Main, 1774), pp. 431–40.

promise in return that he would not "without right" retaliate against Karl Eugen for the long arrest. And there he affixed his signature and a seal, the rampant gray goat.[136]

Moser's refusal to apologize or repent was characteristic enough—and where would confessing disloyalty have left him? He had held onto his self-esteem and dignity all these years by thinking himself a political prisoner—a victim, not a criminal or an intriguer. What would become of that, or any possible future employment, if he acknowledged himself to have been a lawbreaker, false to his duty and to the law? It is worth remembering hereabouts that Moser after all had been one of Germany's most renowned jurists, though he wondered now what might have happened to his reputation during the years of exile. Even a confession everybody knew he did not mean would be a mark of moral enfeeblement, of intellectual compromise. Still it would be interesting to know how much Moser knew of events outside and the pressures to which the duke was subject, or how much he was able to sense or read of them between the lines of Karl Eugen's offer.

Two weeks later, on 6 September, the Reichshofrat delivered a finding in favor of the estates of Württemberg. It ordered the duke of Württemberg to release Moser on condition only that he hold himself available for proper trial; it ordered the suspension of all extraordinary taxes, an immediate recall of the diet, negotiations over their grievances, and a government reply to them within two months. There would have to be a diet, then, an open contest with the assembled estates. Karl Eugen and his counselors put their heads together to think how to equip themselves, and decided it would be best to yield first on Moser in the interest of the other negotiations that lay ahead. They still felt reasonably sure they could keep Moser quiet in return for his release, and doubted that the committee or estates would find much use for him once he was freed. Karl Eugen gave the order for reconvening the diet, and retired to Ludwigsburg out of range of the guarantor and now also the imperial emissaries in Stuttgart.[137] And he gave instructions about Moser.

On 17 September there arrived at Hohentwiel the state councillor Johann Christian Commerell, a former district official who had risen recently and rapidly in Karl Eugen's service by virtue of his support in the property-tax matter. Commerell bore with him a series of formal charges, to which Moser was to make categorical and binding reply. Moser refused to accept jurisdiction of the duke's officers or courts in his case, saying that it belonged properly before His Imperial Majesty and the Reichshofrat; this seems to mean that Moser at Hohentwiel knew at least

136. Documents of 18 and 25 August 1764 in WHS KA III Ls 389.
137. Adam, *Moser*, pp. 76–79; Grube, *Stuttgarter Landtag*, pp. 438–39.

generally what had been taking place in Vienna and Stuttgart, though there were fair legal grounds too for his denial of state jurisdiction. Moser would, though, discuss the charges as a matter of "discourse and information." Commerell could write down what he chose and Moser would make his own record; but formal reply to charges must await his release.

The first charge against Moser was that in the spring of 1759 he had improperly advised the committee to refuse the defense monies required by the government, and that he had told the privy council that he would "give his gray head" before yielding. To this Moser replied that the committee, whose counsel he had been, had unanimously agreed that their constitutional mandate did not allow them to meet this demand in the absence of a plenary diet. Montmartin himself had implicitly acknowledged this to be so at that privy council meeting, presumably with his talk about yielding to force, and Moser then had said he would give his gray head rather than violate his oath.[138] The phrase attested not insolence but his honor. A second charge was that Moser had used disrespectful and slanderous language in committee messages to the duke. The attack on "evil advisers"—Montmartin—had slandered Karl Eugen as a "bad ruler" who could not tell good from evil. Moser said again that he had not written the passage in question, and that what he himself had written contained nothing disrespectful. A third charge was that Moser as early as 1758 had urged the council to seek help for their case from foreign courts. Moser readily conceded this; there was nothing wrong in it; there were imperial laws and precedents aplenty for settling inside disputes by outside mediation—not least among them, the mediation of the Reversalien dispute by the *corpus evangelicorum* in Karl Alexander's time. So "here I stand," Moser concluded, "I can do no other, God help me."[139]

This of course was not the reply the government wanted; but they had already decided for tactical reasons that Moser had to be released in early compliance with the imperial order, so he got out anyway, honor and all. On 25 September the duke ordered Moser to be set free as an act of clemency—thus saving what he could on the issue of guilt—on condition that Moser sign a formal bond pledging himself to appear before Württemberg courts on demand. This reservation conformed with the letter of the imperial order; and it may be that the government, in view of Moser's

138. See above, §23.

139. The reports of this inquisition—in Adam, *Moser*, p. 79–80; in WHS LA 2 41 5; in *Lebensgeschichte*, II, pp. 141–43; and in Moser's own record set down the following day (18 September) in WHS KA III Ls 389—are not quite alike but they substantially agree. I have mainly (but with some reservations and departures) followed the last.

denial of the duke's jurisdiction in his case, expected Moser to refuse to sign the bond. But on 28 September Moser did sign—perhaps because he knew the language of the imperial order (though he nowhere says he did), or perhaps because he reckoned he had pushed matters as far as he dared (as his silence on the matter suggests). He was promptly released and set out for Stuttgart.[140]

It was a very different journey from the one he had endured more than five years before. His gout had disappeared. He found himself famous in the countryside. In the first Württemberg village he entered the school-master came to the inn, saying he rarely entered such places but must make an exception today; he pointed at Moser and cried, *Unverzagt und ohne Grauen!* For Moser's arrest had become, in the intervening troubled years, heroic legend. Along the way he was recognized, cheered, blessed, prayed over. In Balingen, merchants on their way back from the fair at Zürich told him he was famous in Switzerland too. At Tübingen when he drove into the familiar marketplace the people crowded about him, calling out and straining to see him and speak with him. The description of Moser's journey home is a happy passage in his Life History. Only in Stuttgart, though, the passage concludes, "in places where one ought least to have expected it, was my return seen with indifference."[141]

The day after Moser's arrival in Stuttgart he received a caller, his old colleague and now senior secretary to the committee, Philip Friedrich Abel. On behalf of the committee, just now going into a brief recess, Abel offered congratulations and expressed the hope that Moser would soon resume his office as counsel. Now this was something Moser in prison had resolved never to do. Moreover, Friedrich Karl von Moser was even urging him now to leave Württemberg altogether in yet another "flight to Egypt." He told his father that everybody of friendly inclination at Vienna advised this. Moser should trust nobody. Imperial Vice-Chancellor Colloredo had told Friedrich Karl that he "certainly hoped your Herr Father will not stay in Württemberg" after his release; "he would do well to retire altogether." And Wilhelm Gottfried noted the marked indifference now from the side of the estates toward Moser.[142] But when the commit-

140. *Lebensgeschichte*, II, pp. 143–44; Adam, *Moser*, pp. 80–81. The exact date of his release is not clear. Adam, p. 82, says 26 September, Moser arriving in Stuttgart on 28 September; this sounds right; but Moser's bond, printed in *Lebensgeschichte*, II, p. 144, is dated Hohentwiel, 28 September 1764.

141. *Lebensgeschichte*, II, pp. 154–58.

142. WHS LA 2 41 5; Adam, *Moser*, p. 82; *Lebensgeschichte*, II, pp. 159–60; Schmid, *Moser*, p. 377. For a related discussion by Friedrich Karl von Moser of the perils of an official caught between two political sides, and of the relation between the estates of a land and the empire, see his *Was ist gut Kayserlich und nicht gut Kayserlich?* (n.p., 1766), pp. 229–34, 293–94; see also his *Daniel in der Löwen-Grube* (Frankfurt/Main, 1763).

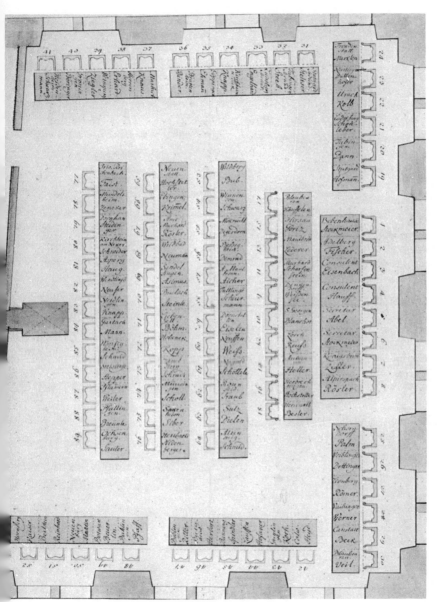

SEATING ORDER OF THE WÜRTTEMBERG DIET, 1763

"Only in Stuttgart, in places where one ought least to have expected it, was my return seen with indifference." Moser, Lebensgeschichte, II, p. 156.

Würtembergisches Hauptstaatsarchiv, Stuttgart

tee reconvened on 16 October, to prepare for the diet that would meet in ten days, there Moser sat. And he promptly launched an offensively ill-natured attack on the committee and staff—for not having done enough to get him out of prison, for having treated him badly during his earlier years as counsel, for loading blame for committee actions on his shoulders. He even accused them, almost certainly unjustly, of betraying him behind his back to Karl Eugen's officials. Out burst a whole boil of suspicions that had festered over the years. But despite it all, Moser concluded, he would forget the past and stay with the committee if they wished it. Then he walked out.

The committee, hoping to avoid a new quarrel with the martyred Moser, sent Abel the next day with a mild reply: they were distressed at what he had said and hoped he would refrain from saying such things in the future, so as not to disturb the mutual confidence that must rest among them all. Moser answered that he was "very sensitive" about this. He had said nothing he could not prove (almost certainly, again, this was not so); and inasmuch as the committee showed so little confidence in him, he would not serve. When that brought no reply Moser announced, two days later, that he would leave it up to the committee whether he served or not. Oh no, answered the committee, you decide. Moser said he would take an opinion from the Reichskammergericht judge Johann Heinrich Harpprecht (not his student crony but a member of the same clan). Harpprecht replied that a man with Moser's past could hardly put himself again "between wind and wave," he would be "more a stumbling block than a bridge." Would that God might allow Moser "some little space yet between time and eternity" to rest in the "harbor of security." The biblical Joseph, Harpprecht pointed out, "served his father and brothers far better in Egypt than at home."[143]

Moser assented to this "sour conclusion" and made ready to go stay with his youngest daughter, Renata Gottlieb, now married to Johann Friedrich Mohl, a Baden official in Karlsruhe. The committee said it would be glad to receive opinions from him—in absentia—and would remit his full salary to him—at Karlsruhe. Committeeman Johann Friedrich Dann, a sometime student of Moser's who had followed him to Frankfurt on Oder thirty years before and who now was mayor of Tübingen, would keep him in touch.[144] But yet Moser hung on in Stuttgart; he caught a fever and could not travel. Around the end of October he got

143. Adam, *Moser*, pp. 82–86; Rürup, *Moser*, p. 188, n. 32; Lehmann, *Pietismus*, p. 113; Schmid, *Moser*, pp. 389–91.

144. On Mohl, below, n. 160; on Dann, above, part I, n. 136, and Rürup, *Moser*, p. 191, n. 139; Adam, *Moser*, pp. 86–87.

back his papers that had been seized in 1759. Not all were returned, for the government kept some that they thought might be used to embarrass Moser or the estates, and kept some others that he or the estates might use to embarrass the duke and the government. Moser carefully sorted and filed the ones he had.[145]

The diet reconvened on 27 October; a week later Moser submitted a lengthy opinion on the propositions the government laid before it. In effect he adjured the diet to stand fast on all points. Although none of this commentary quite contradicted anything Moser had said before, there was little sign in it now of the duke's cameralist commissioner of ten years before, except maybe a mirror image. He scorned the government's claim that it would save money by streamlining administration if its requests were met; this was not feasible, Moser said, and would save only trifles even if it were. To the duke's demand for a large military establishment, Moser replied that Württemberg's security could never depend on its own military resources, but only on the general security and stability of the empire. Anyway "sad experience teaches" that Karl Eugen used forces raised at Württemberg's cost not for the defense of the duchy but for foreign wars. Peacetime military expenditures speeded the circulation of money, to be sure; but they circulated it right out of the pockets of the "middling man," into the hands of folk who contributed little to the general welfare. Gains that peasants realized from rising prices and artisans from demand for their work would be swallowed up in general inflation. The ducal household and court must be obliged to live within their means. As for the cameralist measures of political economy that had so engaged Moser a decade before—all that business must be rolled back to the position where Karl Eugen had found it when he had assumed the government in 1744. His unconstitutional behavior must be stopped at all costs. The expense to the duchy of constitutional resistance, for drawn-out legal and political procedures, would indeed be great; but "either one follows the course of law, or else one leaves it and gives the money over to the military."[146]

Then on 21 November 1764 Moser wrote a sharp-tongued letter to the duke, which, after mentioning his own important political connections

145. A careful analysis of the papers was made by the government before they were returned to Moser; among those withheld (which thus escaped burning by Friedrich Karl after his father's death) were an attack on the quality of Reichshofrat justice (above, part II, n. 94), his "Reflections" on the imperial election of 1745 (above, §16), and Karl Eugen's grateful note to Moser of 15 July 1756 (above, §21).

146. *Votum* of 2 November 1764, in WHS LA 2 41 5. The opinion is ordered into pros and cons, but leaves little doubt of Moser's choice.

and the imperial favor shown his sons, demanded back the bond he had signed and full restitution of his honor. Otherwise he would bring the whole matter before His Imperial Majesty's own eyes—at Vienna, where legal proceedings in any case were under way. Or additionally, Moser would invoke the imperial diet at Regensburg to his defense. Montmartin snarled, and his teeth still grind aloud in the comment he made on this to Karl Eugen: "If we were doing this scenario at another point in time and in other conditions, then the suitable thing for Your Grace's dignity would be to tell this old political mole [Staats-Grübler] that what happened to him was done on good political grounds, approved by the imperial court itself; that he should be satisfied with his release and annoy Your Grace no further." But Moser must be given his precious honor and bond to keep him quiet, Montmartin advised. Far from wanting to try Moser, the government really only wished he would go away. So Moser got back his signed bond and was informed that his imprisonment had been inflicted for political reasons, not subject to criminal penalty.[147]

But early in January Moser found trouble in another quarter. The emperor's ambassador to Württemberg, Baron von Widmann, had called him to Ludwigsburg for a private talk. Moser allowed that he was not well informed these days, but he did have some opinions. He told Widmann that Karl Eugen's government had to be pushed back to the constitutional position at the time of his accession, clear back to the regency. There would be disaster if the duke were not brought soon to heel. One way to do this would be for the ambassador to convince Karl Eugen that the letters from the three kings meant serious business. Another was to publicize certain scandals about the duke's private and public misbehavior. And so the conversation went, the ambassador raising objections as probes, Moser deploying his arguments and warming to the work as he went along. The estates of course were much aroused when they heard that this private meeting had taken place, and at their request Moser, quite properly, made a report of it to the committee. In Moser's report one might read that Widmann agreed at least in principle to most of what Moser had said; the committee transmitted it to the full diet, whence it promptly leaked. There were copies or extracts to be had all over Württemberg and elsewhere, to the acute embarrassment of Widmann and the annoyance of his superiors in Vienna, to the discredit of the estates, and to the rage of Karl Eugen.[148]

At this juncture, the imperial vice-chancellor Colloredo wrote to Fried-

147. Moser's letter of 21 November and Montmartin's memorandum of 23 November 1764 are in WHS KA III Ls 389; Adam, *Moser*, pp. 87–88.
148. Moser's report of 5 January 1765 is in WHS KA III Ls 389; *Lebensgeschichte*, IV, pp. 67–68; Adam, *Moser*, p. 90.

rich Karl, to urge again Moser's retirement from public affairs. Meanwhile the estates, who had offered to pay Moser in absentia, would have none of him in Stuttgart and told him as little as possible about their affairs. Their officials avoided him—although he was still officially counsel, the most learned of them all—and they were engaged in drafting extraordinarily complex and detailed legal materials for the critical proceedings in Stuttgart and in Vienna.[149] Excluded from official work, Moser began to publish his own views on certain sensitive points at issue, and on the first of June he offered to postpone his planned summer cure at the baths, if he was needed. But he was not needed; even the Prussian emissary to the negotiations at Stuttgart said emphatically that Moser was not. In August of 1765 Moser finally made good on his "sour conclusion" and went to stay with his daughter's family in Karlsruhe, and the Württemberg constitutional crisis entered its final stage without him.[150]

§26. Powers of States and Estates, 1765–1769

MOSER had no part, though not for want of trying, in the deliberations amongst Stuttgart, Vienna, and the guarantor courts that ultimately produced the Württemberg Erbvergleich or Hereditary Agreement of 1770. Kept outside the circle of negotiators and draftsmen, he gave his attention to what he thought the constitutional issues and implications were for diet, state, and empire, and in the course of this began to develop the views that formed his jurisprudence of the 1770s. In 1765 he fired off a great volley of pamphlets

149. The *gravamina*, which became the basis of the Hereditary Agreement of 1770, are summarized in Grube, *Stuttgarter Landtag*, pp. 439–40: 1) constitutional violations respecting legislative rights, taxation, and the administration of justice; 2) ecclesiastical grievances (giving legal grounds for the intervention of the Protestant guarantors); 3) military grievances; 4) cameral grievances, such as the misuse of excises and monopolies, and maladministration of ducal properties and rights; 5) forests and hunting rights; 6) government violations of the rights of communities and district officials (the administrative reorganization begun in 1762).

150. *Lebensgeschichte*, II, pp. 159–60; Adam, *Moser*, pp. 90–92; Schmid, *Moser*, pp. 394–96.

and other short polemical tracts—thirteen of them in that year, all ostensibly anonymous. Most of these were directed to particular points where the constitutional conflict of the 1750s had crystallized. Moser had been unable to sort out the political issues between duke and estates constitutionally then and had gone to the Hohentwiel where he had had time to ponder, without the clutter of his card files, how it had all come about and what to make of it. Now that he had his pen back but no office he returned to the juridical problem of reconciling two claims to supremacy, that of established right and that of administrative authority, within the context of imperial law. These juridical writings of 1765 were not conclusive either, but they show a direction and a link, forged in these intensely political Württemberg years, between the earlier Moser of the *Teutsches Staats-Recht*, and his later greater work in the *Neues Teutsches Staats-Recht*.

Two of the short pieces of 1765 treated problems of military rights and duties, with the approximate titles "The obligation of subjects to regular military service" and "What the basic imperial laws say to the question of how many soldiers an imperial prince shall maintain, and who shall determine this."[151] The latter drew largely on the analysis he had prepared for the estates late in 1764,[152] but put it here in more general terms of the imperial constitution. Here too the estates got the better of Moser's argument, implicitly; but that did not exhaust the problem. His question was not really how many troops an imperial prince, a Reichsstand, might maintain, but how many an imperial sanction might oblige his land to supply. Thus, as far as imperial law went, it seemed that a prince might constitutionally have as many as he could support out of his own private and cameral resources, or even from foreign subsidies—*ordinarily*, added Moser, who was clearly unhappy with this legal conclusion. The "ordinarily" meant, for example, that the prince could not by this authority quarter such soldiers of his own on the country, or conscript them from among unwilling subjects. Distinctions had to be made among the kinds of troops and the use made of them. The contingent to the imperial circle, for example, was one for which the whole land was constitutionally responsible. But politically vital distinctions had to be made between troops used abroad, and those used to garrison home fortresses; or between local militias, and standing armed units under direct princely command.

---

151. *Reichs-Grund-Gesez-mäsige Beantwortung der Frage: Wie vil Soldaten eines Teutschen Reich-Standes Land zu erhalten schuldig seye? wie auch Wer den Ausschlag darinn geben könne?* (n.p., 1765); *Abhandlung von Noethigung derer Unterthanen zu regulairen Kriegs-Diensten* (n.p., 1765). My citations to the latter are from the text in *Sammlung einiger neuen Abhandlungen von teutschen Staatssachen*, II (1765), pp. 185–230.

152. The *votum* of 2 November 1764 (above, §25).

In fact, though, it all came back to the relation between prince and subjects; all the distinctions were conditioned by compacts and agreements particular to the state in question. Consequently these compacts and agreements, rather than imperial law, ultimately must set the boundaries of a prince's military rights.[153]

Moser gave special attention to the doctrine of "Nothfall" or emergency, which allowed a prince military powers that overrode normal procedures: a doctrine Karl Eugen had regularly invoked before and during the Seven Years War. He could not deny the doctrine's general validity or its firm foundation in imperial law; and imperial authority had supported Karl Eugen's invocation of it. But he made a long list of conditions for the use of it, and put the conditions, this time, not as constitutional artifacts but as reasoned political prose. The emergency must be real; it must not have resulted from the prince's own actions; effective defense must be in fact feasible and within the land's capacity; and when the danger is past the emergency rights expire. None of these entitled a prince to maintain a standing peacetime army on his own authority. Imperial law entitled no prince to maintain as many soldiers as he saw fit on general grounds of his responsibility for the defense of the land. In Moser's other military treatise, on the obligation of subjects to serve, he conceded that even the standing-army question was complicated by special agreements and precedents going back to the sixteenth and seventeenth centuries. But still these were territorial rights, particular to the constitutions of the states concerned. They were not absolute nor immutable, nor founded in imperial law.[154]

The direction of the argument persisted when it came to taxation rights. Moser at Hohentwiel had scratched out a short "Principles of the right of taxation," which he now published as an essay for laymen, along with a more formidable and technical treatise to the same effect. In these Moser's emerging theme was the difference between German territorial supremacy or Landeshoheit as foundation for the constitutional right, and the idea of sovereignty. A prince's taxation rights came to him with the Landeshoheit; but the Landeshoheit was subject to limitations, and so, accordingly, were his taxation rights. Moser's more technical treatise came out of the card files of German public law: tax rights by his showing were agreements between rulers and estates. They could be changed, but only by mutual consent—and only, Moser here allowed, where mutual confidence and reciprocity prevailed. Anyway the Landeshoheit gave princes no power to modify them unilaterally. His more general essay went further into political theory and political principle. Not only did

153. *Wie vil Soldaten*, pp. 1–33.
154. *Wie vil Soldaten*, pp. 33–51; *Abhandlung von Noethigung*, especially pp. 189–201.

the Landeshoheit confer no absolute taxation right, Moser declared, no European ruler, however "sovereign," could credibly claim such a right. The very crown of France, though founded on the doctrine of monarchic sovereignty, and though its *parlements* could not be deemed true estates, had in fact no such unlimited taxation rights.[155]

Moser's own professional ambiguity in the 1750s between state and estates, and his musings on it in confinement, had brought him willy-nilly to the theoretical problem of sovereignty as a basis of right—somebody's plenitude of political authority. And while he sometimes accepted the term "sovereignty" in an international sense, to identify a state's action among other states taken independently of all others (as France might, for example, but never Württemberg), he never used it in a domestic sense, except rhetorically or as equivalent to lawlessness. Nobody was sovereign *within* a civil society. In the 1770s he was to turn to the problem of how to locate authority where the very concept of civil sovereignty was radically denied, as Moser denied it, but yet where positive rights were mutable with time and circumstance, as Moser insisted they were and must be. Now in 1765 he began with a headlong attack on the concept of sovereignty in German law, in the form of a searing commentary on the views of the jurist Johann Adam von Ickstatt, director of the Bavarian university at Ingolstadt and now an electoral adviser at Munich, and of his nephew Peter Josef Ickstatt, who had succeeded to his uncle's professorial chair at the university.[156]

The elder Ickstatt, a scholar for whose competence Moser had always had considerable professional respect, had joined Catholic jurisprudence of authority together with a deductive natural law on the Wolff pattern, into a combined doctrine of sovereign majesty. But worse yet, he had expounded this position in a Latin treatise, tacitly aimed at the Württemberg conflict and defending Karl Eugen's authority, which had appeared in July 1759, the very month of Moser's arrest. Ickstatt called it "Saving the Landeshoheit from abuse by capitulations, state compacts, and agreements."[157] Moser, now out of arrest, wrote voluminous notes to a German edition of Ickstatt's work, renaming it "A short guide for

155. *Abhandlung von Recess-widrigen, oder doch unbewilligten Land-Steuern* (n.p., 1765); and *Grund-Säze des Besteuerungs-Rechts derer Teutschen Reichs-Stände* (n.p., 1765); see *Lebensgeschichte*, II, p. 149.

156. On the Ickstatts, Fritz Kreh, *Leben und Werk des Reichsfreiherrn Johann Adam von Ickstatt (1702–1776)* (Paderborn, 1974); Roderich Stintzing and Ernst Landsberg, *Geschichte der Deutschen Rechtswissenschaft*, III (Munich, 1910), pp. 277–82; Johann Stephan Pütter, *Litteratur des teutschen Staatsrechts*, 4 vols. (Göttingen, 1776–91), especially I (1776), pp. 459–63. A rather different Ickstatt holds the stage in Notker Hammerstein, *Aufklärung und katholisches Reich* (Berlin, 1977), pp. 33–131.

157. Kreh, *Ickstatt*, pp. 126–30.

princes who want to break their obligations and overthrow the constitutions of their lands at will." No ruler had a right to abrogate established rights and compacts merely because they no longer suited political conditions; times changed, to be sure, but rights could be modified with the times only by new negotiations.[158] The younger Ickstatt for his part gave as a first political principle that "the government of a state consists in the right to direct the activities of subjects in such a way that the common weal of the state is thereby maximized." Here, answered Moser, was a perfect *petitio principii*, a begged question, justifying government in the name of a common weal that the government itself identified. As for sovereign monarchy in the world of facts, again, not one ruler in Europe exercised unlimited power; not even the czar of Russia (Peter III had recently been deposed, murdered, and replaced by his widow Catherine) could threaten the religious and social rights of his subjects without placing his person and state in desperate danger. Moser denounced the whole huckstering "sovereignty-makers guild," amongst whose masters he included Niccolò Machiavelli, Thomas Hobbes, and both Ickstatts— followed by all those ministers, counselors, and legal scholars who built their careers on the ruin of their lands.[159]

None of these public polemics—and there were more—seemed likely to commend Moser to the committee of estates in their perilous negotiations. If Moser hoped otherwise, then he willfully disregarded both the tortuous working style of the negotiators and their dependence on the support of powerful princes. But now, behold, there arrived through the agency of another Mohl son-in-law[160] an overture from the duke of Württemberg, inviting proposals from Moser on how his troubles with the estates might be settled. Moser replied from Karlsruhe in November of 1765. After some ambiguously conciliatory language blaming Mont-

158. *Johann Adams Freiherrn von Ickstatt . . . Rettung der Landes-Hoheit gegen den Missbrauch derer Capitulationen, Landes-Verträge und Reversalien* (Frankfurt/Main, 1765), pp. 105 and passim.

159. *Herrn Peters von Ickstatt . . . Säze von dem Majestäts-Recht der Obristen Herrschaft und dessen Folgen* (n.p., 1765); *Von der Landeshoheit derer Teutschen Reichsstände überhaupt* (= NTSR XIV: Frankfurt/Main, 1773), p. 256. In *Von der Teutschen Reichs-Stände Landen* (= NTSR XIII, 1769), p. 1188, Moser wrote of "dieses orientalische Staats-Recht" of Machiavelli, Hobbes, and the Ickstatts. But in 1770 he was more graceful toward the elder Ickstatt: "Ein vernünfftiger und geschickter Mann, deme es nur an mehrere Freiheit fehlet, zu schreiben, was er denckt. Er ist ein Liebhaber der Mathematik und lasset es in seinem Vortrag starck spühren." *Neueste Geschichte der teutschen Staats-Rechts-Lehrer und deren Lehre* (Frankfurt/Main, 1770), pp. 107–9.

160. Christiana Beata's Carl Gottlieb Mohl, an official in Stuttgart. Their son Benjamin Ferdinand (b. 1766) was to be the father of the nineteenth-century political scientist and publicist Robert von Mohl (1799–1875), who thus was Johann Jakob Moser's great-grandson.

martin for the past unpleasantness between himself and Karl Eugen, Moser observed that anything he now said could not be construed as coming from the estates, where he was thoroughly distrusted as it was. But he would say some general things on his own account. First, Württemberg must be ruled Württemberg-style, *auf württembergisch*; second, Karl Eugen must use and rely on honest and able ministers; third, he must completely revamp his fiscal system. He must learn to rule constitutionally. The old constitution provided resources enough for firm authority and effective government—but string the bow tighter and it will snap. The reasons were not only domestic. The imperial court's own interest and authority required that German princes must not become sovereign (*souverän*); "no emperor ever can or ever will let it come to that."[161] Karl Eugen must never count on the emperor to set him free of the estates.

Whatever Karl Eugen's reasons for asking Moser's advice, the main pressure upon him to conciliate his estates was at this time coming from the king of Prussia, a monarch who brooked no estates of his own, and whom Friedrich Karl von Moser at the time likened to Tacitus's Caesar: better either that he had never been born, or that he never died.[162] Frederick the Great threatened the Reichshofrat with unilateral action by himself to defend the Württemberg ecclesiastical settlement and estates if imperial authorities did not do it. Karl Eugen tried to deflect the wind from the north by asking his estranged duchess whether she might not like to forgive and forget and come home now to Württemberg. But her uncle at Potsdam promptly diagnosed this as a political tactic (as it was, and as the duke's gesture to Moser at the same time presumably also was), and Frederick would have none of it. Indeed, the messages that flew among Prussians at this time seem to say that whereas the guarantor team at Stuttgart aimed mainly to do maximum damage to Karl Eugen, their master at Potsdam was mainly determined to keep his niece out of the duke's clutches. Vienna on the other hand was working for the reconciliation. On 10 May 1766 Karl Eugen lightened ship: Montmartin was dismissed from office, a move that Frederick, again correctly, interpreted as a political feint which would not end Montmartin's influence over the duke. In reply to news of this from Stuttgart, Frederick wrote irritably to his emissary there that "I have seen what your report of the tenth of this month tells me about the affairs of that duchy down there [*du Duché de là-bas*]," but what about the matter of his niece the duchess? Three weeks later he ordered the duke to be told in his name "that I can never acquiesce in his reconciling and making peace with her, in the

161. Rürup, *Moser*, pp. 189–90, with Moser's text on pp. 245–48; *Lebensgeschichte*, II, pp. 160–61.

plain intention of using her, so to speak, as a puppet, to entrap the estates of Württemberg"; and so it went until the duchess was safely ensconced in Potsdam itself.[163]

The Protestant protector had his own particular interests; and hardly anybody in the 1760s could suppose him to be a defender in principle of the Public Peace and constitutional order of the empire and its estates. King of Prussia seemed essentially incongruous to politician of the empire; that bothered Moser. Maybe the phrase "nicht nach dem *Gout* des heutigen *Seculi*" rang in his mind—surely something like it. Anyway he had not forgotten what Prussian constitutionality signified. In 1767 (to skip ahead of the story briefly) Moser wrote a biting attack on the uses of "rational" jurisprudence in the constitutional law of the empire, in which his obvious political target was the Prussian state and its constitutional apologists. He invoked German nationality to sustain the imperial constitution in all its parts. "Europe knows that the Holy Roman or German Empire is the German nation, constituting its own political body," wrote Moser. Despite all pretensions of mighty German princes, "in Germany itself there are no European states or independent lands."[164] About the same time he published an essay "On the guarantee of the Peace of Westphalia, according to the sense and the letter thereof," which focused on the constitutional dangers raised by the Seven Years War. He argued that it was the first and particular duty of imperial estates, and not of European sovereigns—here he used the word in the international sense— to uphold the imperial constitution and peace. An imperial estate could not, in that capacity, act as a sovereign. If a sovereign outside the empire was an imperial estate within it (Denmark, England-Hanover, and Brandenburg-Prussia) then his rights and duties respecting the empire flowed from his place in it and not from his sovereign status elsewhere. And other members of the empire had no responsibility for his actions outside it as a sovereign. An imperial prince with this double capacity thus had a right and an obligation to uphold the constitutional order of the empire, including the recognized rights of estates and subjects, but he had no right to involve them or the empire in his quarrels as a sovereign.

162. *Was ist gut Kayserlich?*, p. 100.

163. "Pour tâcher d'engager par-là les Etats de Wurttemberg." Mohl, *Beiträge*, I, pp. 46–49, 73–182; Grube, *Stuttgarter Landtag*, p. 442.

164. See above, §9. *Gedancken über das neu-erfundene vernünftige Staats-Recht des Teutschen Reichs* (Frankfurt/Main, 1767), pp. 27–28, 40; this essay will be considered in more detail below, §28. In 1769 Moser directly indicted Prussia ("certain places, especially since 1713 and 1740"—the accession dates of Frederick William I and Frederick II) for violating the rights of subjects "when their whole right consisted in having 100,000 men under arms." See also below, §29.

The guarantees of the German constitution, a German responsibility, must be kept free from the doings of independent sovereigns.[165]

And, considering Prussia, Moser was especially concerned for confessional guarantees, which were at the base of the Peace of Westphalia and of the Württemberg constitution too. They had been the grounds for the intervention by the "sovereign" guarantors, the three kings, in Württemberg's affairs. That intervention probably had rescued the Württemberg estates, and Moser too; and if religious issues alone had been at stake he might have been content with that. But the same episode showed how religious confession and its guarantees could become instruments of the competitive politics of states. The rights of Protestants in particular seemed to be becoming a domain of Prussian state interests. Moser himself had found it most unpleasant to be thought a tool of Prussian policy.

Alternatively, the right imperial institutions must be found to sustain these guarantees, and for Protestant rights Moser summoned to this role the *corpus evangelicorum*, the constitutionally organized Protestant party of the empire. In that same volley of pamphlets in 1765 were two on the Zedtwitz affair. The family of this name held jurisdiction in the district of Asch, protruding westward from Bohemia, held it as a fief from Maria Theresa's Bohemian crown (which Moser had defended twenty-five years before); yet they were recognized as immediate to the German Empire. Their ruling male line was Protestant, as was the population of the district. Insofar as the Zedtwitz-Asch merely exercised Bohemian crown jurisdictions, the Austrian government—here the Catholic Bohemian crown—was entitled to control religious institutions and exercises there as part of the Landeshoheit. But insofar as they were immediate to the empire, their Protestant religious jurisdiction and immunity were constitutionally guaranteed. It had long been a sore issue; family religious disputes there repeatedly tempted Habsburg intervention, which in turn stimulated family religious disputes. Moser had written in defense of the immunity of Asch twenty years before at Ebersdorf and again at Hanau; now in the politics of the mid-sixties, upon a formal Zedtwitz complaint against the crown, it erupted as an issue which was politically dangerous and to which Moser gave serious constitutional meaning.[166] He called

165. *Von der Garantie des Westphälischen Friedens, nach dem Sinn und Buchstaben desselbigen* (Stuttgart, 1767); for the contemporary political import, see the review in *Allgemeine Deutsche Bibliothek*, XII (1770), pp. 798–99, and *Von Teutschland und dessen Staats-Verfassung überhaupt* (= NTSR I: Stuttgart, 1766), pp. 447–55.

166. See the titles listed in the bibliography in Rürup, *Moser*, pp. 260–61; Schmid, *Moser*, pp. 545–47. On the Zedtwitz issue summarily, Pütter, *Staatsverfassung*, III, p. 210. The careful list of imperial estates in Bruno Gebhardt, *Handbuch der deutschen Geschichte*, 9th ed., II (Stuttgart, 1970), pp. 769–84, does not include either Zedtwitz or Asch. But the town of Asch ranked among the first half-dozen of the Kingdom of Bohemia: tables in

repeatedly upon the *corpus evangelicorum,* as the responsible imperial body, to make the constitutional defense of Protestants in this sensitive region. Institutions of the empire, not rivalry between Austria and Prussia, should sustain the constitutional equilibrium upon which so many political and religious rights (as in the case of Württemberg) depended.

During 1766 at Karlsruhe Moser restrained his polemical pen altogether, perhaps in hope of making himself more palatable to the committee—for he still hoped to be called to active service in the negotiations, and in March he visited Stuttgart in a vain attempt at reinstatement.[167] But in exclusion from Württemberg affairs, he was thinking again on the massive scale of the German public law, and that year he published the first volume of what was to become his *Neues Teutsches Staats-Recht.* The first five or six volumes would summarize and bring up to date the old series, which had lapsed when he came to Stuttgart; then he planned to treat other topics he had not considered there but which now seemed to him of great importance. The opening volume was about the basic laws of the empire; but then he jumped clean out of sequence for a volume on the imperial estates, in 1767, and one on the business of the Reichstag, in 1768. Then in 1769 he skipped far ahead of the scheme, just in time for the climax of the Württemberg negotiations, with two volumes on the lands of imperial princes, "their estates, their subjects and their rights, grievances, obligations, and convocations."[168] Also he went to work on his own Life History, drawing extensively on the "Account" he had scratched out for posterity at Hohentwiel.[169]

Johann Stephan Pütter, *An Historical Developement of the Present Political Constitution of the Germanic Empire,* 3 vols. (London, 1790), appendix, p. 7.

167. *Lebensgeschichte,* II, p. 160; Adam, *Moser,* p. 93; Moser's appeal to the committee is in Schmid, *Moser,* pp. 405–6.

168. *Von Teutschland und dessen Staats-Verfassung überhaupt* (= NTSR I: Stuttgart, 1766); *Von denen Teutschen Reichs-Ständen, der Reichs-Ritterschafft, auch denen übrigen unmittelbaren Reichs-Glidern* (= NTSR IV: Frankfurt/Main, 1767); *Von denen Teutschen Reichs-Tags-Geschäfften* (= NTSR VI: Frankfurt/Main, 1768); and *Von der Teutschen Reichs-Stände Landen, deren Landständen, Unterthanen, Landes-Freyheiten, Beschwerden und Zusammenkünfften* (= NTSR XIII: Frankfurt/Main, 1769). The 1967 reprint of the NTSR series by Otto Zeller in some instances departs from the traditional numbering of volumes that Moser intended and used: see *Allgemeines Register über das Moserische alte und neue Teutsche Staats-Recht* (Frankfurt/Main, 1775), preface. Thus Moser's vol. III becomes Zeller's V, IV becomes III, V becomes VI, and VI becomes IV.

169. The surviving manuscript of the "Nachricht" that I have seen was at some time transcribed in Moser's hand from, presumably, the Hohentwiel scratchings, but with signs of emendations. This completes the sections on his "natural" and on his "spiritual" life, but the "civic life" breaks off mid-sentence and mid-page at 1725. I do not know whether there was more in the scratched original or in any other possible draft that has since disappeared; Moser in *Lebensgeschichte,* I, preface, seems to say there was.

This first volume and edition of the Life History, chronologically ordered, fell into two sequential parts that paralleled one another in structure: one told of his journey from birth and baptism to dismissal from Frankfurt on Oder, the other from Ebersdorf to Hohentwiel arrest.[170] It is a book that charms from a distance, partly for its language of innocent naivety; and though composed as a straightforward narrative, it allows to the reader the self-satisfaction—or annoyance—of discovering things in it that Moser himself seemed unconscious of, or meant to conceal. It admitted faults and errors on Moser's part that are easy to forgive, but few others; and it was filled with pointers to Moser's own virtues and moderation. These features at the time were not so easy to smile at; and also there were opinions and gossip in it that many contemporaries, notably on the committee, were not pleased to see. The book achieved a current notoriety; it was promptly pirated and reprinted in a 1769 Münster edition.[171]

In 1767 Moser returned to the defense of Zedtwitz-Asch, with a perverse and impolitic vehemence that managed to destroy his standing with the Austrian court in turn. He denounced both the Bohemian government and the administration of imperial justice, and for remedy called again upon the *corpus evangelicorum* to intervene.[172] This was a serious embarrassment to Friedrich Karl von Moser, who by now had made an eminent name for himself in Germany as a political writer and learned official, and who in the autumn of that year was appointed, though Protestant, to a seat on the Reichshofrat by the new emperor Joseph II.[173] The elder Moser's four polemical pamphlets of 1767 on Zedtwitz-Asch were anonymous, so it was possible to overlook them. But the 1768 *Neues Teutsches Staats-Recht* volume on the business of the Reichstag, a signed and solemn work of learned authority, contained a passage on "political considerations" affecting religious grievances that could not be ignored.

170. For a literary analysis that puts the *Lebensgeschichte* in the tradition of pietist autobiography, Marianne Fröhlich, *Johann Jakob Moser in seinem Verhältnis zum Rationalismus und Pietismus* (Vienna, 1925), pp. 135–56. There was a critical and shrewd contemporary review by August Schott in his *Unpartheyische Critik über die neuesten juristischen Schriften*, I (1769), pp. 412–20, which pointed to the amalgam of openness doubled into guile, and remarked on how Moser's humble tone did not really hide his vanity or his low opinions of others. Moser replied to this in the preface to his third edition (1777).

171. *Lebensgeschichte*, I, preface. Moser's own first edition was published in Offenbach (Hessen) in 1768 and reached a third edition (Frankfurt/Main, 1777), which I have mainly used, followed by an additional fourth part (Frankfurt/Main, 1783).

172. The titles are listed in the bibliography by Rürup, *Moser*, p. 261.

173. Friedrich Karl had published *Der Herr und seine Diener, geschildert mit patriotischer Freiheit* at Frankfurt/Main in 1759, and *Was ist gut Kayserlich und nicht gut Kayserlich?* at Frankfurt/Main in 1766.

This alleged a pattern of religious usurpations on the part of Roman Catholic princes, and defended the authority of the *corpus evangelicorum* to thwart them. Moser praised Joseph II in the course of this but warned him against bad advisers, and he cast more slurs on the government of Bohemia.[174] Friedrich Karl was admonished (in August 1768) to tell his father that the imperial court was seriously displeased at this inflammatory meddling in a delicate unresolved issue; Moser had shown open disrespect toward the emperor and particularly toward the person of his mother the queen; and the hostile way in which Moser treated Austria was notably different from his indulgence toward blatantly illegal actions by "a certain other court."[175] Around the same time Moser published a separate volume, on the political affairs of the empire since the end of the Seven Years War, which recurred to the theme of defending Protestant interests through imperial institutions. Here he argued that Protestant appointees to the Reichskammergericht at Wetzlar could constitutionally be sworn to follow in their official judgments the principles and decisions of the *corpus evangelicorum*. This opened a controversy of which there will be more to say later on; here let it be noted that what had put the notion in Moser's head was the interesting situation of a fellow Swabian, Johann Ulrich Cramer, who in 1765 had been named by Brandenburg-Prussia to a seat on that imperial court.[176]

In reply to the furor at Vienna and Regensburg over his behavior, Moser sent an aggressive apology to the emperor Joseph, who then told Friedrich Karl orally that this was not acceptable: Moser must delete the offensive passages from any further printings, and must submit all future manuscripts on German public affairs to the Reichshofrat or the imperial censors prior to publication. Moser replied now in a tone of humble bewilderment that he had no idea which passages had caused offense and surely would never have written them if he had known they would offend; of course he would cut them out if somebody would tell him which they were. At his age, Moser went on, he had just as soon stop writing altogether if that was what the world wanted, and forget about the *Neues Teutsches Staats-Recht*. When Vienna finally did tell Moser

174. *Von denen Teutschen Reichs-Tags-Geschäfften* (= NTSR VI), pp. 440–47.

175. *Lebensgeschichte*, II, pp. 163–64. The last complaint probably meant particularly Moser's discussion of the ban proceedings of 1756–59, where Moser put Prussia on an equal constitutional footing with Austria, and emphasized the role and rights of the *corpus evangelicorum*: *Von denen Teutschen Reichs-Tags-Geschäfften* (= NTSR VI), pp. 206–18.

176. *Lebensgeschichte*, II, pp. 164–65; IV, pp. 70–71. The volume was the *Neuestes Reichs-Staats-Handbuch, oder Nachricht von den seit dem Hubertusburger Frieden öffentlich bekannt gewordenen Staats-Handlungen*, 2 vols. (Frankfurt/Main, 1768–69). The case in point was that raised by the Reichskammergericht judge Johann Ulrich Cramer, and the story will be pursued further in this work below, §§30–31.

officially just which passages were offensive, he decided that by then there were too few copies left undistributed to worry about; and he decided that for subsequent volumes he would comply with prior censorship by using asterisks and special fat black type to mark the places where imperial censors had modified his manuscripts.[177] At the end of 1769 the harassed Friedrich Karl von Moser was raised to the rank of imperial baron (Freiherr) and sent to be governor of the County of Falkenstein; gratefully he resigned his place on the Reichshofrat and left Vienna. He had had a miserable time there, and the emperor was saving his life, he said, by sending him away.[178]

By now the Württemberg constitutional negotiations were coming finally to a head, while Moser stewed at Karlsruhe.[179] The diet had been in recess since December 1767 while the committee worked secretly; and the committee still would have nothing to do with Moser. Karl Eugen, though, showed renewed signs of a friendly disposition toward Moser: he readily granted retroactive pay to Wilhelm Gottfried, at Moser's request, as compensation for the three years he had spent unemployed and forbidden to leave Württemberg after his dismissal in 1759. The duke also granted certain favors to Moser's other children, respecting disposition of Moser's property after his death. To Moser's letter of thanks Karl Eugen sent a cordial handwritten reply, in January of 1769, saying that if Moser cared to come by in person he would be glad to see him. Moser promptly presented himself, and the duke declared that inasmuch as he now realized Moser was an honest man, a good patriot, and a loyal subject, Moser might always count on his gracious protection. He invited Moser to stay for dinner.[180]

And that spring Moser's aforementioned big book in two volumes on the qualities, rights, and grievances of estates in German lands appeared. This was Moser's backdrop for the constitutional conclusion, and it also

177. *Lebensgeschichte*, II, pp. 166–71. Moser threatened then to break off the NTSR, even though, he said, the important parts were yet to come: preface to *Von der Teutschen Reichs-Stände Landen* (= NTSR XIII); and see below, §28. For whatever reason, the imperial censors soon lost interest in censoring the NTSR. After 1769 Moser published no more volumes until 1772, but then thirteen volumes of it appeared in the next three years. The only places I have noted his highlighting of censored passages is in *Von denen Kayserlichen Regierungs-Rechten und Pflichten* (= NTSR III: Frankfurt/Main, 1772–73), dealing with imperial rights in religious matters. There is other evidence of the effect of censorship in the delay in publishing the latter half of the volume, and in the uncertainty of pagination in the table of contents and elsewhere.

178. *Allgemeine Deutsche Biographie*, XXII (Leipzig, 1885), p. 771.

179. For the proceedings of 1765–70, see Grube, *Stuttgarter Landtag*, pp. 441–44.

180. *Lebensgeschichte*, II, pp. 173–74; Moser's letter from Stuttgart, 14 February 1769, to Maria Dorothea Mögling, is in the possession of Helmut Haecker at the Hirsch-Apotheke in Urach/Württemberg.

set the scene for his own final foray into Württemberg politics. The book on the whole was a sober description of the constitutional and social order within the German principalities, with modest efforts to classify them and generalize about them. It was written on the scale of imperial law, and part of its purpose was to lay the foundations for the new work that was to follow in the *Neues Teutsches Staats-Recht.* Moser gave no disproportionate space to Württemberg—rather less than one might have expected of the most famous of the German estates, just then in its most dramatic hour. Still, many of his general remarks of a political nature— what estates were good for and how they ought to behave—came to bear from his Württemberg experience and seemed addressed to the Württemberg case. At any rate the readers of 1769 were prompt to find such passages and interpret them that way.

Moser declared unequivocally that the estates of a German land, wherever they existed and however they had begun, now by virtue of their existence "represented" the whole land.[181] With representation, Moser conferred upon them, or imposed upon them, a public capacity, superseding the exercise of private rights.[182] This public capacity affected how they were to regard themselves. But here Moser introduced a corollary. (Readers interested in the constitutional principle will wish to see his exact wording in the note below).[183] This public office of representation, which was what gave to the actions and decisions of estates a force binding "all inhabitants of the land," was present only in plenary diets. It could not be exercised by special committees or officers. This provision of Moser's seems not at all necessary in law or in logic. Probably he meant here in a theoretical way to sharpen the role of representation by distinguishing it from anything more like government or administration. For anybody thinking concretely and explicitly about Württemberg in

181. "Sie seynd Repräsentanten des Landes *in favorabilibus & odiosis, Custodes Legum & Jurium Patriae,* Vorstehere, und gleichsam Vormundere, des Landes." *Von der Teutschen Reichs-Stände Landen* (= NTSR XIII), p. 843. Also: "Wo nun Land-Stände seynd, repräsentieren dieselbige das ganze Land." Ibid., p. 1300.

182. See the observations of this point by Renger, *Osnabrück,* p. 46. He says that Moser was the first to specify this public role clearly and that he thus prepared the way for Justus Möser's, Johann Stephan Pütter's, and David George Strube's development of representation theory as a check on princely absolutism, relying here on a somewhat fanciful passage in Otto F. von Gierke, *Das deutsche Genossenschaftsrecht,* I (Berlin, 1868), p. 820. There were of course also particular rights that pertained privately to membership in estates: *Von der Teutschen Reichs-Stände Landen* (= NTSR XIII), especially pp. 547–606.

183. "Ein Land-Ständisches *Corpus* stellet in Landes-Sachen die gesamte Landes-Innwohnerschafft vor; so, dass dasjenige, was man auf einem allgemeinen Land-Tag beschliesset, eben so angesehen wird, als wann die samtliche Landes-Eingesessene Mann vor Mann darein bewilliget hätten; dahero dergleichen Schlüsse eine allgemeine Verbindlichkeit nach sich ziehen." *Von der Teutschen Reichs-Stände Landen* (= NTSR XIII), p. 716.

1769, though, he was denying that the committee and its acting counsels had any right to represent or to bind the people of the duchy.

The influence of German estates and diets, Moser wrote, had an uneven history, with ups and downs in different times and places; but they were particularly challenged by the institution of peacetime standing armies.[184] Although they were entitled to take any action that contributed to the general weal of the land and was not forbidden by their constitution, their basic instrument was the statement of general grievances addressed to executive authority. This could be negotiated with their prince or, if he proved unwilling, brought before an imperial court; in such action estates were never answerable to a state's courts. Usually a ruler was well advised to negotiate, rather than allow the airing of dirty linen in direct confrontation. And in open disputes "often the subjects' eyes are opened for the first time; they become wiser than is in their master's interest; they learn their rights and where to seek and find help." (And so the strength of the grievance weapon, implicitly, depended on whether the estates represented the rights and interests of the land truly enough to risk public scrutiny.) Still, subjects and estates must remember that though they were no slaves, neither were they co-regents. Again this may have clarified by contrast the principle of representation in a theoretical way, but Moser's explication was political and concrete. "The lord is still master," *Herr bleibt doch Herr*; and he can retaliate in a thousand ways no imperial court can prevent. "We live in no Platonic state," recited Moser; and both sides to a dispute must play close attention to shifting political circumstances in the "political theater," at Vienna and the other major German courts.[185]

To the much-debated question of whether constitutional estates were good and useful things, Moser replied that this depended on circumstances. From the ruler's point of view, estates were a "gold mine" if he behaved himself and got along with them. If he was evil and greedy and his estates resisted, that frustration might humiliate his person but at least his successors thereby would inherit something better than "a plundered nest." From the point of view of the land as a whole, it was important to have a constituted body in position to prevent abuses of the Landeshoheit, that princely territorial authority "which nowadays has

184. Ibid., p. 410. Perhaps by historical implication it was the institution of standing armies that thrust their public role upon them.

185. Ibid., pp. 715, 833, 839–42, 1299–1325. Moser here made no connection between assent to taxation and the presentation of grievances. In fact, surprisingly, he makes no direct mention at all of the fiscal rights of estates, only that they must do what the weal and the particular laws of the land require.

reached such exaggerated pretensions," a body able to restrict government to its original purpose, to wit: "that every subject shall live in
security, support himself honorably, enjoy in peace that which is his, and,
if he becomes involved in a dispute, to receive evenhanded justice." Above
all, Moser insisted, the interests of the estates must be kept continually
in close accord with the interests of the land as a whole, or as nearly
aligned as possible. Then the whole business of oaths, plenipotentiary
powers, instructions to delegates, and the rest falls away. The constitutional estates then further the land's interest as they further their own:
shared self-interest was another corollary to the representative principle.
Self-interest is "a driving wheel with incomparably more effect on most
people than anything else one may urge upon them."[186] Moser was
warming now to his chapter "The uses and abuses of a land's estates."
One sort of thing estates were *not* good for were matters requiring political skill (Staats-Klugheit), or clear knowledge of the complex political relations of the empire and Europe. Keep them out of that. Anything
that required secrecy should be kept from them, lest it get into "all too
many big mouths [Mäuler]," ruining the enterprise. They could not reach
speedy decisions, which sometimes were necessary. Still, there was a lot
to be said for a diet composed of very ordinary people—"*vox Populi,
vox Dei*; and just as a sound peasant philosophy often makes more sense
in praxi than the hair-splittingest Cartesian, Thomasian, or Wolffian,
etc., so too the common man and a diet composed of not especially
political people" often made sounder judgments than an over-ambitious
ruler "along with his whole ministry."[187]

There (and then) Moser oddly sounded almost like a radical outsider.
But he also declared that it was important to have knights in the estates, a
Ritterschaft—of course there were none in Württemberg's. A mediate
nobility was experienced in government by inheritance; they had useful
outside connections and prestige. But most important, if the land was
ruined they were ruined with it, and this was not always true of people
who turned up in the estates, "especially in certain places." Individual
nobles were often selfish and corrupt to be sure, just like other sorts of
people; still estates were better off with that class among them than
without them. Where there were no knights, and where estates consisted
only in people who have studied nothing useful, "and have no understanding of economic policy, commerce, manufacture, or cameralistics,
then usually these pillars of a well-founded state will turn out badly,"

186. Ibid., pp. 491–93.
187. Ibid., pp. 497–98.

unless the governing ministry is well staffed and the incompetent estates let themselves be manipulated at the government's pleasure, so as to make up for their own deficiencies.[188]

Summarizing the right personal qualifications for members of a diet and its officials, Moser used language the committee of the Württemberg estates had heard before. They must have courage, spirit, insight, honesty, industry, "neither too violent nor too conciliatory"; they must never be "slaves to some patriotic obstinacy and stupidity," nor unwilling to hear good advice when it is offered them. Wherever estates "have no great mother-wit," where they were "*dumm-patriotisch*," where they "know right away that everything that seems new is a heresy, and just hang onto received opinions," and the like—then "woe to the land, that finds its fate in such hands." And this applied particularly and expressly to estates' committees.[189] As for the counsel or syndic to the estates, where he was accorded trust and authority, "this is as important a position as any minister; in fact he can do more good or harm than the whole ministry ... and where there are no knights at all in the estates, much more depends on this man than where there are knights." But the more important such an officer's role was, "the greater the danger to him in critical times." For documentation Moser referred readers to events in Holstein and Mecklenburg, and to his own Life History.[190]

188. Ibid., pp. 411, 496–97. Lehmann, "Die württembergischen Landstande," p. 200, opines that the Württemberg estates were strong, first, among other reasons, because the absence of nobles (Adel) allowed a socially homogeneous body. Rudolf Vierhaus, "Ständewesen und Staatsverwaltung in Deutschland im späteren 18. Jahrhundert," *Dauer und Wandel in der Geschichte: Festgabe Kurt v. Raumer* (Münster, 1966), pp. 337–60, says that in general German estates were *weaker* where the nobility (Adel) had left them—with the exception of Württemberg. The analysis of Osnabrück in Renger, *Osnabrück*, pp. 67–84, favors Moser's view. Moser used the term "Ritterschaft" and not "Adel" here, and he addressed not the point of power but of civic responsibility; yet the main example that seems to have been on his mind at the time (other than Württemberg) was Mecklenburg, where issues of power may have been more prominent than responsibility. Near the end of his career Moser repeated his preference for an estates with Ritterschaft, now citing electoral Braunschweig, where as Land-Syndicus "ich würde hoffentlich brillieret haben." *Lebensgeschichte*, IV (1783), p. 111.

189. *Von der Teutschen Reichs-Stände Landen* (= NTSR XIII), pp. 498–99.

190. Ibid., pp. 813–14.

§27. 1770: The Constitutional Settlement, Moser's Readmission Dispute and Dismissal

AT the beginning of 1770 the terms of the Hereditary Agreement seemed, finally, all but complete. They were being released piecemeal at Vienna, and they amounted to a sound defeat for the duke of Württemberg. He was obliged to acknowledge his estates and their committee to be "*corpus repraesentativum* of the whole beloved fatherland," and must promise to deal with them "according to the old customary ways." The ecclesiastical settlement was restored. The military budget was fixed—but the Small Committee could grant emergency defense funds without recourse to a diet. The government was forbidden to violate community constitutions or the organization of diet constituencies, or to hire, dismiss, or transfer local officials on its own authority. The monetary cost to the estates for this victory was substantial. For although their regular contribution to the government was set back to the 1739 level, the committee's expenditures during the long struggle had to be met, many of them discretionary and unaccounted for. Moreover, the estates agreed to contribute annually toward a dissolution of the duke's debts, and to reimburse persons from whom he had collected illegal taxes.[191]

Still the constitutional triumph was clear; in Stuttgart the committee was victorious. The political conjuncture that had freed Karl Eugen's hands in the 1750s had been reversed. Joseph II's imperial government was back in the business of reducing the powers of imperial princes, at least of this one it could get at. The guarantor powers in this instance were quite willing, and their support of the Württemberg estates was holding. A plenary diet was convened on 25 January to ratify the settlement. Karl Eugen continued to struggle; he was grasping for straws when there was a sudden disruption in the estates. On 8 February, the Tübingen burgomaster Dann in the committee and the university chancellor Reuss in the diet placed simultaneous motions for the full readmission of estates counsel Johann Jakob Moser to the deliberations.[192] To the committee, complacent in its success, this came as a fire bell.

The event cannot have surprised Moser. He had been back in Stuttgart for some time, apparently; and he had been openly critical of the com-

191. A summary of the Erbvergleich is in Mohl, *Beiträge*, I, pp. 54–58; text in Reyscher, *Sammlung der württembergischen Gesetze*, II (Stuttgart, 1829), pp. 550–609.
192. Grube, *Stuttgarter Landtag*, pp. 443–45; UBT Mh 253.

mittee's actions, about which his friend Dann had kept him informed. He probably thought, for one thing, that provisions of the Agreement were too extreme for the duke's government to abide by them in the long run, so that they would only breed more trouble and more chicanery. But above all he suspected (with good reason) private dealings, under-standings, and corruption on the committee's part; and he had come to think that unless some provision was made, the Agreement would estab-lish the committee as a permanent self-interested oligarchy, able to make its own ongoing arrangements with the government and with others, to the exclusion of the estates of the duchy. This would violate the notions of representation and identity of interest he had been thinking about; and his constitutional objections fed upon his personal resentment of the committee and staff. Specifically, he thought the committee should now be obliged to give a public accounting of all they had spent during the negotiations. The main villains he saw were his old rivals: the counsel Eisenbach, the chief prelate Fischer, and the secretary Friedrich Amandus Stockmayer. He had discussed these views with Dann and with dis-affected members of the estates, and had repeated to them his willingness to return to his duties as counsel if called.[193] In all this Moser's personal jealousies and taste for vengeance against the committee are easy enough to see, but that does not mean his diagnoses or his prognoses were mistaken. He was quite right.

On 12 February there was, as the burgomaster of Calw wrote home, *"collisio et controversia magna"* in the diet over Moser's readmission. Moser's advocates in the debate were four: Dann, Reuss, the prelate and theology professor Johann Gottlieb Faber, and the good gray pietist theo-logian Friedrich Christoph Oetinger, Moser's old friend. Reuss's brother, it happens, was court physician; Faber's brother was a state official in close touch with Karl Eugen. A day's uproar in the diet settled nothing; and on the following day the committee ruled that the accrediting of a counsel was a decision for itself to make, not one for the diet plenum. On the fifteenth the duke intervened, with an order for Moser's readmission. For Karl Eugen thought or hoped that finally he had found a way to split the diet or divide it from the committee—or at least to obstruct it, to throw the deliberation of the Agreement into confusion at this last moment. His aim was clear enough to everybody, and that made Moser's readmission part of a government plot. The committee turned confidently to the plenum, which on 20 February duly affirmed the committee posi-

193. Adam, *Moser*, pp. 96–103. Moser admitted his early private discussions with estates members and his stated willingness to return in his 27 June 1770 memorandum, LBS Cod jur fol 193. For exchanges between Moser's champions in the estates and Karl Eugen, see Lehmann, *Pietismus*, 113–14.

tion by a vote of seventy to four. The effect of Karl Eugen's Moser maneuver had been to bring the diet solidly behind its committee.[194] On 27 February Karl Eugen yielded and ratified the Agreement, and on 2 March the diet followed suit.

The diet's work was not over, though, for it still had to prepare the mandate for the committee's power to act in its behalf during its recess— which, judging by past experience, might last for decades. The terms of this mandate therefore would define the committee's authority to represent the duchy, and Moser's emphatic views on this were of course known. Moreover, even when the Agreement had been ratified by contending parties, but before it was sent to Vienna for final confirmation, negotiations were reopened on certain points, to the great aggravation of the guarantor ambassadors. The question of Moser's readmission became inextricably entangled with these matters; Karl Eugen continued to support him, with special eye, the ambassadors believed, to the guarantor courts, hoping thereby to attract their support against the committee and diet majorities. Moser's readmission would be a significant victory for those dissident diet and committee minorities who were trying to restrain the committee's powers.[195]

It was not certain how sentiments lay in the country, or how outside powers would react; and all sides competed for the favor of Württemberg public opinion and of the German courts. Karl Eugen issued pamphlets and posters, and promised new appointments and security to local officials. He showered Vienna with correspondence and he wooed his duchess. The committee sent emissaries to Hamburg, Berlin, and Hanover.[196] The duke sent out a printed proclamation to deny the charge that his intervention on behalf of Moser and the Four was designed to confuse and delay the Agreement; rather, it was to prevent an unconstitutional abdication of estates authority to the committee. He urged constituencies to call their deputies to their constitutional duties, and to withhold any mandate unless they were sure of their deputies' position on Moser's readmission.[197] The guarantor ambassadors, however, entreated their

194. Adam, *Moser*, pp. 104–7; reports by the guarantor ambassadors in Mohl, *Beiträge*, I, pp. 290–95; Adam, "Herzog Karl," pp. 273–74. Lehmann, *Pietismus*, examines the relations among the Four and Moser, p. 113, n. 135; he describes the group as wishing to "mit dem Herzog zusammenarbeiten und christliche Landespolitik treiben," p. 115. Accounts differ on the sequence and detail of some of these actions.

195. Mohl, *Beiträge*, I, pp. 304–7; Adam, *Moser*, pp. 108–9; petition of Reuss, Oettinger, Faber, and Dann to Karl Eugen, 24 March 1770, in UBT Mh 253/k. Karl Eugen was kept fully informed on the votes and groupings in the diet through the brothers Faber: WHS KA III 1 81.

196. UBT Mh 253, passim; WHS LA IV 11–22.

197. UBT Mh 253/p, q.

governments not to be taken in by this Moser maneuver nor leap to his defense; "it is quite impossible for this man to live without strife." Frederick of Prussia replied dryly that he did not expect to be taken in.[198] From Vienna the duke's special emissary, Commerell (whom Moser had encountered in his last days at Hohentwiel), reported that Vice-Chancellor Colloredo recommended that Karl Eugen drop the cause of this disagreeable old man: let the situation cool and wait for a better opportunity.[199]

At the end of April the diet resolved that Moser should not be readmitted. A letter was sent to the district assembly at Tübingen to inform them that Dann would be excluded henceforth from any meeting where the Moser question arose, and they were invited to choose another delegate. The Ludwigsburg assembly, whose delegate had been an intimate of the duke, was queried whether their deputy really represented them.[200] On 7 May the decision not to readmit Moser was transmitted to the duke, with a request for him to cease his championship of this man who had been rejected by the diet by vote of seventy to four, and who was a source of constant dissension on account of his "changeable principles and conduct"—the old epithet from the 1750s. For many reasons, this acid message went on, they would not mention the opinions that Karl Eugen himself had once expressed about Moser (clippings were circulating about of that newspaper announcement of 17 July 1759). The estates agreed with the imperial vice-chancellor that Moser should spend the rest of his life in peace.[201]

Peace! Now Moser himself, who apparently had been staying out of sight during the wrangling over his case, burst upon the scene. His outrage and frustration at the situation in which he now found himself was surely compounded by the realization that he had let himself in for it, and that the probable outcome for him was the worst imaginable, with respect both to his personal dignity and to his constitutional views. He sent a long, furious memorandum to the diet, defending himself and attacking the committee, in language more violent and bitterly personal than any of his I have seen. So the committee claimed, did they, that he had made trouble for them? Indeed he had; they were "men and not

198. Mohl, *Beiträge*, I, p. 308. Karl Eugen complained to the estates about "foreign intervention": ibid., pp. 311–13.

199. Adam, *Moser*, pp. 113–14.

200. UBT Mh 677. The Ludwigsburg deputy was Georg Thomas Schoenleber, a committee member whose political rise had come as office salesman for Karl Eugen and as mayor of the residence town Ludwigsburg, and whose committee loyalty was dubious at best. But Schoenleber played no visible role in the Moser readmission controversy.

201. Adam, *Moser*, pp. 114–16, 130; see above, §§23, 25.

angels," and deserved to be summoned to answer for abuses and corruption in office. He called upon the plenum to make remonstrance against the committee and to require a full financial accounting. He said that weak and malicious men had deliberately misrepresented his position; the last thing he wanted was constitutional disruption or innovation; what he demanded was a restoration and a strengthening of the old constitution of the land and estates. The whole constitutional system, in this very moment of apparent victory, was in a process of decay; the estates by their own acquiescence had become "an empty name, a mere shadow of what diets mean elsewhere and once were in Württemberg itself." They were prey to ignorance, laziness, and greed. The Small Committee was worst of all, and its proper subordination to estates and land must be reestablished. "It is not admissible that the weal and woe of the whole land should be played out in the hands of two or three persons." To revitalize the constitution, accordingly, the usurped rights, responsibilities, and authority of diet and Greater Committee must be restored. For this several steps were necessary. Moser himself must be reinstated, for Eisenbach had shown that he could not be trusted with the counsel's job. There must be a thorough and detailed investigation of all committee expenditures, and especially of the uses for which the enormous outlays of the constitutional conflict had been spent. Finally, there must be a regular constitutional mandate negotiated between *duke* and estates, not between committee and a compliant diet, to govern the committee's powers and procedures. Even the present rules, though sworn to by the committee, were not observed. Present abuses, unless they were formally corrected, would come with usage to stand as established custom and thus as law.[202]

Turning to his personal defense, Moser made of it an attack on the committee and its officials. The renewed accusation of "changeable principles" particularly stung his honor and aroused his ire. *His* changeability? He was no false patriot, no hypocrite, no . . . "Wilkes, who lines his private pocket and tries to make himself popular by bravely denouncing the Court so as to gain favor from the rabble and stir them up; and because he gabbles at them all about freedom and upholding the coun-

202. Moser's emotional memorandum is reprinted in Adam, *Moser*, pp. 117–43; manuscript copies abound in the Württemberg archives, in number approaching Xerox scale. The insistence that the power of the committee must be formally and constitutionally checked by agreement between diet and duke is the main basis for Rürup's position (*Moser*, pp. 190–97) that Moser aimed at a reform of the Württemberg constitution. Moser himself was very explicit to deny any suggestion of that nature; he said repeatedly that he meant only to restore the true constitutional relations between estates and committee, by formal agreement to forfend abuses.

try's rights and pulls the wool over their eyes and so makes, out of imputed slaves of the Court, low lickspittles of his own." After this unlikely comparison of the Württemberg Small Committee with John Wilkes (unless, fantastically, he really had contemplated a Wilkes-like role for himself), Moser pointed out that he had suffered much on the estates' account; and if some people were trying to force his retirement, that was because he was champion of the estates, not of the duke. "Finally, that the estates, or rather the ruling party there, desires me to spend my remaining life in peace, that I quite believe; then everything will stay in the same disorder, and thus be legitimized by the land." It need not come to that even yet, no matter how the readmission turned out; "and once the old inner constitution of the estates is restored (which can happen in a few weeks if there is the will), then I will gladly spend my remaining days in peace."

After Moser's memorandum of 17 May there could be no serious hope of his returning to his office as counsel. Still Karl Eugen continued to champion his case, perhaps hoping for a new change of attitudes in Vienna but more likely for another reason, shortly to appear. On 19 May a ducal order went out announcing special protection for the learned, loyal, and afflicted Moser; it was signed by Montmartin of all people, who had been lurking about all this time but who now at the bitter end openly emerged. Jakob Heinrich Dann spent that long hot day at Tübingen arguing before the district assembly there. At the end the assembly decided for the committee. Moser should not be admitted, and the committee need not account for its expenditures in detail to the plenum. Dann was forbidden to represent the Tübingen district in any other sense.[203]

The story grows dreary and need not go on much longer. Karl Eugen refused to let the diet go home until the Moser question was settled. Then on 18 June, in return for a *don gratuit* of sixty thousand gulden, he let Moser drop and approved the dismissal of Dann from the committee; and he agreed that the committee's expenditures need not be explored. The diet recessed on 25 June, leaving the Small Committee in possession of the constitutional powers of the estates.

On 16 July Moser was dismissed altogether from the office of counsel to the estates of Württemberg; after some bargaining Montmartin extracted another twenty thousand gulden from the committee in return for Karl Eugen's official assent to this expulsion. Moser's and Dann's

---

203. WHS KA III 1 81; there is a collection of material bearing on Dann's relations with and exclusion from the committee and diet in WHS LA 2 26.

portraits were removed from the gallery in the dining hall of the estates; they were restored by unanimous vote of the next plenary diet, which met, in other circumstances, in 1797. Shortly thereafter, though, Moser's official portrait disappeared again.[204]

204. Adam, *Moser*, pp. 144–55; Grube, *Stuttgarter Landtag*, pp. 447–48, 459, 614. Napoleon Bonaparte's advice to the elector and king Frederick II of Württemberg about his estates is said to have "Chassez les bougres"—Wilhelm Lang, "Die auswärtige Politik der württembergischen Stände," *Preussische Jahrbücher*, L (1882), p. 372—and in 1805 he did. I believe Moser's official portrait to be the 1751 likeness reproduced in this volume, of which Württembergische Landesbibliothek has only recently acquired a copy by courtesy of the private owner.

PART IV

Reason, Nature, and a World without End

§28. The Anti-Philosophe

THROUGHOUT his life, Johann Jakob Moser the jurist had been a declared enemy to rationality and system applied to the public law. For him "Vernunft," both as a justifying principle for law and as a vehicle for its exposition, was opposed to right. Its contrast with "right" was what distinguished and defined "reason" in that rational and systematic sense of the word. Moser's rejection of formal reason as a constitutional mode had permeated the shape and substance of his written jurisprudence. At nearly every crisis of his career Moser found himself in collision with reason, in some one of its contemporary political or philosophical costumes. That was the Moser who had gone to the Hohentwiel. His hostility toward reason had come to locate him near one end of the spectrum of professional opinion in the world where he lived and worked, a world dominated philosophically by a tension between fact and system, and politically by a tension between mixed particular interests (sometimes called freedom) and dynamic purpose (sometimes called ambition). It was an embattled position in the 1770s.

Yet this attitude of Moser's toward reason and his expressions of it had always been flawed by an uneasy and vulnerable tone of personal resentment, envy, or insecurity, a fear of intellectual inferiority. To counter the spokesmen of Vernunft Moser did not simply expound. He huffed, he pouted, he protested. Quite apparently he was jealous of their rhetorical elegance and their philosophical credentials. Much of the Life History, especially the early parts, was addressed to explaining and defending his own shortcomings in those modes, going back to university years and before, blaming his professors, his haste, and, of course, his forthright character and truthful tongue and pen. Surely this fed on doubts within himself, contest between parts of him. And it was awkward to make reasoned arguments against reason.

But by the end of the 1760s, Moser's hostility toward reason had taken on real conviction and vehemence; it had been affirmed by "experience"; it was truly "pragmatic." His own softening toward reason in Württemberg service in the 1750s had ended by restoring him firmly to the party of rights, by way of Hohentwiel. His foray into Staats-Klugheit in the sphere of administrative policy, as committeeman to the duke of Württemberg while counsel to the estates, had brought him there. Not only had he been unable to live in both compartments at once. More telling, Staats-Klugheit had betrayed him; in its name his master had sent him to prison—in contempt of law and right and of Moser's own virtuous intentions. Moser's attack on the Ickstatts had come almost at the moment of his release, even as the Ickstatt treatise he denounced had appeared at the moment of his arrest; and the target of his attack was a

doctrine which, in Moser's reading and political understanding, justified the
eclipse of contracted and established political rights in the name of reason and
the common weal. So Moser had no difficulty perceiving his personal mis-
fortunes and his scholarly quarrels as analogous parts, both of them bred from
a broad, serious, and dangerous tendency in political practice and opinion. He
confronted that quite real conjuncture of political practice with ideas that
schoolbooks once called, summarily, enlightened despotism.

Moser had not abandoned his distinction between public law and
political sagacity, nor had he banished the latter from his consideration.
It had fallen sharply in his esteem, and now he pointedly avoided using
the word; but still in 1768 he was writing, with regard to the Reichstag:
"I am writing in the German public law to be sure; but in many matters
the public law, without taking note of the political grounds and circumstances, is worth no more than a bell without a clapper."[1] The necessary political wisdom Moser meant here drew on "experience" and on
"practice"; he could never abandon those. But he was immeasurably
more concerned now to distinguish and uphold the law against those
excesses of the Staats-Klugheit that marched under the banner of reason
or Vernunft—their corrosion of public rights, and of the whole body and
study of jurisprudence. Moser examined the theoretical and methodological implications of this for imperial law in an anonymous "Thoughts
on the Newly Contrived Rational Public Law of the German Empire,"
published in 1767.[2] For just then he was planning and launching his new
and massive compendium of German public law, the *Neues Teutsches
Staats-Recht*.

In the "newly contrived rational public law," Moser claimed, students
were made to learn nothing about the imperial or state constitutions.
That was deemed pedantry; and "to talk of the freedoms or rights of
estates and subjects is the highest treason." According to this school the
whole art of the jurist consisted, finally, in justifying the actions of rulers
by recourse to the name of reason; and there was nothing judicious about
that. "Just as a chameleon takes on the color of the thing it is clinging
to," so reason took on the color of the reasoner's circumstances and
interests, steered by "help or hurt, hope or dread, fear of men and flattery,
etc. . . . Reason [here *Verstand*] is supposed to be master of the will;
in praxi, however, it is usually the other way around." Where reason

1. *Von denen Teutschen Reichs-Tags-Geschäfften* (= NTSR VI: Frankfurt/Main, 1768),
p. 439; Reinhard Rürup, *Johann Jacob Moser: Pietismus und Reform* (Wiesbaden, 1965),
p. 117. But see the cursory and dubious passage on Staats-Klugheit conceived as *ratione
Status* in *Von Teutschland und dessen Staats-Verfassung überhaupt* (= NTSR I: Stuttgart,
1766), pp. 556–59.

2. *Gedancken über das neu erfundene vernünfftige Staats-Recht des Teutschen Reichs*
(Frankfurt/Main, 1767).

decides, there "*le plus fort* has and keeps the right." Reason dissolved the law without providing reliable new right. Adduced to any positive law, "clever reasoning can always find a way to prove that the sense is not really what had been supposed, but rather this and that by law of convenience; that something is no longer applicable to modern times or to *Legi supremae, Salutis Reipublicae* (meaning in plain German [Moser added]: the passions of the ruler)."[3]

It was just that magnetic mix of power with reason—so attractive to many of Moser's contemporaries (and successors)—that seemed to him most terrible; for it was a corrosive compound too, and one to which, he believed, Germany and its constitution were peculiarly vulnerable. For "German freedom [die teutsche Freiheit] is set forth in the very laws of the empire, and consists in this: that the emperor shall leave to the estates what is theirs, that the stronger shall not oppress the weaker nor the ruler his subjects, but rather the emperor shall give protection against this. This freedom is a common good; it is the bond of unity among members of the empire so unequal in power, and it is the means of maintaining our quite particular imperial constitution."[4]

Reason, then, destroyed rights and the security of legal norms; without secure legal norms, the empire could not survive; without the empire there was no defense against destructive political reason, and so back to the beginning. If Moser saw a circular trap here he was not prepared to name it. Instead he talked about experience. Teachers of "the new mode," he said, were in fact "not even beginners in the German political sagacity."[5] In 1771, Moser joined his condemnation of political naivety in the law with a more general argument on rational statecraft. The occasion was an anonymous physiocratic treatise that had appeared, as a translation from the French, under the title "On the Origins and Progress of a New Science." It had been published at Karlsruhe in Baden. At that court physiocratic doctrines were particularly in style, with the patronage of the margrave Karl Friedrich, urged on and advised by the German political economist Johann August Schlettwein;[6] and there Moser's youngest

---

3. Moser's parentheses. *Gedancken*, pp. 5, 23–25, 56; Erwin Schömbs, *Das Staatsrecht Johann Jakob Mosers (1701–1785)* (Berlin, 1968), pp. 272–74.

4. *Gedancken*, p. 32. Schömbs, *Staatsrecht Mosers*, pp. 276–80, develops this argument in terms of assuring *Rechtssicherheit*, reliable or predictable law.

5. Moser, *Lebensgeschichte Johann Jacob Mosers . . . von ihm selbst beschrieben*, IV (Frankfurt/Main, 1783), p. 218.

6. *Von dem Ursprung und Fortgang einer neuen Wissenschaft. Aus dem Französischen übersezt von F. M. Vierordt* (Karlsruhe, 1770). I have not found this German edition. On Karl Friedrich and physiocracy generally, see Wilhelm Roscher, *Geschichte der National-Oekonomik in Deutschland* (Munich, 1874), pp. 484–92. Vierordt was Karl Friedrich's secretary, and the translation apparently was made at the margrave's order: Karl Friedrich,

son, the unsteady Christian Benjamin, had recently entered the margrave's service. The French original was probably written by Dupont
de Nemours; Moser attributed it to the Marquis de Mirabeau. This let
him entitle his reply *Anti-Mirabeau*, echoing the *Anti-Machiavel* that the
young Frederick of Prussia had once written while waiting to succeed his
father Frederick William I.[7]

The physiocratic book, in Moser's reading, related how thirteen years
earlier the "Ritter" Quesnay, followed by others, had discovered the
true principles of natural government. These principles were founded in
political economy and postulated natural freedom of individuals to work
for their own gain. Property consisted in the product of earth and water;
the common weal was founded on the accumulated surplus after the
costs of working these resources, and would be greatest where freedom
and security prevailed. To achieve this state of freedom and security was
the whole and unconditioned task of government and the laws, and
rulers would perform this duty willingly once they recognized that their
own interests coincided with the interests of their subjects (the common
weal) and thus with the freedom and security of their subjects. Public
taxes were to be laid evenly on the surplus produce of agriculture, so as
not to hinder free individual incentive; persons, trade, and consumption,
as creative agents, were to be left untaxed. Hereditary monarchy was
deemed the best constitutional form for establishing and assuring continual harmony between the requirements of government and the freedom of subjects. This natural system would work anywhere and at any
time. It had been working in China for four thousand years.[8]

The points of similarity here with Moser's "Reasoned Art of Government" of 1753 are quite palpable even in Moser's summary, and in his
anonymous reply Moser had the fussy job of defending his own priority
while refuting the doctrines here expounded. He solved that by resorting
again to experience: he had been there before, and he knew how things
worked. He identified himself, the anonymous author, to be somebody
who had studied these matters for many years, and listed his own name
among a number of other Germans who had studied them; he made

---

Grand Duke of Baden, *Brieflicher Verkehr mit Mirabeau und Du Pont*, edited by Carl
Knies, I (Heidelberg, 1892), p. 18. On Schlettwein, *Allgemeine Deutsche Biographie*, XXXI
(Leipzig, 1890), pp. 467–71.

7. [Moser], *Anti-Mirabeau, oder unpartheyische Anmerckungen über des Marquis von
Mirabeau natürliche Regierungs-Form* (Frankfurt/Main, 1771). The Catalogue Générale of
the Bibliothèque Nationale attributes *De l'origine et les progrès d'une science nouvelle*
(Paris, 1768) uncertainly to Pierre Samuel Dupont de Nemours.

8. This follows Moser's summary in *Anti-Mirabeau*, pp. 5–15. It is consistent with the
French original.

some jocular remarks about a "new science" which had been practiced in China for four thousand years. The practical purpose of this "new science," he allowed, was to draw attention to the manifest evils of French tax farms. But in rhetoric of "reason" it went on then to provide solemn ceremonial excuse for unlimited power in the hands of the French monarchy, particularly its power to tax. The structure of ideas was "a fine political fiction [Staats-Roman], a philosophical dream of a Platonic state."[9] The heart of Moser's criticism was political but ideological too: he meant to show how this kind of reason had little to do with real political wisdom.

A key sentence in the physiocratic discourse, which launched Moser's own, declared that any sovereign, once "arithmetically convinced" that his power rested on the weal of his subjects, would do everything possible to assure their full exercise of free property rights. Was Mirabeau really that inexperienced, Moser asked, or was he merely given to gross flattery of the great? Whichever it was, or both: this proposition wholly mistook the nature of rulers, and of subjects and of governmental forms. Rulers were human beings, and "history showed" clearly enough that many of them were stupid, others were lazy; still others knew well enough what they ought to do but out of weakness or passion did not, and being arithmetically convinced would not change that. There were also princes who quite denied that to have prosperous subjects was in the interest of rulers, and for their part this might not be irrational at all, for sometimes it was wealthy subjects who were likely to become "proud, disobedient, and rebellious."[10]

This "Mirabeau" was just as naive when he came to those who were ruled—especially peasants, whose anticipated behavior was central to the whole economic scheme and to the rest that followed. Moser conceded that there was something to be said about the primacy of self-interest with "great lords or private persons," but that would not work with peasants. "Any forced or hasty stimulation of improvement here can only bring general confusion and general misery, or a dangerous political revolution." In the first place, as rulers were inclined to be stupid, peasants were inclined to be lazy, by the ingrained habit of centuries, and they had rather be poor than work. Preach at them about hard work and they laugh at you, just as they laugh at you when you preach at them about their immortal souls. What they cling to is tradition—those solemn peas-

---

9. *Anti-Mirabeau*, p. 21.

10. *Anti-Mirabeau*, pp. 23–34; *De l'origine*, pp. 61–62. A theory that subjects should be heavily enough taxed to keep them working and producing a maximum was common among German political economists in Moser's time: see for example Johann Justi, *System des Finanzwesens* (Halle, 1766), pp. 386–89.

ant incantations about times for sowing and planting and bleeding and purging, just as wrong now as they were when they were invented. And "the common man, especially the greater mass of the countrymen, thinks, as we Germans are accustomed to say, small-town [kleinstättisch]"—he is concerned only for near and visible values and is stubborn and conservative about projected gains. Leave them to their own free and natural wills and they neglect their own advantage, or else turn it to wasteful luxury.[11]

Now to forms of government. The supposed Mirabeau had deplored the thought of dispersed authorities in one state, saying that only by entrusting all power to one united authority could freedom and security be assured. In this "simple and natural" single government Moser saw simple and natural despotism, an "oriental" constitution. The nature and order of godly creatures provided for every weight a counterweight, for every power a counterpower; God's order of nature did not enjoin one mortal being to judge the fate of a million co-beings. Then Moser completed his criticism of the physiocratic text with this matter of individual freedom. Here were balance and counterweights again: as power could not be left unconditioned, neither could freedom. Moser had a particular and vital challenge in mind here. The basic principle on which the whole physiocratic program depended Moser quoted thus: "The rights of each person, which are older than contracts, are freedom to seek his own maintenance and weal, possession of his own person and of the things acquired by the labor of his own person."[12] To begin with, for the presumed Mirabeau to talk about absolute rule and absolute freedom side by side was plain self-contradiction; that was easy enough to see. Interests, simply, collided, among subjects and between subjects and rulers. Rulers, simply, were by nature no better or wiser than the least of their subjects; and vice versa.

But to give natural freedom priority over contracts! If there was a truly prior and indispensable freedom, it was the right to *make* contracts that would hold. Now Moser had found his way to his own ground, and defended it with passion. In a world of power it was contracts that provided freedom as they conditioned it; and Moser meant real, literal contracts. "This Mirabeau principle is supremely dangerous for nearly every European state and the German lands." Most of them had estates, judicial courts, or other authorities that contained power, and freedom, legally in check; and while they functioned to sustain rights and to limit

11. *Anti-Mirabeau*, pp. 34–43. And see Justi's remark, *System des Finanzwesens*, p. 389, that there were certain odd sorts of people who kept on working and gaining wealth even when they did not have to—compare Max Weber on the spirit of capitalism.

12. P. 18 of *De l'origine*; Moser, *Anti-Mirabeau*, p. 46.

powers there was no need for these political whimsies. "If these freedoms of estates and subjects remain intact, answering to the needs of human nature and its original inborn independence and defended by contracts and long tradition, then the whole Mirabeau system falls useless to the ground," along with its appeal to despotic power. But should despotism triumph, "this can happen no otherwise than by a riddling and annihilation of the holiest, sworn, basic laws of empire and land till then held inviolate." Anybody who advocated such a thing was "a traitor and an enemy to the fatherland," who would "set its whole constitution in full upheaval; and it could, or almost must, lead to the most perilous inner disorders in an independent state; or, in the German lands, to very difficult, costly, and wearisome legal proceedings."[13]

This odd rhetorical anticlimax about legal proceedings is Moser's own indeed; it bespeaks both his fear of political violence and his mixed hope and fear for the capacity of the particular laws, procedures, and institutions of Germany to suppress it. He went on to refute physiocratic claims that free exploitation of natural resources or total freedom of commerce could serve the common weal in a civilized society—a primitive society to be sure might be otherwise—and to denounce the single-tax plan. He made some pointed observations about the credibility of these doctrines for France in the year of this writing, 1771. For this was the time of the Maupéou reforms and the suppression of the *parlements*, and of dearth and the *pacte de famine* affair; and it is a fair guess that these events, coinciding with the appearance of a physiocratic school and literature with a princely sponsor in Germany, were what induced Moser to write the *Anti-Mirabeau*. In the end he came back to the German Empire and its law, citing his own works on the limited and diffused rights of taxation, and on the right of German subjects to appeal against governments to estates and to imperial courts. These constitutional conditions made it impossible anyway, he said, for the Mirabeau system to be carried out in Germany.[14]

Moser's encounter with *philosophes* had made him write more nearly in their language than was his custom; but in the end he fell back on the

13. *Anti-Mirabeau*, pp. 47–51, 66–67. Moser acknowledged firm restrictions on freedom to write and to publish, and worked out the conditions at just this time: *Von der Reichs-Verfassungsmässigen Freyheit, von teutschen Staats-Sachen zu schreiben* (Göttingen, 1772), a work prohibited by the Tübingen faculty. For analogous conditions for the propagation of religious doctrines, Moser's "Wie weit sich die Freyheit derer Evangelischen in Teutschland in Lehrsachen nach denen Reichsgrundgesezen erstrecke, oder nicht?" in *Abhandlungen aus dem Teutschen Kirchen-Recht* (Frankfurt/Main, 1772), pp. 203–34.

14. *Anti-Mirabeau*, pp. 107–15. On conditions in France, Steven L. Kaplan, *Bread, Politics and Political Economy in the Reign of Louis XV*, 2 vols. (The Hague, 1976), especially chapters X–XIII.

empire. All was not well with the empire, though—if all had ever been well with it in Moser's lifetime, for that matter, or ever. The circumstances of German imperial politics at this particular time, however, were quite probably another reason for Moser's outburst against "rational" and "natural" public law. All eyes were fixed on the unwonted and possibly portentous cooperation between Joseph's Austria and Frederick's Prussia, an amity then on its way toward the first partition of Poland in 1772.[15] On past occasion Moser had seen the empire's salvation in Austro-Prussian accommodation, back at the imperial elections of the 1740s; but this new royal cooperation between rationality and sagacity, between Vernunft and Staats-Klugheit incarnate, cast another light on that proposition. In the present case all other German princes had cause to reflect—and they did—on what could happen to them (and Moser perhaps to think on how, if this had come about a bit earlier, he might have been at the Hohentwiel even yet).

Anyway it was high time to look at the empire thoroughly again, in the light of what had happened since the 1740s, and Moser had written the two essays just considered while mainly engaged in getting under way what turned into his new massive work on the German public law. This *Neues Teutsches Staats-Recht* of the 1770s was a rather different work from the *Teutsches Staats-Recht* of the 1740s—less stuffy, more opinionated and more personal, more given to political observations and generalities, readier with political advice. But in some ways too it seemed to be describing a different constitutional system or at least another set of problems from the work set down in the 1740s. I cannot say how much of the difference resulted from actual changes in the political and legal life of the empire, or how much from changes in Moser's view of it; or considering his view, how much of that came from his study of events or how much from a change interior to his mind and language. They all came together in this: that Moser seemed now to conceive that a different empire had come into being since about 1740, the time of Frederick II's coming to the throne of Prussia and the experiment with the Wittelsbach emperor. It was a date he often mentioned, in many contexts. And even as he still turned reflexively to the empire to forfend the dangers of rational statecraft and natural politics, Moser was losing confidence in the efficacy of the laws and institutions of the empire in these more recent circumstances—at least, of the imperial laws and institutions as he had thought of them and described them before.

An immediate problem that vexed him as a professional scholar and writer, as he worked out the early volumes of the *Neues Teutsches Staats-*

15. Theo Rohr, *Der deutsche Reichstag vom Hubertusburger Frieden bis zum bayerischen Erbfolgekrieg (1763–1778)* (Bonn, 1968), especially pp. 152–54.

Recht, was superficial perhaps but symptomatic: he was writing books to sell, and he was afraid he might find few readers or buyers. For a long work of many volumes that would mean, even for a small press run, tying up large amounts of capital for a long time. Partly for that reason, and partly because of his advanced age, Moser arranged the work topically by volumes, each of which could be sold separately. This obliged him to hew to his line in each, unlike the run-together alphabets of the older work; the parts were separating.

The larger problem, though, was that this generation's market seemed to have little use for his extended and comprehensive brand of jurisprudence. Even his old university text, first published in 1731 and then updated for several subsequent editions, had gone out of style.[16] For this the professors were partly to blame, Moser thought; the book treated such a variety of subjects that professors would not prepare themselves to discuss them all, nor would they revise their notes to keep up with Moser's new editions. But behind the problem of professors was the problem of the students who paid their fees; and behind that was the world in which students expected to market their training and talents. Students expected to get in and out of the university fast, and to cover the public law in one semester: imagine! Frivolous books of belles-lettres, natural science, theater, novels, and the like were driving public law off the booksellers' shelves. And the truth was, Moser admitted, the public law was less important for a successful career than it had been, so that in many great lands it was hardly taught. In 1773 he wrote a special plea called "The Authority of Learned Jurists in German Political Affairs," explaining to princes and ministers why they should pay attention to scholars.[17] And it was also true that detailed treatises in the public law were bound to be very expensive and slow in the preparation. Moser the scholar had a double-leveled problem: how to write a major work that would be readily marketable but would still be faithful to his convictions and skills, and that would sustain the imperial structure while still taking into account the political shifts he had observed.

He completed the twenty-odd volumes of the *Neues Teutsches Staats-Recht* in a space of less than ten years. He condensed the matter of the old set of fifty volumes, on the central institutions and laws of the empire, into the first half-dozen of the new. These condensed opening volumes of Moser's new constitutional law gave more notice than had the old to

16. *Compendium juris publici Germanici, oder Grundriss der heutigen Staats-Verfassung des Teutschen Reichs* (1st-7th ed., 1731–54).

17. Moser, *Neueste Geschichte der teutschen Staats-Rechts-Lehre und deren Lehrer* (Frankfurt/Main, 1770), pp. 30–36; *Lebensgeschichte*, IV, pp. 164, 224–25; *Von dem Ansehen der Rechtsgelehrten in teutschen Staats-Sachen* (Regensburg, 1773).

what he called "Gebrechen," the infirmities of nonobservance in imperial law. And these infirmities appeared alongside general standards and principles. The greater brevity required more generalization and summary, against which particular transactions Moser was bound to report appeared as violations, where in a looser work they might have appeared simply as additional information. Moreover, the Gebrechen were forcing Moser to face questions of principle and summary. He even came reluctantly to some kind of terms with his old bugbear Pufendorf and discussed (protesting all the way) the abstract question of forms of government. "Pufendorf aroused a great noise among the political academics [Schul-Staatsmänner] when he held that our form of government is irregular, in fact quite monstrous. . . . And yet he was quite right after his fashion. For in the terms that the old political scientists understood, Germany is not a monarchy, nor an oligarchy, nor a democracy, etc.; and whatever finds no counterpart in its own species is a *Monstrum*." This need be no insult, however, for "a *Monstrum* can be as lovely or lovelier than any other creature of its species." No doubt the word did imply bodily deficiencies, and "our political constitution does have undeniable infirmities." But still this talk about forms of government was an academic question: for "Germany is governed *auf Teutsch*, and in such a manner that no school word, or small number of words, or the ways of other governments, suffice to make our own way of government comprehensible."[18]

More telling was a change in Moser's strategy for expounding the imperial law. Where once he had insisted on the principle of saying simply and thoroughly what the law said and not what somebody might like it to say, now he described his "whole purpose" to be: "first, to set forth our German political constitution as by the imperial laws it ought to be; second, to show how in practice it often departs from this, thus how it actually is; and third, to offer observations on how the German Empire so far as possible may sustain its present constitution, and show here and there how correctable defects may be overcome."[19] His imperial law (but still all of it) had moved from a body of artifacts toward (but only partway) a body of precepts, from an indicative to a subjunctive mood, from "are" to "ought," from a positive toward a normative jurisprudence. Thus, for example, "the more respect an emperor enjoys in the Reich, the more advantageous to the Reich, so long as this is not misused"; and shortly thereafter, "the greater the infirmities our consti-

18. *Von Teutschland und dessen Staats-Verfassung überhaupt* (= NTSR I), pp. 550–56. There is no comparable discussion in the *Teutsches Staats-Recht* of 1737–54. On "majesty," *Von denen Teutschen Reichs-Tags-Geschäfften* (= NTSR VI), pp. 27–29.

19. *Lebensgeschichte*, III, p. 80, and similarly in other contexts.

tution has . . . the more careful the emperor must be to see that all does not go still further off the rails, and that not only the mere shadow, but the actuality of the imperial constitution be maintained."[20]

Still, Moser carefully distinguished the "is" from the "ought," even though it obviously weakened his jurisprudence to have to say "here is the law" but then "here is what has happened." To hold this distinction was, in its way, another rejection of natural-law jurisprudence or state-craft, inasmuch as natural law tended to merge the two by the proposition that behavior and principle were the same, permeating the body politic with particular precepts following general axioms.[21] Natural law remained for Moser admissible only occasionally, in the form of common sense, to fill spaces where positive law did not speak, or else as tangential philosophy in an academic compartment only faintly related to the law. And he was even more dubious about it now in both forms, on political grounds, than he had been thirty years before. Natural law as a science grew from the "shallow earth" of interest and passion, "wherein all men have the same rights and stand in their natural condition of independence."[22] This to Moser must lead to defiance or dissolution of the law. He compared it with Holy Scripture as a remote source of law, in the sense that this too was shared among different states and peoples; but Scripture was better. "A natural right is something each person makes out of his own allegedly sound mind, or rather out of his passions, according to what pleases him," where by comparison "the word of God, particularly in matters of that sort, is clear and immutable." But religious passions, Moser argued, were something an emperor ought to keep altogether out of his political conduct, or "he will be no good for Germany, nor will he ever be beloved or successful."[23] His most urgent counsel, if the empire was to survive, was that it must shun war. "The infirmities [Gebrechen] that emerge in an imperial war and an imperial army are so great, so many, and so various, that as long as the German Reich remains as it is now constituted, it should be forbidden to wage any imperial war if this can be avoided in any way." And "when the Ger-

20. *Von dem Römischen Kayser, Römischen König, und denen Reichs-Vicarien* (= NTSR II: Frankfurt/Main, 1767), pp. 371–72.

21. A fruitful comparison with Pufendorf might be made here: Leonard Krieger, *The Politics of Discretion: Pufendorf and the Acceptance of Natural Law* (Chicago, 1965), especially chapters II–III.

22. *Von Teutschland und dessen Staats-Verfassung überhaupt* (= NTSR I), p. 527. The *Allgemeines Register* (Frankfurt/Main, 1775) to the NTSR, unlike the *Hauptregister* (n.p., 1754) to the TSR, contains no heading at all for *Natur-Recht*.

23. *Von Teutschland und dessen Staats-Verfassung überhaupt* (= NTSR I), pp. 525–26; *Von denen Kayserlichen Regierungs-Rechten und Pflichten* (= NTSR III: Frankfurt/Main, 1772), pp. 40–41. Compare above, §14.

mans make war amongst and against one another, they are the plunder and mockery of all Europe, and in the end they are left with nothing but the rueful wish that they had agreed voluntarily to that which they now must agree to, perforce."[24]

What could be done to correct the infirmities? "Great personages who need not worry about the imperial courts do what they will; the middling ones follow suit as best they can and for as long as that serves; and the weak are often the worst of all."[25] Natural law and rational statecraft "throw out the baby with the bath," in a phrase Moser addressed somewhat inappropriately to Hippolythus à Lapide.[26] Moser could not invoke power against law, nor reason against right, nor religious sanctions for political goals. These possible agents for correction were disqualified by their natures, and Moser was left without any effective moral grounds to sanction or to direct change, or at least could not use any of these commonest three. He saw no cure for constitutional ills but constitutional observance. "Those who care for maintaining Germany in its present constitution, and for the best of the whole Reich, must take and leave the German constitution as it now is. It has many and great infirmities—that is true. But that does not mean Germany could not be a happy state if the emperor and the imperial estates earnestly wished it to be. If that is not their will, then no conceivable constitution, made however you will, could make Germany happy and sound." The laws of the empire proffered a palatable and practical balance between authority and freedom, if its members would only observe them. Finally, "of course there must be goodwill; for otherwise . . . nothing can be achieved."[27]

This was no cheerful conclusion for a constitutional lawyer. Moser was too weary or too wise, entering the 1770s, to put much stock in goodwill, and he introduced his volume on the lands of imperial princes with an announcement that he could write no more. He expected now to lay aside his pen so as to enjoy peace in his last few years; and he did not care a bit. "So dam up the springs, boys!"—he reverted to a schoolboy's

24. *Von denen Teutschen Reichs-Tags-Geschäfften* (= NTSR VI), pp. 810, 815. Some of the material I have adduced here as evidence of Moser's pessimism about the Reich is invoked by Rürup, *Moser*, especially pp. 141–52, as evidence of a spirit of reform.

25. *Von der Landes-Hoheit in Steuer-Sachen* (= NTSR XVI, part 4: Frankfurt/Main, 1773), p. 13.

26. In *Lebensgeschichte*, IV, p. 219; see n. 112 below.

27. *Von denen Kayserlichen Regierungs-Rechten und Pflichten* (= NTSR III: Frankfurt/ Main, 1772), pp. 31–32. On the indispensability of goodwill for right exercise of the Landeshoheit, see *Von der Teutschen Reichs-Stände Landen* (= NTSR XIII: Frankfurt/ Main, 1769), pp. 1148–49. Compare *Unmasgebliches Bedenken über einige Hauptpuncten, so bey Einrichtung des Visitations-Wesens bey dem Kaiserl. Reichs Cammergerichte zu beobachten seyn* (Regensburg, 1767), §4: "Geschickte und ehrliche Leute brauchen wenig Gesetze. . . . Bey ungeschickten oder gewissenlosen Leuten aber sind bey nahe alle Gesetze vergeblich."

tag from Virgil—"the meadows have drunk their fill."[28] But after a year or two of near-silence (angrily interrupted by the *Anti-Mirabeau*), he did go on—not to repudiate or change any part of the German public law, but to seek out and explore areas in it that he had never thoroughly considered before.

For there is another way to describe the condition that confronted Moser now and that would not let the jurist rest. The traditional division in German political science, between statecraft or *prudentia* and law, had opened with time into an excruciating gap. Moser in Württemberg had tried to bridge it in his own person and had failed. When that happened he, like many other imperial jurists, reverted to law as the fundamental base of politics.

But for this to be credible and effective, the sphere of the public law would have to be modified and extended to incorporate realms it had not directly addressed before in positive terms, political realms formally ruled in the irresponsible name of *prudentia*, or in the indeterminate names of natural or divine law.

---

§29. Authority of States: The Landeshoheit

THE new categories and materials Moser addressed in the *Neues Teutsches Staats-Recht* were three: the Landeshoheit; the rights of German subjects; and a novel constitutional topic he gave the name "Neighborhood Public Law," Nachbarliches Staats-Recht. His new emphasis on these topics represents an effort to adapt imperial jurisprudence to the political conditions of the late eighteenth century. They matter not because Moser found in them solutions to Germany's constitutional troubles and deficiencies. He did not find solutions; it would strain all historical ingenuity and credulity to argue that he did; and he never claimed solutions. Rather, these new emphases show where and how it was he tried. They show the terms in which he perceived the constitutional troubles and possible remedial spheres—not as constitutional reforms, but as other areas of jurisprudence, within the vast con-

28. "Claudite jam rivos, Pueri! sat prata bibere." *Von der Teutschen Reichs-Stände Landen* (= NTSR XIII), preface. This volume, as noted before, had been written out of sequence so as to address the Württemberg constitutional issue: see above, §26. The line is from Virgil's *Eclogues*, III, 111.

stitutional inclusivity of the German public law, which he thought now ought especially to be defined, explored, and expounded.

Landeshoheit has been variously translated as territorial supremacy or superiority, or *superioritas territorialis* (the parent Latin term), or some limiting variant on the idea of political sovereignty. But since it baffles clear definition in any language, here it will be best to stick to the German label, going on to consider its nature and content.[29] Moser had made a definition forty years before, in his handbook *Compendium juris publici*, which he now cited along with definitions others had offered: it was the right possessed by imperial estates—the princes, nobles, towns, and other public beings that stood in immediate sworn relation to the emperor—"to command and to forbid, to do and to allow in their lands and territories whatever any regent is allowed by divine or natural law or the law of nations insofar as their hands are not bound by imperial laws, imperial traditions, agreements with their own estates or subjects, or the latter's old and well-established rights and traditions etc." This was a description he "still found no reason to regret," he said.[30] The trouble with it was, of course, that on the one hand it opened up broad avenues for political exploitation through the sanctions of divine or natural law or the law of nations, unless, on the other hand, one went directly to the specifics of each place or agreement anyway, making the general doctrine redundant. So Moser had never before pursued the doctrine in general terms. Instead he had turned (apart from the law of the empire proper) to the public law of German states in particular, even aspiring at one time to write up the constitutional law of every one of the imperial estates, rather than tackle the Landeshoheit as something common to all of them.[31] But now, he observed, the public law of particularities (besonderes Staats-Recht) had been eclipsed by the expansion of the Landeshoheit toward a pretense of general sovereignty, toward an unrestrained and arbitrary authority usurped by rulers.[32] And Moser had little confidence in the capacity of

29. See Emilio Bussi's discussion in *Il diritto pubblico del Sacro romano impero alla fine del XVIII secolo*, II (Milan, 1959), pp. 339–50; and Karl S. Bader, "Territorialbildung und Landeshoheit," *Blätter für deutsche Landesgeschichte*, XC (1953), pp. 109–31. Johann Stephan Pütter published a large collection of essays on the Landeshoheit shortly after Moser's NTSR appeared: *Beyträge zum Teutschen Staats- und Fürsten-Rechte*, 2 vols. (Göttingen, 1777–79).

30. *Compendium juris publici*, p. 449; *Von der Landeshoheit derer Teutschen Reichsstände überhaupt* (= NTSR XIV: Frankfurt/Main, 1773), pp. 9, 11.

31. See above, §11.

32. For Moser on the decay of the *besonderes Staats-Recht*, see *Von dem neuesten Zustande des besonderen Teutschen Staatsrechts* (Frankfurt/Main, 1770), pp. 8–9; for his historical and political explication of the corresponding rise of the Landeshoheit, *Von der Landeshoheit derer Teutschen Reichsstände überhaupt* (= NTSR XIV), pp. 248–74.

imperial authority to restrain territorial authority, nor even much faith in what the outcome would be, for the empire or within the states, if imperial authority should succeed in doing so. He confronted what may be called a mediatization or devolution of the German public law. As the sphere of public activity had grown, the centers of juridical gravity had migrated from imperial to territorial location, so that the focuses of constitutional issues and activity were no longer immediate to the empire but lay in the relations between princes and their subjects or estates.[33]

Moser denied, though, that the Landeshoheit consisted in powers that had descended to the princes from imperial authority or that it had been delegated in any way to the princes by imperial authority. It lived in its own part of the German constitution, and its links with the rest were not derivative or imitative. Moser rejected out of hand the motto "An imperial estate is the emperor in his own land"—indeed, he remarked dryly (citing Pütter), few princes would be satisfied with powers so slight as those exercised by the emperor.[34] Written imperial law itself was remarkably silent on the whole subject, so that from the purview of imperial rights, the Landeshoheit rested almost entirely on tradition or Herkommen (remember that tradition here means exercise of rights that are not founded on explicit awards of authority). A ruler exercised the Landeshoheit, both ecclesiastical and secular, by his territorial right.[35] Moser's old summary definition had seemed theoretically to postulate a total, undifferentiated fund or reservoir of plenary authority limited only by explicit restraints. That is what the making of definitions had got him into; but Moser could not really accept that picture in theory nor did he in juridical fact—not, at least, when the question turned from the imperial right (as Moser now turned it) to questions of what happened *within* the territorial states. That derivation from sovereignty would justify unspecified powers arbitrarily assumed; but the Landeshoheit rested on tradition, he insisted, and "tradition consists entirely in plain facts, which must be described and proven."[36]

33. To the proposition that in Europe in general, the decay of old juridical forms and the advance of sovereign authority in the later eighteenth century created a demand for "constitutions," Werner Näf, "Der Durchbruch des Verfassungsgedankens im 18. Jahrhundert," *Schweizer Beiträge zur Allgemeinen Geschichte*, XI (1953), pp. 108–20. For Germany in particular, see Eberhard Schmidt-Assmann, *Der Verfassungsbegriff in der deutschen Staatslehre der Aufklärung und des Historismus* (Berlin, 1967).

34. *Von der Landeshoheit derer Teutschen Reichsstände überhaupt* (= NTSR XIV), preface, pp. 11–14, 311.

35. Ibid., pp. 11–13, 43; *Von Teutschland und dessen Staats-Verfassung überhaupt* (= NTSR I), p. 506.

36. *Lebensgeschichte*, IV, p. 297. Thus the only way the old definition can be made consistent with the Landeshoheit Moser now expounded is to suppose it meant not a

But neither, conversely, could Moser rest on the theoretical proposition or definition that the Landeshoheit consisted only in a heap or a complex of specified particular rights. This was tempting, and in some instances—when making definitions or avoiding them—Moser seemed to invoke it.[37] But he knew very well that much governing was done without explicit sanction, and he could not allow to the dead hand of old agreements and precedents a power to stifle constitutional adaptation and change—not because of a liking for change, but because change happened and had to happen. There was no question but that the Landeshoheit was subject both to imperial law and justice and to the constitutional rights and agreements of a land, its estates, and its subjects; but these were not immutable. For often "the course of world events," or the condition of the imperial constitution, or the internal condition of a land, made changes necessary. The Landeshoheit emphatically did not allow a ruler to do anything he chose; but it allowed him to do some things and obliged him to do some things. There was no single substantive Landeshoheit anyway, but rather a kind of power, or set of powers, held within that category, whose substance varied from place to place and from time to time.[38] As between a plenitude of power on the one theoretical pole and a bundle of specifics on the other, Moser seemed to seek out an administrator's middle ground: "Enough," he wrote; "included in the Landeshoheit are all those rights which are required [erforderlich] for the governing of a state to its own best advantage." The norm for its exercise, except for specific provision, was *salus publica suprema lex esto*—the public weal is the highest law.[39]

There are three things to say about this un-Moser-like invocation of the public weal—in a Latin legal motto to boot. First (like his old general

justification of rights but a formal category of rights, attested not by delegation but by exercise.

37. See the definition taken from Johann Jakob Schmauss, *Akademische Reden* (Lemgo, 1766), p. 599, in Bussi, *Diritto pubblico*, II, p. 344; in Moser with respect to territorial estates, *Von der Teutschen Reichs-Stände Landen* (= NTSR XIII), p. 1148: "eine Massa, die sich in allerlei Formen drücken lässt, und jede derselben ist recht"; respecting Landeshoheit in general, *Von der Landeshoheit derer Teutschen Reichsstände überhaupt* (= NTSR XIV), p. 218: "Nun alle Regalien machen zusammen die Landeshoheit aus"; regarding ecclesiastical matters, *Von der Landeshoheit im Geistlichen* (= NTSR XV: Frankfurt/Main, 1773), p. 7: "bestehet . . . aus vilen einzelnen Theilen . . . und darunter gehören."

38. *Von der Landeshoheit derer Teutschen Reichsstände überhaupt* (= NTSR XIV), pp. 50–51, 295–99.

39. Ibid., pp. 15, 211. On the relation of administrative requirements to legislation in this context, Wilhelm Ebel, *Geschichte der Gesetzgebung in Deutschland*, 2d ed. (Göttingen, 1958), pp. 67–69.

definition of the Landeshoheit), it was used less to justify than to cate-
gorize a kind of right for which he could not locate the kind of arti-
factual foundation he preferred; second, it expressed a limitation on
power rather than a license for it; and third, he used it in the uncomfortable and unaccustomed effort to find a general principle from which
to develop his real exposition. He followed it with a disclaimer on the
uses of the common weal. In fact, he said, men differ so easily and so
frequently in their conception of the common weal, and they use it so
cynically, that this was the main source of quarrels between rulers and
their estates and subjects; consequently there had to be recourse to the
land's constitution or the higher judicial courts anyway.[40]

Actually Moser was not much interested in theoretical purity; and his
lack of interest extended not only to his efforts theoretically to denounce
the uses of theory, but also to his own lax efforts to apply it. There is no
use obliging Moser to say whether the Landeshoheit relied on a reservoir
of princely authority limited in specific ways, or on a body of specific
powers coming from someplace else. It was not the kind of thing he felt
obliged to make up his mind about. It was like the question of where the
ultimate source of authority lay. This was something more than lack of
interest on Moser's part, though; it reflected positive conviction. This
was the sort of question that he thoroughly believed the German constitution did not raise, and must not undergo. Where majesty resides, he
announced, a favorite topic of constitutional lawyers, was "one of the
most miserable school questions there is."[41] Whether the Landeshoheit
was a prince's own possession or rested on some higher right was not
only a sterile question but also a destructive one. The Landeshoheit was
there, conditioned and articulated in various complex ways; and the only
reason for going into its foundations at all, Moser said, was that many
sycophantic publicists were using the doctrine to excuse rulers from all
constitutional and political responsibility, toward the empire on one hand
and toward their subjects on the other, as if they were "oriental despots."

As for the comparison of Landeshoheit with sovereignty: certain for-
eigners, notably French royal jurists, tried to make them out to be the
same, mainly to make sure of a distinction between the very limited
rights of their own estates and the far greater powers of German princes.
To do this served the purposes of the French monarchy both at home and

40. *Von der Landeshoheit derer Teutschen Reichsstände überhaupt* (= NTSR XIV), pp.
15–16.
41. *Von denen Kayserlichen Regierungs-Rechten und Pflichten* (= NTSR III), pp. 27–28.
On the majestas controversy generally, Hanns Gross, *Empire and Sovereignty: A History of
the Public Law Literature of the Holy Roman Empire* (Chicago, 1973).

abroad; but where Germany was concerned this again was word games and flattery.[42] Or take the judicial question: as between the Landeshoheit of the prince (or prelate, or imperial town council) and the freedoms of the land, which side has the burden of proving its right, or which has presumption in its favor? "Answer: neither of the two, but both together. It is a large error and a crude one [abgeschmackt] to suppose them contrary to each other." Although freedom and authority are separate topics, they were not incompatible in practice, "but rather they let themselves blend together like water and wine; the wine is not so strong that way, but so much the less intoxicating." Still Moser allowed that in cases of doubt, the ruler should have the presumption on his side where the general weal was affected; but where the question was some particular interest of the ruler, presumption should be for the liberties of subjects. Similarly he agreed that Landeshoheit authority in some respects approached sovereignty, and he accepted the use some jurists made, to that effect, of the term *majestatis aemula*.[43]

One reason the Landeshoheit was so confusing a subject was that (like sovereignty) it had two faces, outward and inward. The outward face was a German territorial ruler's capacity to act in certain matters independently of imperial authority and even in defiance of it; this Moser in the 1770s considered undeniable. The inward face was the direct authority a ruler had over his subjects and estates. Moser blamed other jurists for treating the Landeshoheit only as it laid out a ruler's independence of the empire, while ignoring the counterforce of his territorial obligation within. This was the imbalance he meant to correct and the gap he meant to fill, in his treatment of the Landeshoheit, and also in his following treatments of the rights of subjects and the law of neighborhood.[44]

He had come to consider this Landeshoheit facing within the territories, though, because of the victories of Landeshoheit facing the empire. They were mirrored faces, reciprocally related in a way that was somehow, alas, both historical and geometrical. "The less respect the imperial government and the judgments of the imperial courts enjoy, the more the Landeshoheit grows, or rather, the more the rulers squeeze out of it," in the form of power over their subjects. Conversely, the greater the dignity

42. *Von der Landeshoheit derer Teutschen Reichsstände überhaupt* (= NTSR XIV), pp. 16–18, 30–31.

43. *Von der Teutschen Reichs-Stände Landen* (= NTSR XIII), p. 1150; *Von der Landeshoheit derer Teutschen Reichsstände überhaupt* (= NTSR XIV), pp. 25, 242; see also Bussi, *Diritto pubblico*, II, pp. 344–45. Writing on the Völkerrecht ten years later Moser adopted the term *Halb-Souverain*: see below, §32.

44. *Von der Landeshoheit derer Teutschen Reichsstände überhaupt* (= NTSR XIV), pp. 30–32. See Johann Stephan Pütter's comments in *Litteratur des teutschen Staatsrechts*, II (Göttingen, 1781), p. 95.

of imperial government and courts, "the more the old German freedom peeps through, and so much more cautiously territorial rulers and their ministers, and even their attendant jurists, behave."[45] To explain the peculiarity of the German Landeshoheit Moser even made a comparison with ancient Germanic tribes and "the present Indian nations and tribes of North America."[46] An interesting feature of all Moser's general discussion of the Landeshoheit, and the related topics of rights of subjects and law of nations, was how frequently he slipped away from his accustomed positivist principles and his juridical artifacts, how often they seemed not to suffice. Methodologically abhorrent things came peeping through the Landeshoheit, even Moser's. Legitimate tradition was becoming more nearly a matter of age; ancient Teutons were acquiring a freedom somehow natural, like American Indians; and almost always to finish things up there had to be some reference to natural rights, or reasonable policy, or the common weal. Natural rights or law were a real temptation perhaps because of their generalizing capacity, because of the way they coped with individuals and wholes as the Landeshoheit tended to do, bypassing the gradations of rights and the intermediate groups hard to generalize about.

But Moser protested: "Just as we in Germany do not live together in a *statu naturali* but in a state with its own general and particular laws, contracts, freedoms, and a fundamental constitution deriving from this," thus the particularities of the law must come first; and where particularities sufficed there was no need for appeal to these abstract notions, or to any fund of plenary authority anywhere.[47] So from a general introduction Moser went on to spell out the Landeshoheit as ten categories of rights held by territorial rulers in that capacity; each category was composed of a list of particular rights, more or less related within the category. Within the secular Landeshoheit Moser distinguished the categories of government, justice, military affairs, taxation, cameral affairs, police, matters of grace or favor, the persons and possessions of subjects, and natural resources. Landeshoheit in ecclesiastical affairs was a separate topic. Moser issued a separate volume for each of the ten categories. He had divided it up that way because, he explained, for him to have

---

45. *Von der Landeshoheit derer Teutschen Reichsstände überhaupt* (= NTSR XIV), p. 41. Karl Kormann, "Die Landeshoheit in ihrem Verhältnis zur Reichsgewalt im alten Deutschen Reich seit dem Westfälischen Frieden," *Zeitschrift für Politik*, VII (1914), pp. 139–70, considers only the relation with imperial authority; Moser's insistence that the Landeshoheit was held by the imperial estates on their own account is the grounds for Kormann's view that Moser was "durchaus auf der Seite der Landeshoheit," p. 152.

46. *Von der Teutschen Reichs-Stände Landen* (= NTSR XIII), p. 3.

47. *Von der Landes-Hoheit in Steuer-Sachen* (=NTSR XVI, part 4), p. 449.

incorporated the whole Landeshoheit under one heading would have produced a work so big and expensive that nobody would buy it.[48]

All powers composing the Landeshoheit were governing powers in a general sense; Moser further distinguished, under this initial category of "Regierung," two areas he called administration and legislation. These in turn he conceived narrowly, limiting his exposition to the particular matters where a ruler's authority derived from the Landeshoheit. Even these governmental powers he insisted were subject to oversight by emperor and Reich, by the imperial courts, and to restrictions embodied in a land's particular constitution including written agreements, freedoms, and traditions.[49]

By "administration" Moser meant control over the conduct and responsibilities of two kinds of officials, servants of the ruler whose recognition in the public law had developed in step with their master's Landeshoheit. He called these two types "councillors," *Raths-Collegien*, and "civil officials," *Beamten*. Both ordinarily were appointed and dismissed at the ruler's pleasure. The estates of a land, not being co-regents (as Moser had insisted in his 1769 work on that subject), had no direct authority over administration; but their right of remonstrance against actions of their ruler extended also to the behavior of his public servants. In practice this voice of the estates was addressed mainly to the collegial councillors, whose relation with the ruler was advisory and broad in nature and whose posture affected the whole land, rather than a particular place or group of subjects. Complaints by estates or subjects about a ruler's evil councillors indeed were not at all uncommon; "and sometimes, as is well known, such villains have paid with their heads."[50] Civil officials were the active agents of government, for the exercise of Landeshoheit powers in particular matters and places. Such persons were selected and maintained by the ruler, under a variety of systems of training, tenure, and immunity; in this respect they were quite unlike local officials chosen by communes or their representatives and responsible to them. Complaints about civil officials tended to be loosely about excessive severity, or corruption, indolence, or meddling outside their proper spheres.[51]

New legislation, the "Gesetzgebungsrecht": this was one of the vital parts of the Landeshoheit, encompassing "the right to issue general laws and ordinances that every resident of the land is obliged to observe." The

48. *Von der Landeshoheit in Regierungssachen überhaupt* (= NTSR XVI, part 1: Frankfurt/Main, 1772), preface.
49. Ibid., pp. 8-9.
50. Ibid., pp. 17, 28–36, 133–40.
51. Ibid., pp. 148–51, 174, 187, and passim.

term "general" here meant not to open the legislative power in all directions, but rather by definition to limit its application to matters which affected all subject persons or a large and continuing category of them. Decrees addressed to particular cases were not true legislation. The legislative power included not all areas of government but only specified ones, and must follow specified forms and techniques. Moser noticeably did not mention taxation powers here, for they flowed not from legislative authority but from other sources and usually involved some special mechanism of consent or agreement.[52] Moser thought there ought to be a lot more regular legislation, so as to keep alien, inappropriate, or licentiously vague precepts and decrees from sneaking in to fill up gaps. Legislation, following learned counsel, made for sound and explicit law. It gave the various mechanisms for communication, oversight, and restraints a chance to work, so to assure that the policy or action in question did not violate anybody's rights. Moser observed that he had given a lot of thought to this topic while he was at the Hohentwiel, and he set down his lengthy and convoluted conclusions about the rights of estates in legislation: they boiled down to proper procedures for defending, together in each act, both the rights of subjects and the weal of the land. He was markedly reserved and circumlocutory about appeal to imperial courts against a ruler's legislative acts, speaking mostly of particular situations and procedures. For the ground for this appeal, given present constitutional conditions, would probably have to be denial of territorial justice. This was a loose claim that raised a whole additional complex of problems; there were in fact many provisions of imperial law that protected the legislative powers of territorial rulers against imperial interference.[53] But the justice which territorial legislation was bound by imperial law to observe was mainly territorial justice.

Territorial justice, like administration and legislation, flowed from the Landeshoheit, and all inferior justice in the state derived its authority from that. But in its exercise a ruler must uphold the rights of all, because "that is the purpose for which men have placed themselves in civil society," and because this is required of all who acknowledge Holy Scripture, and because of provisions of the imperial basic laws. The main areas of territorial justice were the protection of each person's rights and

52. See the discussion of Moser's *Gesetzgebungsrecht* in Ernst W. Böckenförde, *Gesetz und gesetzgebende Gewalt, von den Anfängen der deutschen Staatsrechtslehre bis zur Höhe des staatsrechtlichen Positivismus* (Berlin, 1958), pp. 55–56.

53. *Von der Landeshoheit in Regierungssachen überhaupt* (= NTSR XVI, part 1), pp. 192, 303–14, 325–27. To the question of whether an imperial law could modify or abolish earlier state laws, which had got Moser into such difficulty in 1757 (above, §22), Moser now replied that this could happen if it was the specific intention of the emperor and estates to do so: ibid., p. 330.

possessions, the settlement of disputes over them, and the punishment of crime. Justice must be unpartisan, accurate and learned, and prompt. It was subject to the provisions of the land's constitution in all these respects. Moreover, imperial law forbade cabinet justice, meaning adjudication by the ruler's administrative arm (the councillors and civil officials). There must be regular judicial tribunals, although in certain situations special courts might be commissioned.[54]

Maladministration, delay, or failure of territorial justice was always grounds for appeal to the authority of the empire. Here again, Moser was noticeably reticent about the *privilegia de non appellando*, the special rights accorded imperial electors and certain others to forbid their subjects to appeal to imperial courts. He hardly mentioned these exemptions from imperial jurisdiction in the Landeshoheit volumes, and seemed tacitly to work from the position that while the terms of imperial justice could not overrule the terms of territorial justice in such cases, nor could imperial courts accept territorial cases in the first instance, still imperial authority was bound and entitled to see that territorial justice was properly maintained. Moser excepted no German principality from this rule. An interesting feature of this, though, is that he located the power and duty of oversight not only with the emperor, by terms of his capitulation, but also with the imperial estates in general, by judicial agency of the imperial courts. Some ramifications of this will appear as we go along.[55]

Military rights were the wing of the Landeshoheit that brought it closest to sovereign authority. Imperial laws to govern them were, Moser found, scarce and of doubtful modern validity. Territorial constitutions provided some checks, but the "rising barometer" of the stronger German princes was dissolving legal restraints everywhere. The law of nations might move in and help if people could agree on just what it said— that needed doing—but there was no sense turning to Grotius, Pufendorf, Wolff, or anybody else's *Raisonnement* for this kind of help. Tradition was being overwhelmed by events de facto, inasmuch as "nowadays so much happens in this area without any grounds except that somebody will have it so because he has the cannon law [Canonen-Recht] on his side." It was a process that fed on itself; the wide scope of military rights worked to produce the crises that justified them. "For on account of the principle *Inter arma silent leges*—amidst arms the laws fall silent—it is a

54. *Von der Landes-Hoheit in Justiz-Sachen* (= NTSR XVI, part 2: Frankfurt/Main, 1773), pp. 1–3, 25–27.

55. Ibid., pp. 35, 75. See Moser's gingerly and circuitous discussion of conditions affecting the *privilegia de non appellando* in *Von der Teutschen Justiz-Verfassung* (= NTSR VIII, part 1: Frankfurt/Main, 1774), pp. 177–239; and on this point see Johann Stephan Pütter, *Historische Entwicklung der heutigen Staatsverfassung des Teutschen Reichs*, 3d ed., I (Göttingen, 1798), p. 330.

very common thing for many a prince to be inclined to fish in troubled waters."[56]

The wily Leibniz in considering the Landeshoheit had once tried to make a distinction between strong independent princes who by holding and defending large territories possessed something called *Suprematum*, and lesser ones who did not. Moser had rejected this as a matter of constitutional law and theory, "but yet in practice . . . it has perfectly good grounds . . . and its effects are more visible all the time." But then again the little princes were following the great ones as fast as they could to develop this part of the Landeshoheit, thus making out of territorial military rights "a new imperial tradition with force of law" encompassing everybody. These military powers flowed irresistibly into other areas when trouble was about—especially taxation, but finally into the whole constitutional system of the German lands. "For where are the old freedoms and rights of estates and subjects in the lands of princes who can put whole corps or armies in the field?"[57] About all Moser seemed able to do about it was to adopt the word "Provinzien" whenever he could when he wrote about military law, hearkening to the imperial circles and to military power as an imperial responsibility and not a territorial arm— a feeble verbal attempt to contain this wing of the Landeshoheit—and to lay out detailed legal rules and forms for different kinds of military organization.

With taxation law, fourth category of the Landeshoheit, Moser made his most strenuous effort to hold territorial authority within rules and procedures. The main weight of it was to pull together "the particular constitutions of many German lands with respect to taxation," and here he offered examples and summaries from about fifty different places that took up some four hundred pages. For, he said firmly, it would be quite incorrect to found taxation powers in the "general" public law; they rested on the constitutions of each place. That meant, conversely, that as Landeshoheit they were exercised by each ruler in his own capacity, not as delegation from imperial authorities.[58] Respecting the tax power

56. *Von der Landeshoheit derer Teutschen Reichsstände überhaupt* (= NTSR XIV), p. 322; *Von der Landes-Hoheit in Militar-Sachen* (= NTSR XVI, part 3: Frankfurt/Main, 1773), preface and pp. 1–6.

57. *Von denen Kayserlichen Regierungs-Rechten und Pflichten* (= NTSR III), pp. 17– 18; *Von der Landes-Hoheit in Militar-Sachen* (= NTSR XVI, part 3), p. 3 and passim. Leibniz had set forth his stepwise analysis of political authority in the empire pseudony- mously in Caesarinus Fürstenarius, *De jure suprematus ac legationis principum Germaniae* (n.p., 1677) and in subsequent works. See J. J. Schmauss's remark that Leibniz was prone to botch this kind of question: Bussi, *Diritto pubblico*, II, p. 345.

58. *Von der Landes-Hoheit in Steuer-Sachen* (= NTSR XVI, part 4), pp. 13, 21–418, 420.

Moser made the plea mentioned earlier, that the Germans did not live in a state of nature but in a condition governed by particular laws, treaties, and freedoms; and he made a long list of the kinds there were. They began with territorial capitulations and agreements, wherein a ruler, at the time of his installation or on some subsequent occasion, declared or accepted the terms of his exercise of taxation rights. Following that with equal force were imperial court judgments—those based however on the territorial law—of taxation disputes between ruler and subject. Then came territorial tradition, imperial law, and so on down to Holy Scripture. Where there were estates, no new taxes could be imposed without their knowledge and consent; only where there were no estates could a ruler impose taxes without this procedure of consent from the land; and even that imposition must follow constitutional provision, still subject to imperial review. His experience with the Württemberg committee, probably, goaded Moser into the improbable generality that "new taxes, or the increase of old ones . . . cannot be imposed anywhere in Germany except by consent of the whole land, or its representatives in a general diet." This ignored the problem of how representation would occur where there were no organized estates or diets, and Moser, wrapped up in the doings of estates, kept on ignoring it during his discussion of assent. He remarked that sometimes estates, "holding the principle that 'Fish for the money' makes as good sense as 'Money for the fish,'" extracted special freedoms and privileges from rulers in return for allowing special taxes; but he said this kind of extraction rarely did the land much good. In the "rare but not impossible case" where estates offered *more* money than the ruler would accept or spend, imperial courts would have to decide.[59]

When he arrived at cameralism and police, Moser insisted that in this work on the public law he would not consider the actual sciences of public finance and political economy, or "political sagacity [Staatsklugheit] in police matters," but only the constitutional powers and constraints upon the Landeshoheit in their exercise. Irresistibly, however, the particular goals and materials of these sciences came peeping through the law, not only in Moser's general definitions but by imposing their own forms upon the jurisprudence. That was a way they had. The powers of police were "those rights and duties, and the institutions deriving from them, whose purpose is to bring and maintain order in the political behavior of subjects in everyday life, and to further their temporal weal." It is hard to find perimeters in such a definition; and there was, Moser admitted, almost no other word current in German jurisprudence that had so loose a meaning as *Polizey*, or where constitutional regulations were

59. Ibid., pp. 10–16, 449, 586–89, 604.

JOHANN JAKOB MOSER, AGE SEVENTY-FOUR
"Similar, but not wholly like me: and note especially, that I have been represented as a much sterner person than I really ought to have been. . . . But even in my seventy-sixth year, I can grind up veal bones etc. with my teeth."
Moser, Lebensgeschichte, III, pp. 3–4.
Württembergische Landesbibliothek, Stuttgart

so hard to locate (recall again his Württemberg experience). Where there were no estates, a ruler might by this authority do anything pursuant to public order and weal that did not violate positive imperial law or tradition or give cause for appeal to imperial courts (presumably on grounds of denial of justice). Where there were estates, the ruler had a free hand insofar as he did not violate their specified rights and agreements. Estates were entitled to advise rulers on police matters by their own initiative—it was their sworn duty to forfend evil from the fatherland and to promote its best interests. "Indeed when out of short-sightedness, indolence, timidity, or envy toward those who have proposed such actions, they neglect or fail to support a ruler in his good intentions or hinder him, they must answer for it at Last Judgment, before the ruler, the fatherland, the public, and posterity."[60]

This leakage of police power into constitutional right clearly threatened to become a deluge. Moser tried again to sort out the respective claims of police and justice, but still had little success at it. It was an area, apparently, where only vast volumes of detailed formal legislation could regulate Landeshoheit authority. For though the mandate was broad, "no general rule" for controlling it seemed to work. So again Moser turned to the particular categories of the Landeshoheit power to nail down the substance; and here, in police, the themes of political economy thoroughly dominated the rules and the language. "A wise ruler" would always keep his eye on the population and how it could be developed in the best interest of himself and his land—migration, marriage, Jews, land clearing, and so on. Every ruler, by his obligation to serve his own and the common weal, was responsible for "the enlightenment of the minds and the improvement of the wills" of his subjects. Religion was "the easiest and most important aid" in this, through its principles of fear of God and love for one's neighbor—especially the Christian religion (and especially the Protestant kind). Other religions should be tolerated, but atheists could and should be expelled; and Moser went on to schools, libraries, censorship. Works that threatened religious peace and public order should be prohibited, although censorship did harm true learning too, and it caused money to emigrate to other states when arbitrarily applied. Occupations: the Landeshoheit entitled a ruler to forbid any activity contrary to divine or other law, or which in any way harmed one's fellow man or the public weal: prostitution, false representation of goods, or "too many people set on studying who will starve at it." Swearing, drinking, too much travel, clothes, food, coffee, sexual promiscuity,

60. *Von der Landeshoheit in Cameral-Sachen* (= NTSR XVI, part 5: Frankfurt/Main, 1773), preface and pp. 2–3; *Von der Landes-Hoheit in Policey-Sachen* (= NTSR XVI, part 6: Frankfurt/Main, 1773), preface and pp. 2–10.

zealotry, prisons. "The promotion of inland manufactures nowadays is a main governmental activity of all territorial rulers who understand and care about their lands." Artisan guilds were subject to the Landeshoheit. Public security and order, housekeeping, coinage and post, amusements, cleanliness, provision for the unfortunate. How to deal with oriental locusts.[61] There were laws affecting all these based on the Landeshoheit in police, and Moser recorded them.

For although Moser usually invoked the principles of common weal or natural law only as a last resort and for the purpose of restraining governmental power, where it came to territorial authority in police or political economy he lost all control of it.[62] That failing of positive limits on police in the law of Landeshoheit, and the German political and constitutional circumstances that engendered it, caused him to follow up his treatment of the Landeshoheit with a work on the rights and duties of German subjects. To set about this was in itself an innovative and a technically creative undertaking—or, in another aspect, a juridical solecism and garble of categories. For to give the rights of subjects substance and standing in the public law, Moser took up matters theretofore confined to private or civil law and brought them to the heart of his treatment of public or constitutional law.[63] He incorporated the rights of German subjects as persons into the German constitution.

61. *Von der Landes-Hoheit in Policey-Sachen* (= NTSR XVI, part 6), pp. 21, 25–73, 88–115, 179–89, 444, and passim.

62. But see the argument in Walther Merk, "Der Gedanke des gemeinen Besten in der deutschen Staats- und Rechtsentwicklung," *Festschrift für A. Schultze* (Weimar, 1934), pp. 516–17 and passim, listing Moser along with Pütter and Kant as those who strove against the transformation of the common weal into a police state motto. August Schott, *Unpartheyischer Critik über die neuesten juristischen Schriften*, V (1773–75), pp. 20–21, remarked that Moser's volume on Polizey was new to the public law—and that Staatsklugheit seemed persistently to leak into it.

63. See the remarks in Pütter, *Litteratur*, II, p. 95. Moser in the preface to *Von der Teutschen Unterthanen Rechten und Pflichten* (= NTSR XVII: Frankfurt/Main, 1774) was uneasy and defensive about methods and categories, and about the paucity of sources. I shall not here consider Moser's *Von der Landeshoheit in Gnaden-Sachen* (= NTSR XVI, part 7: Frankfurt/Main, 1773), concerning a ruler's actions of grace not subject to complaints in law, such as legitimation of birth, removal of dishonor, granting of titles, and the like; nor shall I consider *Von der Landeshoheit in Ansehung Erde und Wassers* (= NTSR XVI, part 9: Frankfurt/Main, 1773), concerning land surveys, highways, forests and hunting, mining, navigation, and the like. The Landeshoheit in ecclesiastical matters and over the persons and properties of subjects will appear on convenient occasions below.

§30. The Rights of Subjects, Neighbors, and the *Corpus Evangelicorum*

MOSER had touched upon the rights of subjects as a topic in public law as early as his 1731 *Compendium juris publici*, but the name of his five-page treatment there had been "The rights to which all mediate members of the German Empire are entitled."[64] Now he was thinking about them not as remote members of the imperial system but as objects and subjects of territorial rule. For his topic thus formulated in 1774, legal sources and bibliographical equipment were scarce and indirect because of the eccentricity of Moser's category, which was more akin to categories of political theory than of law. He drew mainly on fragments from earlier work of his own, on the more recent excellent commentary on the Bavarian civil code by Wiguläus Kreittmayr (Moser's favorite Catholic jurist), and for the imperial side on the writings of the Reichskammergericht judge Johann Ulrich Cramer.[65]

Essentially everybody who resided in the territory of a German territorial ruler (Reichsstand) was that ruler's subject (the citizens of imperial towns being the main technical exception), whose rights and obligations Moser sought to capture and identify now in public law. Norms for judging their constitutional rights as subjects began "without doubt" with particular freedoms and agreements affecting localities, families, and the like. Just below these were the constitutional privileges and agreements affecting the whole land, then unlegislated traditions attached to communes or estates, then territorial legislation, imperial decisions based on territorial law, and so on down to common law and the law of nations. The conditions of territorial rights were normally established or affirmed at the time when a new ruler was installed, or on certain other occasions such as a request for extraordinary taxes or the settlement of some quarrel or suit. Every subject owed his territorial ruler "deference, love, loyalty, and obedience"; if he refused it the ruler could apply to territorial justice, help from his neighbors; or, if he had to, he might appeal to imperial justice and take his chances there. Any territorial subject was also a mediate subject of the empire, so the empire was

---

64. Pp. 592–96.

65. Kreittmayr, *Anmerkungen über den Codicem Maximilianeum Bavaricum civilem,* 5 vols. (Munich, 1759–68), especially part 5; on Cramer: Roderich Stintzing and Ernst Landsberg, *Geschichte der Deutschen Rechtswissenschaft,* III (Munich, 1910), pp. 273–76, and below, §30.

bound to protect his rights against any deprivation, and conversely also to enjoin upon him proper obedience to the territorial ruler. The most servile subjects, those with no articulated rights, got last-resort protection from "Holy Scripture, and the general natural public law, enjoyed by subjects in lands which accept the Christian religion, or which are civilized, respectively."[66]

Moser then enumerated the rights and duties pertaining to particular groups of subjects—*corpore* and *Gesellschaften*. He began with estates, summarizing what he had said in his 1769 treatise. He proceeded to districts: groups of communities brought together under a single court jurisdiction, for example, or who shared forest rights—something with respect to which they held a common constitutional identity, common rights and privileges, and so were treated together. Then came "single communes, especially towns," whose particular corporate laws were to be found scattered through a variety of local constitutional sources pertaining only to themselves. Every town had a magistracy of its own, variously chosen by local rules. Ordinarily towns were entitled to accept or reject new citizens according to their own judgment, and they had important corporate control over marriages and over the toleration of Jews and other noncitizens. (In his discussion of Landeshoheit in police, though, Moser had remarked respecting population policy that "one should not always pay attention to the howling of the natives.") Finally, there were other communities identified by lesser rights: markets, villages, fisheries, forest settlements.[67]

As a third main way to describe the rights and duties of subjects—after sources of right and location of right—Moser recategorized them according to "the particular sorts of German subjects." This procedure more nearly approached a social analysis but still used dominant terms of law. He began with the higher clergy and ended with serfs, Leibeigenen. No Protestant clergy enjoyed noble status by virtue of ecclesiastical office; in Catholic places there were some who did. Certain ecclesiastical officials, some members of cathedral chapters and endowed orders, monasteries, convents, and other groups were identified somewhere in the public law by rules affecting their rights and properties. Next came nobility: how to identify them, the various ranks and titles and ceremonial rights,

---

66. *Von der Teutschen Unterthanen Rechten und Pflichten* (= NTSR XVII), pp. 2, 9–18, 43–44, 49.

67. See above, §26; *Von der Teutschen Unterthanen Rechten und Pflichten* (= NTSR XVII), pp. 85–261, especially pp. 163–66, 188–201, 237–41; and then Moser went on to miscellaneous groups such as learned societies, commercial companies, charitable funds, guilds, and religious communities, pp. 261–71; see also *Von der Landes-Hoheit in Policey-Sachen* (= NTSR XVI, part 6), p. 35.

the generally recognized rules of inheritance and exclusion. Most noble rights, however, attached to their persons rather than their categorical status as nobles, except that as a rule they were exempted from the jurisdiction of territorial civil officials and the inferior courts. There was no real German nobility of office (a contrast with France), with the minor exception of certain Catholic ecclesiastical positions accorded noble equivalence. Moser was not impressed by the claims of urban patricians or of learned academicians to noble status: the status of the patricians was a matter of local recognition only; and "now that academic rank is so common, and every ignoramus who has spent a couple of years at the university . . . claims it," there was "no shadow" of nobility left in academic degrees.[68]

The "bürgerlicher Stand" or citizens' estate encompassed people who were neither nobles nor peasants; but labels were tricky and inadequate here. Moser was unwilling to restrict the term to franchised citizens of the towns because he found common usage now looser than that. The relation between the social and the legal meaning was muddled; but he seemed to hold that "bürgerlich" status and rights related to the place and group where they were enjoyed and did not travel with the person. He ranked the citizens' estate into five categories ranging from "Honoratioren," usually wealthy or learned persons or important officials who held ranks and immunities especially recognized in law, down to "common citizens," who enjoyed economic franchise in their own towns, eligibility for town office, and claims on common properties and endowments.[69]

In an afterthought to the 1769 book on lands and estates, Moser had cursorily mentioned just three categories of Bürger: the honorables, local citizens and communal officials, but then a third class of "lower servants, comedians, or firetenders in a ruler's service, and in towns people who work at dishonorable occupations (*levis notae macula*), unfranchised inhabitants [Beisassen], wage laborers," and in the countryside "people who work the land with their own hands, low communal servants, shepherds, doorkeepers, gravediggers, guards, etc." He did not mention this class when he described the rights and duties of German subjects in 1774. Nor did he mention Jews, who had appeared previously in terms of the

68. Thus "nobility" here meant *Landsassen*, mediate nobility with subjects of their own. *Von der Teutschen Unterthanen Rechten und Pflichten* (= NTSR XVII), pp. 7, 272–77, 391–97, 411; *Von denen Kayserlichen Regierungs-Rechten und Pflichten* (= NTSR III), pp. 1173–79. For a comparison with another analysis by Moser, *Von der Teutschen Reichs-Stände Landen* (= NTSR XIII), pp. 903–28.

69. *Von der Teutschen Unterthanen Rechten und Pflichten* (= NTSR XVII), pp. 459–73.

authority of lands and princes. There Moser had categorized them as "neither fish nor crab" and had outlined their legal status by way of territorial control over their admission, their number, their occupations and behavior, and their exemption from military and labor obligations and certain taxes, and their particular reliance on imperial protection.[70]

The final category of subjects who did have public rights and duties was peasants: "common subjects who live on the land, mainly as cultivators, or, where there are few fields and meadows but many forests, with grazing or wood." Were German peasants freemen or serfs? There had been much debate and opinions varied; Moser's opinion was that in many places, for example in Franconia, Swabia, along the Rhine, or in Saxony, they were as a rule free, but in Austria, Moravia, Bohemia, Lusatia, and like places the common countrymen lived in "a kind of slavery." Legally, then, there were two kinds of peasants, free and bound (leibeigen); but behind that the rights and obligations especially of free peasants were so murky and complex that no categorical rules were possible. Some had rights as members of communes; in a few instances they were represented in territorial estates. Other peasant rights either were personal or related to their properties: anyway these were the things that turned up when peasants got into lawsuits, and so got into the law. Most peasants had some particular obligation of regular work service to the state.

Bound peasants or serfs were subjects who "were not full masters of their own bodily persons." To identify them was easy in a place like Bohemia, where all subject countrymen were bound; but in most places it was hard to tell, and usually the only way was a long study of legal documents. Serfs of German race and tradition lived under generally better conditions than Slavs or Wends, who often were treated "harder and with less mercy than cattle." Their bodily rights usually depended "only on the way of thinking of one master or another, about how to treat and deal with others; apart from that usually they must let themselves and their children be used or misused in whatever manner may occur to their master or his officials and servants." Moser thought it was "a wonder" that such people did not lose patience and riot and rebel more often than they did.[71] He had nothing to say about their

70. *Von der Teutschen Reichs-Stände Landen* (= NTSR XIII), p. 928; *Von der Landeshoheit in Ansehung der Unterthanen Personen und Vermögens* (= NTSR XVI, part 8: Frankfurt/Main, 1773), pp. 9–27; *Von denen Kayserlichen Regierungs-Rechten und Pflichten* (= NTSR III), pp. 636–40.

71. *Von der Teutschen Reichs-Stände Landen* (= NTSR XIII), pp. 928–31; *Von der Teutschen Unterthanen Rechten und Pflichten* (= NTSR XVII), pp. 475–507.

standing before the imperial courts or in the constitutional freedoms of the German lands.[72]

If the focal point of German constitutional life was now the states of the empire, then after this distribution of duties and rights within them, the next problem was their relations with one another. The relations among German states had customarily been perceived through the medium of central imperial institutions and law; Moser himself had treated the topic that way, more comprehensively and in greater detail perhaps than anybody else. Now in the political circumstances of the 1770s (and possibly the religious, as will soon appear) Moser sought out another way of thinking about it. He undertook to consider the relations of the German imperial estates or princes not in a vertical but in a lateral way—not through their relation with "the emperor or empire *in Corpore*" but directly with their fellows; and not only with respect to their own subjects but with their fellows' estates and subjects, and between their subjects and the subjects of their fellows. That is to say (Moser did not say it this way), he would consider their relations not as amongst *Reichsstände* but as amongst *Landesherren*: not as imperial estates but as territorial rulers. This did not mean the dissolution of the empire or its law; it did mark their migration from one juridical sphere to another. To accomplish this, again, meant cutting across a great many of the topical divisions in the German public law, and bringing in other sources, and then reconstituting the fragments. Since lawbooks were easier to cite if they had short titles, Moser explained, for these newly collected topics he had invented the "Neighbor Public Law." But though the form was new there was nothing whatever speculative about this, he quickly added. Perhaps nobody had ever put it together before, but anybody could see at a glance that these were ordinary practical matters that turned up often, some of them every day.[73]

Neighbor Law was founded in the imperial constitution by the Public Peace and the Execution Ordinance, but Moser added another summary source: "the *officia humanitatis*, or the rights and duties necessary for the civil life of men, even without special agreements [Verträge]." The emperor was bound to sustain Neighbor Law by his capitulation promise to uphold peace and harmony. This background cleared the way consti-

72. An ordinary German subject could almost always renounce loyalty and duty to his ruler by leaving the territory (a "traditional right of a freeborn German," according to Moser), though he might be obliged to leave property behind. Bound peasants, however, could emigrate only on religious grounds or by purchasing their freedom. *Von der Teutschen Unterthanen Rechten und Pflicten* (= NTSR XVII), pp. 479–80; *Von der Landeshoheit in Ansehung der Unterthanen Personen und Vermögens* (= NTSR XVI, part 8), pp. 214–44.

73. *Teutsches Nachbarliches Staatsrecht* (= NTSR XIX: Frankfurt/Main, 1773), preface. See the review in Schott, *Critik*, VI (1773–75), pp. 370–74.

tutionally in imperial law. But Moser's real concern here was to establish how the peace and law of the empire could be sustained without effective guidance from the central institutions or officers of the empire.[74]

He sketched the procedures whereby princes could settle ordinary disputes between themselves peacefully and bilaterally. The party that considered itself injured should make written representations to the other, or send an emissary; there could be meetings of deputies from each side. There could be appeal to the good offices and opinions of the emperor, or of other imperial princes. In earlier times a common practice had been to turn a dispute over to an arbiter whose decision both parties agreed in advance to accept, or whom they would fear to defy; but this was less common nowadays. There could be appeal to the empire as a whole for nonjudicial mediation, or to one of the religious *corpore* of the empire if both parties accepted it, or to Kreis institutions. Most ordinary frictions over commerce, borders, competing jurisdictions, coinage, post, and the like could be solved or quieted in these ways.[75]

But what happened if none of these peaceful remedies succeeded in settling a dispute? That brought risk of violence, invoking the dangerous doctrines of self-defense and self-help. In every orderly state, Moser said, in any polity equipped with effective government and competent courts, acts of violence among members had to be suppressed; and should there be no adequate means for this in Germany "then we are on our way to the confederationist brigandage, cruelty, and inhumanity with which unhappy Poland is destroying itself as I write this." Forceful means were legally recognized, though, in self-defense or recovery of one's own. They were compatible with the Public Peace when they followed rules laid out for them in imperial law and recognized by the imperial courts. But then "Germany may or may not be in a condition where judicial remedies are available. Where judicial procedures meet the need, self-help is always prohibited, however protracted and uncomfortable that road may be; but if the judicial remedy fails, then the Public Peace and all other imperial laws lapse" and the German states "live then *in statu naturali* amongst themselves." Similarly in the case of a prince who was exempt from the jurisdiction of imperial courts: if good will and mediation failed the Public Peace fell away, and the parties moved into "the *statum naturalem* of self-help and destructive private warfare."[76]

Relatively mild and constitutional means of self-help against an offending neighbor were *Repressalien* and *Retorsionen*, meaning measured

74. *Teutsches Nachbarliches Staatsrecht* (= NTSR XIX), pp. 74–78; and see above, §15.

75. *Teutsches Nachbarliches Staatsrecht* (= NTSR XIX), pp. 81–82 and passim.

76. Ibid., pp. 81–82, 94, 124–25, 144–45, and passim.

retaliation against the neighbor's vulnerable properties or subjects, or sequestration of them pending redress of the offense. Usually, though, self-help doctrine came up in the course of bringing one's own unruly subjects to order, where regular procedures failed. It was invoked in appeals to neighboring states for help in doing this; and often it implied that the neighboring state had some influence or authority over the unruly subjects or was actually involved somehow in their dissidence. That helped bring self-help doctrine under the Neighbor Law rubric. Coming at the same problem by the other way, as the rights of one prince respecting the subjects of another: the rule was that no prince could meddle in the domestic affairs of another. "The grounds for this rule, to tell the truth, rest not so much on express imperial laws as on the general public law and the European law of nations." There were important exceptions to the rule. The Public Peace might even require intervention in the territory of another. Or one prince might have rights or duties respecting the subjects of another, by tradition or by special legal provision or agreement. Of these the most important instances were guarantees undertaken by one or more princes to uphold the constitutional agreements made between another prince and his subjects.[77]

Now then: the most memorable instance in turn of such a guarantee was surely the three Protestant kings' guarantee of the Württemberg ecclesiastical settlement. Moser avoided any mention of that somewhat unneighborly affair in discussing the Neighbor Law among princes. But it is hard to doubt that the events of the Seven Years War—the crisis and failure of the imperial proceedings then at Regensburg and Wetzlar, and the related Württemberg constitutional crisis at Stuttgart—had very much to do with Moser's discovery and exposition of Neighbor Law. And in another context, a few months later, Moser argued that the right of subjects to make constitutional appeal to outside rulers against their own was not restricted to formal guarantors. They could appeal to any neighbor prince whenever normal procedures through the imperial courts would be too slow, or difficult, to prevent irreparable harm to their constitutional rights (though he admitted that unless prudently used, this medicine might be worse than the sickness). Then yet elsewhere, in a discussion of ecclesiastical problems, Moser argued that the imperial prohibition against one territorial ruler's meddling in another's domestic affairs could not apply in a case where that ruler was violating imperial law, including any agreement recognized by the empire.

By this doctrine, it appears, the recognition of the Württemberg Reversalien that Moser had helped extract from Charles VII thirty years

77. *Von der Landeshoheit derer Teutschen Reichsstände überhaupt* (= NTSR XIV), pp. 328–33; *Teutsches Nachbarliches Staatsrecht* (= NTSR XIX), pp. 126–35, 159–98, 249–51.

before could be enforced by any prince or number of princes of the empire who decided to intervene on that basis.[78] Indeed, it was an issue of the German ecclesiastical constitution that turned out to unite for Moser the themes of Landeshoheit, the rights of subjects and of neighbors, and the powers of imperial courts; and it precipitated the last political altercation of his career. This curious incident, I venture, goes close to the nub of the German constitutional dilemma and the trammels of the central institutions of the empire; Moser's role in it is curious and characteristic too; and it is worth some attention.

In 1765, just after the end of the Seven Years War, Emperor Francis had died. His son and successor, Joseph II, had come to the throne set upon reestablishing imperial authority through the kind of administrative energy and "rational statecraft" that had served imperial princes— notably Prussia—so well in their extension of the Landeshoheit during past decades. Fundamental for this would be reform of the high imperial courts, to make them effectively functioning tribunals of constitutional justice; and Joseph launched a "visitation" of the Reichskammergericht at Wetzlar for this purpose.[79]

At first he had very little success with this, being blocked particularly by a dispute with England-Hanover in which Prussia sided with the latter; but when that residue of the war was settled Joseph returned to the project, encouraged by the establishment of friendly relations with Prussia, based on foreign considerations in turn: the ambitious behavior of Catherine of Russia and the problem of Poland. The Austro-Prussian cooperation that set in about 1768–69 was, as already noted, a shock to the lesser principalities of the empire. They had reason to fear what might happen to them (as it did to Poland) if the German constitutional duality, which now relied on a hostile counterbalance of Austrian and Prussian state power, should surcease. Most concerned were the Protestant principalities, who had come to depend on Prussia, as leader of the Protestant party, for support against the Austrian territorial *and* imperial will that Joseph sought to galvanize together. Inasmuch as Prussian support seemed compromised or lost to Prussian sovereign international interests, the Protestant principalities turned now to the *corpus evangelicorum* itself, the organized Protestant party of the empire. This was a step that Moser, seeing these political and constitutional events in

78. "Von dem Recurs Teutscher Landstände und Unterthanen an andere Reichsstände, oder auswärtige Machten . . . ," *Abhandlung verschiedener besonderer Rechts-Materien*, IV (1774), pp. 462–77; *Von des Corporis Evangelicorum Vertretungs-Recht seiner Glaubens-Genossen* (Regensburg, 1772), p. 34; above, §12.

79. See generally Rudolf Smend, *Das Reichskammergericht* (Weimar, 1911), pp. 232–37; and Rohr, *Der deutsche Reichstag*, passim and as cited below.

the making, and disliking reliance on Prussia anyway, had for some years recommended.[80]

Protestant principalities had almost always avoided submitting their disputes to imperial jurisdictions, and for this they had two important grounds, constitutional grounds with confessional and political content. One was the principle of religious parity of rights embodied in the Peace of Westphalia and spread throughout the imperial constitution. Of this the central working feature was the *itio in partes*, the going-into-parts that enabled Protestants to block majority decisions in matters confessional in nature. This procedural right had done more than any other to immobilize Reichstag procedures (for example, imperial execution proceedings against Prussia in 1756). The other main ground was self-help: where effective and impartial imperial justice was not available—as the Protestants claimed it was not, in matters relating to religion—a principality could seek remedies on its own resources or by whatever appeal it saw fit, and apply force as a last resort. (Here was the self-help Moser had tried to work out and to control under the Neighbor Law heading.)

The right of going-into-parts was in turn, though, an important reason why Protestant princes especially did adduce confessional grounds to their disputes and complaints, inasmuch as this blocked adverse majority or imperial decision and opened the way to self-help, or to appeal and decision within their confessional group. That advantage helps explain the persistence of confessional issues in German politics that often seems puzzling. But moreover, for the going-into-parts to be constitutionally valid, the confessional division had to be clear. All coreligionists on one side had to agree that the issue was a confessional one; and the ongoing need to work up partisan support on religious grounds, to oblige or deal with coreligionists in order to get them to go along, was a basic reason for the building and maintenance of German political groupings or parties on confessional lines. This tendency seems actually to have increased in the later eighteenth century. For Protestants the matrix of the party process and structure was probably the Gremium or standing conference of ambassadors and trained jurists from the Protestant governments to the Reichstag at Regensburg. The *corpus catholicorum*, a looser organization, relied more on regular imperial institutions.[81]

80. Above, §§22 and 26.

81. Klaus Schlaich, "Corpus Evangelicorum und Corpus Catholicorum. Aspekte eines Parteiwesens im Hlg. Römischen Reich Deutscher Nation," *Der Staat*, XI (1972), pp. 218–30; Ulrich Belster, *Die Stellung des Corpus Evangelicorum in der Reichsverfassung* (Bamberg, 1968), passim. Karl O. Fr. v. Aretin, "Die Konfessionen als politische Kräfte am Ausgang des alten Reichs," in *Festgabe Joseph Lortz*, edited by Erwin Iserloh and Peter Manns, II (Baden-Baden, 1958), pp. 181–241, remarks the increased importance of confessional partisan division by *corpore* in the later eighteenth century, connecting it

Now Johann Jakob Moser's Protestantism and his constitutional views begin to come together, particularly in the 1770s and in his work just considered (and we shall be back to the Reichskammergericht shortly). He insisted, as noted, that the general Landeshoheit was a ruler's own, not derived from superior authority. He had good constitutional, political, and historical grounds for this. But he also insisted that the Landeshoheit in ecclesiastical matters was part of the general Landeshoheit: "The Landeshoheit in ecclesiastical things goes to nobody but to him who has the Landeshoheit overall; and whoever has the Landeshoheit overall, has the ecclesiastical Landeshoheit as well." This rule and benefit applied, he said, to Catholic principalities as well as Protestant. But for Protestant princes, territorial possession of the ecclesiastical Landeshoheit was particularly important, because their unrivaled control of ecclesiastical and secularized properties, endowments, and jurisdictions (except as conditioned by special arrangement as in Württemberg) was a vital source of their wealth and political authority.[82] So this link between the Landeshoheit and ecclesiastical issues had strengthened with the growth of the Landeshoheit itself. For Moser, it would have been awkward enough to suppose that a Catholic prince's ecclesiastical rights flowed from the emperor or the pope; for a Protestant ruler to hold his ecclesiastical powers and properties from the emperor was for Moser quite intolerable, and in constitutional fact quite anomalous and in politics quite untrue.

Yet Moser left no doubt that the exercise of the Landeshoheit, ecclesiastical and all, was subject to imperial law and imperial justice; his whole sense of the constitution and his fear of its disintegration bound him to hold that view. Self-help was still only a last constitutional resort, invoked where there was no other remedy. But the territorial rulers, especially Protestant ones, did in fact refuse to apply or submit to imperial justice. And so they wanted no reforms to make the Reichskammergericht efficient and effective, which could deprive them of that right in law and in practice. When Joseph's visitation showed signs of getting seriously under way, therefore, the *corpus evangelicorum* came alive and mounted an attack on it, particularly with regard to the views and person of the Protestant Reichskammergericht judge Johann Ulrich Cramer. Just what Cramer's position was at this conjuncture is not altogether clear. He had

---

directly with Austro-Prussian rivalry, whereas I here, following Moser, have emphasized the *corpore* as alternatives to Austrian or Prussian domination of the religious parties. See also Fritz Wolff, *Corpus Evangelicorum und Corpus Catholicorum auf dem Westfälischen Friedenskongress* (Münster, 1966), pp. 198–200.

82. *Von der Landeshoheit im Geistlichen* (= NTSR XV), pp. 4–9, 53–56, 169–99, 250–51.

been a student of Christian Wolff and then had become an expert on Roman law and on Reichskammergericht practice. He was a loyal and energetic member of the court, a believer in the unity of imperial law as spoken by his court and in rational justice. He had joined the court in 1752 with an appointment from the Franconian free towns; but in 1765, significantly perhaps, he had moved up to the Brandenburg-Prussian seat. To Protestant leaders now, devotion to the authority and dignity of the court seemed a kind of treachery—especially coming from the Prussian nominee on this court, from whose jurisdiction Prussia itself was immune. Another straw in the wind is that Cramer was a friend of Johann Adam Ickstatt, and had once collaborated with him in writing an anonymous defense of the ecclesiastical authority of the elector of Bavaria.[83]

Confronting the disagreement between the Protestant Cramer and the *corpus evangelicorum*, certain other Protestant judges on the Reichskammergericht picked up a suggestion Johann Jakob Moser made in connection with the visitation: that the *corpus evangelicorum* should require of all Protestant nominees to the court a promise to follow the decisions of the *corpus* in their official judgments.[84] This proposition takes some getting used to now; and at the time, it flew so radically in the face of any rational conception of impartial justice that not only Catholic opinion was outraged—even most Protestant judges were put back on their judicial honor. Meanwhile efforts by the *corpus evangelicorum* to influence cases and proceedings before the court roused such conflicts between the *corpus* and the court that the Protestant judges joined Catholic colleagues in warning the *corpus* to cease meddling with imperial justice. Thus Moser's proposal seemed to have been defeated, if not by general perceptions of how justice ought in principle to be administered, then by institutional rivalry between the Reichskammergericht, Protestants and all, and the *corpus evangelicorum*. Anyway it was submerged in the morass of bargaining, claims, and counterclaims that attended the organization of the visitation commission and its agenda.[85]

There it might have remained, perhaps; but Moser did all he could to

---

83. Stintzing and Landsberg, *Rechtswissenschaft*, III, pp. 273–77, and notes p. 187; Karl S. Bader, "Johann Ulrich (Freih. v.) Cramer. Jurist und Cameralist, 1706–1772," *Schwäbische Lebensbilder*, X (1966), pp. 38–60; Notker Hammerstein, *Aufklärung und katholisches Reich* (Berlin, 1977), pp. 60–61, 271.

84. Above, §26 and n. 176 thereto. Moser had made his mistrust of Reichskammergericht personnel quite open since the beginning of the visitation proceedings: see *Unmasgebliches Bedenken* (above, n. 27).

85. Rohr, *Der deutsche Reichstag*, pp. 156–61 and passim; Moser, *Von der Verbindung derer Evangelischen Reichs-Gerichts-Beysizer an die Schlüsse des Corporis Evangelicorum* (Frankfurt/Main, 1775), pp. 1–5; *Lebensgeschichte*, IV, pp. 70–71.

keep it alive. He published a string of more or less polemical tracts in 1772, about the constitutional rights and role of the *corpus evangelicorum*. In one of them he argued that the *corpus* had exclusive authority to control its inner organization and to represent the constitutional position of German Protestants in confessional matters; thus it could bind the Reichstag votes of Protestant principalities to decisions reached in Protestant caucus. Moreover, the *corpus* had a right and a responsibility to intervene in Catholic territories to protect the confessional interest of Protestant subjects—as Catholic princes to be sure also could intervene for Catholic subjects in Protestant lands. This neighborly breach of the Landeshoheit, Moser argued, had been explicitly reserved from all modern prohibitions against meddling with the subjects of other princes. In a 1774 volume of the *Neues Teutsches Staats-Recht*, on the religious constitution of the empire, Moser declared further that without the assent of the *corpus evangelicorum*, no new imperial court could be established nor the existing ones modified; and Protestant deputies to a visitation must be equal in number to Catholics and had authority to instruct judges of the court on procedures affecting confessional interests.[86]

When the visitation got formally under way, Catholic deputations cited Moser's propositions to show the unreliability of some of the Protestant judges. Some Protestant deputations and some Protestants on the bench—not all—adopted Moser's view. A special imperial commission declared that Moser's position was unconstitutional, that it aimed at a total undermining of high imperial justice. There were hints of criminal action to be taken against him, or so he believed (and ultimately action was taken).[87] In reply Moser fired off, openly under his name, the treatise "On the Binding of Protestant Imperial Court Judges to the Decisions of the Corpus Evangelicorum," setting forth the constitutional argument in full.[88]

What was at issue here? Moser inquired. It was not how to apply clearly known and existing law; that raised no judicial problems. Nor, secondly, did the question arise where the Protestant estates of the empire did not have a conjoined confessional opinion, enunciated by the *corpus evangelicorum*. The question arose only where there was a serious interpretive question of law and one that clearly divided German Protestants from German Catholics, and where the respective imperial estates *in*

86. *Von der Evangelischen Reichsstände Collegial-Rechten, besonders in Ansehung ihrer innern Verfassung* (Regensburg, 1772); *Von des Corporis Evangelicorum Vertretungs-Recht; Von der Teutschen Religions-Verfassung* (= NTSR VII: Frankfurt/Main, 1774), pp. 427, 566–68.

87. *Lebensgeschichte*, IV, pp. 70–71; *Von der Verbindung*, pp. 4–6.

88. *Von der Verbindung derer Evangelischen Reichs-Gerichts-Beysizer an die Schlüsse des Corporis Evangelicorum* (Frankfurt/Main, 1775).

corporibus had assumed collegial confessional positions. In such a situation, judges were expected to act as representatives of their religious confessions; no other principle could make sense of the Peace of Westphalia, which carefully allocated judicial office in terms of confession, nor indeed of the whole religious scheme of the imperial constitution. As confessional representatives, then, inasmuch as they were bound to follow confessional positions constitutionally arrived at (by the *corpore*), the judges could also, it followed, be asked at the time of their appointment to make agreement that they would do so.

That is to say, Moser extended the going-into-parts to the imperial judiciary. That would defend the constitutional position of German Protestants there; but Moser's outraged critics claimed, predictably and credibly, that it aimed at the destruction of imperial justice. Moser professed to find irony in this calumny. Heretofore, he said, it had been Protestant political circles who had deemed him a "political enthusiast and heretic" because he was "known to be so eager a defender of the imperial judicial office and the high imperial courts." Nothing would make him drop his proposal sooner than persuasion that it tended to undermine imperial justice. But his intention was just the reverse. "For we are dealing here, namely, with no part of the high judicial function, but with a piece of the legislative power." That brought the principle of imperial religious parity into play, and the going-into-parts; and in legislative roles the judges of the Reichskammergericht were constitutionally "Repräsentanten" of the Protestant estates of the empire.[89]

Moser's argument was tainted by its confessional partisanship and its unlikelihood of success; but yet it has a modern ring, with its invocation of representation (compare his view of the Württemberg estates) and the distinction of legislative from judicial powers. Where the judicial reformers meant to give new efficient force to the imperial judiciary, though, Moser meant to adapt it more closely to the rest of the constitutional structure. Whatever one makes of his constitutional analysis after thinking it through, it was a long way from wood-chopping collectioneering of juridical artifacts. To support it lies the political position prepared a few pages back for Moser's constitutional argument: that the fundamental problem of imperial justice was how to get the princes of the empire and particularly the Protestant ones to come before the imperial courts and to submit to their enunciation of imperial law. If the princes did not, the empire could never hold the Landeshoheit within bounds, nor safeguard the rights of subjects and estates, nor sustain the imperial constitution itself.

89. *Von der Verbindung*, pp. 6–8, 18–20, 28–31, and passim.

It all went back to the confessional division, which in Germany, alone among major European countries, had never been overcome or suppressed—where in fact, rather, it pervaded the constitutional foundations of the empire. "As long as both confessions enjoy the same rights in Germany," Moser concluded in 1775, his solution to the odd condition of imperial justice was "a necessary and unavoidable consequence, though also an accidental one." As for the Josephine goal of efficient imperial justice and administration—nobody in Germany, he predicted, was going to sacrifice important rights for the sake of that. "To attempt this would add a Volume Two to the present history of Great Britain's American colonies; and then what would be the end to it?"[90]

---

§31. Taking the Measure

T H E last part of a life seems not usually to make sense of the foregoing in the manner of a monograph or a sonnet; old age and death its companion more commonly empty the life before of the form and meaning it had attained. Surely, though, it tells something about the life that has been lived; at least people often try to make it so. Moser took to old age with a kind of virtuosity and lived it well—so it seems at this writing. It is almost as though that had been his object all along, as he meant us to see him at least.

To temper his chosen mode of bland benevolence and serene conviction, however, we may finish first the story of Moser's engagement with the Reichskammergericht, the *corpus evangelicorum*, and the imperial judicial reform. After the partition of Poland in 1772 the pattern of Austro-Prussian cooperation gradually dissolved, in disputes first over details of disposing that booty, but then over other Austrian territorial and imperial ambitions. These converged on an uncertain Bavarian inheritance that was impending, which was to produce in 1778 the Bavarian succession war between Austria and Prussia. Parallel to his estrangement from Austria, Frederick of Prussia resumed active leadership of the *corpus evangelicorum*, and in 1776 the Reichskammergericht visitation collapsed, largely because of the intransigence of the Protestant party (in which, however, a number of the smaller Catholic principalities joined).

90. *Von der Verbindung*, p. 35.

Before its demise, though, the visitation had turned up a bribery scandal affecting three Reichskammergericht judges, Catholic and Protestant, which led to their dismissal from the court. Between this scandal and the collapse of the visitation, the Reichskammergericht was much concerned for its institutional dignity in the later seventies.[91]

Johann Jakob Moser had meanwhile got himself involved with another confessional matter, this one growing out of the dissolution of the Society of Jesus by Pope Clement XIV in 1773. The status of German ex-Jesuits and especially what would become of their schools and properties inevitably became a controversial issue, and Moser promptly chimed in. His view, based on the doctrine of the ecclesiastical Landeshoheit, was that the Jesuit schools and properties, whatever the pope may have said about it, had legally been in the jurisdictions of the territorial governments; with the order's dissolution, all agreements respecting their status lapsed, and the territorial governments might dispose of the former Jesuit rights and goods as they saw fit.[92] This brought a sharp reply from the ex-Jesuit Aloys Merz, an energetic polemicist who some years before had made a bitter personal attack on Moser in the form of commentary on the first edition of Moser's Life History.[93] Then in 1775 Moser published a number of confidential Reichshofrat memoranda, embarrassing to the imperial government, concerning the Jesuit problem; the memoranda had reached him through Protestant governments who probably meant to get them published that way. Vienna authorities were outraged, and tried in vain to cause the Württemberg government to seize and examine Moser's private papers.[94]

Moser's argument for the binding of the Protestant Reichskammergericht judges to the views of their confessional party and sponsors thus coincided with his invocation of the Landeshoheit in the interest of territorial rights to the Jesuit inheritance. There were ambiguities here tempting to exploit. "In so confused a situation," observed one Catholic political writer regarding Moser, "where not even the holiest of laws

91. Rohr, *Der deutsche Reichstag*, pp. 225–83; Smend, *Reichskammergericht*, p. 236.

92. But Moser recommended that Protestant princes entrust the disposition of Jesuit properties to the leaders of their Catholic subject communities, for schools and the like. "Rechtliches Bedencken von Aufhebung des Jesuiten-Ordens; besonders so viel es die Befügnisse eines Evangelischen Reichs-Standes dabey betrifft," *Abhandlung verschiedener besonderer Rechts-Materien*, II (1774), pp. 3–62.

93. Aloys (sometimes Aloysius) Merz, *Der Jesuit vor dem Richterstuhle des Johann Jacob Moser* (Berlin, 1774); Merz, *Unentbehrliche Anecdoten zu Johann Jacob Mosers ... Lebensgeschichte* (Münster, 1769); Moser, *Lebensgeschichte*, I, pp. 3–4; and *Abhandlung verschiedener besonderer Rechts-Materien*, III (1774), pp. 223–52 (a reply to Merz).

94. *Zwölf Reichs-Hofraths-Gutachten wegen des Jesuiter-Ordens, dessen Aufhebung etc.* (Ulm, 1775); *Lebensgeschichte*, II, pp. 174–75; IV, p. 173.

are spared: here the honor of one's fellow man and even of one's own brotherhood comes under attack." Moser snapped back intemperately that there had never been reason to suppose that all members of the imperial judiciary were uniformly virtuous, and the recent visitation had shown that "there are men of both religious parties who are not to be trusted, who in fact are cause for shame, as false and bad brothers"—an allusion to the bribery scandal and perhaps to the resistance of some Protestant judges to his scheme for binding them. The pamphlet containing this language was seized by the imperial censors at Frankfurt on Main; and the Reichskammergericht at Wetzlar, enmeshed with a sensitive problem of new appointments, called upon the Württemberg government to deliver Moser's seventy-six-year-old person before them to answer charges.[95]

A pompous political parody ensued. Duke Karl Eugen sent an official to take a deposition from Moser in Stuttgart. In this Moser averred that his earlier statement had meant to impugn no present court official. The Reichskammergericht, after a series of debates from which Protestant judges tended pointedly to absent themselves, resolved to summon the Reichsfiskal, an imperial criminal prosecutor before that court especially charged with breaches of the peace, to take action against Moser. The Reichsfiskal filed a writ for Moser's offensive pamphlet to be publicly torn to shreds by the beadle, for a fine of ten golden marks, and requiring public retraction. Moser appealed to the *corpus evangelicorum*.[96] Now the Wittelsbach elector of Bavaria died, precipitating a showdown between Austria and Prussia; and Moser learned from a "well-wisher in Berlin" that measures in his defense were on the way. In March of 1778, as war between Austria and Prussia awaited only the final political dispositions and agreeable weather, a Protestant Reichstag caucus at Regensburg invoked the *corpus evangelicorum* in Moser's cause against the Reichskammergericht, calling Protestant judges to account for neglect of their confessional duties respecting the good gray Moser. During the war summer of 1778 Moser's correspondents at Wetzlar and elsewhere encouraged him to be defiant and keep the case alive; and in consequence a judgment of contumacy was issued against him in September

95. *Nochmals bevestigte Verbindung derer Evangelischen Reichs-Gerichts-Beysizere an die Schlüsse des Corporis Evangelicorum* (Frankfurt/Main, 1777); *Lebensgeschichte*, IV, pp. 71–73.

96. *Lebensgeschichte*, IV, pp. 73–76; Moser, *Memoriale an das Corpus Evangelicorum* (Stuttgart, 1777). On the Reichsfiskal (at this time Johann Conrad von Birckenstock), *Von der Teutschen Justiz-Verfassung* (= NTSR VIII), pp. 442–47; Smend, *Reichskammergericht*, pp. 359–63; Friedrich Thudicum, "Das vormalige Reichskammergericht und seine Schicksale," *Zeitschrift für deutsches Recht und deutsche Rechtswissenchaft*, XX (1861), p. 164.

for failing to submit to Reichskammergericht authority. By then, though, the Austro-Prussian war was petering out in ways suitable to Prussia; and the Prussian agent at Wetzlar wrote to Friedrich Karl von Moser that it would be best now for his father to avoid further provocation of the Reichskammergericht. If he did, the matter could be expected to fade away; if he persisted, there might be some nasty moments ahead for the Moser family. After the exchange of a few more threats and protests, and after the Treaty of Teschen early in 1779, the matter was dropped—a farcical replay in miniature of Moser's experience with the Seven Years War.[97]

These controversies of the 1770s, however, involving *corpus evangelicorum*, Jesuits, Reichskammergericht, and the ecclesiastical Landeshoheit, all emphasized Moser's confessional position and allegiance. This conjuncture came not merely from a series of political accidents; it followed his own changing sense of the role of religion in the sphere of public life. And there is little doubt that his identification with a kind of Protestantism that was both traditional and pietistical was closer than ever before. A reason for this turn of mind might be partly an old and pious man's concern for the place of his faith in a world where faiths were changing, but that begs the question and trivializes it. More specifically, Moser had growing doubts about the efficacy of institutions, and growing conviction that the wills of persons inhabiting them mattered more. In some proportion with Moser's declining confidence in the secular institutions of the empire and their control over the behavior of its members, his conviction grew stronger that religion was vitally important for maintaining civil peace and constitutional order. Decent relations among the members of the empire, and between them and their subjects, depended on religion—the Christian faith, in Germany and Europe— both for its tempering and gentling effect on individual wills, and as a basis for their political and moral community. Yet neither Moser's own temper nor the German (or European) religious order and peace could tolerate any dictated official orthodoxy in the detail of religious observance or belief.

The problem of balancing freedom of conscience against the perils of sectarian religious rivalry was a real and most sensitive one for Moser because of his own religious history and conviction: his skeptical attitude toward ecclesiastical institutions and official doctrines, his personal

97. *Schreiben corpus evangelicorum an das Reichs-Cammer-Gericht, Evangelischen Theils* (Regensburg, 1788); *Lebensgeschichte*, IV, pp. 77–90. In 1783 Moser remarked, defending his compliance in this incident, "Dass man solche Drohungen nicht achten, sondern darüber weggehen solle, wäre ein guter Rath für ein Engeiländer. Aber wo ist in Teutschland leicht ein Ort, wo ihn ein kluger Mann befolgen könnte?" *Lebensgeschichte*, IV, p. 222.

commitment to individual salvation out of utter consciousness of the failure and sin nobody could avoid, and his long uneven association with teachers and groups of pietist persuasion. He had managed to contain the legal and constitutional problem in a general way within the proposition that religious beliefs were free to all Christians as long as they professed one of the three recognized faiths, as long as they accepted what he considered the basic Christian principles, and as long as they made no attempt to set up separate hierarchies and disciplines actively hostile to the established ecclesiastical structure, which he believed must lead to a kind of theocratic Babel.[98] Jews, Greeks, and Muslims also enjoyed liberty of conscience and moreover were entitled at least de facto to their separate religious institutions. But Moser had always opposed Separatist establishments among German Protestants, had suffered from Ebersdorf theocracy, and fully accepted the many prohibitions written firmly into imperial law against religious manifestations on Anabaptist pattern. The fragile boundary of tolerance he thus drew, between the sphere or compartment of secular confessional order and the sphere of free religious conscience, depended on the acceptance by both spheres, order and conscience, of common basic theological tenets. Neither sphere could tolerate the departure of the other from these. The free conscience could not abide in a church that left the foundations of personal faith; the church could not tolerate attacks on the foundations of confessional order. The civic truce between these spheres was the religious core of the basic constitutional laws of the Religious Peace and the Peace of Westphalia. Should it fail on account of a loss of the shared religious principles accepted on both sides, the loss seemed inevitably to lead to what the basic laws had been drawn to prevent: to cruel religious oppression from one quarter, and to impassioned public disorder on the other.

This great importance of knowing basic and simple religious principles pressed Moser's religious attitudes in a conservative direction, a tendency guided and reinforced by his private religious experience, by his skepticism of theological embellishments both scholastic and humanistic, and now no doubt by his growing old. But it was not easy to say how to know and sustain basic principles of shared belief—proof against the vagaries of false imagination and interest—without inviting the contradictions and evasions that would empty or destroy them. For Moser in his time there came a grave dilemma, between his concern lest a secular loosening of religious faith end by destroying these bonds of accommodation on the one hand, and his hostility to religious tutelage and fear

98. See for example *Von der Teutschen Religions-Verfassung* (= NTSR VII), pp. 23–38; and above, §17.

of its consequences on the other. Here a clear link across compartments between Moser's religious and political convictions emerged.

In a collection of "Essays on the German Ecclesiastical Law," published in 1772, Moser examined efforts which Protestant governments and orthodox theologians had made to identify the confessional tenets established and recognized in the basic laws, and to condemn deviations from them. He found these efforts laborious, exaggerated, and generally unsuccessful, especially when it came to identifying "so-called pietism"— a word as hard to define in the eighteenth century as it is now. Moser found no valid doctrinal or legal definition for it, and so went on to deny that pietism was anywhere forbidden in imperial law, or subject to judgment by the Reichskammergericht.[99] "How far" then, inquired his next essay, "does the doctrinal freedom of Protestants extend according to the basic imperial laws?" The problem was not the pietists, who freely lived and believed within the Christian core; it was the new religious scholarship and theology, whose claims of doctrinal freedom pointed to a "revolution in the principles of the Christian religion." The result of this freedom would be a religious society of "civilized heathen and honorable naturalists."

Protestants, to be sure, had always declared that no man—only God —could rule another's conscience; this meant that faith could not be commanded and enforced. But surely, Moser argued, it had never meant that anybody could write and preach at others however he pleased. No constitutional agreement had ever contemplated this. Personal belief was free, but public propagation of doctrines that were alien or hostile to the basic tenets of the constitutionally recognized confessions was subject to suppression or penalty. Moser even fell back lawyer-fashion on the constitutional rights of Catholics here: they had contracted to acknowledge the Augsburg confession in the empire, but not "freethinkers and indifferentists." Recourse to Scripture was not enough; the devil, Matthew 4, quoted Scripture, and so did all the "Anabaptists, Anti-Trinitarians, Arians, Socinians, Separatists, and so on." If the mouthing of Scripture justified, five thousand German sects would be at one another's throats in fifty years. Neither did worldly virtue justify. With scorn Moser quoted something he had read in Friedrich Nicolai's *Allgemeine Deutsche Bibliothek*: that anybody who knows that he has striven to be good, in conscience and out of love of God, can be sure of grace and blessing. More than scorn, shock: "Is that not the exact and total natu-

99. "Von der Beurtheilung, welcher Religion Jemand zugethan seye," *Abhandlungen aus dem Teutschen Kirchen-Recht* (Frankfurt/Main, 1772), pp. 126–94; "Ob der Pietismus durch Kayserliche Edicte und Reichs-Cammergerichtliche Urtheile verworffen worden seye?" ibid., pp. 195–203.

ralism? Cannot honorable and conscientious heathen proclaim exactly that? Where then is the redemption from guilt and the delivery from the penalty of sin through the blood of the Son of God?"[100] Here was rock-bottom: Moser could not conceive in well-mannered heathen any firm foundation for peace, for peace between a created human and the world, or peace of an immortal soul with its destiny.

A curious manifestation of Moser's concern was a disquisition on Freemasonry and the Peace of Westphalia, which he wrote in 1776 after an imperial effort to suppress Freemasonic lodges at Regensburg, seat of the imperial diet. It was not at all obvious, some newer critics remarked half-amused, what Freemasonry had to do with the Peace of Westphalia; but Moser's mind took this straight to the place of religious belief in the German constitution. However decent or however frivolous individual Freemasons might be (Moser observed that there were no "so-called pietists" among them), imperial law could prohibit the lodges if it could be shown that they propagated a faith at odds with the three confessions recognized in the Peace. The trouble here was finding out what the Freemasons were up to. Was it a faith, with public doctrines? Their ceremonials surely sounded religious, and in a sense public: important people were mixed up in it. But the town council of Regensburg by virtue of the Landeshoheit could suppress the lodges anyway if they were shown to be inimical to the common weal, even without being sure what went on in them. But whatever happened, Moser opined, there were still plenty of people left who would want to die in the old faith despite the changing temper of the times. No Voltaire or any of his ilk could replace faith, and the world would not be long in learning to its sorrow what the new "religious" styles would bring.[101]

During the middle seventies, his own and the century's, Moser was taking stock of himself and of his career against the background of the time. It seemed a time set on landmarks and conclusions. The *Neues Teutsches Staats-Recht* was finished in 1775. In 1774 came a terrible personal blow: the slow wasting death of Christian Benjamin the beloved, conceived at Ebersdorf in Moser's middle years, twenty years younger than his brothers and ten years younger than his nearest living sister. Moser had taught Benjamin himself after the others were grown, and had

100. "Wie weit sich die Freyheit derer Evangelischen in Teutschland in Lehrsachen nach denen Reichsgrundgesezen erstrecke, oder nicht?" ibid., pp. 203–34; see n. 13 above.

101. *Von Geduldung der Freymaurer-Gesellschaften, besonders in Rücksicht auf den Osnabrückischen Frieden* (Frankfurt/Main, 1776). Reviews in Schott's *Critik*, VII (1775–76), pp. 893–95; in Nicolai's *Allgemeine Deutsche Bibliothek*, XXXIII (1778), part 2, pp. 445–46. See also Moser's remarks on Lessing's defense of Freemasonry in *Lebensgeschichte*, IV, pp. 99–101.

found great pride and happiness in launching the boy's career with the governments of Baden and the empire; that was gone now and the generations were out of joint. Two daughters were dead too: Wilhelmina Louysa Achenwall and her Göttingen professor husband also, and the unmarried Christiana Friderika who had died young; the two Mohl daughters were alive and so was Maria Dorothea, wife of a Württemberg official. As for the older sons, Friedrich Karl was now first minister and chief of cabinet at Hessen-Darmstadt, and Wilhelm Gottfried was a privy councillor there.[102] In 1775 Moser wrote and published an account of the life and death of his wife Friderica Rosina. He included it as an appendix to a new third volume for a third edition of his Life History, which he began in 1776, remarking that in that year he began to notice some signs of aging.[103]

The new volume of the Life History contained no new narrative, except for the appended story of Friderica Rosina, in which Moser himself figured prominently, and a smattering of new anecdotes. Instead it was all about what Moser thought of himself, and what others had said or written about him. Some critics of the earlier version had complained of too much irrelevant personal detail, others that he had hidden his own sentiments and motives from his readers. Moser concluded from this and from the popularity of the work that "the public consists of all kinds of people" with many different interests in the private life of another. "The Christian, the philosopher, the psychologist [Psycholog], the natural scientist, people concerned for their health or peace of mind, a husband or a wife, a scholar of one kind or another" (no mention of "the historian") ought to be at least as interested in so real and controversial a person as himself as they were in some literary invention of a Robinson Crusoe or in some novel.[104]

Moser meant to exemplify himself for present and future as well as to defend his past, but he was careful not to exclude his lesser weaknesses and shortcomings, and his account of himself rings true at least in ex-

---

102. *Lebensgeschichte*, II, pp. 178–81, 239–41. After Moser's death, Friedrich Karl published a moving collection of letters from Moser to Benjamin or about him, of which the closing salutation of one written to Benjamin on the eve of his death may give the tone, and tell a union of compartments: "Meines herzlich geliebtesten Sohnes und zukünftigen lieben Bruders und Mitgenossens an dem Reiche Jesu, getreuer Vater und zärtlichster Freund, J. J. Moser." *Patriotisches Archiv für Deutschland*, V (1786), pp. 365–478, quotation from p. 430.

103. *Etwas von dem innern Leben der seel. Frau Friederike Rosine Moserin* (Stuttgart, 1775); *Lebensgeschichte*, III, pp. 6, 200–246. The account was drawn mainly from Moser's "Nachricht von meinem natürlichen, bürgerlichen und geistl: Leben"; see above, §24.

104. *Lebensgeschichte*, I, preface; III, pp. 1–2.

ternal ways. He claimed absolute probity in all his professional life; he had never taken a bribe or accepted an illicit gift, nor delivered an opinion he did not believe in return for flattery or favor. Such civic righteousness had not always been to his professional advantage; and he took considerable satisfaction (now) in that too. An honest man is like a virgin, he said—give way just once and there is no recovery. The disagreeable Aloys Merz had inquired rhetorically why it was that Moser had never got along with people at Vienna, Stuttgart, Frankfurt on Oder, Ebersdorf, Homburg, Hanau, or anyplace else. In more civil language that meant, Moser supposed, why had he changed positions so often? The answer was simply that people were always engaging and dismissing him, probably because, like Jeremiah, he uttered too many unwelcome truths. But he admitted to a certain lack of grace in his dealing with others; and he had run a tight chancellery in his time.[105]

The great number and diversity of his publications, Moser pointed out, showed what an industrious fellow he was. He printed an incomplete list of about four hundred of them (noting another dozen titles that had often been falsely attributed to him, including the most important works of Friedrich Karl). His books were not all perfect. In fact, a fair share of them ought not to have been published really—too hasty, not worked through to the end—"but then I needed the money, or some poor printer's widow did, etc." He had always written as clearly as possible, so that his readers "would not have to break their heads to find what hidden treasure, or wormy core, might lie beneath some flowery expressions, or profound philosophical or mathematical jargon [Kunstwörter]." Since leaving the university world he had written only in German, so that more people would read and buy his books. Besides, one commenter had said that Moser's Latin was enough to give anybody a headache, and Moser was content to spare that pain to "tender Latin nerves." Anyway, he went on, this had forfended the risk of being made a member of any of the honorable Latin societies, which would have expanded his title to a length quite annoying for someone who had signed as many official documents as he had. He used traditional German spelling and avoided neologisms, and he took no instruction from North Germans on proper language: "Our language too is a piece of the German liberty, common to Upper and Lower Germany, and neither got it from the other. Where we understand each other, well and good; where not, let each take his council without it until he learns to understand his neighbors, or until there is a voluntary agreement [Vergleich] on common writing and expression in Germany."[106]

105. *Lebensgeschichte*, III, pp. 54–70; IV, p. 110.
106. *Lebensgeschichte*, III, pp. 109–11, 120–79; IV, pp. 126–31.

More than forty pages of the new Life History volume were given to excerpts from the written opinions of others, most either favorable or else openly vituperous or misdirected; but also some that were troublesome. Among his critics Moser was particularly vexed with the physiocrat Schlettwein (recall the *Anti-Mirabeau*), who had declared Moser deficient not only in his reasoning faculties but in human charity. The disastrous results of Schlettwein's projects in Baden, Moser replied *ad hominem*, sufficed to answer that opinion.[107] He quoted apologetically but at length from Johann Stephan Pütter's fulsome estimation of him, written for Pütter's large work of 1776, "The Literature of the German Public Law." Cheerfully Moser assented to Pütter's reservation and quoted it, that "in view of the wealth of materials contained in Moser's writings, it could hardly be expected that everything could be as thoroughly thought out into principles and brought into the systematic order that might have been possible with, perhaps, more philosophical, historical, and juridical grasp." Fair enough, replied Moser; and Pütter might have left out the "perhaps." Moser did not see or comment on any sly meaning, if such there was, in Pütter's concluding encomium, that "now others are in a position to build on his shoulders. . . . In the history of this literature he forever marks an epoch." He reprinted without any comment Daniel Nettelbladt's 1758 praise for Moser's epochal expulsion of history from the sources of law, which according to Nettelbladt had cleared the way for "a purified philosophy," *gereinigte Weltweisheit*. Moser did not always note ironies. He did, though, remark a possible double meaning in an epigram somebody had made about him: "You survive yourself; you die, and will not die."[108]

During the 1770s the patronizing mode of opinion about Moser took form that has dominated at least until very recently and may yet prevail. It was a regular litany with interchangeable parts—the "worthy old man," whose "indefatigable energy" and "unswerving honesty" had made an "epoch" in the history of jurisprudence with his vast "collections," but who lacked "philosophical depth" to achieve "meaningful concepts."[109] From one scholarly quarter came remarks about Moser's

107. *Lebensgeschichte*, IV, pp. 104–5, 138–39; above, §28.

108. *Lebensgeschichte*, III, pp. 82–84, 189; Pütter, *Litteratur*, I (1776), pp. 408–30; Schömbs, *Staatsrecht Mosers*, p. 224, n. 9. With "judicial" Pütter presumably had private law in mind. On the Wolffian systematizer Nettelbladt, who seems earnestly to have believed still that there could be accommodation between natural law and postive German public law, Stintzing and Landsberg, *Rechtswissenschaft*, III, pp. 288–99; and see above, §14.

109. *Lebensgeschichte*, III, especially pp. 82–111, 183–95; IV, pp. 94, 184–85. Moser's work was reviewed regularly in the *Allgemeine Deutsche Bibliothek* (edited by Nicolai), in the *Göttingische gelehrten Anzeigen* (Haller and then Heyne), in *Unpartheyische Critik*

inattention or ignorance of history, and from another about his short-comings as a "thinking head" or "reasoning philosopher." (All, including Moser, agreed that the systematic historical jurisprudence of Heinrich Cocceji and of Johann Ludewig at Halle were dead, and often credited Moser with its demise.)[110] In 1776 Moser tried to answer both critical sides with two works. One was the first general political history he had written, the other was "Observations on Collecting and Thinking in the German Public Law."

The German history was to show, as reviewers promptly remarked, that Moser knew about history and could write it too if he chose. He also hoped it would succeed as a university handbook, and subtitled it "As preparation for the German public law." He had not retracted his lifelong insistence that history was no source of law, and the definition he gave of history was guarded. History was "a connected narrative of many parti-cular events," and there were three main kinds. History could be a plain description of events without commentary, the soundest but dullest kind; or a relation of events interwoven with the author's judgments, the most interesting but least reliable kind; or else a narrative followed by com-mentary, which was the best kind. Moser, however, declined the last and best in favor of the first, the soundest and dullest, "so as not to impose my views on anybody nor attack anybody's own, but leave it up to the reflective reader to think through the facts for himself." Moreover, one could write history for everybody, which would offend specialists, or come down on a theme—in this work Staatsgeschichte, political or con-stitutional history. This history, he said, would leave out the private and dynastic doings of the great, and all the military campaigning, to con-centrate on Germany within its own true boundaries and on the specific events affecting the constitutional rights of authorities and subjects. And so it did, in a wooden form of roughly equivalent chronological sections, each section then subdivided into topics—the political boundaries, the emperor, the Reichstag, the subjects, and so on. There is no hint in the

---

über die neuesten juristischen Schriften (Schott), and elsewhere. Schott's *Critik*, II (1769–70), pp. 789–804, had picked up Nettelbladt's 1758 periodizing estimation and had applied the term *epoch* to Moser's career; the term became common coin with Pütter's use of it in 1774. On *Critik* as a leading German organ for "naturrechtliche Aufklärung," see Stintzing and Landsberg, *Rechtswissenschaft*, III, p. 481. Two especially patronizing reviews that may have galled Moser at this time—or anyway should have—were in the *Allgemeine Deutsche Bibliothek*, XXVI (1775), pp. 160–64; and XXXIII (1778), part 2, pp. 439–42.

110. On Moser's role in the fate of the Halle school, Schömbs, *Staatsrecht Mosers*, pp. 178–221; Moser, *Lebensgeschichte*, IV, pp. 205–6; "Betrachtungen über das sammlen und dencken in dem Teutschen Staatsrecht," *Abhandlung verschiedener besonderer Rechts-Materien*, XVIII (1776), pp. 341–42.

book of the elegant and shapely constitutional exposition through history then being accomplished by Pütter and others of his school. And Moser's history was not a success, critical or commercial. "The worthy old man himself," wrote one reviewer who routinely complained of Moser's lack of originality and spirit, "may not take offense if, by his example, one is a better friend of truth, than of Plato and of Aristotle."[111] The word "Collecteenmacher" was now firmly fixed on Moser as author of truth.

This name of being a "collectioneer" and thus no thinker did more than vex Moser—it obsessed him. In some degree it always had; but his annoyance and anxiety on this score had grown more intense and bitter with time. Part of it was personal and professional resentment. "I am not writing too much when I claim," he wrote in the 1776 essay on collecting and thinking, "that apart from the Latin and the German H. à Lapide [Chemnitz and perhaps Justi], who throw out the baby with the bath, all teachers of the German law put together, Monzambano [Pufendorf] included, have not reasoned as much as I have." There was "a sky-high difference," though, "between thinking and thinking, between reasoning and reasoning." To prove his reasoning capacities, Moser justly cited his work on the Landeshoheit, on estates, on the relations between imperial and territorial authority. But more than his vanity was involved. "We have a German Empire and it has a head, the emperor; his deputies the imperial vicars, in spiritual matters for Catholics still another head, the pope; we have imperial princes of differing religions, status, dignities, power, etc. . . . high and low imperial courts of various kinds. In the territories we have rulers of every sort, amongst whom some get authority by election, some by inheritance." And some sciences required more data than others. Moser piled up the complexities of his science with grim relish and yet disquiet: "We have various kinds of lands, various forms of government, with estates and without them, imperial towns, a nobility of whom some are immediate, subjects of all different sorts, and a thousand other such things—to think for oneself, what good is it here? Not the slightest! What can a Philosoph do about it? Not the slightest! These are

111. *Erste Grundlehren der Teutschen Staatsgeschichte, zur Vorbereitung auf das Teutsche Staatsrecht* (Stuttgart, 1776), pp. 1–5 and passim. The comparison I have particularly in mind is with Pütter's *Historische Entwickelung der heutigen Staatsverfassung des Teutschen Reichs*, which did not appear until 1786–87 (3 vols., Göttingen); but Pütter's success with this mode was already apparent, and Moser knew and admired it, without, I think, fully appreciating what Pütter was doing. Schömbs, *Staatsrecht Mosers*, pp. 218–19; Stintzing and Landsberg, *Rechtswissenschaft*, III, pp. 338–41; Moser, *Neueste Geschichte der teutschen Staats-Recht-Lehre*, pp. 47, 125–26. The quoted review was in Nicolai, *Allgemeine Deutsche Bibliothek*, XXXI (1777), pp. 162–64.

plain facts, things that I must accept . . . as they are, unless I want to deform and ruin our German Empire."[112]

More than Moser's own vanity was involved, and a profounder kind of vanity: this was Moser the imperial patriot as well, and so Moser the collectioneer. Bound together were the way of his mind, the work of his life, and the German Empire now: all collectivities and reciprocities, whose parts were connected by incomprehensively many and tortuous ligatures to baffle the twinned dissolvents of the age as he saw them— reason and power.[113] Still, "for all I care," Moser wrote for yet another volume of his Life History in 1783, "others in the thinking world can reason out [vorraisonniren] a philosophical German public law, or else spell out the history and fate of all the pieces and principles from Tacitus and times even earlier, through all the centuries till now"; and "for all I care they can shut me out of the high-learned guilds altogether, and send me to the company of collectors, because I cannot and will not do this." From his humble seat in Stuttgart no envy would come, he promised, and nobody was more content with his lot than he.[114]

---

112. *Lebensgeschichte*, IV, pp. 218–19; "Sammlen und dencken," pp. 314–16. Monzambano was Samuel v. Pufendorf's pseudonym for *De statu Imperii Germanici* (many editions, the first at Amsterdam, 1667). Hippolythus à Lapide was Bogislaw P. v. Chemnitz's pseudonym for *Dissertatio de ratione status in Imperio nostro romano* (many editions, the first at Stettin, 1640). A German abridged and heavily annotated translation of the Hippolythus was published during the Seven Years War as *Abriss der Staats-Verfassung, Staats-Verhältnisse, und Bedürfniss des römischen Reichs deutscher Nation* (Mainz, 1761). This edition is customarily attributed to Johann Philipp Carrach, but Pütter in 1776 (*Litteratur*, I, pp. 212–13) publicly attributed it to Justi, and I am assuming that Moser did too. In 1761 both Justi and Carrach were living in Prussia, in the pay of that government but without official duties. This translation and notes were not Justi's usual kind of work. But it is quite unlikely that Moser would have put J. P. Carrach in intellectual ranks with Chemnitz and Pufendorf; he could have put Justi there.

113. Hegel scholars are inclined to identify Moser as the source for Georg W. F. Hegel's early (1802) *Verfassung des Deutschen Reichs* (Stuttgart, 1935), which begins from the proposition that the empire did not exist because it could not be comprehended. Grounds for the attribution are that Moser alone (a Stuttgart neighbor of the boy Hegel, by the way) had calmly denied that the empire could or should be sorted out into principles and categories. Franz Rosenzweig, *Hegel und der Staat*, I (Munich, 1920), pp. 105, 237; Rolf K. Hočevar, *Stände und Repräsentation beim jungen Hegel* (Munich, 1968), pp. 46–47, 165–68. The evidence is slim; Hegel hardly needed Moser's authority, and a more likely relationship would be baffled repulsion on Hegel's part at Moser's jurisprudence than admiration of his analyses. See the young Hegel's epitaph at the time of Moser's death in Hočevar, p. 46: "Mortuus est eodem temporis spatio celeberrimus ille, decus maximus patriae nostrae Moser, qui tot, quot perlegere humana no sufficit aetas, perscripsit libros, qui tot tamque variis casibus jactatus vitam egit."

114. *Lebensgeschichte*, IV, pp. 212–13.

For if Moser in the later seventies was other than content with himself, he was at pains to keep that out of his "natural life." His hair was long since white, he was used to that; his color was high, his skin was smooth, his gait was lively. His eyes were still good enough to read the old Hohentwiel scratchings. His teeth were still so sound, he boasted, that not only could he grind up veal bones with them, he also could pick up the coffee tray in his jaws—no hands—and pass refreshment to his guests. (This exhibition of vigor still persists in some forms in Moser's part of the world.) At seventy-eight he decided to learn to play the clavier, and reported to Dorothea that "it goes very well too, but it does bother my head." Age alone was no malady, he reported. He read in a medical book that persons who read and wrote a great deal were subject to the "hypochondriacal evil," and announced himself to be an exception. He was "quite free of hypochondria, thank God! so my religious sentiments surely cannot be ascribed to that." Then his steady hand went directly on to retell the story of his encounter with Frederick William I forty years before, to which he gave the heading "Presence of Mind."[115]

The quarrel with the Reichskammergericht seemed even to give him cheer; he had the support of his countrymen and of his duke in that. Out of it he got a kind of life's peroration he liked and repeated: "This is my character then: Fear God! Honor the emperor! Do right and fear nobody, not even the Reichsfiskal! And since I seek nothing from the great (whatever their rank or religion), and hope for nothing from them, and beg for nothing, then there is nothing for me to fear! *Dixi!*"[116]

Moser worked quietly and alone at Stuttgart into his eighties, living "from day to day, like a bird, out of God's hand," though pain and fatigue grew harder to drive away. His Mohl grandchildren regularly brought him the newspapers and earned each time a sugar cake, of which Moser always laid by a year's supply at the end of Christmas holidays. His great-grandson Robert von Mohl remembered that a theme of family reminiscence was how childlike the old man was, and how little he understood of the world. He was glad to see visitors and to gossip with neighbors, but he tired of them soon and wanted to go back to writing. Friedrich Nicolai called on Moser ("who made epochs in the German public law") during the famous 1781 journey through Germany, and found himself unprepared for Moser's "fiery glance, and shrewd at the same time." Moser's piety did not offend the enlightened Nicolai: Moser "was what he appeared, which is not true of all people with pious talk."

115. *Lebensgeschichte*, III, pp. 3–7, 22–23; Siegfried Röder, ed., *J. J. Moser, ein schwäbischer Patriot* (Heidenheim, 1971), p. 15.

116. *Lebensgeschichte*, IV, pp. 141–42, repeating the conclusion to *Nochmals bevestigte Verbindung*, p. 75.

Nicolai concluded that what Moser had put into his Life History was true.[117]

Moser had always wanted the character of one who was what he appeared to be. That had been the reason for some of his oddest deeds and words; it was the person he represented to himself, his fellows, to his sons, and to God. On 30 September 1785 he died.[118] Then, if he understood his faith, the parts would come together in truth and there would really be no difference between what he was and what he seemed.

Still, at the very end of his life in Time he was working to sort out what time had brought: a renewed *ex factis oritur ius* about mankind.

---

§32. Law of Nations, Rights of Man, America

MOSER had kept on writing until the end. His great work on the German public law seemed complete, even in the sense of going out of style; but he could not be idle, and in his eighties he tried new and different things. What he wrote in the last five years of his life moved away from the modes and principles which he had always avowed, and which he still proclaimed even when the work of his pen belied him. He drew much closer now to matters he had regularly scorned as sterile intellectual constructions, or as rationalizations, both in that word's everyday sense of expedience and in its technical sense of reasoned order. He turned his attention to natural law and natural rights, logical systems of analysis and exposition, appeals to the general political rights of men and plenary powers of authority. Here was the European Enlightenment, the German Aufklärung. The relation of Moser's last work to this climate of thought was ambiguous and changed almost from one word to the next. His dilemma shows well enough, though, that there really was such an Enlightenment in history; it was palpable to him, and he could not escape using its language even when he denied its

117. *Lebensgeschichte*, III, pp. 63–65; IV, pp. 42, 91–94; Robert von Mohl, *Lebenserinnerungen*, I (Stuttgart, 1902), pp. 8–10; more on the "simplicity of heart" and the "naivety of the honest old man" is in Mohl, "Die beiden Moser in ihrem Verhältnisse zu deutschem Leben und Wissen," *Monatblätter zur Ergänzung der Allgemeinen Zeitung*, 1846, pp. 363 and passim. Friedrich Nicolai, *Beschreibung einer Reise durch Deutschland und die Schweiz, im Jahre 1781*, X (Berlin, 1795), pp. 87, 165–66.

118. Moser's last months and death were described in a letter written by his housekeeper and published by Friedrich Karl in *Patriotisches Archiv*, VI (1787), pp. 439–50.

principles. This was partly because of the way this climate and language affected him, but also because of the direction the work and worries of his own mind had been taking him.

Moser wanted to show that he could use the current rhetoric of learned political, social, and religious discourse when he chose, if only to give him credentials for refuting it. That had appeared in the *Anti-Mirabeau*, in the essay on collecting and thinking, and in many protests on the same theme in the two late volumes of the Life History. Also he wanted to address this intellectual world and its inhabitants, and to be heard. More striking and important, though, was a progression through the topics Moser had addressed in his own work since the end of the 1760s. For his own modes had changed, willy-nilly, as he had turned from the constitutional jurisprudence of the empire, to relations within the German states—Landeshoheit and rights of subjects—and to the immediate relations among states. As he had traveled this path it had become steadily harder even for Moser to avoid recourse to general principles, reasoned connections, and natural sense. He was a part of the movement of ideas, for reasons of his own finding and choosing. It was not that he wanted to talk that way (while insisting always that he could if he chose), but rather that the matters he wanted to talk about took him there. At the end of the 1770s Moser took another step along that way, with his last ambitious scholarly enterprise: a comprehensive work on the European law of nations, the Völker-Recht.[119]

Moser had written briefly and occasionally on the law of nations before. He even announced, in 1778, that it would have been his favorite subject if he had found time for it (that seems very doubtful, but now at any rate he did find time for it). In an unfinished handbook of 1732 on the political constitution of Europe, he had put the law of nations into company with natural and rational law, as kinds of law vaguely adduced to the acts of sovereigns, who were defined as those *die bloss unter Gott und dem Degen stehen*, "subject only to the greater force of God and violence." Now he looked to the Völker-Recht for a body of rules of behavior operative among all European states. In an essay of 1739 he had proposed the existence of a law of nations which, in the absence of

119. *Versuch des neuesten Europäischen Völker-Rechts in Friedens- und Kriegs-Zeiten, vornehmlich aus denen Staatshandlungen derer Europäischen Mächten, auch anderen Begebenheiten, so sich seit dem Tode Kayser Carls VI. im Jahr 1740 zugetragen haben.*, 10 parts (Frankfurt/Main, 1777–80). Rürup discusses Moser's Völkerrecht in *Moser*, pp. 99–103. Franz Valjavec, *Die Entstehung der politischen Strömungen in Deutschland, 1770–1815* (Vienna, 1951), makes much use of Moser for discussing the place of imperial institutions and sentiments in the transition from Aufklärung to liberalism (especially pp. 39–51), but his location of Moser in a "altfränkische Gedankenwelt" with feudalistic overtones is careless and misleading, both about Moser's own intellectual posture and his relation with that of others.

any general rules or any general contract, would be based on the positive experience of norms customary among civilized peoples. Now he set out to learn what these might be and to make them known.[120]

The law of nations included, Moser wrote, all expressions of conduct that were "actually binding" on European sovereigns in their relations with one another, or of their behavior "according to plain natural sense," *der blossen natürlichen Billigkeit gemäss*, or other "customs or practices" commonly accepted by them. For this modern European law of nations he would use no material earlier than the death of Charles VI in 1740—a favorite date of his for some time now—claiming he had neither time nor space to hunt back to the sixteenth century, which seemed the alternative starting point for the subject. He proposed to use only demonstrable and positive facts. But the interesting thing here is that he could not and did not abide by this old principle of his, not for a generally applicable law of nations, for here founts of positive evidence were incomplete and unsure. This problem got him into an uncharacteristic quandary and disquisition over method: whether principles could be proven by examples, a kind of problem he had treated with indifference before. Moser tried to solve the quandary, though, in a characteristic way: by distinguishing between a deductive or academic "school" law of nations, drawn from absolute principles, and his own "actual" inductive kind, based on "experience." In his kind, principles could properly be established by examples. Nor, he announced, did he propose a "philosophical" law of nations, based on speculative constructions of the history and nature of man.[121]

In fact, though, the very form of the work was a series of general and descending propositions, printed in boldface, each followed by commentary or illustrations that rarely did establish the principle, and sometimes there were no examples at all. Underlying the form, after all protestations Moser made against the subjective invocation of reason and natural law, was a sense in Moser's mind or an irresistible tendency in the material that in the law of nations, at least, there *must be* a natural law and an order, which therefore particular examples *could* fairly demonstrate without closed deductive proof. In this Moser seems to have been thinking less about philosophy than about the natural sciences—the relation between his old friend experience, and experiment.[122] Moser entitled his

120. *Lebensgeschichte*, III, pp. 96–97; *Anfangs-Gründe der Wissenschaft von der gegenwärtigen Staats-Verfassung von Europa und dem unter denen Europäischen Potenzien üblichen Völcker- oder allgemeinen Staats-Recht* (Tübingen, 1732), preface §4, and pp. 56–60; Alfred Verdross, "J. J. Mosers Program einer Völkerrechtswissenschaft der Erfahrung," *Zeitschrift für öffentliches Recht*, III (1922), pp. 96–102; Franz v. Holzendorff, *Handbuch des Völkerrechts*, I (Berlin, 1885), pp. 456–62.

121. *Versuch des Völker-Rechts*, I, pp. 11, 13, 17–18.

122. Thus the unusual explicit acceptance by Moser in 1779 of a valid "Lehre und

ten systematic volumes an "essay" and nine supplementary ones "contributions." Disarmingly he described the main work as "just a little political stroll through all Europe, brought into a certain order."[123]

Nor did he propose a prescriptive "political" law of nations in the manner of some *Raisoneur* like the Abbé de St. Pierre, "that famed apothecary for all Europe." He was sensitive to the criticism, which was promptly made and which persisted, that his law of nations could offer no guide to what was just or unjust; but he dismissed this. In the first place, a large share of the transactions making up the law of nations had nothing to do with justice at all, nor with reason, but only with arbitrary convention. And where justice was an issue, "my friend! are you the judge over powers independent of human jurisdiction, and over their actions? or am I?" For Moser the jurist (and one with an eye to his market), the answer was in the question, a tautology almost; it was a simple literal fact that neither he nor an ordinary reader could hold such a court, and "such a foolish thought I never let into my mind—as though my assent or dissent made the slightest difference." It was for God "at the great general Day of Judgment" to tear aside the veils drawn about the motives, just or unjust, of the powerful figures that made the law of nations.[124]

From among useful sources of the law of nations, Moser excluded both divine and natural law. The first he dismissed on the grounds that though it was commonly preached to the common man, it was rarely followed, by the great especially. Natural law he excluded on the grounds that in practice it amounted either to a law of arbitrary convenience, or else to a formal academic exercise to which no statesman paid serious attention. Rights deriving from these sources, both in the writings of jurists and the actions of statesmen, so contradicted and canceled one another out that nothing was left but what they agreed upon in positive fact, for which, consequently, divine or natural law were not the true effective sources anyway. Only the agreement about them was. One real source was treaties. But the more important source (as in the case of

---

Theorie des natürlichen Völkerrechts," in *Der Teschenische Friedensschluss vom Jahre 1779, mit Anmerckungen, als eine Fortsetzung der Staatsgeschichte des zwischen Österreich und Preussen in denen Jahren 1778 und 1779 geführten Krieges* (Frankfurt/Main, 1779), pp. 231–32; Rürup, *Moser*, pp. 102–3, n. 28. Here Moser made a positive comparison of the natural law of nations with the theoretical "premises" underlying experimental physics and empirical medicine. His main message, though, seems to have been that prior study of the natural Völkerrecht should not dissuade anybody from studying Moser's.

123. My quotation combines phrasing in two parallel statements in *Versuch des Völker-Rechts*, I, pp. 18, 38.

124. *Versuch des Völker-Rechts*, I, pp. 17–20.

Landeshoheit) was Herkommen, custom or tradition. When governments seriously invoked the law of nations it was usually immediate precedent or practice that they meant, and observed.

There was another kind of source, though Moser did not call it that. He quoted some remarks by Frederick the Great about the haphazard and unspoken motives of statesmen, and the pretexts of right or reason with which they might, or might not, seek to clothe them. To be sure, said Moser, the "four main pillars" upon which the political structure of Europe "had always rested, and would continue to rest," and which therefore provided much important material for the European law of nations, were: "1) the passions of great lords and their ministers; 2) greed for more land, riches, and power; or 3) greater power than those with whom one may have dealings; and 4) timely application of political prudence."[125] Moser could not resist the rhetorical overkill: he had to show he knew all about that, and flourish his political realism before those readers or rivals who might profess loftier sentiments. But then he had to address the main task, to find rules European nations really had contrived or accepted in consequence of their necessary intercourse with one another.

Moser's law of nations was an unstable mix of positives and principles, of political cynicism and the will to find a true order. It was most successful where it treated politically indifferent subjects like the conventional privileges of ambassadors or rules for exchanging prisoners of war—useful matters to be sure. It was least successful where for example it attempted to sort out rights of sovereignty (thirteen European states), of "half-sovereignty" (the German principalities and a scattering of others like Monaco), and what these categorical principles had to do with the effective capacities of European states, in their dealings with one another, with their subjects, or with one another's subjects.[126] Moser hoped to find his main market in the chancelleries and embassies of European officialdom—among just those, as he openly acknowledged, who were engaged in constructing public veils for the motives of statesmen or else in transacting conventional business where "interests and passions play no notable part." He hoped for subsidies and a prompt translation into French. But the governments did not subscribe, nor was

125. *Versuch des Völker-Rechts*, I, pp. 21–35; *Erste Grundlehren des jezigen Europäischen Völcker-Rechts, in Friedens- und Kriegs-Zeiten* (Nürnberg, 1778), pp. 3–4; Ludwig Becher, *Johann Jakob Moser und seine Bedeutung für das Völkerrecht* (Würzburg, 1927), pp. 50–52 and passim. Moser attributed his quotations of Frederick the Great to *Mémoires, pour servir à l'Histoire de Brandenbourg*; but if that is correct I have not found the edition he used.

126. *Versuch des Völker-Rechts*, I, pp. 37–66; IV, passim.

the work a critical success. Commentary took the form and language now fixed on Moser: his epoch in the public law, his services in bringing materials together for a better mind someday to bring into system and meaning; but now also these complaints that he would take no stand for right and justice. For such comments, reviewers had no need to read much of the main body of the work, and indeed they sound as though they had never got beyond Moser's introduction. They knew about him already, how to review him, and they remarked no change in the form of his exposition or the style of his thought.[127]

In 1782 Moser published an essay he called "The Rights of Man, in Religious Matters, both in the State of Nature and in Civil Society." These were extraordinary phrases for Moser to use, especially in a title. More extraordinary still, and despite the word "religion" in the title, most of the seventy-odd pages were not about religion at all, but about secular political theory in its root form—the question of natural human rights and their relation to the worldly civic order. Religion's place was to provide analogy, hardly explicit but vital, finally, to Moser's meaning.

Moser here had no trouble, to begin with, dismissing fashionable notions about inborn natural freedoms as a starting point for political discourse. No single person on earth, he said, was independent at birth, not even savages "in a kind of state of nature" (he had been following closely reports on American Indians). Never was anybody free of all other men, "nor can that ever be or come about; and such imputed independence is less than a hypothesis, a dream, a fiction: it is in fact a true and total impossibility." Still less could any appeal be made in a historical way to antecedent rights of men. No member of society could credibly claim that his forebears had not yielded some disputed power over him to civic authority; authority need only reply "Dear citizen! Show me when your ancestors transferred themselves from the free state of nature into our civil society, what they then relinquished, and what rights they reserved!" There could be no proof of such a thing, and in the absence of any, authority would exercise the adverse powers it possessed. It was "unphilosophical, extravagant, and ridiculous . . . to invoke rights

127. *Lebensgeschichte*, IV, pp. 160–63; *Versuch des Völker-Rechts*, I, pp. 35–36; reviews in Schott, *Critik*, IX (1778–81), pp. 232–39, and X (1781–82), p. 339; Nicolai, *Allgemeine Deutsche Bibliothek*, XXXVII (1779), p. 124, and XLV (1781), pp. 294–95; Pütter, *Litteratur*, II, p. 382. Moser's claim that future generations would have better appreciation of his Völkerrecht turned out to be true: see the citations to Rürup, Verdross, Holzendorff, and Becher in notes 119, 120, and 125 above; and Stintzing and Landsberg, *Rechtswissenschaft*, III, pp. 327–28 ("Moser der Vater des positiven Völkerrechts"). But the posthumous praise, oddly like the criticism by Moser's contemporaries, seems addressed more to Moser's stated intentions than to the substance of his work.

of man that apply, only, to a condition of men that exists nowhere in the whole world."[128]

Yet Moser did want to write about the "state of nature," despite himself or a part of himself; and the reason, it seems, was that "natural" did have a specific, concrete, and critical meaning for him in religion; and that was how religion got into his title and his subject. Religion was crossing again over the compartmental boundaries into civic life, carried by this word "nature," and the way of its crossing tells something important about Moser's lifelong antipathy to "nature" and "reason" as implements of jurisprudence.

The "state of nature" Moser now described in political terms was a condition of rational choice. This he thought might be identified with heads of families in some primitive circumstances, in North America or in Greenland, perhaps in any remote villages or settlements where all association was voluntary, "according to one's own free will." His important point though—and here is the reason Moser got himself into the hypothetical question at all—was to forfend the "supreme error" of "confusing voluntary social life with civic society." The former was "natural," but the latter was not. The putative free, natural, and rational individual, to be sure, was always in fact subject to duties and restraints laid upon him by the surrounding society; but he obeyed them by choice. He obeyed them, in nature, by prudent will, because he had better, because it was in his interest to do so. "The several rights of independence are not, like moral truths, immutable; they are within the powers of men." Such a person could depart from the society, or such a society could expel him, by arbitrary choice and prudence. Neither side had any bound obligation to the other.

This was not civil society. Civil society, *bürgerliche Gesellschaft*, was a body of persons who, in accordance with "expressly contracted or otherwise established [hergebrachten] rules" lived together in a "union and community," *Verbindung und Gemeinschaft*, thereby composing amongst themselves a state, "distinguishable from the civil communities of other groups of persons." In this true state or civil community, "plain reasoning" about questions of constitutional right or wrong, "as it could or should be," had no validity; "each must be content to accept the institutions of the state, and let himself be directed by others."[129]

Moser's analogy, though nowhere clearly stated or closely reasoned, was between the meanings of "natural" in religion and in politics: be-

128. *Die Rechte der Menschheit in Religions-Sachen; so wohl im Stande der Natur, als auch in einer bürgerlichen Gesellschaft* (Stuttgart, 1782), pp. 5, 9–11, 34.

129. *Rechte der Menschheit*, pp. 12–13, 17, 25, 31–33.

tween the "natural religion" whose growing popularity in recent years had troubled him, and doctrines of "natural rights" in politics. Natural religion was that voluntary and wise "lawful condition" he knew from his life before grace: there one chose his religious course freely, according to prudential calculation of self-interest. And that is how Moser thought of natural law. Beyond natural religion and natural law were, respectively, submission to divine grace, and to the civic order. There is an odd flaw in the analogy that takes on significance as one thinks about it in terms of Moser's experience: the disparity between the infinitely simple condition of grace and the infinite complexity of the public law as Moser had always expounded it. But the disparity is on the whole formal and intellectual. Psychologically and morally, both the positive law in its complexity and the state of grace in its simplicity freed the man from domination by other men. Immediacy to the mind and will of God had its counterpart in a body of law immunized against the minds and wills of men. The more complex and particular the law, and the simpler the unity of grace, the better able were both to protect one's spirit against the wills and calculations of the world's others. To accept the law as it was, defending it against critical examination or human rejection, was a liberation. The entry into civil society from a state of nature was an equivalent of conversion, a *Bekehrung*.

From the law of nations and the rights of man, Moser turned finally to North America, whose history during the last years of his life suggested a parable, a *Bekehrungsgeschichte* perhaps, a coming of civic age and an entry into civilized nationhood. He wrote three long volumes on "North America after the Peace Treaties of 1783," bringing together every scrap of information he could find about that continent and about the events that separated the thirteen colonies from England.[130] Hegemony over the continent, Moser wrote, was approximately divided between Europeans and aborigines, although the latter had been severely decimated by "the so-called Christians, or rather Unchristians." He deplored the "loathsome condition of life" of black slaves, of whom one in seven died each year, he said, under the hands of "barbarian" masters; and he tried

130. Moser's late son-in-law at Göttingen had published a book on American affairs fifteen years before, based on interviews with the obliging Benjamin Franklin, which had been widely circulated, translated, and republished: Gottfried Achenwall, *Anmerkungen über Nordamerika und über dasige grosbritannische Colonien, aus mündlichen Nachrichten des Herrn Dr. Franklins* (Frankfurt/Main, 1769). In another connection, Moser himself was flattered but bemused to find himself listed by one writer on America along with Haller, Putendorf, and Pütter, as German authors particularly influential in America (meaning, apparently, among the German-speaking population): *Lebensgeschichte*, IV, pp. 232–35.

to trace the slave population back to African tribal origins.[131] American Indians and their political institutions fascinated him. "Each individual is supposed to be independent of every other; the loss of this unrestricted freedom they hold to be irretrievable; and since all Europeans live in subordination to the authorities over them, they hold the latter to be lesser men than themselves." Still as natural men Indians lived in various kinds of voluntary associations—notably the Six Nations—and Moser made a long catalogue of the tribes he could discover, from Abenakis to Zopas.[132]

The history of American independence in Moser's description (which makes America's experience sound a little like Württemberg's) began with British victories in the Seven Years War, followed by arbitrary infringements of American rights imposed by England. American protestations at this, corrupted from proper remonstrance into conspiracy by "the smugglers Hancock and Adams," were deemed rebellion by Great Britain; and the thirteen colonies responded by declaring themselves independent. And independent they had now become, in the course of military events, and were so recognized in international law by the treaties of 1783. "These lands formerly inhabited by Europeans," this "*corpus* of 13 formerly British colonies" now "constitute one free and great state"— a new situation sure to change the situations and ambitions not only of England but of France and Spain.[133]

Whether the Americans now independent would fall out among themselves and their state collapse, Moser would not predict; only time would tell. Had they left a state of nature, or had they entered one? In his work on the law of nations written during the American war, Moser had connected invocation of a right to make war with declaration of sovereign independence. He had compared the constitutional position of England's American colonies with that of the German principalities, the British empire with the German. To have renounced loyalty to a ruler, he had insisted, did not separate anybody from the state.[134] Now without comment he printed translations and summaries of American state constitutions: Massachusetts Bay, with its rights of man and its social com-

131. *Nord-America nach den Friedensschlüssen vom Jahre 1783*, 3 vols. (Leipzig, 1784–85), I, pp. 109–47.

132. *Nord-America*, I, pp. 267–696 (the quotation p. 346). Labrador Eskimos lived in small loose groups "ohne bürgerliche Verfassung": p. 409.

133. *Nord-America*, I, pp. iii–iv, 697–98, 734–45. Moser was particularly interested in the question of smuggling, with respect to the Völkerrecht and to the imperial situation of the American colonies: *Nord-America*, III, pp. 374–434. This was a growing problem in German imperial relations.

134. *Versuch des Völker-Rechts*, VI, pp. 122–47; IX, pp. 6–15.

pacts; and Pennsylvania, toward which he recognized his own religious and cultural affinities, with its language of inborn equality and natural rights.[135] The fates of empires seemed held in analogy by the conjunction of reason, freedom, and power.

To these last questions that had brought Moser through the law of nations and the rights of men to America, he had given no answer when the third volume of "North America" was published in the year of his death. He had written, so he reported in the very last words of the last volume of his Life History in 1783, "Philosophical Observations on Human Nature, as far as the natural law among individual men and families, as well as whole peoples and nations, may be derived from it"; this was ready for the press.[136] The essay was not published and seems to have disappeared. It was probably destroyed after Moser's death by Friedrich Karl von Moser, one of Germany's most distinguished political writers, a friend of Goethe and of Joseph II, and his father's devoted son.

135. *Nord-America*, I, pp. 728–29; III, pp. 496–542, 567–70, and passim.
136. *Lebensgeschichte*, IV, pp. 237–38; Rürup, *Moser*, p. x; Mohl, *Lebenserinnerungen*, I, p. 10.

Bibliography

I. Unpublished materials

A. In the possession of Helmut Haecker at the Hirsch-Apotheke in Urach/Württemberg:
  "Nachricht von meinem natürlichen, bürgerlichen und geistl: Leben, Für meine
  Kinder und Nachkommen," by Johann Jakob Moser. Corrected but unfinished
  draft, introduction dated Hohentwiel, 12 September 1763.
  Other materials from the same collection are identified and described where cited in
  the notes.

B. LBS Landesbibliothek, Stuttgart:
  Cod jur 4° 239. Kurze Einleitung in die Württembergische Staats- und Landes
  Verfassung, fürnemlich zum Verbrauch derer, die es zu wissen nötig haben,
  entworfen. Von Johan Jakob Moser. Stuttgardt 1752.
  Cod jur fol 193. Landtags-Acta in der Moserischen Readmissions Sache.
  Cod his fol 557b. Kurze Ausführung der Württembergischen Staats- u. Landesverfas-
  sung. . . . 1752 (another version of LBS Cod jur 4° 239, among the papers of
  Johann Theodor Scheffer, with no author identified).

C. UBT Universitäts-Bibliothek, Tübingen:
  Mh 202. Grund-Riss der Würtembergischen Staats- und Landes-Verfassung, autore
  Johann Jacob Moser. (In Mh 202 are several more versions of the treatise cited
  from LBS Cod jur 4° 239 and Cod his fol 557b. I have found the one bearing the
  title given here the most useful and authoritative.)
  Mh 202. Von den Land-Ständen dess Herzogthums Würtemberg (bound together
  with the title cited just above, but without attribution of date or author).
  Mh 253. Dreysig Zwey Piecen den im jahr 1770 bey der Landschaft vorgefallenen
  Streitt, die Readmission dess Consulenten Mosers zu denen Landsversamlung
  betreffend. (This includes a briefer draft of the estates' constitution cited just above,
  unsigned and undated, but here attributed to Moser).
  Mh 267. Aktenstücke die zwischen den beyden Landschafts Consulenten Stockmajer
  und Mos. entstandenen Differentien betreffend de anno 1757.
  Mh 268. Vorstellung der Landschaft wegen Befreyung des Consulenten Mosers vom
  Ende Julius 1759.
  Mh 677. Consulent Mosers Readmission zum Landtag. Acta de 1770.
  Mh 712. Kurtze Einleitung in die Württembergische Staats- und Landes Verfassung,
  fürneml. zum Gebrauch derer es zu wissen nöthig ist, unterworffen von Johann
  Jacob Moser . . . Stuttgardt 1752 (a draft rougher and rather different from the
  constitutional treatises listed above, this one bearing Moser's own marginal
  alterations, made apparently in an effort to satisfy censors).
  Ml 1. (An imperial Adelsbrief, confirming patent of nobility in the names of
  Friedrich Karl von Moser, Wilhelm Gottfried von Moser, and Christian Benjamin
  von Moser.)

D. WHS Württembergisches Hauptstaatsarchiv, Stuttgart:
  A34 B86. Verhandlungen und Irrungen mit der Landschaft, 1758.
  A34 B87. Verhandlungen und Irrungen mit der Landschaft, 1759.
  KA III 1 71. Gutachten des Landschaftskonsulenten Johann Jacob Moser . . .
  1755–56.

347

KA III 1 81. Wiederanstellung des Rechtskonsulenten Johann Jacob Moser bei der Landschaft. . . .

KA III Ls 389. Verhaftung des Landschafts-Konsulenten Moser und dessen Befreiung betr. Acten von 1759–1764.

KA III Ls 390. Befreiung des Landschafts-Konsulenten Joh. Jac. Moser und Rückgabe seiner beschlagnahmten Privatacten; vorwiegend Gutachten.

KA III Ls 394. Zwistigkeit der Ausschüsse mit dem Landschafts-Konsulenten Johann Jacob Moser und dem Ausschuss-Beisitzer Dann von Tübingen, 1770.

LA 2 26. Ausschliessung einzelner Ausschussmitglieder durch Herzog und Landschaft, besonders des BM Dann von Tübingen im Jahr 1770.

LA 2 41 5. Landschafts-Konsulenten, 1759–1764.

LA IV 11–22. Irrungen mit Herzog Karl.

II. Published materials

This list includes all works cited more than once in any one part of the present volume, works that therefore appear with shortened titles somewhere in the footnotes, plus a number of other works deemed of special interest to readers of this volume. Thorough bibliographies of Moser's own published work are in the Rürup and Schömbs books listed below.

Adam, Albert E. "Herzog Karl und die Landschaft." *Herzog Karl Eugen von Württemberg und seine Zeit*, I, pp. 103–310. Esslingen, 1907.

———. *Johann Jakob Moser als Württembergischer Landschaftskonsulent, 1751– 1771*. Stuttgart, 1887.

Allgemeine Deutsche Biographie. 56 vols. Leipzig, 1875–1912.

Bader, Karl S. "Johann Jakob Moser." *Lebensbilder aus Schwaben und Franken*, VII, pp. 92–121. Stuttgart, 1960.

Barthold, Friedrich W. "Die Erweckten im protestantischen Deutschland während des Ausgangs des 17. und der ersten Hälfte des 18. Jahrhunderts, besonders die Frommen Grafenhöfe," part II, *Historisches Taschenbuch*, 3d series, IV, pp. 169–390. Leipzig, 1853.

Bauser, Friedrich. *Geschichte der Moser von Filseck*. Stuttgart, 1911.

Becher, Ludwig. *Johann Jakob Moser und seine Bedeutung für das Völkerrecht*. Würzburg, 1927.

Becher, Ursula A. J. *Politische Gesellschaft. Studien zur Genese bürgerlicher Öffentlichkeit in Deutschland*. Göttingen, 1978.

Belster, Ulrich. *Die Stellung des Corpus Evangelicorum in der Reichsverfassung*. Bamberg, 1968.

Beyreuther, Gottfried. *Sexualtheorie im Pietismus*. Munich, 1963.

Bleek, Wilhelm. *Von der Kameralausbildung zum Juristenprivileg. Studium, Prüfung und Ausbildung der höheren Beamten des allgemeinen Verwaltungsdienstes in Deutschland im 18. und 19. Jahrhundert*. Berlin, 1972.

Böckenförde, Ernst W. *Gesetz und gesetzgebende Gewalt, von den Anfängen der deutschen Staatsrechtslehre bis zur Höhe des staatsrechtlichen Positivismus*. Berlin, 1958.

———. "Die Historische Rechtschule und das Problem der Geschichtlichkeit des Rechts." *Collegium Philosophicum. Studien Joachim Ritter zum 60. Geburtstag*, pp. 9–76. Basel, 1964.

Borch, Herbert v. *Obrigkeit und Widerstand. Zur politischen Soziologie des Beamtentums.* Tübingen, 1954.

Bornhak, Conrad. *Geschichte der preussischen Universitätsverwaltung bis 1810.* Berlin, 1900.

―――. "Johann Jakob Moser als Professor in Frankfurt a. O." *Forschungen zur Brandenburgischen und Preussischen Geschichte,* XI (1898), pp. 330–39.

Brunner, Otto. "Der Historiker und die Geschichte von Verfassung und Recht." *Historische Zeitschrift,* CCIX (1969), pp. 1–16.

Buff, Walter. *Gerlach Adolph Freiherr von Münchhausen als Gründer der Universität Göttingen.* Göttingen, 1937.

Bussi, Emilio. *Diritto e politica in Germania nel XVIII secolo.* Milan, 1971.

―――. *Il diritto pubblico del Sacro romano impero alla fine del XVIII secolo.* 2 vols. Milan, 1959–70.

Carsten, Francis L. *Princes and Parliaments in Germany.* Oxford, 1959.

Conrad, Hermann. *Deutsche Rechtsgeschichte.* 2nd ed. 2 vols. Karlsruhe, 1962–66.

Cotta, Christoph F. *Einleitung in das allgemeine Staatsrecht der teutschen Länder.* Tübingen, 1786.

Dehlinger, Alfred. *Württembergs Staatswesen.* 2 vols. Stuttgart, 1951–53.

Dittrich, Erhard. *Die deutschen und österreichischen Kameralisten.* Darmstadt, 1974.

Ebel, Wilhelm. *Geschichte der Gesetzgebung in Deutschland.* 2nd ed. Göttingen, 1958.

―――. *Der Göttinger Professor Johann Stephan Pütter aus Iserlohn.* Göttingen, 1975.

Elliott, Philip. *The Sociology of the Professions.* London, 1972.

Erler, Adalbert, and Kaufmann, Ekkehard. *Handwörterbuch zur deutschen Rechtsgeschichte.* Berlin, 1964–.

Feine, Hans E. "Zur Verfassungsentwicklung des Heil. Röm. Reichs seit dem Westfälischen Frieden." *Zeitschrift der Savigny-Stiftung für Rechtsgeschichte, Germanische Abteilung,* LII (1932), pp. 65–133.

Frensdorff, Ferdinand. *Die ersten Jahrzehnte des staatsrechtlichen Studiums in Göttingen.* Göttingen, 1887.

Fröhlich, Marianne. *Die Entwicklung der deutschen Selbsterzeugnisse.* Leipzig, 1930.

―――. *Johann Jakob Moser in seinem Verhältnis zum Rationalismus und Pietismus.* Vienna, 1925.

Gerhard, Dietrich, ed. *Ständische Vertretungen in Europa im 17. und 18. Jahrhundert.* Göttingen, 1969.

Gross, Hanns. *Empire and Sovereignty: A History of the Public Law Literature of the Holy Roman Empire.* Chicago, 1973.

Gross, Lothar. *Geschichte der deutschen Reichshofkanzlei von 1559 bis 1806.* Vienna, 1933.

Grube, Walter. *Der Stuttgarter Landtag 1457–1957.* Stuttgart, 1957.

Günther, Hans R. G. "Psychologie des deutschen Pietismus." *Deutsche Vierteljahrsschrift für Literaturwissenschaft und Geistesgeschichte,* IV (1926), pp. 144–76.

Häberlin, Karl F. *Handbuch des teutschen Staatsrechts nach dem System des herrn geheim justizrath Pütter. Zum gemeinnützigen Gebrauch der gebildeteren Stände in Teutschland.* 3 vols. Berlin, 1794–97.

Häcker, Otto. "Neues über Johann Jakob Moser." *Schwäbischer Schillerverein. Rechenschaftsbericht,* XXXIV (1930), pp. 112–14.

Hammerstein, Notker. *Aufklärung und katholisches Reich.* Berlin, 1977.

―――. *Jus und Historie. Ein Beitrag zur Geschichte des historischen Denkens an deutschen Universitäten im späten 17. und im 18. Jahrhundert.* Göttingen, 1972.

Hanselmann, G. *Johann Jakob Moser.* Stuttgart, 1958.

Hantsch, Hugo. *Reichsvizekanzler Friedrich Karl von Schönborn (1674–1746).* Augsburg, 1929.

Hartung, Fritz. "Die Wahlcapitulationen der deutschen Kaiser und Könige." *Historische Zeitschrift,* CVII (1911), pp. 340–44.

Hasselhorn, Martin. *Der altwürttembergische Pfarrstand in 18. Jahrhundert.* Stuttgart, 1958.

Hertz, Friedrich. "Die Rechtssprechung der höchsten Reichsgerichte im römisch-deutschen Reich und ihre politische Bedeutung." *Mitteilungen des Instituts für österreichische Geschichtsforschung,* LXIX (1961), pp. 331–358.

Herzog Karl Eugen von Württemberg und seine Zeit, published by the Württembergisches Geschichts- und Altertumsverein. 2 vols. Esslingen, 1907–9.

Hinrichs, Carl. *Preussentum und Pietismus.* Göttingen, 1971.

Hočevar, Rolf K. *Stände und Repräsentation beim jungen Hegel.* Munich, 1968.

Johnson, Paul E. *Psychology of Religion.* Rev. ed. New York, 1959.

Justi, Johann Gottlieb. *System des Finanzwesens.* Halle, 1766.

Kaufmann, Hans-Heinrich. *Friedrich Karl von Moser als Politiker und Publizist.* Darmstadt, 1931.

Kelsen, Hans. *Die philosophischen Grundlagen der Naturrechtslehre und des Rechtspositivismus.* Charlottenburg, 1928.

Kleinheyer, Gerd. *Die kaiserlichen Wahlkapitulationen. Geschichte, Wesen und Funktion.* Karlsruhe, 1968.

Kormann, Karl. "Die Landeshoheit in ihrem Verhältnis zur Reichsgewalt im alten Deutschen Reich seit dem Westfälischen Frieden." *Zeitschrift für Politik,* VIII (1914), pp. 139–70.

Kreh, Fritz. *Leben und Werk des Reichsfreiherrn Johann Adam von Ickstatt (1702–1776).* Paderborn, 1974.

Kreittmayr, Wiguläus X. A. *Anmerkungen über den Codicem Maximilianeum Bavaricum civilem.* 5 vols. Munich, 1759–68.

Kürschner, Theo. *Die Landeshoheit der deutschen Länder seit dem Westfälischen Frieden unter dem Gesichtspunkt der Souveränität.* Schwetzingen, 1938.

Langen, August. *Der Wortschatz des deutschen Pietismus.* Tübingen, 1954.

La Palombara, Joseph, ed. *Bureaucracy and Political Development.* Princeton, 1963.

Lehmann, Hartmut. "Der Pietismus im Alten Reich." *Historische Zeitschrift,* CCXIV (1972), pp. 58–95.

———. *Pietismus und weltliche Ordnung in Württemberg vom 17. bis zum 20. Jahrhundert.* Stuttgart, 1969.

———. "Die Württembergischen Landstände im 17. und 18. Jahrhundert." In *Ständische Vertretungen in Europa im 17. und 18. Jahrhundert,* edited by Dietrich Gerhard. Göttingen, 1969.

Merk, Walther. "Der Gedanke des gemeinen Besten in der deutschen Staats- und Rechtsentwicklung." *Festschrift Alfred Schultze.* Weimar, 1934.

Mohl, Robert von. *Beiträge zur Geschichte Württembergs.* Vol. I. Tübingen, 1828.

———. *Lebenserinnerungen.* Vol. I. Stuttgart, 1902.

Moser, Friedrich Karl von, ed. *Patriotisches Archiv für Deutschland.* 12 vols. Mannheim and Leipzig, 1784–90.

———. *Was ist gut Kayserlich und nicht gut Kayserlich?* n.p., 1766.

Moser, Johann Jakob. *Abhandlungen verschiedener besonderer Rechts-Materien.* 20 parts. Frankfurt/Main and Leipzig, 1772–77.

_____. "Abhandlung von Noethigung derer Unterthanen zu regulairen Kriegs-Diensten." *Sammlung einiger neuen Abhandlungen von teutschen Staatssachen*, II (1765), pp. 185–230.

_____. *Abhandlungen aus dem Teutschen Kirchen-Recht.* Frankfurt/Main, 1772.

_____. *Altes und Neues aus dem Reich Gottes und der übrigen guten und bösen Geister.* 24 parts. Frankfurt/Main, 1733–39.

_____. *Anfangs-Gründe der Wissenschafft von der gegenwärtigen Staats-Verfassung von Europa und dem unter denen Europäischen Potenzien üblichen Völcker- oder allgemeinen Staats-Recht.* Tübingen, 1732.

_____. *Anti-Mirabeau, oder unpartheyische Anmerkungen über des Marquis von Mirabeau natürliche Regierungs-Form.* Frankfurt/Main, 1771.

_____. "Betrachtungen über das sammlen und dencken in dem Teutschen Staatsrecht." *Abhandlung verschiedener besonderer Rechts-Materien*, XVIII (1776), pp. 305–64.

_____. *Bibliotheca juris publici S. R. German. Imperii.* 2 vols. Stuttgart, 1729–34.

_____. *Compendium juris publici Germanici, oder Grundriss der heutigen Staats-Verfassung des Teutschen Reichs.* Tübingen, 1731.

_____. *Einige Grund-Saetze einer Vernünftigen Regierungs-Kunst, nach der jetzigen Gedenckens-Art und Handels-Weise verständiger Regenten, Ministers und Land-Stände.* Stuttgart, 1753.

_____. *Gedancken über das neu-erfundene vernünftige Staats-Recht des Teutschen Reichs.* Frankfurt/Main, 1767.

_____. *Die gerettete völlige Souveraineté der löblichen Schweitzerischen Eydgenossenschaft.* Tübingen, 1731.

_____. *Hanauische Berichte für Religions-Sachen.* 2 vols. Hanau, 1750–51.

_____. *Ihro Römisch-Kayserlichen Majestät Carls des Siebenden Wahl-Capitulation, mit Beylagen und Anmerckungen versehen.* 2 vols. Frankfurt/Main, 1742.

_____. *Lebensgeschichte Johann Jacob Mosers . . . von ihm selbst beschrieben.* 3d ed., 4 parts. Frankfurt/Main, 1777–83.

_____. *Merckwürdige Reichs-Hof-Raths-Conclusa.* 8 parts. Frankfurt/Main, 1726–32.

_____. *Monathliche Beyträge zur Förderung des wahren Christenthums.* 2 vols. N.p., 1751–53.

_____. *Nebenstunden von Teutschen Staats-Sachen.* 6 parts. Frankfurt/Main and Leipzig, 1757–58.

_____. *Neues Teutsches Staats-Recht.*

Vol. I: *Von Teutschland und dessen Staats-Verfassung überhaupt.* Stuttgart, 1766.

Vol. II: *Von dem Römischen Kayser, Römischen König und denen Reichs-Vicarien.* Frankfurt/Main, 1767.

Vol. III: *Von denen Kayserlichen Regierungs-Rechten und Pflichten.* Frankfurt/Main, 1772.

Vol. VI: *Von denen Teutschen Reichs-Tags-Geschäfften.* Frankfurt/Main, 1768.

Vol. VII: *Von der Teutschen Religions-Verfassung.* Frankfurt/Main, 1774.

Vol VIII: *Von der Teutschen Justiz-Verfassung.* Frankfurt/Main, 1774.

Vol. XIII: *Von der Teutschen Reichs-Stände Landen.* Frankfurt/Main, 1769.

Vol. XIV: *Von der Landeshoheit derer Teutschen Reichsstände überhaupt.* Frankfurt/Main, 1773.

Vol. XV: *Von der Landeshoheit im Geistlichen.* Frankfurt/Main, 1773.

Vol. XVI, part 1: *Von der Landeshoheit in Regierungssachen überhaupt.*
Frankfurt/Main, 1772.

Vol. XVI, part 2: *Von der Landes-Hoheit in Justiz-Sachen.* Frankfurt/Main, 1773.

Vol. XVI, part 3: *Von der Landes-Hoheit in Militar-Sachen.* Frankfurt/Main, 1773.

Vol. XVI, part 4: *Von der Landes-Hoheit in Steuer-Sachen.* Frankfurt/Main, 1773.

Vol. XVI, part 5: *Von der Landeshoheit in Cameral-Sachen.* Frankfurt/Main, 1773.

Vol. XVI, part 6: *Von der Landes-Hoheit in Policey-Sachen.* Frankfurt/Main, 1773.

Vol. XVI, part 8: *Von der Landeshoheit in Ansehung der Unterthanen Personen und Vermögens.* Frankfurt/Main, 1773.

Vol. XVII: *Von der Teutschen Unterthanen Rechten und Pflichten.* Frankfurt/Main, 1774.

Vol. XIX: *Teutsches Nachbarliches Staatsrecht.* Frankfurt/Main, 1773.

_____. *Neueste Geschichte der teutschen Staats-Rechts-Lehre und deren Lehrer.* Frankfurt/Main, 1770.

_____. *Nochmals bevestigte Verbindung derer Evangelischen Reichs-Gerichts-Beysizere an die Schlüsse des Corporis Evangelicorum.* Frankfurt/Main, 1777.

_____. *Nord-America nach den Friedensschlüssen vom Jahre 1783.* 3 vols. Leipzig, 1784–85.

_____. *Die Rechte der Menschheit in Religions-Sachen; so wohl im Stande der Natur, als auch in einer bürgerlichen Gesellschaft.* Stuttgart, 1782.

_____. *Reichs-Grund-Gesez-mäsige Beantwortung der Frage: Wie vil Soldaten eines Teutschen Reich-Standes Land zu erhalten schuldig seye? wie auch Wer den Ausschlag darinn geben könne?* n.p., 1765.

_____. *Schrifftmässige Gedancken von der Verbindung der Welt-Weisheit, besonders der Wolfischen, mit der Theologie.* [Saalfeld], 1741.

_____. *Schwäbische Nachrichten von Oeconomie- Cameral- Policey- Handlungs-Manufactur- Mechanischen und Bergwercks-Sachen.* 10 parts. Stuttgart, 1756–1757.

_____. *Staats-Historie Teutschlands unter der Regierung Ihro Kayserlichen Majestät Carls des Siebenden.* 2 vols. Jena, 1743.

_____. *Teutsches Staats-Recht.* 50 vols. Nürnberg, etc., 1737–53.

_____. *Zusätze zu seinem Teutschen Staats-Recht.* 2 vols. Leipzig, 1744.

_____. *Theologische Gedancken von der ehlichen Beywohnung unbekehrter, erweckter und widergebohrener Personen.* Züllichau, 1741.

_____. *Unmasgebliches Bedenken über einige Hauptpuncten, so bey Einrichtung des Visitations-Wesens bey dem Kaiserl. Reichs Cammergerichte zu beobachten seyn.* Regensburg, 1767.

_____. *Unpartheyliche Urtheile, von Juridisch- und Historischen Büchern.* 6 parts. Frankfurt/Main and Leipzig, 1722–25.

_____. *Versuch des neuesten Europäischen Völker-Rechts in Friedens- und Kriegs-Zeiten, vornehmlich aus denen Staatshandlungen derer Europäischen Mächten, auch anderen Begebenheiten, so sich seit dem Tode Kayser Carls VI. im Jahr 1740 zugetragen haben.* 10 parts. Frankfurt/Main, 1777–89.

_____. *Vischerische Ahnen-Tafeln.* Tübingen, 1728.

_____. *Von der Reichs-Verfassungsmässigen Freyheit, von teutschen Staats-Sachen zu schreiben.* Göttingen, 1772.

_____. *Von der Verbindung derer Evangelischen Reichs-Gerichts-Beysizer an die*

Schlüsse des Corporis Evangelicorum. Frankfurt/Main, 1775.

_____. *Von des Corporis Evangelicorum Vertretungs-Recht seiner Glaubens-Genossen.* Regensburg, 1772.

Näf, Werner. "Der Durchbruch des Verfassungsgedankens im 18. Jahrhundert." *Schweizer Beiträge zur Allgemeinen Geschichte,* XI (1953), pp. 108–20.

Necker, Karl Friedrich. *The constitution and government of the Germanic body. Showing how this state has subsisted for three hundred years past, under the emperors of the house of Austria* (translated by Stephan Whatley). London, 1745.

Nicolai, Friedrich. *Allgemeine Deutsche Bibliothek.* Berlin and Stettin, 1765–96.

Orzack, Louis H. "Work as a 'Central Life Interest' of Professionals." *Social Problems,* VII (1959), pp. 125–32.

Philipp, Wolfgang. *Das Werden der Aufklärung in theologiegeschichtlicher Sicht.* Göttingen, 1957.

Pütter, Johann Stephan. *Entwurf einer juristischen Encyklopädie und Methodologie.* Göttingen, 1757.

_____. *Historische Entwickelung der heutigen Staatsverfassung des Teutschen Reichs.* 3d ed. 3 vols. Göttingen, 1798–99.

_____. *Litteratur des teutschen Staatsrechts.* 4 vols. Göttingen, 1776–91.

Rachfahl, Felix. "Alte und neue Landesvertretung in Deutschland." *Schmollers Jahrbuch für Gesetzgebung, Verwaltung und Volkswirtschaft im Deutschen Reiche,* XXXIII (1909), pp. 89–130.

Renger, Reinhard. *Landesherr und Landstände im Hochstift Osnabrück in der Mitte des 18. Jahrhunderts.* Göttingen, 1968.

Reyscher, August L. *Vollständige, historisch und kritisch bearbeitete Sammlung der württembergischen Gesetze.* Vol. II: Stuttgart, 1829. Vol. XIV: Tübingen, 1843.

Ritschl, Albrecht. *Geschichte des Pietismus.* 3 vols. Bonn, 1880–86.

Rössler, Helmuth, and Franz, Günther, eds. *Universität und Gelehrtenstand 1400–1800.* Limburg/Lahn, 1970.

Rohr, Theo. *Der deutsche Reichstag vom Hubertusburger Frieden bis zum bayerischen Erbfolgekrieg (1763–1778).* Bonn, 1968.

Roscher, Wilhelm. *Geschichte der National-Oekonomik in Deutschland.* Munich, 1874.

Rürup, Reinhard. *Johann Jacob Moser: Pietismus und Reform.* Wiesbaden, 1965.

Schlaich, Klaus. "Corpus Evangelicorum und Corpus Catholicorum. Aspekte eines Parteiwescns im Hlg. Römischen Reich Deutscher Nation." *Der Staat,* XI (1972), pp. 218–30.

Schmauss, Johann Jacob. *Corpus Juris Publici, enthaltend des Heil. Röm. Reichs deutscher Nation Grund-Gesetze.* Rev. ed. Leipzig, 1794.

Schmid, August. *Das Leben Johann Jakob Mosers, aus seiner Selbstbiographie, den Archiven und Familienpapieren dargestellt.* Stuttgart, 1868.

Schmidt, Martin. *Pietismus.* Stuttgart, 1972.

Schmidt-Assmann, Eberhard. *Der Verfassungsbegriff in der deutschen Staatslehre der Aufklärung und des Historismus.* Berlin, 1967.

Schömbs, Erwin. *Das Staatsrecht Johann Jakob Mosers (1701–1785).* Berlin, 1968.

Schott, August. *Unpartheyischer Critik über die neuesten juristischen Schriften.* 10 vols. Leipzig, 1768–82.

Schubert, Friedrich H. *Die deutschen Reichstage in der Staatslehre der frühen Neuzeit.* Göttingen, 1966.

Selle, Götz v. *Die Georg-August-Universität zu Göttingen.* Göttingen, 1937.

Smend, Rudolf. *Das Reichskammergericht.* Weimar, 1911.

Söll, Wilhelm. *Die staatliche Wirtschaftspolitik in Württemberg im 17. und 18. Jahrhundert.* Tübingen, 1934.

Stälin, Paul F. "Karl Eugen, Herzog von Württemberg." *Allgemeine Deutsche Biographie,* XV (Leipzig, 1882), pp. 376–93.

Stieda, Wilhelm. *Die Nationalökonomie als Universitätswissenschaft.* Leipzig, 1906.

Stintzing, Roderich and Landsberg, Ernst. *Geschichte der deutschen Rechtswissenschaft.* 3 vols. Munich, 1880–1910.

Stolleis, Michael, ed. *Staatsdenker im 17. und 18. Jahrhundert: Reichspublizistik, Politik, Naturrecht.* Frankfurt/Main, 1977.

Thudichum, Friedrich. "Das vormalige Reichskammergericht und seine Schicksale." *Zeitschrift für deutsches Recht und deutsche Rechtswissenschaft,* XX (1861), pp. 148–222.

Tüchle, Hermann. *Die Kirchenpolitik des Herzogs Karl Alexander von Württemberg (1733–1737).* Würzburg, 1937.

Valjavec, Franz. *Die Entstehung der politischen Strömungen in Deutschland, 1770–1815.* Vienna, 1951.

Verdross, Alfred. "J. J. Mosers Program einer Völkerrechtswissenschaft der Erfahrung." *Zeitschrift für öffentliches Recht,* III (1922), pp. 96–102.

Vierhaus, Rudolf. "Ständewesen und Staatsverwaltung in Deutschland im späteren 18. Jahrhundert." *Dauer und Wandel im der Geschichte: Festgabe Kurt v. Raumer.* Münster, 1966.

Walker, Mack. "Rights and Functions: The Social Categories of Eighteenth-Century German Jurists and Cameralists." *Journal of Modern History,* L (1978), pp. 234–51.

Wintterlin, Friedrich. *Geschichte der Behördenorganisation in Württemberg.* 2 vols. Stuttgart, 1904–6.

_____. "Zur Geschichte des herzoglich Kommerzienrats." *Württembergische Vierteljahrshefte für Landesgeschichte,* N.F. XX (1911), pp. 310–27.

Wolzendorff, Kurt. *Über den Umfang der Polizeigewalt im Polizeistaat.* Marburg, 1905.

Index